Y0-ELD-020

THE SEVEN GATES OF SOUL

Reclaiming the Poetry Of Everyday Life

Joe Landwehr

Ancient Tower Press
Abilene, Texas

www.ancient-tower-press.com

The Seven Gates of Soul: Reclaiming the Poetry of Everyday Life © 2004 by Joe Landwehr. All rights reserved. No part of this book may be used or reproduced in any manner whatsoever, including Internet usage, without written permission from Ancient Tower Press, except in the case of brief quotations embodied in critical articles or reviews.

FIRST EDITION
First Printing, 2004

Cover design by Michael McClure
Interior design by Joe Landwehr
Copy-editing by Annie Woods Tornick

Publisher's Cataloguing-in-Publication
(Provided by Quality Books, Inc.)

Landwehr, Joe
    The seven gates of soul : reclaiming the poetry of everyday life / Joe Landwehr
    p. cm.
    Includes bibliographical references and index.
    LCCN 2004091983
    ISBN 0-9747626-0-1

    1. Soul—History of doctrines.   I. Title

BD421.1.L36 2004   128'.1
                    QB104-700149

Ancient Tower Press
1904 North 5th Street
Abilene, Texas 79603

www.ancient-tower-press.com

About the Author

J oe Landwehr is an astrologer of 33 years experience, seeking new, deeper, and more innovative ways to approach the basic symbolism of astrology. The author of three other books and numerous articles, Joe currently teaches an intimate course in the fundamentals of astropoetics, designed to guide each individual student toward an appreciation of the ancient wisdom that dwells within, while exploring astrological symbolism in the sacred context of everyday life.

The author can be contacted by e-mail at jlandwehr@ancient-tower-press.com.

Additional information about astropoetics, the correspondence course, and the author's current workshop schedule can be found at www.astropoetics.com.

Acknowledgements

Any book is an alchemical synthesis, in which the work of countless others percolates through a body of life experiences, gathers insight from interactions with friends and enemies, chance encounters, snippets of news, movies, synchronistic moments, and the unpredictable free-flight of imagination. To fully acknowledge all those who have influenced this book, I would have to write another. Having said that, there are few key souls I wish to honor for their instrumental part in the birthing process of this small piece of alchemy:

Ross Bishop, shaman, visionary healer, and author of *Healing the Shadow* and *Truth*, for your well-intentioned honesty. It was hard to hear at times, but in the end, I believe it has helped make this a stronger, clearer book.

Josef Tornick, photographer extraordinaire, wise trickster, and man of many talents, for your uncensored enthusiasm and encouragement. Even though history of philosophy is not your favorite bedside reading matter, you immediately recognized the luminous spirit of this work, and in that recognition, helped lift me through my doubt.

Eliza King, poet and teacher of poets, for your editorial skill and your uncanny attunement to the nuance of the well-turned phrase. You intuitively sensed where I was wanting to go, and offered the perfect mix of praise and constructive criticism to help guide me there.

Fran Laakman, teacher, astrologer, and world traveler, for your unflinching support, and the depth of your own knowledge and wisdom. You asked all the right questions and played just enough of a devil's advocate to keep me digging for a deeper level of clarity. I deeply appreciate your commitment to this project, sustained through several demanding crises and a full schedule of your own.

Thomas Moore, wise philosopher of the soul, for graciously taking the time to read my book and offer your encouragement.

Annie Woods Tornick, writer, teacher and raven sister, for your gentle literary liposuction. Thank you for seeing what I could not, and helping me cut away unnecessary verbiage, so my ideas could breathe.

Mike McClure, artist, and fellow men's group survivor for your amazing ability to translate my vision into tangible images. Your patient attention to detail, and tolerance for my demanding nature has graced the cover of this book with a special magic.

Ann Postma, my loving partner, for your unconditional love and support. You are my living proof that the soul can be embodied as a dancing sunburst of joy.

This book is dedicated to wolf and raven people everywhere.
You know who you are.

Table of Figures

Table of Contents

CONTENTS

CONTENTS

CONTENTS

◇◇

Soul is a force that can light up a room.
The force radiates from a sense of selfhood,
a sense of knowing where you've been
and what it means.
Soul is a way of life . . .

Ray Charles (1930-2004)

INTRODUCTION

Introduction

Like many who have come before me, and many who will come after, I always intuitively believed that I was born for a reason. I am here not just as a biochemical convergence of routine happenstance, but as part of a conscious design. Whose conscious design has never been a question with easy answers, but I cannot help but notice its presence everywhere. I marvel at the fact that the Earth is just the right distance from the Sun, and has all the necessary ingredients — a breathable atmosphere, accessible water, a moderate temperature, and more — to support organic life. I am awed by the fact that day follows night, and season follows season, in predictable rhythm. It amazes me to notice that every detail of this wondrous creation — from the tiniest pebble on the beach to the infinity of stars overheard — seems to play its part in an exquisite mosaic that is always changing, yet always whole. Systems of river tributaries, the circulatory system of a human body, and the network of veins in a leaf echo each other in one of many recognizable patterns that unite all of nature into an integrated masterpiece of ingenious creation. While some might take such simple observations for granted, or assign them to chance, I have always held them in an aura of sacred revelation.

I won't pretend to understand this revelation, nor even that I think it is understandable with any degree of certainty, but I do celebrate the irresistible invitation it extends. For at the heart of this invitation is the implication that I, too, have my place and my purpose within the outworking of conscious design that is everywhere around me. This part of me that partakes of the creative intelligence at work throughout the universe has traditionally been called the "soul," and so that is what I will call it in this book. That I apparently possess a soul that is somehow mine, yet also connects me to something much larger, older and wiser, I take to be the greatest miracle of all.

In one way or another, the attempt to understand and articulate the nature, place and purpose of soul has been my lifelong quest. With more than mere academic interest, I have journeyed through many realms — religion, science, philosophy, metaphysics, astrology, psychology, mythology, music and poetry among them — in pursuit of a language to articulate the unfathomable mystery posed by my existence. What I have discovered is that none of these disciplines can fully encompass the soul, yet all have something to contribute to an exploration of the riddles that the soul poses.

Standing outside the circle, beholden to no one worldview, has brought me closer to an evolving truth I could live with. The most valuable truth is less a definitive statement than a kaleidoscope of a question capturing light from every possible angle. To create such a kaleidoscope, I have found it necessary to meander around a focal point of intention, rather than charge my subject matter head on. As I see it, circling is the heart of meaningful inquiry, and paradoxically a more direct pathway to an understanding of soul than assuming definitive answers. Ranier Maria Rilke, one of western civilizations' greatest poets, describes the journey this way:

> I live my life in growing orbits
> which move out over the things of the world.
> Perhaps I can never achieve the last,
> but that will be my attempt.
> I am circling around God, around the ancient tower,
> and I have been circling for a thousand years,
> and I still don't know if I am a falcon, or a storm,
> or a great song.

Not knowing is rarely acknowledged as a virtue by our achievement-oriented culture, but it was for Rilke and is for me a rich and fertile place. When I do not have definitive answers, I am free to turn the kaleidoscope of possibilities, and discover something new. When I think I know something in absolute terms, the pattern gels, and I become a prisoner of that pattern. As beautiful as the pattern may be, something inside of me dies, when I stop circling that "ancient tower" in some misguided attempt to possess it. The cosmic design that has given birth to falcons, storms and great songs cannot be possessed. Like a butterfly, whose seemingly random movements through the garden scatter beauty and pollen upon the dancing wind, something essential is lost forever when truth or beauty get pinned to a dissection board for closer scrutiny. This is not to say that the mystery of soul is inscrutable. We can glimpse it now and then, if we lean into it with open minds and hearts. The mystery is best approached humbly, however, with hat in hand, not with fiercely defended expertise or authority.

Speaking about soul, I readily acknowledge that I am entering a conversation that has been running unabated since the beginning of human discourse. Anthropologists have gradually pieced together an understanding of so-called primitive cultures, that places speculation about the soul — in some cases, rather sophisticated speculation — and preparations for its care, at the very heart of their existence. Religious traditions throughout the ages and around the world have long concerned themselves with the fate of the soul and its relationship to larger questions of life, death and eternity. From circa 600 BCE to the 18th or 19th century, Europe became a hotbed of discussion about soul, and secular and religious philosophers rubbed noses and bumped heads with scientists and theologians, to hash out basic questions about the cosmos, man's place within the natural order, and other endless conundrums. Even after science went its separate way in the 17th century, became king, divorced itself from religion and philosophy, and declared all questions about soul to be irrelevant to an understanding of the universe, curiosity continued to abound. A quick search on the Internet today spits out thousands of references to books offering advice, solace, and/or enlightened perspective to the soul, suggesting that far from being dead, the river of soul has snaked its way through human consciousness, spawning hundreds of tributaries.

At times, the conversation about soul has been a vital raging torrent, sweeping some of the world's greatest minds into its current. At other times, the stream of soul has all but disappeared from the visible landscape, to wind underground through cloistered monasteries, arcane esoteric brotherhoods, and remote mystery schools. Never quite disappearing entirely, this flow has been the metaphysical lifeblood of our species — whether in celebration or neglect. It has coursed through our veins ever since human beings became conscious enough to think and wonder. If I dare to jump into this stream, it is not because I have definitive answers, but because I burn with the same relentless questions that drove those who came before me. The questions, not the answers, are what drive me.

Interest in the soul is as perennial as the return of greenery in the spring, because it speaks to the hidden, durable roots of our existence. The questions posed by soul: "Who am I?", "Why am I here?", "What is the meaning and purpose of my existence?" and "What is my place within the larger scheme of things?" generate a subliminal undertone to every life, regardless of its external shape. There is rarely a moment when these questions do not provide the over-arching context for everything we do in the course of our lives. At times the undertone is scarcely audible; at other times, usually in moments of crisis, it becomes deafening. These questions and our relationship to them define us, not just in temporal, worldly terms, but as spiritual beings, a part of something much larger than can be contained in the mere existence we are trying to understand.

Like Rilke circling his ancient tower, we will circle around these questions posed by soul — which ultimately have no final or absolute answers — at least until the day we die. It is this circling that gives our life its spiritual focus.

Too many who circle these questions believe that finally arriving at the tower, and claiming it for their particular corner of the kingdom, is the object of their quest. This is as true for spiritual seekers, as it is for philosophers, theologians, or scientists. Dogma of any persuasion is not truth, and to muck around in it for any length of time is to lose the capacity to move. That is too steep a price to pay. Truth is a living, breathing work-in-progress. To seek it with integrity is to acknowledge at the outset that it will change into something else the moment you think you have it. My truth will not necessarily be your truth; and what is true for me today may not be true for me tomorrow. It is not "the Truth" that will be of greatest use to the soul, but many smaller truths, which are temporary and relative to the moment. Although I have clung to various truths, from time to time as though they were "the Truth," I have gradually learned that to be true to my soul's particular quest for meaning and purpose, I have had to disavow absolute answers, in whatever guise they try to seduce me. Each pathway to Truth I have explored has proven to be fatally flawed in some way, yet it has been the discovery of such flaws that has kept the kaleidoscope turning, and produced a steady stream of smaller truths of deeper importance to the soul

I once wanted to be a Catholic priest. But then I wondered, "How could a God capable of creating this magnificent universe be so jealous as to exclude from His circle those who had seen the ancient tower from a different perspective?" I once wanted to be a scientist. But then one day in a sophomore titration experiment, watching the colors transmute from black to purple to magenta to red to orange to yellow to amber to clear, I realized that science could not adequately account for the miracle of this ineffable beauty, and unless it could, I had no doubt that in its hands the Truth would become a terminally dry affair. I once wanted to be a psychologist. But I found too much effort to classify people that sacrificed the delicacy of unpredictable nuance in human nature, and too many statistical probabilities that left real people out in the cold. I have immersed myself in the study and practice of astrology for over thirty years, and am still fascinated enough by it to want to write this book to share with you its potential as a language of soul. But I have never been entirely comfortable calling myself an astrologer, because of its association with pop psychology and a personal fate decodable by perfect strangers armed with cookbooks and computers. To the extent that any of these disciplines have attempted to lay claim to the Truth, they have lost a bit of my allegiance, and left me hungering for a less authoritative, more intimate way of knowing.

I quested for a pathway into the nature of reality that would not require me to sell my perpetually evolving soul for access to the Truth. I wanted a path whose guardians were brave enough to acknowledge that getting there was not the point of the journey. I wanted someone to say to me, "I have no answers for you, but I can teach you how to identify the really interesting questions." No one came forward, and I heard my plea echoing onto a battlefield of competing ideologies. The quest for Truth, I soon learned, was rarely pursued as an open-ended inquiry into the kaleidoscopic nature of reality, but more often as a mechanism for validating and asserting a particular point of view. History is filled with religious persecutions of scientific heresies, and vigorous scientific dismissals of metaphysical assumptions. Religions vie amongst themselves for souls — sometimes violently through wars and inquisitions — while physicists, biologists and psychologists often eye each other with suspicion. Astrologers are rarely taken seriously by any of these other disciplines, although within their ranks is great debate over which approach to astrology is most valid.

The most interesting discoveries — that is to say, those most capable of breathing fresh life into the quest for truth — span the conceptual gap between disciplines. Einstein triggered a scientific paradigm shift, not by clinging to the orthodoxy of his profession, but by walking the razor's edge between science and metaphysics. Gandhi brought an empire to its knees, not by selling religious *dogma, but by bridging the gap between religion and secular politics. Jung unhinged the science of psychology by daring to infuse his science with the distinctly unscientific wisdom of ancient myths, fairy tales, alchemy and his own internal voices. None of these pioneers could have unearthed these bits and pieces of soul wisdom without abandoning the quest for Truth, and daring to circle the ancient tower in a more open-ended, multidisciplinary way.

In my own quest, I have found that a willingness to embrace diverse perspectives yields the most useful truth. When any seeker of truth forgets this, in a zealous attempt to embrace the Truth, he or she slips over the thin line between truth and dogma. Religious seekers forget that all paths ultimately lead to God, and begin to proselytize the One True Faith. Scientific seekers lose the spirit of discovery for discovery's sake and begin to design their experiments to prove what they already believe. Psychologists forget they have a complex living person in front of them, and begin to unconsciously mold their clients to fit their pet theories about human nature. Astrologers with chart in hand begin to think they know who their client is, before he or she even walks through the door.

Regardless of the path that is followed, when it alone becomes the sole determinant of Truth, the circling of the ancient tower that gives vitality to the quest ceases, the kaleidoscope stops turning, and truth begins to rot as dogma on a cultivated vine.

A natural born skeptic and outsider by nature, I am free to discover beauty and value in each approach, yet escape the predisposition to close-mindedness that seems to plague most "true believers." I see that each discipline has glimpsed some essential understanding that is missing in the other perspectives, and from that I can weave a much more interesting collage than any dogmatist. Since the very thought of such work excites me, I feel certain that I must be hot on the trail of something useful to my quest — and hopefully of interest to others. At the very least, I am compelled to follow this particular trail around the ancient tower, just to see what I can see.

What I value from the religious perspective in general, and my own religious upbringing in particular, is the concept of soul. To a scientist, the world is devoid of soul. To the psychologist versed in the more traditional branches of the art, soul is but the primordial soup out of which a more functionally useful ego must arise to shape and steer the personality. Even to the religious seeker, soul is a means to an end — defined as salvation, enlightenment, or transcendence. From the religious perspective, however, we have an acknowledgment that the same forces that have shaped this miraculous creation have shaped us as well, and it is this aspect of the perspective I find attractive.

In Part One of this book, I travel through the religious worldview with more focused attention. My intent is to help free the soul from the straightjacket that religion has imposed upon it, and point the way toward a more useful understanding of the soul's spiritual dimension. If I understand myself to be a soul, grown from the same soil as everything else in this manifest universe, then I will recognize myself, and learn something new, each time I encounter a falcon, a storm, or a great song. This possibility of recognition is what gives my soul's journey its momentum and its promise of joyful reunion with a larger Self[1] — call it God or Spirit. If I take this possibility to its most enticing extreme, everywhere I go, there "I" am, and my circling around the ancient tower becomes a process of meeting my Self in every possible dimension. The Sufi poet, Rumi once put this thought in a poem called "The Turn:":

> I stand up, and this one of me
> turns into a hundred of me.
> They say I circle around you.
> Nonsense. I circle around me.

What I value from the scientific perspective is the discipline of empirical inquiry guided by logic. Science labors under the illusion of objectivity, although its own experiments have proven that the mindset and expectations of the observer affect the outcome of the observations. Science also refuses to acknowledge any pathway to knowledge but that which can be traversed by the left-brain, analytical, rational mind, while the right-brain, intuitive, metaphorical mind is actually better suited to the courting of mystery. But science does recognize the value of forming a relationship to the truth that is based upon empirical evidence, and as I hope to demonstrate later in this book, this is an attitude that is just as useful to the evolution of an intimately personal truth as it is to the validation of objective truth.

Traditional religion abdicates this responsibility to provide evidence for one's claims about the nature of reality. In place of empirical inquiry, religion requires faith. If you trace the history of most religions back far enough, faith is just another word for placing greater credence in someone else's experiences than your own.

To the extent that psychology has arisen from and wedded itself to the scientific worldview, it has built its truth with the same insistence on left-brain objectivity that renders science useless as a tool for exploring subjective truth. Individual experience is often forced into a common mold in order to fit psychological theory, instead of being allowed to reveal its own subjective logic in terms that are unique to it.

In Part Two of this book, I outline what I feel are the limitations and virtues of the scientific method. Then I invite the reader to imagine what an empirical pathway of inquiry into the nature of the soul's journey might look like, once it has been freed from the tyranny of objectivity and the rational mind. Soul, by its very nature, speaks to us in a fluid language of image, symbol and metaphor, colored intimately by sensory awareness and feelings. The truth revealed by this language is multidimensional, often paradoxical or self-contradictory, and open to many interpretations, each of which can be a useful turning of the kaleidoscope. If we are going to establish a relationship with soul that can be articulated, we must be open to a more meandering approach as we pursue the various clues the soul will drop — in our dreams, through synchronistic encounters with others who serve as mirrors to our truth, in seemingly random patterns that play themselves out all around us in concert with our movements. This process is absolutely empirical in nature, though not in the way that science understands the term.

Our goal is to develop a focus which is intent enough to penetrate the veils, but not so narrowly defined that we cannot catch the subtler choreography of soul that often takes place at the periphery of our awareness. Science tries to squeeze out the periphery; we want to stake our claim somewhere between what we can observe through direct attention and what we can't quite bring into focus, except by an endless circling of the mystery that soul is. We don't want to lose the valuable discipline that observation brings, but we also want to observe ourselves observing, and find our truth somewhere between the one who is seeing and the one who is being seen.

◇◇◇◇◇◇◇◇◇◇◇◇◇◇

What I value about psychology that seems missing from science, religion, and often astrology, is its focus on addressing core issues — those seemingly intractable patterns in our lives that cause pain and suffering. Through the god-like auspices of medicine, and increasingly through a form of psychology that is rooted in neurochemistry, science seeks to alleviate pain, if not eliminate it altogether. Religion considers it a virtue to endure pain, rationalizing that a painful life is the price of sin, and that if one suffers silently and plays by the rules, one's reward will come in the next life. For all their theories about where pain comes from and what can be done about it, most psychologists at least recognize the value of entering more deeply into our suffering in order to understand it, work through it, and then let it go. My sense is that core issues are not quite so easily released, but are meant to be the catalyst to a lifelong process of learning that is often psychological in nature as well as a pivotal path to evolution in the life of the soul. The work of soul is, in fact, living with, coming to more conscious terms with, and slowly transmuting core issues. Psychology can give us some of the language and perspective with which to do this work, even if it doesn't always recognize the true spiritual purpose of the work.

In Part Three, I explore certain psychological perspectives and concepts that can be useful cornerstones in a language of soul. The life of the soul parallels, and is not entirely separate from a developmental approach to psychology, which recognizes human growth as more than just a pathway of adaptation to social norms. No one has articulated this perspective more clearly than Carl Jung, who was brave enough to engage the soul not only in his academic role as a psychological pioneer, but also quite intimately in his personal life. In particular, his concept of the archetypes as guides to various phases of the soul's evolutionary process, will serve as a valuable template to an astropoetic language of soul. Jung's work has been carried forward into contemporary times by a small army of dedicated psychologists, none more important than James Hillman, from whom we will occasionally draw important inspiration for the trek into more decidedly astrological waters. The humanistic and transpersonal schools of psychology are likewise a valuable source of understanding about the generic evolution of soul within the human psyche. However, it is an understanding that we will necessarily have to glean through peripheral vision, as we make important distinctions between soul and Spirit on the transpersonal side of the equation, and between soul and the human being (as understood without reference to Spirit) on the humanistic side.

Before these psychological concepts are ready for prime time soul work, we will have to extract them from the scientific mindset out of which they evolved, for many of the pitfalls that hamper science's ability to serve as an adequate language of soul also impede psychology. Like science, psychology seeks a rational explanation for the function of a biochemical machine, or the cause of behavior that deviates from a mythical norm, or the confirmation of its own theories. The human soul is not that easily captured in a neat analytical box, and is often absent from psychological discourse. Each soul is in fact, a one-of-a-kind work of art in progress, and this bugaboo has yet to register in the psychological kingdom.

Before psychological concepts can be truly helpful to the soul, the widespread preoccupation with articulating the universal human experience as if all life was stamped out of a monolithic genetic template must be exposed as a shallow, self-serving exercise. Labeling a common problem, ADD (Attention Deficit Disorder), for example, may benefit the drug companies providing treatment, but it does not help the individual soul to understand how its particular struggle with this malady is part of a larger, more important journey toward wholeness and integration. Similarly, personality types, statistical observations of human behavior, and psychological profiles do not speak to the individual soul in a language it can understand.

To render psychology useful, we must give it back to the individual. Only as we each find an intimately personal language to talk about the psychology of soul, will we step onto a path we can truly call our own. We all use the same words. But words have different meanings in different contexts, and before we can talk intelligently about the soul, we must reinterpret basic principles through a deeper allegiance to the context in which each individual life gropes toward meaning. If the individual soul is to be empowered to recognize and actualize itself, we must realize that each life has its own internal logic. This logic must be honored beyond allegiance to pet theories of personality development, or treatment modality,

◇◇◇◇◇◇◇◇◇◇◇◇◇◇◇◇

Astrology at its best is a language by which we might describe the psychology of soul in the most personal terms. The birthchart is literally a map of the heavens at the time of one's birth that is thoroughly infused with deep metaphorical significance. Each birthchart is as unique as the person reflected in its image, and through the application of astrological principles, something of the nature of the individual soul and its process can be discerned and articulated. Much of the language of astrology is rooted in mythology, which is where our pre-scientific understanding of collective human psychology is found. But since the birthchart is so intimately personal, astrology allows us to approach the soul life of each individual on its own terms, showing not only how an individual participates in the life of the collective, but also how he or she is struggling to give birth to a shining potentiality that is as unique as their fingerprints or the sound of their voice.

Some who read this book may feel uncomfortable that I include astrology as an equal partner in a discussion with "more respectable" disciplines such as religion, science, and psychology. It may help to know that the astrology I promote bears no relationship to the superficial daily horoscope columns on the entertainment page of your daily newspaper, and is even quite different in many ways than that commonly practiced by most professional astrologers. For reasons that I will outline throughout this book, the astrological worldview per se lends itself quite nicely to a discussion of soul, and it may inspire you to consider the enormous contribution astrology can make, even though it may take you outside of your intellectual comfort zone. The very premise on which astrology is based — namely that there is a discernible relationship between the evolving cosmic order (the macrocosm) and the journey of the individual soul (the microcosm) — adds a dimension to the discussion of soul that is missing from the other disciplines we shall consider in this book. Because this is so, I would ask you to be open-minded as I demonstrate the ways in which astrology can fill some of the conceptual gaps left by these other disciplines.

Having said that, I would also argue that there are many ways in which the practice of astrology must change, before its potential contribution to a language of soul can be realized. Throughout this book, but particularly in Part Four, I will not hesitate to point out these shortcomings. I will differentiate an approach to the use of astrology – called astropoetics - that deviates from common astrological practice in several important ways. Like religion, science, and psychology, astrology is subject to calcification, and astrological dogma abounds. In practice, astrology's usefulness as a language with which to discuss the soul's journey depends upon the sensibilities of the individual astrologer, and many astrologers are conditioned by bad habits that have become institutionalized within the discipline.

Astrologers are also conditioned, like everyone else, by exposure to a common cultural heritage in which religion, science and psychology have dominated the discussion about soul for millennia. When astrologers speak of soul, they generally either follow psychologists in confusing soul with personality, or they attempt to graft religious and/or metaphysical principles onto their interpretations without considering the astro-logical[2] basis for their inclusion. With a few isolated exceptions, the practice of astrology has also become too analytical, too focused on the rational interpretation of symbols that have been reduced to a form of shorthand notation, and too far removed from the visceral, emotional, unconscious potency of the fertile imagery in which its symbols are rooted. All these conditioned responses and bad habits must be addressed before astrology can make a meaningful contribution to a useful language of soul.

Within the astrological community, there is a particularly strong internal pressure to establish credibility with the scientific establishment. To my way of thinking, this means adopting a mindset and approach to inquiry that is antithetical to astrology's purpose. Astrology is often labeled "unscientific" by its detractors, and at the risk of evoking the protestations of some astrologers, I would have to agree. It *is* unscientific, and so it should be. To the extent that astrology is understood as a symbolic language, it does not easily conform to the same worldview that science considers philosophical bedrock. Science looks at the world from a perspective that is rational, quantitative, causal, impersonal, and objective. When understood on its own terms, astrology provides a radically different turning of the kaleidoscope, one that is wholistic, qualitative, acausal, intimately personal, and subjective — everything that science is not.

To state that astrology is "unscientific" does not negate its worth as a pathway of inquiry into the nature, meaning and purpose of human experience. Quite the contrary.

Because astrology is not bound by the narrow dictates of a paradigm designed to measure external consensus reality, it has an advantage in addressing matters of soul, which are unique to the individual, intimately personal, and not measurable in any meaningful sense by the quantitative tools of science. Astrology is predicated on its own non-scientific brand of logic, rooted in symbol and metaphor, suggesting an alternative discipline of inquiry into matters relevant to the soul that I call astro-logic. Astro-logic is a logic of context, which derives its potency through correlations between symbolism and real life experience. It is ultimately astro-logic — and not an astrology forced awkwardly into a scientific mold — which must serve as the basis for an astrological understanding of soul.

A significant number of astrologers within the scientific camp emphasize the predictive superiority of astrology, proposing an approach to astrology that perhaps has its place within the study of stock markets, earthquakes, and sunspot activity. Astrology's predictive capacity begins to break down, however, once we enter the realm of individual human psychology. The debate between advocates of free will and harbingers of fate is as old as time itself, but it simply makes no sense to talk about the soul, if the soul is not capable of evolving in consciousness through the exercise of choice, and this is where I beg to differ with those who tout astrology's virtues as a predictive science. At any given time, we are capable of making choices that break the patterns that we ourselves have previously established. Because we have this power, all attempts at prediction of human behavior based upon an understanding of those patterns becomes a crap shoot. I will not argue with the premise that life is fated in certain ways that are beyond our control, but it is how we *respond* to this fate that determines who we are as souls, and I would assert that this cannot be predicted.

A second major movement has been set in motion through the scholarly efforts of those intent upon restoring astrology to its traditional roots, through the translation of Medieval, early Greek, and pre-Hellenic texts. While no one can discount the unprecedented contribution these dedicated souls have made to our understanding of astrology's origins, most of the material generated through this exploration seems too rule-bound, and too strictly focused within an astrological context — that is to say, a consideration of the birthchart alone — to provide useful articulation of an intimately personal understanding of soul.

On the other side of the cultural divide, but in some ways aligned with both the predictive camp and the Western historians, are the Vedic astrologers. This group has its own rules, steeped in Eastern cultural beliefs about human nature, and is perhaps more overtly geared toward prediction than its Western counterpart. Both Western historians and Vedic astrologers, though outwardly very different from one another, promote a rational, rule-based consideration of the birthchart, which is construed as a predictive tool not particularly dependent upon input from the person to whom the chart refers. The astro-logic I discuss in this book, by contrast, cannot be understood without reference to the life in which it is unfolding, and must be flexible enough to re-create itself in language that is intrinsic to the individual. Hard and fast rules are obviously anathema to this kind of approach.

More closely aligned with my astrological perspective is an equally vociferous subculture of psychologically oriented astrologers. Of these, a handful are identified with humanistic and transpersonal schools of thought, pioneered in the 1960s and 1970s by a Jungian Renaissance astrologer named Dane Rudhyar. Rudhyar had wide ranging roots in the theosophical writings of Alice Bailey and Helena Blavatsky; the Western hermetic tradition as espoused by Manly Palmer Hall and Aleister Crowley; the teachings of Lao Tzu; the emerging philosophy of holism promoted by Ian Smuts; the humanistic school of psychology being developed by Abraham Maslow and others; and the astrological tutelage of his mentor, Marc Edmond Jones. Rudhyar was also a poet, painter, and composer, whose eclectic exposure to diverse sources of inspiration empowered him to breathe fresh life into an ancient tradition that had begin to show the inflexibility of its age.

Though a few bright lights in the astrological community continue to be inspired by Rudhyar's seminal work, many of the philosophical insights that deeply influenced astrologers a generation ago have since been compromised by a creeping mindset which prefers predictability to process. Astute psychological analyses of everything astrological abound, and it is now possible — thanks to modern technology — to simulate a psychological analysis of any birthchart by computer. To my way of thinking, however, the astrological profile — whether encapsulated in some cookbook, faithfully spit up by some well-crafted computer program, or parroted to a real live client by a real live astrologer — is of limited use in reaching the soul where it actually lives. As convenient as it would be, one size does not fit all when it comes to interpretation of astrological symbolism, because the consciousness of the person living the symbolism will forever be the deciding factor, and consciousness cannot be assessed with reference to the birthchart alone. Life context is as important as astrological context, and without it even the most psychologically enlightened analysis of the birthchart might as well be talking to the wall.

Where I beg to differ with most psychologically oriented astrologers is in attempting to fit the chart to the person, rather than the person to the chart, and whatever astrological profile it reflects. There are as many astrological signatures for any psychological condition you could possibly profile as there are individuals to color them with their own particular brand of eccentricity. And without the life story that gives the birthchart meaning, the profile means nothing. It means even less if the story is not considered in relation to the evolutionary agenda of the soul, which can be deduced through reference to the chart and the story considered together side by side. This agenda is best delineated in a language that evokes the imagery, feelings and sensory memories that form the lifeblood of the soul, rather than the rational definitions that have become gospel among traditional astrologers. This is where I intend to steer the astrological discussion that weaves throughout this book, and culminates in Part Four. Along the way, I will outline in some detail these and other astrological biases, and point the way toward a poetic use of the astrological language that is capable of speaking more clearly to the soul.

Some astrologers who read this book may be disappointed by the fact that this is not primarily a book of astrological shop talk. I confess that my original intent was to write such a book. But as I began to put together the more overtly astrological material I had culled from more than thirty years of practice, I realized that such a book would be premature without first establishing a philosophical foundation on which the practice of astrology might begin to make a more coherent contribution to the discussion about soul. Before we can even begin to address the soul from an astrological perspective, we must be clear what it is we are addressing and who it is that is asking the questions. More important than how we work with astrology, or which techniques we use is how we understand what we do and why we do it, and it is these larger issues that I hope to begin addressing in this book. I will not do this strictly as an astrologer, but within the context of a more general discussion of the presuppositions with which we approach the soul — presuppositions that affect astrologers and non-astrologers alike.

The intent of this book is to introduce a more open-ended approach to the understanding of soul that does not depend upon any particular system, or philosophical perspective. The essence of the soul is something that cannot be captured in words, much less words that have been codified into dogma, or a systemic thought process. The great Catch-22 in beginning any journey into the heart of Mystery, however, is that words are all we have to articulate our understanding in any given moment. Flawed though our perpetually transient knowledge of soul might be, there is something about transmuting that knowledge into words that provides an opening to the next step on our path. Western metaphysicians, Eastern gurus, Third World shamans, astrologers, and other assorted doctors of soul have all understood the magical power of words to bring the energy underlying those words to life. In talking about the soul, we embody the soul, and infuse it with a life of its own, which in turn re-infuses us with a certain spiritual vitality that is worth talking about.

How we talk about soul matters. For the soul can be trapped by words as easily as it can be set free. The words we choose must have the transparency to reveal multiple

◇◇

dimensions. They must invoke the creative imagination to see beyond the words themselves into the essence of soul-full experiences that cannot be captured by them. No language in existence does this better than poetry, and any language — astrological or otherwise — that intends to speak to the soul, must necessarily be poetic. The poetic art lies in using words to slip between the cracks of language, into the depths of meaning and mystery. And for all our fishtailing around in the realm of words, it is ultimately into this wordless place that we are going. Words that have solidified into precise associations cannot take us there, but words shaped poetically can at least bring the ancient tower into kaleidoscopic view.

When we arrive at our destination, if there is such a place, then we can let the birthchart and every other philosophical artifice go, as we would a fading dream in morning light. We can allow all theory to drop away like petals on a perpetually self-generating rose, and simply experience what is there — here — to be experienced on the threshold of soul itself. If we are brave enough to make the leap from this threshold into the heart of Mystery, we will at last know what Rilke knows when he speaks to us about the Buddha inside the light:

> The core of every core, the kernel of every kernel,
> an almond! held in itself, deepening in sweetness;
> all of this, everything, right up to the stars,
> is the meat around your stone. Accept my bow.
> Oh, yes, you feel it, how the weights on you are gone!
> Your husk has reached into what has no end,
> and that is where the great saps are brewing now.
> On the outside is a warmth helping,
> for, high, high above, your own suns are growing
> immense and they glow as they wheel around.
> Yet something has already started to live
> in you that will live longer than the suns.

To get to this timeless place of awe and wonder within us, we must shed everything nonessential that has been wrapped around the concept of soul - by religion, science, psychology and astrology — so that we can see and feel what is there beneath the "meat around the stone" of these disciplines. If we are to evolve a truly useful language of soul, then we must find a way to allow the soul to speak for itself, without unnecessary translation, especially where the true agenda of the translator is rooted in a primal fear of the soul's potency. Religion keeps the soul bound to dogma for the same reason that science denies the soul's existence, psychology subordinates the soul to the ego, and astrology confuses soul with the map used to navigate its journey. Left to its own devices, soul transcends all attempts by religion, science, psychology, and astrology to contain it, and in so doing, pricks the balloon of self-importance by which these disciplines keep themselves afloat. The individual soul does not need religion, science, psychology, or astrology to form a meaningful relationship to itself. Quite the contrary, it is only as each soul liberates itself from the religious, scientific, psychological, astrological and other conceptual chains which bind it, that it is free to find out What is living inside it that will live longer than the suns.

The Seven Gates of Soul

My intention is to initiate a journey that will help us loosen some of these conceptual chains. As we enter this process, it will be helpful to imagine that our journey bears some affinity to that undertaken by the Mesopotamian goddess, Inanna, as she enters the realm of the dead. Inanna. "Queen of the Sky," and Goddess of War as well as Love, is driven by an inordinate lust for power, in much the same way as the authoritative champions of religion, science, psychology, astrology or any other discipline are driven to claim the Truth as their personal domain. Having tricked her father, Enki, the God of Wisdom to relinquish the Tablets of Destiny and other sacred treasures, Inanna grows bold and turns her ambitions to the underworld of soul governed by her sister, Ereshkigal. Dressing in her finest regalia, and fortified by all the accoutrements of her authority (Powell 37), Inanna storms the gates of the underworld, arrogantly demanding:

> Gatekeeper, let me in! Open your gate for me!
> Open your gate and let me in!
> If you don't open the gate and let me in,
> I will smash the gate and splinter the bolt!
> I will smash the doorjambs and knock down the doors.
> I will raise up the dead, who will devour the living:
> the dead will outnumber the living!

The gatekeeper responds by asking Inanna the archetypal question posed by soul: "Who are you?" Inanna, puffed up to her fullest sense of self-importance, responds, "I am Inanna from the place of sunrise." The gatekeeper tells Inanna to wait, while consulting with Ereshkigal, who recognizes her power-hungry sister, and informs her that in order to enter the underworld, or realm of soul, she will have to pass through seven gates in accordance with "the ancient rites."

At the first gate, Inanna is forced to relinquish her crown, and with it a fairly hefty chunk of the self-importance that makes her who she thinks she is. At each subsequent gate, Inanna is compelled to remove an additional piece of clothing or jewelry, and with it shed another layer of the worldly identity on which her supposed authority depends. Inanna protests loudly, but is told, "Be quiet, Inanna! This is the way of the underworld." By the time she passes through the seventh gate, Inanna is naked, stripped of all pretension to certainty about who she is, and face to face with "the core of every core, the kernel of every kernel." When Inanna continues to protest, and attempts to forcibly remove Ereshkigal from her throne, Ereshkigal summons her guards and turns Inanna into a slab of flesh, green and rotting with decay, hung on a peg in the corner of the room. Inanna finally makes it to the realm of soul, but not in the triumphant style of the conquering queen she wanted to be. There is more to the story than this, but for now, it is enough to note the fate of one who storms the realm of soul under the authoritative mantle of certainty.

As the myth implies, only in a place of naked humility can the soul can be revealed. Only as we shed the various ideas that buffer us from an encounter with the soul, will we hear what the soul is trying to tell us, and then speak, in turn, a language that the soul understands. Each circling of the ancient tower that we undertake through the chapters of this book will afford us an opportunity to shed another layer of conditioning that buffers our experience of the soul, and pass through yet another gate. By the end of the book, we will hopefully enter the presence of soul, possessing the kernel of a language with which we can speak of that which cannot be encompassed by words.

Endnotes

1   From time to time throughout this book, I will capitalize words like Self or Being or You, which are ordinarily not capitalized. My purpose in doing this is indicate that what I am referring to is a larger sense of identity with God or Spirit or some transcendent reality that cannot be contained within the limitations of everyday speech.

2   When the word astrological is spelled "astro-logical," it refers to a system of symbolic logic on which astrological correspondences are based. In practice, astrologers often memorize correspondences or defer to tradition, without reference to the astro-logic behind their interpretations. The word is therefore meant to embody and encourage a more conscious approach to astrology, rooted in symbolic principles. The word astrology is used, by contrast, to refer to common practice.

PART ONE

THROUGH THE GATES OF RELIGION

Chapter One
Toward a Working Definition of Soul

Soul is defined by most traditions as a spiritual essence. It is the animating principle of life, that which gives us our vitality, motivates us to move toward gradual fulfillment of our sense of purpose, and infuses our life with meaning. Within the context of this definition – which is nearly universally shared by all religions – it is easy to forget, or take for granted, or even deny the fact that the life we hope to infuse with meaning and purpose is the one we live inside this body, on a physical planet bound by time and space. It is, in fact, the animating presence of Spirit[1] within the body that makes life, as we know it, possible. The perennial questions that soul poses – "Who am I?", "Why am I here?", "What is my place within the larger scheme of things?" and "What is the meaning and purpose of my existence?" – make sense only within the context of an embodied life. We would not be asking these questions were we not alive in physical form. To realize the full implication of this self-evident truth, is to require a broader definition of soul – one that encompasses both its spiritual essence and its physical containment within a body. Because this is so, I will talk about soul in a slightly different way than it is normally discussed.

Redefining the Soul as an Embodiment of Spirit

As James Hillman has suggested, soul "is neither physical and material on one hand, nor spiritual and abstract on the other, yet bound to them both" (68). It inhabits the middle ground between Spirit and body, a sacred territory that has been largely abandoned by religion. Most religious traditions identify the soul exclusively with Spirit, and place it in opposition to the mortal body in which it is housed. In the formative years of the Judeo-Christian tradition, the body was thought to be a source of imprisonment, while many of the early Greek mystery cults felt the body was something to be endured until one had enough knowledge to move beyond it. Buddhists consider the body a source of suffering to be transcended by detachment. Hindus believe the body and the physical realm to which it was bound to be a dance of *maya*, that is to say, an illusory dream. When these and other traditions speak about soul, they use the term as a synonym for the presence of God, or Spirit, within the body, but deny, downplay or denigrate the role that the body plays in housing Spirit. Yet, as contemporary mystical theologian Matthew Fox reminds us, "there can be no living worship without the body. We *are* our bodies – though more than our bodies. Our bodies are the temple that contemples us with other temples, other bodies of the universe, bodies of stars, of suns, of earth, of winged, finned, four-legged and two-legged brothers and sisters, children all of a living God" (217).

To simply dismiss the relationship between soul and body as many religions do is to deny the very act of incarnation that provides the opportunity for a spiritual life in the first place. It is not possible to experience the presence of Spirit within the embodied life, while trying to escape or transcend or otherwise deny the body that makes the experience possible. As Walt Whitman once put it, "If anything is sacred, the human body is sacred." Before we can comprehend the soul in its human dimension, we must first find a language broad enough to recognize Spirit and body as partners in a sacred dance they must negotiate together. Soul, as I am choosing to define it, is *the embodiment of Spirit*.

Distinguishing the Embodied Soul From the Postmortem Soul

To talk meaningfully about the soul in this way, it is important to make a few distinctions. First, in differentiating Spirit and soul, I do not wish to deny the possibility that something essential within us survives physical death. Nearly all religious traditions throughout the world agree on this point, although there are important differences when discussion turns to what, exactly, that something is. Most Western religions believe that the soul is a discrete entity that survives intact as a unit after death. Buddhists and many early indigenous cultures believe that what survives is the Life Energy contained within the soul, but not the individual soul itself. Many esoteric traditions – such as those practiced among Taoist yogis, Yaqui shamans, and Tibetan Buddhist monks - believe the survival of the soul's identity after death is a possibility, but not a given. To reach immortality within these traditions requires mastery of advanced spiritual practices, and only the most fiercely dedicated souls complete the arduous journey. Many mystics suggest that when the state of being we call immortality is reached, there is no one there to experience it. Or as American mystic, Ram Dass succinctly put it, "The difference between you and... a perfected being is that they aren't and you still think you are" (Grist for the Mill 166). That is to say, immortality is attainable, but only at the supreme cost of individual identity, which flows back into the cosmic ocean out of which it emerged.

It is likely that something survives the transition from life to death, but exactly what that is remains part of the Great Unknown. Even those who return from near-death experiences convinced of the soul's capacity to survive physical death are only able to convey their message because the etheric cord connecting Spirit and body was never completely severed. What happens after the cord *is* severed cannot be discussed with final authority by the living. As Zen master Gudo responded to a student who asked him where souls go after death, "I know not... because I have not died yet" (Reps 55). We can believe whatever we choose to believe about what happens after death, but all we can actually *know* about ourselves as *living* souls must be experienced within the context of our embodiment.

Reconsidering Past Life Experiences From the Perspective of the Embodied Soul

Many people, myself included, have had past life experiences that seem to affirm that an immortal soul evolves through multiple incarnations. If these experiences are what they appear to be, then we might be justified in taking them as evidence that some essential piece of our individual identity survives physical death. Regardless of how convinced we are of the reality of such experiences, we must remember that they are taking place within the mind, heart, and soul of a being alive in *this* life. How such experiences might be construed, or even whether they are comprehensible once this life has ended is not something we can possibly know. To interpret them in a broader context that assumes a personal existence beyond the life of the body is inherently a leap of faith. Whether we live other lives or not, the embodied soul is bound to *this* life, through its relationship to the body, and it is within *this* life that it must evolve a sense of relationship to Spirit, a spiritual identity, and a sense of meaning and purpose. Once the soul is no longer embodied, it ceases to exist in the form in which we have come to know it. Spirit itself may well cycle endlessly through the life and death of countless bodies, but the individual soul depends upon the body with which it identifies in *this* life for its experience of Spirit cycling through it.

Perhaps our apparent connection to other lives in other times and places is not chronological, as it seems to be from a linear perspective, but concurrent. The Seth material – channeled by Jane Roberts before channeling was popular – teaches that we live all of our incarnations simultaneously. Seth suggests that as we emerge into the realm of space and time from a timeless existence in Spirit, or *Source Self* as Roberts calls it, the various dimensions of our being appear to be laid out chronologically as a succession of lives. According to this view, however, *Source Self* is the only "One" experiencing these lives and beyond the realm of space and time, they are all happening simultaneously (157-160). Spirit assumes many temporary forms, but the coming and going of these forms is nothing more than the eternal play of Spirit, taking place in the here and now. From this perspective, it is not necessary to consider more than one incarnation in order to understand the experience of past lives.

Prominent psychiatrist and consciousness researcher, Stanislav Grof, summarizes his study of past life experiences by emphasizing that he does not consider these experiences "to be necessarily a proof that we have lived before," although he does not go so far as to discount the possibility. "It is interesting to notice," he observes, "that in the mystical tradition literal belief in reincarnation of separate individuals is seen as an inferior and less sophisticated interpretation of karmic experiences. In its complete form, the reincarnation theory suggests that all divisions and boundaries in the universe are illusory and arbitrary. In the last analysis it is only the creative principle, or cosmic consciousness, that actually exists. An individual who penetrates to this ultimate knowledge will see the realm of karmic appearances as just another level of illusion" (Adventure of Self-Discovery 90-91).

This is not to say that information about past lives cannot be valuable to the soul in negotiating this life. Information about past lives provides a rich metaphorical description of the spiritual dilemma faced by the soul in the present moment. I have personally found this information useful in explaining stubborn psychological patterns with no discernible source, though I hesitate to consider it as literal description of my embodied soul's experience. Matthew Fox suggests that a preoccupation with literal interpretations of past lives can become a form of what he calls *pseudo-mysticism*, a substitute for the lack of a genuine, direct connection to Spirit in this life. "Invariably I have found that persons dealing with 'past lives' are working out – often in a very commendable and creative way – the deep suffering and pain from their present life. This connection is lost when the preoccupation with past lives loses its metaphorical base. The result is a severe underestimation of one's present responsibilities and opportunities" (46).

Regardless of what we personally believe about the survival of the soul after death, it is self-evident that the postmortem soul is different than what we call the soul while we are alive in a body. The sacred dance between Spirit and body ends at death, and because this is so, the experience of soul after death must be different than it was during life. Religious traditions that identify the postmortem soul with immortal Spirit may be correct. But the embodied soul's experience is more complex, and I think it is worth making a distinction. According to the definition of soul proposed here, I would reserve the concept of soul for the experience of conscious embodiment in a living body.

Distinguishing the Embodied Soul From Disembodied Spirits

The second distinction I wish to make is between embodied Spirit and disembodied spirits. Focusing on the embodied soul, does not imply that I believe a body is essential to the life of Spirit in manifest form. Scripture, myth and folklore of all traditions are filled with references to angels, ghosts, demons, fairies, devas, and countless other disincarnate beings on other, non-physical planes of existence, who apparently exist perfectly well without bodies. In proposing a narrower focus that encompasses only the embodied soul, I do not wish to deny the potential reality of such beings. Nor do I discount the possibility that non-physical entities can interact with and impact the embodied soul. In fact, there is a vast body of shamanic literature to suggest that this is so (Eliade, Shamanism; Harner).

I once had an encounter with a disembodied spirit[2] in college. During this phase of my own spiritual journey, I was enamored of communing with the spirit world, and started experimenting with automatic writing. I joined a group called Spiritual Frontier Fellowship, which encouraged the cultivation of psychic abilities, and over a period of time, I became a recognized "channel" for weekly messages to the group. One evening, after an especially powerful session, I began to feel rather strange. I said my good-byes and began walking home, when I noticed – much to my horror – that I was not walking the way that I normally walk, nor was I thinking thoughts I would characteristically think. The only way I could understand what was happening was to speculate that some non-physical entity was trying to possess me. I told my roommate what was happening when I got back to my apartment, and together we worked to "exorcize the demon." The non-physical being with whom I was compelled to struggle eventually told me his name was "Manhandler," and that he was determined to replace me as the resident of my body.

It took a supreme act of will to banish this being, and secure the sanctity of my own physical space. After a couple intense and grueling hours, Manhandler finally got the message and left. Then and there, I vowed to give up automatic writing, and to bring my spirituality firmly back into the embodied world. In retrospect, I can see this experience as an important step onto the path that has lead to the understanding of soul presented in this book, since it was apparent to me even then that embodiment was a state of being craved by at least one class of non-physical entity. At the time, however, the struggle to claim my own body was an incomprehensible and terrifying experience, and I lost all interest in trying to attain spiritual enlightenment outside of its comforting embrace. In any case, within the context of the distinction I am making here, I consider these non-physical beings to be in the realm of spirit, and reserve the concept of soul for sentient beings inhabiting a physical body. I leave the discussion of interactions between non-physical beings and the embodied soul to those more skilled in negotiating these realms.

Distinguishing Between the Embodied Soul And the Subtle Body

The final distinction between the embodied soul and the subtle body (also known as the etheric or astral body, the etheric double, the aura, the electromagnetic field, the energy or light body, etc.) is one central to mystical, magical and esoteric traditions throughout the world. In attempting to address the arena in which many spiritual experiences take place, these traditions discuss the existence of an intermediary dimension of being between Spirit and body that is neither physical nor spiritual, but psychic (Myss 33-35). I would consider my experience with Manhandler to fall into this category, as well as certain other out-of-body experiences, altered states of consciousness, and lucid dreams that I have had at various stages of my spiritual journey.

Within this psychic dimension of being, the soul has the freedom to move beyond the ordinary limitations of matter, time and space, while the body is more susceptible to the influence of Spirit within it. Or as humanistic psychologist, Jean Houston, succinctly puts it, psychic phenomena are "by-products of the simultaneous-everywhere-matrix" (190). Shamans, for example, work within this realm as out-of-body healers. In this work, they are connected "by a string, rope, an invisible band, or a thread as delicate as that of a spider's web" (Kalweit 48) to their bodies, while simultaneously being free to traverse at the speed of thought an invisible world of spirits and other non-physical entities with the power to affect the living.

When I describe the soul as the embodiment of Spirit I do not mean that soul does not exist as a psychic entity, or that the life of the soul cannot be understood on this level. Quite the contrary. The psychic realm is a manifestation of this same interplay between Spirit and the body that gives rise to the embodied soul I am discussing. As I see it, however, the subtle body addressed by psychics, shamans and many alternative healers is at one end of the spectrum of possibilities for interaction between Spirit and body, while the embodied soul is at the other. Those who work with the subtle body attempt to explore this relationship from a vantage point as far into the nonphysical realm as it possible to go, without severing Spirit's connection to the body. By contrast, the goal of the embodied soul is to enter as deeply into the body and the embodied world as it can, without severing the body's conscious connection to Spirit. Or put another way, the embodied soul seeks to fully incarnate, and bring as much consciousness as possible to its life within the material realm.

Both the psychic and the embodied definition of soul require a living relationship between Spirit and body to realize their respective agendas. This is only possible when the body is acknowledged to be as necessary to the living vitality of soul as Spirit. Both also seek harmony between Spirit and body, but they seek this harmony in radically different ways. Since I am not a shaman, nor a psychic healer, I will leave the discussion of the relationship between the embodied soul and the etheric realms to those qualified to speak about it. Instead, I will discuss how embodiment itself can be understood as a spiritual experience, and how we might begin to devise a language with which to talk about it in this way.

The Roots of the Embodied Soul in Spiritual Tradition

Embodiment means more than just having a body. As most religious and many esoteric traditions declare, we are born of Spirit. God, or the Creative Force that has given rise to this manifest creation, so they say, has also created us in Its likeness, and in a very deep sense we are as much a product of this Creative Spirit as we are of the body. But we are *both* Spirit and body, coming together in a miraculous fusion of opposites. The first piece of religious conditioning that we must shed before we can pass through Inanna's first gate is an insistence on narrowly identifying soul with Spirit. Religions that do so often forget their own roots as philosophies of embodiment.

In many early religious traditions, the soul was considered to be thoroughly dependent on the body for its existence, and it was the embodied soul, and not the postmortem soul that was the focus of attention. The ancient Mesopotamians, Hebrews and Greeks all generally conceived of the individual as a psycho-physical organism, whose existence required Spirit and body to be joined. Once death occurred, the connection between Spirit and body was severed, and that which survived death became a lifeless vestige of its former self. This *shade*, as it was called, failed to conserve the personality or integrity of being that one experienced in life. Even where the possibility of an afterlife was envisioned, within the context of this psycho-physical worldview – as in ancient Egyptian tradition, Judaism, Zoroastrianism, Christianity and Islam – it required the reconstitution or resurrection of the body. In ancient Egypt, for example, the magical rites surrounding embalmment and mummification were designed to enable souls to live forever in a form of embodiment within their well-designed tombs. According to Christian and Islamic belief, God would ultimately raise the dead with their physical bodies intact. In all of these traditions, a fusion of Spirit and body was originally considered necessary for the soul to exist as a vital spiritual entity with an identity of its own.

The Association of the Embodied Soul With Breath

In most religious traditions, the fusion of Spirit and body giving rise to embodiment takes place through the vehicle of the breath. In many languages, the words for Spirit, soul, wind, and breath share the same etymology (Eliade, Encyclopedia 2:302-304). The Latin, *spiritus* comes from the verb, *spirare*, which means "to breathe." The Greeks used two words for soul – *psyche* and *anima*. The first derives from the verb, *psuchô*, meaning "to breathe," or "to blow;" the second from the verb, *animaô*, meaning "to draw up" (Craig). The Hebrew word, *nefesh* originally meant "neck" or "throat," but later came to mean the "vital spirit" or "anima" in the Latin sense. The word, *ruach* originally meant "wind" but later came to refer to the whole range of a person's emotional, intellectual, and

◇◇

volitional life. Both terms were widely used and often translated as "soul." The Akkadian word *napashu* was used to mean "the throat," "to breathe," and "life" itself. The Egyptians believed in a dual soul, one part of which, the *ka*, was named by the word for breath. The Arabic word, *nafs*, which is associated with individuality and will, is probably related to the word *nafas* (breath). In Chinese, the word for vital energy or spirit, *qi*, also means breath. In Sanskrit, the word for soul, *atman*, and the word for life force, *prana*, are both derived from the root word, *an*, meaning the ability to breathe.

In these languages, and the religious traditions that spoke them, the soul was identified with breath, and the act of breathing. Creation of the physical universe, in many traditions, entails an act of breathing, while Spirit enters the body as breath, and life is construed as the ability to breathe. According to the Song of Creation in the Rig Veda, which may date from 1500 BCE and is probably the earliest known book in the world, "Death was not then, nor was there aught immortal. The world was a total void, except for One Thing, breathless, yet breathed by its own nature" (Book X, Hymn CXXIX: 2 - Griffith 633). In Genesis, the first book of both the Jewish and the Christian Bible, creation begins as "a wind from God sweeping over the water" (Genesis 1:3 - Pelikan 3), and the human soul comes into existence as God blows into Adam's nostrils, "the breath of life" (Genesis 2:7 - Pelikan 5). Likewise, according to the Koran, humanity was created from "fermented clay dried tingling hard" after Allah has "breathed into him of My spirit" (Al-Hijr 15:28-29 - Ali 224).

If we take these etymological and scriptural clues seriously, then breath is understood to be the presence of the Spirit within the body, and the primary vehicle through which Spirit is known. A spiritual life is one that is inspired by the breath of life, and that breathes in rhythm with Spirit dwelling in the body. Breath, of course, is a vital bodily function, suggesting that a spiritual life - or the life of the human soul - is not possible outside the context of an embodied existence. This may seem a radical statement to most of us, conditioned to think of soul and Spirit as one and the same, or who fail to make a distinction between the embodied soul and the postmortem soul. But according to these ancient scriptures, the very origin of the soul demands the body as a vehicle through which Spirit can breathe the breath of life.

Ironically, this understanding defies the current teachings of most religions identified with these scriptures. Even so, it remains the basis of all spiritual disciplines, which promote a direct relationship between soul and Spirit. Such practices include various forms of meditation and yoga based on *pranayama* (breath control), the circular breathing employed by Buddhist monks while chanting, moving meditation practices such as *qigong*, and *t'ai chi*, and certain Sufi *dhikr* practices that combine chanting, movement, and elaborate breathing practices (Eliade, <u>Encyclopedia</u> 2:304-308). Even Gregorian chants are at core a form of conscious breathing, accompanied by sound. These practices and many others – including fasting, celibacy, and other ascetic exercises – designed to free the soul to more clearly identify with Spirit, paradoxically require that we enter more fully into a relationship with the body, for them to be effective.

Before we can move through Inanna's first gate on our way to a functional language of soul, we must first recognize the role of the body and the embodied existence and restore the body to its rightful place as the vehicle through which Spirit is most directly experienced by the soul in this life. Spirit, immortal and eternal, enters the body and lives within it for awhile, but is not in any way bound by it. The embodied soul, on the other hand, *is* the life of Spirit within the body, and is dependent upon the body for its existence. To know the soul more intimately, we must first enter and learn to inhabit the body as a conscious act of choice.

Embracing the Earth as the Larger Body of the Soul

Within the context of the full range of experiences available to an embodied soul, it will be helpful to consider the body not just literally, but also in a larger metaphorical sense that both encompasses the actual physical body, and extends beyond it. On this symbolic level, the body does not end with the skin, but includes the manifest world of nature, the environment that provides a living context for the entire range of experiences of the soul, and the circumstances through which the soul learns, grows and evolves toward fulfillment. While Spirit - at least according to the dominant religious paradigm – seeks its fulfillment through the transcendence or liberation from physical plane reality, the embodied soul seeks its fulfillment through immersion and meaningful involvement in the embodied life.

The body makes possible any experience of meaning - of love, of creativity, of pleasure and pain, of suffering and of joy, of learning and growth that shape any life of meaning. Without the body, such experiences, and the embodied life out of which meaning evolves, are not possible. Metaphorically, all these experiences and the physical plane reality that make them possible can be considered to be part of the experience of embodiment. Earth itself becomes a part of the extended body that allows Spirit to become embodied as the soul.

Within a religious mindset that divorces itself from the body, Earth becomes marginalized as a kind of way station for the soul, whose final destination is somewhere else, beyond the physical plane. From such a perspective, It does not matter what happens to the Earth or its supposedly less sentient creatures, because we are leaving it all behind anyway. It is merely a disposable nightmare, an elaborate seduction, or as a Hindu would put it, a *lila*, or cosmic play, which will evaporate in the vapors of illusion once the material veil of *maya* has been lifted.   One need not be a rocket scientist to see, nor am I the first to point out, where this attitude has led us (Kinsley; McFague).

At this stage of our collective evolution, we are literally choking in the consequences of our refusal to embrace the larger body to which the soul is bound.   Not only have we added considerably to our own suffering, but as a global culture thoroughly infused with this attitude of religious conditioning, we are failing to take advantage of the only opportunity the soul will ever have.   It is only when the soul can actually inhabit this realm of substance in which it has landed, for better or worse, that the soul can live its life in a meaningful way.   This means not only learning to dwell more consciously within the body in which it is housed, but also finding its place within the larger web of embodied life to which it belongs. It means caring for the larger body of the Earth that hosts the evolutionary drama that shapes and nurtures the soul.   It is, in turn, the soul's caring participation in this larger web of life that makes its education and its evolution possible.

This is a point of view cherished by most mystical traditions.   Unlike the more orthodox religious institutions with which they coexist, mystics understand that one cannot approach the experience of unity with Spirit without also recognizing Spirit to be everywhere, especially at the heart of the living pulse of manifest, embodied creation.   As Nobel Prize-winning mystical poet, Rabindranath Tagore observes:

> The same stream of life that runs through the world runs through my veins
> night and day and dances in rhythmic measures.
> It is the same life that shoots in joy through the dust of the earth into
> numberless blades of grass and breaks into tumultuous waves of leaves
> and flowers.
> It is the same life that rocked in the ocean cradle of birth and death, in ebb
> and flow.
> I feel my limbs and am made glorious by the touch of this world of life.
> And my pride is from the life throb of ages dancing in my blood this moment.

Unfortunately, mystics are often treated as the bastard progeny of conventional religion.   Most serve as a source of embarrassment to the traditions to which they belong, teetering on the edge of heresy while alive, then quietly canonized and tucked away in reliquaries after they are safely dead.   Meanwhile, the mystery embraced by mystics in their identification with the body of the Earth is the only true gateway to soul that most conventional religions provide.   It is a gateway that few of its practitioners are encouraged to enter.   Instead we are admonished to reach toward the sky, while leaving the worldly roots that would nourish soul neglected and abused.   Obviously, this is an attitude with serious, even fatal consequences, not just for the individual soul, but for the entire web of souls that binds us to each other, to all of life, and to the Earth itself. In discussing this crisis of neglect in modern Western religious tradition, Matthew Fox pulls no punches when he says, "The denial of mysticism by churches and synagogues is a deep and enduring scandal that is no longer tolerable... A civilization that denies the mystic is no civilization at all" (43).

Spirit as championed by non-mystical religion may be free to wander ethereal realms without looking back, but soul is inherently in relationship to the rest of manifest creation, and cannot do anything to the Earth without feeling its repercussions. From the soul's perspective, we *are* the Earth. Or as the Navajo chant (qtd. in Fox 12):

> The Earth, its life am I,
> The Earth, its feet are my feet,
> The Earth, its legs are my legs,
> The Earth, its body is my body,
> The Earth, its thoughts are my thoughts,
> The Earth, its speech is my speech.

If the embodied soul recognizes its identity with the Earth, the responsibility to care for the Earth becomes a matter of both physical and spiritual survival. If we poison our water and our air, both the soul and the body will become sick. For every species we allow to drift toward extinction, we diminish ourselves accordingly. Every time we devastate an ecosystem in the name of progress, the soul becomes a refugee in its own backyard. For a soul, intimately bound to the body and to the Earth out of which the body emerges, there is no escape to some future paradise in the hereafter. Nor is there any metaphysical excuse to blithely trash this one. From the soul's perspective, the promise of liberation from this mortal coil held forth by most religions is at best a dangerous oxymoron, and at worst a recipe for self-annihilation, ecological disaster, and serious impoverishment of the human condition.

Though we take for granted the superiority of worldviews that place human beings at the pinnacle of the spiritual food chain, we have lost a sensibility critical to soul that was an intimate part of many so-called primitive belief systems, especially among plant-based cultures. Anthropologists of the 19th and early 20th century observed that early man did not differentiate between humans, and plants and animals, whom they also endowed with souls (EB 24:731). They arrogantly assumed this meant that our forbearers lacked the intelligence necessary to tell the difference. This supposed deficiency or "hazy vision" as it was called, formed the conceptual basis for religious phenomena such as animism, totemism, nagualism, and other spiritual beliefs that postulated a soul-based relationship between humans, animals and other nonhuman entities. If this is hazy vision, then it is

✧✧✧

nonetheless a vision that suits the soul, since it recognizes the interconnection of soul, body, and Earth, which is where its identity is most deeply rooted.

Albertus Christian Kruyt, a Dutch anthropologist, coined the term, "soul-stuff" to refer to a belief common among the rice cultivators of Indonesia, but also witnessed among plant-based cultures elsewhere (Myth and Mythology, EB 24:731) that echoes this sensibility. "Soul stuff" is an indestructible reservoir of life that perpetually circulates throughout existence. It is eternally renewed, cycling through the Creator, who then sends it back out into creation to animate the full range of human, animal and plant forms in existence on this planet. Whatever form it inhabits, the same "stuff" is common to all beings. Within such an enlightened worldview, the concept of "body" is likewise extended to encompass not just this particular set of skin and bones that I personally happen to inhabit, but everything physical around me – the plants, the animals, the rocks, the stars, the very air I breathe. Spirit inhabits it all, and it all is essential to the existence and well-being of soul. Given the sad state of affairs our post-modern understanding of soul has produced as the exclusive property of humans, we might consider that the more primitive belief is the religious view of a soul in need of liberation from the body.

Returning Soul to its Rightful Place Within the Web of Life

Any true language of soul must recognize this connection between human beings and the larger body of the Earth, which sustains and nourishes human activity. The embodied soul is in relationship to everything that exists within the embodied world. How consciously we are able to maintain and nurture this relationship will determine the quality of our experience here on earth. When the relationship is conscious and vital, we will experience joy, abundance, and well-being. When it becomes weakened or strained, or goes unconscious, we will experience pain, impoverishment, and disease. An awareness of our place as souls, within the web of life on this planet, must become central to our understanding of who we are, before we can speak in a meaningful way about the spiritual nature of the soul's journey. The pathway to this awareness is a stronger sense of connection to our own bodies, and a conceptual framework that facilitates an understanding of the soul's experience within the context of the body – both literal and figurative – that we inhabit.

Instead of seeking a religious form of spiritual transcendence that takes the soul beyond the body and the physical realm, the soul must be empowered to enter more deeply and more consciously *into* the life it is living. The will to live in the body, with intention, with passion for, and commitment to the life that one has chosen, knowing full well that the body is a temporary home for Spirit, is to follow what Yaqui brujo, Don Juan called "a path of heart" (Castenada, Separate Reality 105-107), and what I would call a life conducive to the cultivation of soul. A language of soul is one that makes it possible to articulate a path of heart, through a conscious embrace of the physical body, the embodied world, and the experience of embodiment.

Astrology provides a foundation for a language of the embodied soul by systematically observing a correlation between heaven (the realm of Spirit) and earth (the realm of the body). The guiding principle behind most astro-logical thinking is the Hermetic axiom "As above, so below; as without, so within." This catch phrase is a pithy expression of a rather elaborate system of symbolic correspondences between the cosmos and all things terrestrial. In exploring these correspondences, one cannot help but recognize that the process of liberation from earthly existence pursued by religion is paradoxically a matter of entering into the embodied life with greater clarity of intention, and availing oneself of the opportunity for deepening of soul that it – and only it – provides. From this perspective, the life of the body is not separate or antithetical to the life of Spirit. Quite the contrary. It *is* the sacred vehicle through which Spirit evolves to more consciously recognize and express itself in space and time.

The Spiritual Challenge Posed by Mortality

Embodiment does not come without a price. When Spirit dwells within a body, the soul is forced to contemplate and somehow come to terms with the hard truth posed by the inevitability of death. If the soul is only Spirit – as religion often claims – then death is but a speed bump on the road to eternal life. To the extent that the soul identifies with the body, and the embodied life, however – which most of us do, regardless of our beliefs – then death becomes a limiting context in which the embodied soul must define itself. For regardless of how much we accomplish in our lifetime, how well loved and respected we are, how meaningful this life was, or how big a wake we leave in our passing, the hard, disconcerting truth that each of us must face is that one day, the embodied life will end. In that moment, our participation in all of the countless melodramas and involvements that are possible only on a planet of substance, and that define life as we know it, will cease. Everything we have identified as "I" and "my life" will dissolve. Again, I do not wish to deny the possibility that something within us survives death. But from the perspective of the embodied soul, death is an event that changes everything, and it cannot simply be swept under the rug of concern by mere belief in some post-mortem existence.

This inescapable fate is what begs the very questions that soul poses. "Are we just this being that we call 'I', or are we more than that?" and "Is this life all there is, or is there life after death?" and "Whether it ends or not when we die, what is this finite existence for?" We are compelled to consider these ultimate questions only because the embodied soul takes its shape through our relationship to the inevitability of death, and to the inscrutable

Mystery that lies beyond death. This mystery is a conundrum fraught with vulnerability, uncertainty, and the potential for great emotional, psychological, and physical suffering. Spirit is not fazed by such considerations, nor is the soul that is understood strictly as a spiritual entity. For the embodied soul, however, death is a silently reverberating context that shapes and conditions the entire journey we call life in profound, and at times earth-shattering ways.

Religious beliefs can act as a psychological buffer between us and our deaths, at least until death is imminent. But beliefs are not the same as experience, and it is experience that speaks most convincingly to the embodied soul. Just as you can't induce an experience of spiritual enlightenment by simply believing in the possibility, so too is it impossible to convince the embodied soul that death is the not the end, just by reassuring the mind. On the visceral level, all experiential evidence says otherwise. Sickness and the aging process, the death of those we love, the gradual breakdown, decay, and disintegration of everything in physical form around us all speak to the fragility of the body that houses the life with which the embodied soul identifies. Regardless of what we tell ourselves, the embodied soul already knows that its days are numbered. We can distract ourselves for awhile, but in the end, death will catch up with us all. I remind you of this, not to be morbid, but to suggest that for the embodied soul, death is real, inescapable, and inherently fraught with uncertainty.

Paradoxically, it is by living with an awareness of the embodied soul's relationship to death, that we become more conscious and more capable of a vital, passionate life of meaning and purpose. In the face of death, as Steven Levine reminds us, "We begin to live our life firsthand, tasting our food instead of thinking it, listening to the music instead of just humming it, seeing a new face without characterizing it. We break the dreamlike quality of a half-attended life" (40).

Death is the final moment of any existence that puts the embodied life as a whole into perspective. Regardless of whether or not we believe in a God, an afterlife, and our own inherent immortality, it is how we personally choose to approach this inescapable ending and the human life it swallows - whether by faith or intellect or tenacious belief or denial or a free-form groping toward the light - that ultimately defines who we are as an embodied soul.

Don Juan counseled Carlos Castenada to live with death as his advisor, meaning that it was within the context of death that the embodied soul must face its most critical choices. "A warrior thinks of his death when things become unclear," Don Juan tells Carlos, who immediately protests, "That's (hard), Don Juan. For most people, death is very vague and remote. We never think of it."

"Why not?" asks Don Juan.

"Why should we?" counters the ever-questioning Castenada.

"Very simple," Don Juan said. "Because the idea of death is the only thing that tempers our spirit" (Separate Reality 63).

To temper something is to make it accessible for use. Within the embodied life of the soul, it is the soul's relationship to the mortal body that tempers the Spirit, and makes it accessible to us. The body makes possible all the experiences of love, compassion, caring, friendship, creativity, accomplishment, abundance, pleasure, and enjoyment that provide opportunity for spiritual fulfillment within the embodied life. But the price we pay for this opportunity is an inescapable vulnerability to death that Spirit does not know outside of its relationship to the body. This vulnerability tempers Spirit and shapes the embodied soul in a way that makes death – in all its many guises – our ally and our teacher.

Viktor Frankl, who derived his particular brand of psychotherapy from his experiences in a Nazi concentration camp during World War II, typically asked his suffering patients, "Why do you not commit suicide?" In their answers, which varied greatly from individual to individual, he found the impetus and motivation for a life of greater spiritual vitality and psychological well-being (Allport vii). The irony behind Frankl's approach, of course, is that each of us is dying anyway, but that by keeping death an abstraction, our suffering becomes an invitation to languish in a kind of living death. Conversely, by keeping death in our awareness as an ever-present pivot point within our existence, we are somehow quickened to life. Shamans; wilderness edgewalkers who flirt with death through sports such as white water river rafting, rock climbing or sky-diving; and all those who have had to face some terminal disease such as AIDS or cancer with courage and spiritual determination, have come to the same conclusion.

The Spiritual Ramifications of a Life Shaped by Death

Just as it is helpful to consider the idea of embodiment as an experience extending beyond the body itself, it is also helpful to understand death not just literally sense, but also metaphorically. On this level, death encompasses all those moments in any life, where we experience pain and suffering, loss, a falling away or a falling apart, breakdown, deterioration, derailment, undoing, or any change which requires a surrender to the forces of entropy that condition life on a physical planet. Each of these experiences is a kind of death, which compels us to rethink who we are in relation to our shifting circumstances. The cumulative psychic momentum of these experiences constitutes a deathing process that shapes the soul. In the midst of a busy life, it is easy to forget the soul silently reverberating at the core of our being, but when life breaks down, when cracks begin to appear in the seamless landscape of business as usual, when death in its many clever disguises comes near, all the questions that the soul poses about its identity

∞∞

and the meaning and purpose of its existence automatically bubble to the top of the cauldron of awareness.

Death in this broader sense is not the only catalyst that shapes the soul. The ascendant side of life is filled which love, abundance, creativity and productivity, which also shape the soul and define us as human beings. But because everything it is possible to experience as a human being comes to an end with physical death, it is death in all of its many manifestations that drives us to make the most of life while we have the opportunity. Because this opportunity is limited by death we feel compelled to more clearly articulate the embodied life we are living. Because of death we quest to make sense of this life now, and hunger for a sense of purpose that will make it meaningful. Ultimately, the awareness and the articulation we bring to this quest defines who we are as embodied souls.

Since life is limited in scope and duration, we are forced to make choices. These choices shape our lives - consciously or unconsciously, for better or worse. If we were going to live forever, questions of identity and purpose, and these choices would have no meaning, for within the span of an endless life, we would get to be and do it all at our leisure. Spirit never asks who it is, what it is doing, or where it is going, because Spirit is not bound by death, time, or space. But the embodied soul does not have this same luxury of limitless existence. The fact that we must function from within a mortal body designed to self-destruct at some unspecified future date makes the quest for identity and purpose urgent and compelling. The fact that we have a finite lifespan in which to find ourselves, discover why we are here, and make something happen, can put a bounce in our step, provided we are not pushing death away or pretending it will never come. Within the context of our acknowledgment of death, each moment becomes infused with possibility, becomes worthy of our attention, beckons us to seek the gift that it has to offer. Each day becomes an opportunity to deepen our relationship to the soul and its questions.

The Systematic Denial of Death By Contemporary Culture

Not everyone feels this sense of urgency, nor will most of us take full advantage of the opportunity. Because we live in a relatively enlightened age in which we have erected many sophisticated barriers between an extended life expectancy and the inevitability of death, our relationship to the shaping influence of mortality is muffled. Raised in a culture where life is celebrated and death is held at bay as long as technological ingenuity will allow, we do not know how to embrace the down cycles - the death of loved ones, the loss of a job, the onset of life-threatening illness, the bear market, the business failures, the aging process, and every other manifestation of death in our lives - as opportunities for learning and for soul growth.

Americans are especially conditioned to relentlessly pursue the good life. We consider death in the metaphorical sense to be an inconvenience on the road to bigger, better, and more, instead of the vital tempering of Spirit that it is. Because we have no sense of the finality of death, a life of relentless consumption in which "he who dies with the most toys wins" apparently has meaning. Facing death - in all the ways it intrudes into our complacency - takes us to the depths of ourselves, builds character, and defines us as human beings, yet most of us seek to avoid and deny it, pretending it is not an ever-present companion to our daily lives. As a consequence, most of us live soulless lives, whose true spiritual poverty is revealed as we approach the literal, physical death that is impossible to avoid

Your answer to the question, "How would your life be different, if you knew you only had six months to live?" is a measure of the extent to which you are aligned with your own death. If you would change nothing, then the embodied soul is alive and well within you. If you would change everything, then perhaps you have bought into the illusion of the limitless life, and it is time to make serious changes while the opportunity exists. For the hard truth is, it won't last forever. Taking this hard truth seriously is what breathes vitality into the embodied soul. Most of us do not take death seriously enough, in part because we are conditioned not to by religion, science, the media, and the culture at large.

Despite the aging of our population, we still live in a culture oriented toward perpetual youth. The media, though filled with images of violence and death, celebrates the capacity to triumph over these forces. Science has appropriated the soul's relationship to death and redefined it as a medical problem, requiring intellectual prowess and Herculean feats of technological intervention. To the extent that science can admit to itself that there are larger, metaphysical questions about death that exist beyond its reach, it has - through what Ken Wilbur graciously refers to as "the dignity of modernity" (44) - relegated matters of soul to theologians. Theologians, however, have erected their own conceptual barriers to an embrace of death. They have confused the soul, conditioned by its mortality, with Spirit, which is eternal, and immortal, in a way that the embodied soul longs to be, but isn't, and failed to acknowledge the soul's vulnerability in the face of death.

Before we can really begin to evolve a useful language of soul, we must look more closely at these limitations, and the story of their evolution. I will return to the scientists and explore their contribution to our current conditioning in relation to soul in Part Two. First, we must understand how our collective concept of soul came to be rooted in religious attitudes of denial toward death, so that we can gradually dig our way out into a more breathable relationship to the important existential questions that the embodied soul poses. The language of soul we are seeking to create demands that we first go backwards before moving forward through Inanna's first gate, leaving the conditioning of the past behind us.

CHAPTER ONE

◇◇

Endnotes

[1] I prefer the term "Spirit" to "God" because it has less religious connotation and is more universal in its meaning. God refers to the monotheistic, immortal, transcendent deity of Western religion, whereas Spirit can be transcendent or immanent. Spirit is experienced as an endless source of perpetual Life that renews itself through a procession of mortal forms, and is embodied in a vast pantheon of deities. As the reader will see, these distinctions become increasingly important as we move through Inanna's first and second gates, as discussed in Part One.

[2] When the word "spirit" is not capitalized, I am referring to a realm of non-physical being, rather than the omnipresent Life Force, which at times inhabits both physical and non-physical form.

Chapter Two
Through Inanna's First Gate Into the Embodied Life

Given the close association between the very concept of the embodied soul and the mystery of death, it is not surprising to find that many of the most ancient religious practices began as funerary rites designed to appease fears that arose in the face of this mystery. As Joseph Campbell points out, this fear was especially potent among the nomadic hunting tribes, whose livelihood depended upon the art of killing, and for whom death was often a violent act (Primitive 125-126). In such cultures, death was generally attributed to magic, and magic was invoked through elaborate ceremonial rites to ward off death as long as possible. The dead were considered to be malevolent spirits capable of causing disease, precipitating misfortune, and/or seeking revenge for wrongs committed against them while alive, and precautionary funeral rites evolved to protect the living against the dead.

The Fear of Death in Early Cultures

In excavated Paleolithic burial sites, some estimated to be dated as early as 50,000 BCE, skeletons were often found lying on their side in a crouched position. Since the posture resembles that of a fetus in a womb, some have interpreted this burial position to suggest a primitive belief in rebirth. In some crouched burials, however, there is evidence that the corpses were forcibly placed in that position before rigor mortis set in, possibly implying a fear of death, and of the dead and their malevolent power to harm the living (Eliade, History 1:10). Similar archeological excavations elsewhere in Europe and Africa suggest that significant effort went into binding corpses in ropes, bandages or nets; breaking their bones; stuffing the orifices of the dead body; and/or covering them with heavy stones (Campbell, Primitive 126), apparently so that the disembodied spirits of the dead could not return to wreak havoc among those left behind.

In most of these early fear-based religions, death was not regarded as a natural event. Instead, it was often believed to be caused by the attack of some demonic power or god of death. In Etruscan sepulchral art, a fearsome being called Charon strikes the deathblow (Eliade, History 2:130-131). In Medieval Christian art, still visible in old European churches, death is depicted as a grotesque mummy with entrails hanging out, brandishing a spear (Ariès 115-116). The Hindus knew death as the fearsome goddess, Kali, with terminally bad hair and a garland of human skulls around her waist. The Tibetan Book of the Dead warns its practitioners of horrific vision after horrific vision awaiting the dead in the bardo state. Among them, for example, are the Yama Dharmaraja deities, "their fang-like teeth protruding over their lips, their eyes like glass, their hair bound up on top of their heads, with protruding bellies, with thin necks, they carry punishment boards and shout, 'Beat him!' and 'Kill him!' They lick up your brains, they sever your head from your body, and they extract your heart and vital organs. Thus they arise, filling the world". The Book goes on to reassure the by-now quivering soul that "The Yama Lords of Death are but arisen from the natural energy of your own awareness and really lack all substantiality. Voidness cannot injure voidness!" (Ch. 6: Guidebook to the Betweens, Fierce Deity, 12th Day - Thurman 163). But who can fail to appreciate the underlying message within this sacred text that death is a horrible, albeit hallucinatory ordeal.

Proper burial of the dead was deemed essential by many early cultures, to ensure that the dead would depart this Earth and make a successful journey to the underworld where they belonged. Failure to expedite their departure could have dangerous consequences for those that remained behind, and most early fear-based religions spelled out proper funeral arrangements in great detail. The Australian Aranda, according to accounts of anthropologists, went so far as to burn the village where a death occurred, refrain from ever mentioning the name of the deceased again, and require elaborate and difficult ordeals of the surviving family to ensure that the dead stayed in their proper place. The message to the dead that they were no longer welcome among the living was driven home by a ritual dance involving wild shouting and beating of the ground (Campbell, Primitive 126).

The Fear of the Soul's Journey After Death

The dead needed to be persuaded, shall we say, to leave their former stomping grounds, if not rudely booted on their way, because the journey across the barrier between the dead and the living was often conceptualized as an arduous and dangerous undertaking. Egyptian funerary texts describe the journey to the next world as a treacherous ordeal, involving encounters with horrific monsters, burning lakes, locked gates opened only by magic, and a host of other sinister obstacles (Rites and Ceremonies, EB 26:806). The Greeks and Romans believed that the dead were carried across the poisonous river, Styx, by a fiendish boatman called Charon, in exchange for a coin, which was placed in the mouth of the corpse (Harris, 249-250). A treacherous journey across a bridge, often over water to get to the land of the dead is a common image occurring across a wide range of diverse cultural traditions – in the Cinvat Bridge in Zoroastrianism (Eliade, History 1:330), the Bifrost of Eddic lore (Gundarsson 2), the Sirāt Bridge of the Muslims, the Bridge over the Gtöll River of Scandinavian mythology, and in the Brig o' Dread or Brig o' Death in Christian folklore (Rites and Ceremonies, EB 26:805).

The depiction of these journeys reflects a common fear for the grim experience that was believed to await the dead in their next life, and on their way to it. Not only was the journey dangerous, but the final destination was no ideal vacation spa, much less the sort of place where the dead might want to spend eternity. For some, like the early Arabs before Mohammed, there was literally no place for the dead to go. Only the ghosts of slain men lingered after death, and then just long enough to seek revenge against those who had killed them (Oxtoby, Western 343). According to early Mesopotamian traditions, all the dead were banished to a grim and hopeless place called *Kur-nu-gi-a* (the Land of No Return) (Rites and Ceremonies, EB 26:806), where they were forced to live in darkness and eat clay (Powell 48). The underworld of classical Judaism was called *Sheol*, "the land of deepest gloom; a land whose light is darkness, all gloom and disarray" (Job 10:21 - Pelikan 1:1353). In *Sheol*, the good and wicked alike shared a common fate, in which nothing at all happened (Eliade, History, 260). Since this was literally inconceivable, its absolute finality was quite frightening. The early Greek underworld, as described by Eliade, sounds like a prison camp. Hades, he says, was "a musty world clad in darkness, a place odious to mortals and immortals alike,... (a) country without laughter or sunshine, where all are obliged to make their way sooner or later.... As soon as the new arrivals cross the dismal threshold, Hades (the Lord of the Underworld) locks the gates, and his agents, who never sleep, prevent any attempt at escape" (Encyclopedia, 6:143).

Toward a Cyclical Conception of Death as a Part of Life

A less fearful attitude toward death was evident in tribes whose life was naturally more plant-based, where hunting was secondary to some form of agriculture or foraging for wild edibles. In these cultures, such as those originating in the temperate climates of southern Europe, the tropical rainforests of South America and the more fertile regions of Africa, death was often much less feared. Even in the undiminished potency of its capacity to undo everything considered to be a part of life, death was considered to be a natural phenomenon, comparable to the return of a seed to the Earth, when a rotten piece of fruit fell from its vine. It was not considered less valuable than that which brought success, abundance, fertility, and power. For such cultures, life depended on death for its vitality, the way a seedling depended upon the nourishment of the composted soil in which it was planted. Within this dependency was a sense of continuity that stretched from one generation to the next and bound the community together as a whole encompassed by the great cycle of Life. Among these cultures, death was not conceptualized as something to be repelled, thwarted or postponed, but rather as a natural progression of events to be expected, even welcomed, as part of a cyclical process. Life and death were not antithetical to one another, but alternating phases in a larger, more mysterious process that included, yet transcended both.

An African folktale (Wilson) illustrates this point. Life and Death were traveling together and came upon a spring. The owner of the spring greeted them, and informed them that it was the custom for the elder to drink first. Life stepped forward to drink, explaining that it was obvious he was the elder, since only that which lives can die, and therefore, life must precede death. But Death replied, "On the contrary. Death is the unknown, out of which the Creator has molded everything that lives. Therefore, death is a father to life." Asked to settle their dispute, the owner of the spring told them, "You are both right. Neither one of you came first, and neither one of you can exist without the other." Life and Death then knelt down to drink from the spring together.

The perennial juxtaposition of life and death is depicted even more poignantly in another African folktale (Campbell, Primitive 118-119), in which the Chief of Death, who presides over the fate of each individual member of the tribe, has a face that is beautiful on one side, but rotten and crawling with maggots on the other. One day, the Chief prophesizes from the beautiful side of his face and life blooms in magnificent abundance. The next day, he prophesizes from the rotten side of his face and death stalks its prey and takes away what life has bestowed.

These tales illuminate an important feature of our relationship to soul, which must be central to any language we devise to understand it. To the extent that death is a part of life – and no one who has ever experienced loss, or failure, or the necessity for letting go can deny it – then it seems reasonable to assume that the soul's journey through life will also be a journey into the mystery of death. At times, the journey will appear to be about moving forward, creating, building, and growing into a realization of our potential. At other times, it will appear to be about falling backward, suffering the decay and dissolution of what we have created, and failing to realize the promise held forth by life. Life will wax and wane within a cyclical rhythm with death, and soul will come into being through a deepening awareness of who we are in relation to these cycles.

As it says in the famous passage of Ecclesiastes (3:1-8 - Jones 856-857):

There is a season for everything, a time for every occupation under heaven:

A time for giving birth,
a time for dying;
a time for planting,
a time for uprooting what has been planted.
A time for killing,
a time for healing;
a time for knocking down,
a time for building.

A time for tears,
a time for laughter;
a time for mourning,
a time for dancing.
A time for throwing stones away,
a time for gathering them up;
a time for embracing,
a time to refrain from embracing.
A time for searching,
a time for losing;
a time for keeping,
a time for throwing away.
A time for tearing,
a time for sewing;
a time for keeping silent,
a time for speaking.
A time for loving,
a time for hating;
a time for war,
a time for peace.

From this perspective, which seems more enlightened than the fear-based approach governing hunting cultures, the cultivation of soul, like the cultivation of a garden, involves learning to live in harmony with the seasons of one's life. These seasons, like the turning of the seasons each year, occur in a recognizable cyclical rhythm, which we can anticipate and prepare ourselves to experience as consciously and as effectively as possible. As we will explore in more detail later, a cyclical awareness of the seasons of life is the conceptual basis for the astrological worldview, a feature that makes it an attractive model for the language of soul we are attempting to evolve.

The Cyclical Worldview and Its Association With a Desire for Release From Suffering

A cyclical awareness of the soul's journey was taken to a pinnacle of understanding in a somewhat different way in a number of religious traditions, including Hinduism, Buddhism, Orphism, and the Mesoamerican worldview. These cultures attempted to catalog not just the cycles of an individual life, but those of our collective evolutionary process as well. In Hinduism, for example, elegantly imaginative chronological systems were worked out, involving cycles within cycles within cycles. A *kalpa*, or day in the life of Brahma, the Creator, was equivalent to approximately 4,320 million earth years. 360 *kalpas* made up one year in the life of Brahma, who lived for 100 years, and spanned the duration of a world from its creation to its destruction. After a period of dormancy, Brahma then recreated the world for another round (Oxtoby, Eastern 45). Here in the West, the early Mayans worked out a system for contemplating larger cycles beyond the span of a human lifetime, derived from a combination of the earlier Olmec tzolkin cycle of 260 days and the Venus cycle of 584 days, and a Long Count, equal to 5125.36 years (Jenkins 52). Astrologers speak of the precession of the equinoxes, a grand cycle involving the movement of the vernal equinox backward through the zodiac. The entire cycle takes 26,000 years and in turn, is divided into ages, such as the Piscean age, the Aquarian age, and so on.

These cyclical worldviews are innately more useful to a language of soul than those based upon a fearful contemplation of the horrors of death, where death is conceived as an abrupt termination of a linear life. Many of these worldviews, especially those derived from religion, however, are plagued by the belief that the embodied life is a struggle and a source of suffering from which it is desirable to be liberated. Hinduism, Buddhism, Jainism, and Sikhism believe that incarnation (and embodiment) is a form of imprisonment in matter, and that the end goal of the spiritual journey is an emancipation. Hindus conceive life to be the result of previous actions, the consequences of which remain to be played out endlessly, or at least until one completes a course of karmic retribution that entails suffering through multiple incarnations. Although Buddhism denies the existence of an individual soul capable of surviving from one incarnation to the next, it similarly believes that the residual karma of each individual becomes a "seed of consciousness," called *vijnana* (Reincarnation, EB 9:1009), around which future incarnations perpetuate the cycle of suffering that marks the material world of the body. To end this cycle, Buddhists seek the gradual extinction of the worldly desires and attachments that keep the soul trapped here. In the Orphic tradition, successive incarnations were construed as "the cycle of sorrow and misery[1]" from which the soul hoped to escape after initiation into the secret knowledge imparted by the cult.

All cyclical traditions agree that disidentification with or detachment from the body and its desires, in combination with an ethical life, are the keys to liberation from the physical realm and a return to union with Spirit. They embrace a cyclical model, potentially useful as a catalyst to the integration of life and death, but they reject the embodied soul no less fiercely than the fear-based hunting cultures, albeit in the opposite direction. Instead of fearing death and its finality as the hunting cultures did, these early cyclical traditions seemed to welcome it as an end to the terminal suffering inherent in life. Within the context of these cultures, death itself was no guarantee of a release from suffering, since rebirth was imminent to the extent that there remained unfinished business, desire and/or attachment to life. Nonetheless, implied within these religions was the assumption that liberation could not be achieved while the soul was embodied.

The Myth of Immortality

To meet the understandable human need for alleviation of the fear of death, a new paradigm begin to emerge in religious thought, probably somewhere around 3000-2000 BCE[2]. This paradigm, which assumed an afterlife and the immortality of a soul that could survive bodily death, gradually superseded the more abject, fear-based belief that the death of the body marked the soul's demise. Though it brought hope to the faithful within the religions where it took root, the concept of immortality also became a pivot point around which soul became increasingly identified with Spirit. Paradoxically, it was this identification that marked the death of religion as a language useful to the evolution of the embodied soul, since the body was now something to be shed on the way to a more relevant identification with a disembodied God.

The shift toward immortality and the spiritual severance of soul and body probably originated with the Egyptians and the myth of Osiris. In Plutarch's version of the myth (circa 120 AD), Osiris was an Egyptian king responsible for bringing civilization to Egypt (Powell 215-218). Together with his sister and queen, Isis, Osiris abolished cannibalism, introduced agriculture and marriage, and passed laws that made everyday life safer, more productive, and more socially integrated. After this new way of life was established, he left the rule of Egypt to Isis, and traveled for a while to teach and spread his ideas to other parts of the world. Upon his return, his enemies led by the evil Typhoeus, tricked him into climbing into a coffin, slammed the lid shut, and threw the coffin into the Nile. The coffin floated down the river into the sea and across it to Phoenica, where it lodged against a tamarisk tree, which grew around it.

When the king of Phoenica ordered the tree cut down, many years later, to be used as a pillar in his palace, the coffin with Osiris inside was taken with it. Meanwhile, Isis had been desperately searching for her brother, and eventually caught up with him. Disguising herself as a nanny, she gained entrance to the palace, where she revealed herself and demanded Osiris' return. She took Osiris back to Egypt and hid his coffin in the marshes. On the way, according to some versions of the myth, Isis opened the coffin, and taking the form of a hawk, hovered over Osiris' penis, inflaming it into an erection, and allowing it to impregnate her.

Typhoeus later stumbled into the coffin one moonlit night while hunting, and tore the corpse of Osiris into fourteen pieces, which he scattered all over the country. Isis set out in a papyrus boat to search for each piece, and built a temple whenever she found one. She eventually found them all, except for the penis that had impregnated her, for which she substituted a wooden phallus. With his body reconstructed, Osiris arose from the underworld to prepare his son, Horus, whom Isis had now borne, to do battle with Typhoeus and avenge his murder. After many days of fighting, Typhoeus' allies deserted him, and Horus delivered him to Isis in chains.

Every reigning pharaoh since Osiris has been identified with Horus, the hawk god, who represented the unvanquishable immortality of Osiris. In the embrace of this myth, the concept of resurrection became the anticipated expectation after death, at least in the case of the ruling class. By about 2400 BCE, the elaborate funeral rite for which the Egyptians are so well known had evolved to imitate the acts that they believed were performed by the gods to preserve the body of Osiris, with whom the deceased was ritually assimilated. This funeral rite was gradually extended to others, until by 1400 BCE or so, it was available to anyone who could afford it (Doctrines and Dogmas, EB 17:414). After the conquests of Alexander, the Great (circa 334 BCE), the cult of Isis, including the central myth of Osiris' resurrection, spread throughout the Greco-Roman world, became quite popular, and asserted a profound influence on Western concepts of the fate of the soul after death (European Religions, EB 18:798).

Extracting the Myth of Immortality From Its Cyclical Roots

The Egyptian concept of immortality, modeled on the story of Osiris and Isis, was one version of a prototypical fertility myth that provided a context not just for the evolution of the human soul, but for the waxing and waning of the life force permeating all of creation. This myth was repeated in various cultural guises, including the Phrygian story of Cybele and Attis; the Sumerian tale of Innana and Dumuzi; various Greek myths such as that of Aphrodite and Adonis, or in alternate form of Demeter and Persephone; and in the Arthurian legends of the dying Fisher King to name just a few (Powell 212-242). Even the Christian image of the Virgin Mary holding the baby Jesus was an adaptation of earlier images depicting Isis and Horus, although Christianity borrowed from the myth only what it found useful to its purposes and renounced the rest (Powell 215).

The original myth, in all its variations, understood immortality to be a cyclical process, not as a source of liberation from death, but rather within the context of a rhythm between life and death – both of which came together in the experience of embodiment in the here and now. To the extent that fear of death dominated the adaptation of this myth to Egyptian funereal rites, however, it gradually became extracted from its cyclical roots and misinterpreted as liberation from death. Although Egyptian funeral rites acknowledged the relationship between the soul and the body – on whose preservation they believed its continuation in the afterlife depended – these practices were also an attempt to transcend the body's obvious limitations. The Egyptian soul, symbolized by Osiris, longed not just for life after death, but for freedom from death. This freedom was symbolized by Horus, the hawk god associated with resurrection. According to the Egyptian Pyramid Texts (c 2375 - 2200 BCE), the elaborate funeral rites were designed to ensure that the dead pharaoh, now identified with the Sun, could travel across the sky to join Osiris in heaven and the "Imperishable Ones" embodied in the circumpolar stars. In this immortal company, he would be beyond the reach of the destructive impact of time (Doctrines and Dogmas, EB 17:413).

While the conquest of time represented a step forward for those who lived in fear of death, the hope it brought in the face of death came at a price. Immortality solved the problem posed by death, at least intellectually. But it also severed the soul from the connection to the full cycle of life and death, through which questions about the meaning and purpose of its embodied existence derived their spiritual potency. Within the new paradigm, resurrection became the goal, instead of just one phase of an ongoing process in which neither life nor death would ultimately triumph. The soul became increasingly identified with the portion of the cycle in which life conquers death. That part of the cycle in which death overcomes life was reinterpreted as a temporary setback that could be mitigated, if not reversed entirely, provided one made the proper arrangements. Western religion has been promising to make those arrangements for the soul ever since.

As the seminal Jungian analyst, Erich Neumann points out, this shift in attitude toward the soul's cyclical relationship to death paralleled the shift from matriarchal to patriarchal cultures taking place throughout the world, over the course of several millennia before the birth of Christ (Origins 245). The embodied soul, championed by matriarchal cultures, was one that existed in sacred relationship to all of life, and derived its life force from an immanent deity actively present in the endless rise and fall of countless embodied forms throughout creation. The immortal soul, championed largely by patriarchal cultures, was one banished to an embodied world to which it did not belong, and destined for reunion with a disembodied sky god. Once this reunion had been achieved, the body and the manifest creation to which it belonged, could gratefully be left behind, like a butterfly shedding its cocoon.

The embodied soul draws its inspiration and takes its nourishment, not from some other place or time beyond the reach of human longing, but from the embodied world in which it dwells. Heaven is not out there somewhere, but right here, as close as the rose in the garden out your back door, or closer still, in the beating of your own heart. Everything within the embodied world becomes a potential source of meaning and fulfillment to the soul, for those with eyes to see and willingness to participate. Patriarchal cultures, which habitually look for liberation from the embodied world and from the experience of death, invariably miss the exquisite and unparalleled opportunity made available to the soul, at the very heart of the experience of embodiment, even as they lust after the good life it is capable of providing.

The Embrace of Personal Immortality in the East

This transition from matriarchal to patriarchal cultures affected not only Western religious tradition, but also the Asian countries in which Eastern religious culture was gestated. Prior to 2000 BCE, the Indian subcontinent was populated by a matriarchal, "vegetal-lunar rhythmic" (Campbell, Oriental 179) culture known as the Harappa (Oxtoby, Eastern 17-20), where goddess worship predominated along with reverence for the ongoing cycle of life and death. Of the goddess/mother who presided over this culture, Campbell writes, "All life, all moments terminate in her insatiable maw; yet in the frightening return there is ultimately rapture for the one who in trust, can give himself – like the perfect king: the son and yet the bull of his cosmic mother" (Oriental 179). As frightening as death was to the soul in danger of annihilation in it, death also represented an ecstatic completion of the soul's journey for those who could surrender their clinging to life.

From 2000-1500 BCE, there was a mass migration from central Asia intro the midst of this culture by Aryan invaders. Some scholars suggest that the migration occurred much earlier, either from within India itself or from the geographical area known today as Turkey (Oxtoby, Eastern 20-21), and was relatively peaceful. In any event, the migration/invasion precipitated a mingling of matriarchal and patriarchal cultures, which in turn gave rise to a gradual shift in prevailing attitudes toward the soul and its potential immortality. To the Harappa, the patriarchal Aryans, or Indo-Europeans as they were also called, brought with them new unfamiliar sky gods, who transcended the cycle of life and death, and "a confidence in the capacity of aggressive fire to make way everywhere for its own victory over darkness" (Campbell 180).

This Aryan attitude of triumph over death through ritual and sacrifice permeated the Vedas, the earliest surviving sacred texts from Indo-European culture, composed between 1500 BCE and 600 BCE. The Vedas contain hymns to the gods and goddesses of the Aryan pantheon, primarily Indra, a storm god and the bringer of rain; Agni, the god of fire; and Varuna, an all-pervasive creator god. The Vedas also include ritual treatises describing how to conduct sacrifices to the gods and goddesses, and other ceremonial instructions that later became the province of the brahminic or priestly caste. Among these are instructions for the preparation and use of soma, a psychotropic brew through which the Aryans sought immortality. "We have drunk Soma and become immortal," says the Rig Veda, "we have attained the light, the Gods discovered. Now what may foeman's malice do to harm us?" (Hymn XLVIII:3 – Pelikan 5:435).

Despite the ceremonial use of soma to attain immortality, there is little reference to an afterlife in Vedic scripture. Nor is there mention of reincarnation. Instead, the primary focus of most hymns is to attain benevolent intervention of the gods in *this* life, through the appropriate ritual sacrifices, and an identification with the invincible power of the immortal gods while still in the body. Immortality was not so much a triumph over death as it was a conquest of the *fear* of death through identification, while living, with gods who were themselves beyond death.

The idea that the cycle of life and death was a curse to be transcended, common to most Eastern religions, appears only later, around 600 BCE, as the scriptural authority of the Vedas gave way to the more modern Upanishads, which reinterpreted original Vedic concepts in more cyclical terms. During the intervening millennium, as the patriarchal Aryans intermingled with the matriarchal Harappa, in all probability there was a synthesis of perspectives. Over time, conquest came to be understood as triumph over the cycle in which life and death alternated with rhythmic predictability. Although the ritual use of soma had disappeared by the time the Upanishads were written, "the revelation of a full and beatific existence, in communion with the gods, continued to haunt Indian spirituality long after the disappearance of the original drink. Hence the attempt was made to attain such an existence by the help of other means: asceticism or orgiastic excesses, meditation, the techniques of Yoga, mystical devotion" (Eliade, History 1:212). It is likely this integration of matriarchal elements into an essentially patriarchal religion gave birth to the modern tradition of Hinduism.

With its doctrine of karma, reincarnation, and the desirability of liberation from the necessity for reincarnation, Hinduism subsequently spread with missionary zeal throughout Asia, Indochina, Sumatra, Java, and Bali during the next millennium (between the 6th century BCE to the 6th century CE). Although it was modified in each local culture into which it was assimilated, the religious drive toward a transcendence of the cycle of life and death that permeated post-Vedic Indian thought had an important developmental influence on Buddhist, Jain, Sikh and other Eastern religious systems. As Eliade sums up this influence, "After the period of the Upanishads, all methods and soteriologies share a common categorical framework. The sequence avidyā-karman-samsāra, the equation existence = suffering, the interpretation of ignorance as sleep, dream, intoxication, captivity – this constellation of concepts, symbols, and images was unanimously accepted" (History 2:49).

The Quest for Immortality in Early Chinese Shamanism

In ancient China, there appears to have been some discussion of immortality in the original shamanic teachings of Lao Tzu, who says of the superior man in the *Tao Te Ching* (Feng 50):

He who knows how to live can walk abroad
Without fear of rhinoceros or tiger.
He will not be wounded in battle.
For in him rhinoceroses can find no place to thrust their horn,
Tigers no place to use their claws,
And weapons no place to pierce.
Why is this so?
Because he has no place for death to enter.

As Eliade suggests, however, the immortality discussed by Lao Tzu evolves from immersion in a state of shamanic ecstasy in which the superior man seeks "to frolic at the Origin of all things," and does not include the notion of survival of the physical body or the human personality after death (History 30-31). The Taoist sage instead aspired to living identification with the Tao, "something mysteriously formed, born before heaven and earth, in the silence and the void, standing alone and unchanging, ever present and in motion" (Lao Tzu, Feng 25). As with the Vedic seers of India, it was this identification with the Tao that gave the Taoist shamans their earthly power, and their capacity to heal. Original Taoist teachings about immortality had little to do with surviving physical death, but everything to do with maximizing one's spiritual vitality in life.

As with the aspiration of Western mystics to unity with Spirit, attaining immortality paradoxically meant checking one's identity as an individual soul at the door. The individual soul could not merge with Tao without becoming annihilated in emptiness, and it was this ecstatic annihilation in death while still alive in a body that produced the immortality sought by Taoist shamans. Just as individual mystics walked a thin line between unity with Spirit and megalomania, and individual yogis were tempted by the *siddhis,* or personal powers that arose as a consequence of their practice, so too were individual shamans likely seduced by the lure of a more personalized form of immortality. It was only later, after the original shamanic teachings were written down and perverted by a more secular class of shaman-kings who used them for political advantage that a preoccupation with the transcendence of physical death became a more widespread goal.

The Platonic Influence on Religious Concepts of Immortality

A belief in this more personal form of immortality was given tremendous philosophical momentum in the West four centuries before the birth of Christ in the teachings of the Greek philosopher, Plato. Plato taught within a couple centuries of the time frame that the Upanishads and the *Tao Te Ching* were being written, thus signaling a synchronistic global shift toward an embrace of personal immortality that took different forms in different cultures over the course of two to three centuries. In

Egyptian tradition, the concept of immortality was rooted in a mythological association of the ruling pharaoh with the immortality of Horus – an association that hardly applied to the common Egyptian. Even after the ritual procedures for guaranteeing immortality became more widely available, immortality was still construed as the privilege of the few who could afford it. It was through Plato's indirect adaptation of Egyptian ideas that immortality became understood in the West as inherent in the very nature of the soul itself, and no longer something that needed to be attained. This development marked a huge paradigm shift from which, in my opinion, we have yet to recover.

Building on arguments put forth by Pythagoras and Socrates, and influenced heavily by the Orphic tradition, Plato considered the soul to be of divine origin, preexistent (existing before it entered the body), and immortal (Melchert 143-144). Plato did not deny that the soul was bound to the body for the duration of this life, but he felt this association to be a burden that would thankfully dissolve at death. Like the Orphics, he considered the body "an impediment which... prevents the soul from attaining to truth..." (110). In advising his students about how best to handle the soul's experience of embodiment, Plato suggested that the soul should indulge its bodily appetites to the minimum extent necessary for the continuance of life, while constantly monitoring the body's pull upon the soul through the use of reason. The true philosopher, as Plato put it in the *Phaedo*, made his life a practice for death because he knew that after death, the soul would be free of its imprisonment in the body and would return to the realm of Spirit from whence it had come (103-116).

According to Plato, there were four arguments (attributed to Socrates and set forth in the *Phaedo*) for thinking that the soul survives death (116-152). First, like the plant-based cultures of prehistory, he observed that the processes of nature are cyclical, and reasoned that this also applied to human life and death. Second, Plato believed that what we call "learning" was really a process of remembering, and through circular reasoning argued that if so, we had to have been here before and would probably be here again. Third, since the soul could perceive the Ideas, or Forms – Truth, Beauty, the Good, that in his theory underlay all of manifest creation, and were unchanging and eternal – then the soul had to exist on the same level of reality that they did. Fourth, since Plato considered the opposites to be antithetical and utterly distinct from one another, he concluded that the soul, which brings life to the body, could not participate in death.

Of course, it is Spirit that brings life to the body, not soul, but this is exactly the confusion that Plato passed on to the emerging western religious traditions of his day. Soul, as we are discussing it here, *is* the life of Spirit within the body, not the source of its own existence. While Spirit is every bit as eternal and immortal as Plato argued, the life of Spirit within the body – the embodied soul – is a temporary, mortal condition.

⬦⬦

The eager intermingling of cultures around the Mediterranean sea, during the centuries preceding and following the birth of Christ, allowed Greek philosophy in general and Plato's ideas about the immortal soul in particular, came to assert a profound influence upon the development of Jewish, Christian and Islamic thought. From the mid 2nd century CE, Jewish and Christian thinkers began articulating their ideas in the broader, more contemporary intellectual context provided by Greek philosophy (Christian 1:213-216). Stoic philosophers emphasizing duty and ascetic practices appealed to some early Christians, but there were also problems with the Stoic belief in corporeality (i.e. the idea that both God and the soul were bodies of refined substance) and embrace of pagan pantheism. Plato's ideas were much more in keeping with early Christian thought, and provided the philosophical foundation for Christianity that would lend credence to its influence within academic and other spheres of power throughout the Greco-Roman empire. Plato's influence also spread to the Muslim world from 800-1000 CE, when Islamic scholars translated a number of dialogues and Neoplatonic treatises into the Arabic languages (Philosophical Schools and Doctrines, EB 25:903-904).

Augustine's Influence as a Bridge Between Christianity and Platonic Thought

While today we take for granted the fusion of Christian and Platonic thought, this was actually a transition that spanned four or five centuries after the birth of Christ. Philo Judeaus of Alexandria (c 15 BCE - 45 CE), a contemporary of Saint Paul, was one of the first to reorient Jewish and early Christian thought in a more Platonic direction (Christian 1:216), which eventually established the concept of immortality as the gospel truth in both cultures. Many other early Christian thinkers after Philo Judeaus were also instrumental in effecting this transition, but none was more important than Saint Augustine (354-430 CE), bishop of Hippo in Roman Africa. Augustine was a central figure in philosophical history, and is often considered the greatest shaping influence upon early Christian theology. More than any other thinker, he provided an essential bridge between the religion of the New Testament and the Platonic tradition, and through his work, Western Christianity absorbed many of Plato's ideas (Melchert 230).

In his youth, Augustine was attracted to Manichaeism, a radical form of Christianity originating in pre-Islamic Iran (then at the heart of the Persian empire), founded by the Gnostic prophet, Mani. Mani taught identification with Christ as the vehicle through which imprisoned souls could escape their entrapment in the body and return to God. The Manichaean religion believed the body to be a haven of darkness, and required the elect of their faith to adhere to a strict regimen of asceticism and celibacy. Augustine eventually abandoned Manichaeism, which failed to answer his deeper philosophical questions about the being of God and the nature and origin of evil, but he maintained Manichaean beliefs about the body's relationship to the soul, and the desire for transcendence of the body's mortal limitations (Augustine, EB 14:397). The more mature Augustine recognized these same beliefs in the teachings of Plato.

Augustine was introduced to the thoughts of Plato through the writings of Plotinus and Porphyry, who were responsible for facilitating a revival of interest in Plato in the 3rd and 4th centuries CE. While Saint Paul admonished the early Christians, including Augustine, to "let your armor be the Lord Jesus Christ; forget about satisfying your bodies with all their cravings." (Romans 13:14 - Jones 210), Neoplatonism reinforced the Manichaean belief that the soul must escape the body before it could return to God. Plotinus asserted that the intellect was an intermediary between soul and God, while Augustine naturally preferred Christ, but neither doubted that the soul's true destiny was immortality and eternal reunion with the One. Both also agreed that the temporal, mortal body was a primary hindrance to fulfilling this purpose. Augustine's philosophy was an amalgam of Manichaeism, Neoplatonism, and Biblical scripture, with a major Plato's ideas. Through Augustine's influence, the immortality of the soul, and a deliberate disidentification with the body became cornerstones of the Christian faith (Augustine, EB 14:398).

Passing Through the Gate of Immortality On the Way to the Underworld

By now, nearly 2 1/2 millennia after the death of Plato, and at least as long since the concept of reincarnation arose in Eastern religious tradition, these ideas have become so thoroughly ingrained in modern thinking, that we no longer question them, nor assess the price we pay for holding them. Religion attempts to solve the problem of death by clinging to a belief in the soul's immortality, or in its ultimate liberation from the necessity for life and death. When the soul's fate is divorced from its cyclical roots in an attempt to mitigate the fear of life *or* death, however, these beliefs become a serious impediment to a meaningful understanding of the embodied soul's experience. Ancient Vedic yogis and Taoist shamans sought identification with Spirit, not as a means for transcending death, but as a source of empowerment within life. When the quest for immortality instead becomes a quest for liberation from life or death, it short-circuits whatever claim to spiritual vitality the embodied soul can claim.

Such a focus serious impedes the soul's embrace of the spiritual opportunity this life presents. Paradoxically, it is our cumulative earthly experiences that form the basis for any real claim to immortality or enlightenment that the embodied soul might have. To the

◇◇◇

extent that we cultivate our talents and make a contribution to the world of which we are part; to the extent that we learn to love and give of ourselves to others; to the extent that we pass on our values and our love of life to our children; to the extent that we participate fully in this life and leave our impact upon the hearts and minds of those that follow, then we will – in some truly meaningful sense – survive our own death, and live on as a source of illumination in the memory of those whose lives we have touched with our own.

Granted, many of those surviving us will remember us through the distorting filter of their own perceptual biases. These imperfect memories may or may not accurately preserve the essence of who we were as embodied souls. It is not the memories of others, however, that give substance to the soul's immortality, but our own willingness to live a memorable life - made memorable through what we have given to it. Wherever the embodied soul is bold enough to assert itself, compassionate enough to share its love, wise and brave enough to risk making a difference, it will continue to reverberate in the embodied world as a vital force after death. Conversely, what happens then will be of little consequence, to the extent we have wasted our time here avoiding life, and pining for liberation from the curse of embodiment.

As we stand before Inanna's first gate, I contend that it is impossible to discuss the experience of the embodied soul in a meaningful way, or realize its spiritual potential, while longing for either eternal life beyond the body, in the style of Western religion, or for liberation from the necessity for embodied life, sought in Eastern tradition. Before we can pass through Inanna's first gate, we must relinquish these beliefs. To face the embodied soul on its own terms, in all of the naked vulnerability that this encounter demands, we must first embrace an awareness of death's inevitability. We must speak about the soul's journey in terms of the cyclical relationship between life and death in *this* incarnation. It is because the soul is privileged to participate in this eternal cycle – and not because the soul is immortal, or destined to one day be free from the cycle – that it enters a realm where an embodied life of meaning and purpose become possible.

The soul must also be distinguished from Spirit, and understood instead as the *presence* of Spirit *within* the physical body and the larger body of this earthly existence. Perhaps other adventures lie in store for the postmortem soul after death, but until then, the embodied soul must fully inhabit the body in order to reap whatever meaning is possible in this life. Despite the widespread appeal of the belief in the survival of the soul after death, any meaningful discussion of the embodied soul depends upon a willingness to focus, not on some possible existence beyond the body, but on *this* life in *this* body in the here and now. For outside of a belief system that speculates otherwise, *this* life is all the embodied soul is guaranteed. Once we have restored the soul to the body, we can begin to understand the body as the vehicle to discover and articulate the particular meaning and spiritual purpose inherent in this life.

Endnotes

[1] From an inscription on a gold plate found in southern Italy (or possibly Crete), described in Powell 315-317.

[2] I am assuming that this development roughly coincided with the period prior to publication of the Egyptian Pyramid Texts (c 2375-2200 BCE), which represent the first known written documentation of the belief in immortality. While it is likely that some belief in an afterlife was prevalent among prehistoric cultures throughout the world, it was primarily the Egyptian conceptualization of immortality that was passed on to Western religious tradition. It is with the passing of this legacy that I associate the paradigm shift mentioned in the text to which this endnote refers.

Chapter Three
Shedding the Religious Concept of Sin

Religions that attempted to liberate the soul from the body left the opportunity for self-discovery through the experience of living within a body largely unexplored. The body, considered by such religions as something separate from Spirit, became the unfortunate casualty of an ill-conceived strategy designed to create as much separation between Spirit and matter as possible. Within these traditions, the body was often considered sinful, and the descent into matter through which Spirit entered into a body to become soul was conceptualized as a "fall from grace." The concept of salvation came increasingly into play, with each religion espousing its own version of a relatively universal code of conduct, designed to lessen the impact of the fall, and ensure a relatively smooth passage from life to a more benign resting place in the hereafter.

The irony of this solution is that when the treatment is successful, and the individual soul becomes acclimated to the prescribed moral code, the patient dies. This kind of religious redemption – which demands a disavowal of the body – can only mean disconnection from the very experience of embodiment that gives the soul its living vitality as a focal point of spiritual opportunity. The soul that gets saved through sacrifice of the body, its pleasures and its fatal limitations, is not the soul that ultimately defines us, but a transcendent ghost of a soul that was never of this Earth to begin with. Such a soul is merely enduring its time here, a stranded alien castaway from some ethereal realm, whose only desire is to one day return to its immaterial home. This life – which, from the embodied soul's perspective, is the only one it has – will be wasted pining for gratification that can only come after death. All earthly experiences that would otherwise have given *this* life its shape and purpose become marginalized and stripped of meaning.

Exposing the Faustian Bargain
Of the Religious Approach to Soul

Few religions encourage a full no-holds-barred exploration of the embodied life as a prescription for the fulfillment of soul. Instead, most religions that sought liberation from the body kept the notion of the terrible destiny awaiting the dead that characterized earlier fear-based religions, but compartmentalized this destiny as a fate reserved only for those who did not meet certain standards of behavior in this life. In this way, the concept of an afterlife typically came to be inseparable from the idea of judgment. In turn, judgment became construed as the fate of a soul whose journey after death was previously understood as a fearful passage into the unknown. The soul could now alter its fate, and

◇◇

ensure its survival after death, provided it subscribed to a moral code, which nearly always encouraged disidentification with the body. Conveniently for the emerging religions that traveled this route, the paradigm shift toward postmortem judgment also filled churches and temples with those who feared being punished after death for their transgressions of the moral code while alive.

While none of this was premeditated as a global conspiracy, the result over thousands of years of political evolution within these traditions is that institutionalized formal religions have became authoritative, though artificial, intermediaries between the individual soul and its ultimate destiny. Even individuals who are not overtly religious cannot help but be influenced by these attitudes, which have permeated world culture for more than 2500 years and have become an intrinsic part of our collective unconscious conditioning. Religion in general has tried to reassure us that the Great Mystery has been solved, that we - or at least they - know where we are going and how to ensure that we get there. All we need to do to get on the fast track to our Eternal Reward is take refuge in some belief system, or some bygone pilgrim who got close enough to the Mystery to be forever altered. According to these traditions, we need not, dare not, approach the Mystery ourselves, but must instead relinquish our individual quest for meaning and purpose, hand our souls over to the care of the Keepers of the Mystery, who in turn will guarantee our passage on the Good Ship.

But ultimately, the Good Ship, however good it might be, can only take us to the threshold of death, and at that threshold, the religion to which we relinquished our soul will not be able to help us. In that moment, we will be alone, face to face with Mystery, and the soul itself must be our mediator. If we have not taken the time to cultivate our own intimately personal relationship to the unfathomable mysteries of soul, including our mortality and the inherent moral ambiguities our embodiment entails, we will not know how to cross that threshold. In that moment, religious belief will be no substitute for a conscious relationship with death maintained in life, and a loving, nonjudgmental embrace of the internal contradictions of our being. Religious beliefs may bring peace of mind in the face of death's uncertainty while death is still an abstraction, but in the face of death itself, it is only the existential peace we have made with ourselves, our difficult choices, and the mistakes we have made, that will matter.

To be sure, some religions - including certain Buddhist sects, the original Taoist teachings of Lao Tzu, the shamanic traditions of central Asia, northern Europe, and indigenous America, and the mystical practices at the secret esoteric heart of most religions - have maintained a viable relationship to death and the mystery inherent in life. These traditions actively promote the individual cultivation of soul through deepening the relationship to our wholeness - including all those aspects of being that institutionalized religions label "bad." But such traditions are often marginalized, especially in the Judeo-Christian West. In the East and in indigenous cultures into which civilization has intruded, which is to say just about everywhere, they have been overtaken by materialistic values steeped in the Western myth of the endless good life. Since the cultural revolution of the 1960s, there has been a renaissance of interest in experiential mystery teachings. But the conservative mood swing of the past 20 years or so, and the return of our collective mindset to more traditional religious values, has once again blunted our cutting edge relationship to death and the mystery posed by the embrace of wholeness.

In the hands of mainstream, often more dogmatic and fundamentalist religious views that silently shape the cultures in which they are housed, the soul's relationship to death is buffered by the promise of eternal life, while the body is bound to a moral code designed to counter its corrupting influence. These codes hold the individual to safe, but limiting standards of behavior, sanctioned as good, at the expense of the polarities, internal contradictions, and natural moral ambiguities that make any soul's journey a story worthy to be told. While claiming to bind us within the community of the faithful, they actually promote a sense of spiritual isolation, since in a judgmental atmosphere of conformity, we tend to repress or deny the very aspects of our being that give our soul its complex individuality and depth of genuine expression.

For some the mediation of religion is undoubtedly a comfort, and comfort is not necessarily a bad thing in a world wracked by uncertainty and rapid, sometimes incomprehensible change. Yet if securing this comfort means denying the soul's embodiment, and the polarities which condition the body, then it comes at the high price of a psychological split with serious consequences. Most religions have yet to come to terms with the fact that each soul is both spiritual and sexual, conscious and unconscious, rational and irrational, loving and utterly dysfunctional in the expression of love, brave and cowardly, generous and selfish, strong and weak, admirable and flawed by numerous shortcomings, and in general, torn by the interplay of opposites. To the extent that religion declares part of us good and part of us bad, then it pits the soul against itself in an unnatural effort to conform to standards of behavior that are impossible to attain without serious psychological consequences. Before we examine these consequences and their antidote, let's review a bit of the history behind this untenable state of affairs.

The Evolution of the Concept of Judgment in Western Culture

By no small coincidence, the Egyptian tradition, whose legacy includes the concept of immortality and the resurrection of the soul after death, also provided the model for judgment that became the soul's fate for subsequent cultures, including Western

◇◇

Christianity. According to Egyptian lore, the spiritual heart was called *ib*, and was considered to encompass most of the attributes that make us human, including not just intelligence and self-awareness, but also the capacity for feeling and vulnerability. At death, the *ib* was weighed against the feather of Ma'at (a symbol of everything deemed right and true). The soul that passed this test was declared *maa kheru* (true of value) and joined Osiris in the heavens. The soul that did not measure up was devoured by the monster Am-mit, the "eater of the dead."

The concepts of resurrection and judgment in Jewish and Christian thought seem to have evolved during Judaism's Hellenistic period (4th century BCE - 2nd century CE). These ideas came directly from Egyptian culture, which enjoyed widespread popularity throughout the Hellenistic world. They were also greatly reinforced by Plato, who in turn was influenced by Pythagoras and the Orphic tradition, which derived part of its doctrine through identification with Egyptian mystery teachings. Like the Egyptians, the Orphics were dualistic, and fervently sought the liberation of the soul from the body, primarily through abstinence from meat, wine, and sexual intercourse. After death, the soul was judged, and either rewarded with an eternal romp through the idyllic meadows of Elysium, or banished to Tartaros, the Greek version of hell. Only a soul that had managed to make it through three lives without serious transgression could be liberated from the endless cycle of life and death.

The Orphic tradition heavily influenced Pythagoras, who taught that the original home of the soul was in the stars. From there, it fell to earth and became imprisoned in the body. Man was considered a stranger on Earth, his primary spiritual task to liberate himself from the ties of the flesh and return to the soul's heavenly abode. Pythagoras conceived of the journey of the soul as a gruesome series of prison terms on earth interrupted by episodes between lives in Hades, where the soul was purged of its sins. The path beyond this depressing "wheel of things" as Pythagoras called it (Christian 56), was to lead a virtuous life. This became the model for the moral code that Plato passed on to the religious community of Christians, Jews, and Muslims, whose beliefs freely intermingled and influenced one another throughout the Hellenistic world. Ironically, Pythagoras' recipe for the virtuous life included a healthy diet, exercise, and other administrations to the body designed to keep it in harmony with the soul it housed.

Plato was also heavily influenced by Socrates, who denounced the physical body and its various seductions as the antithesis of the life of virtue to which all good philosophers should aspire. Purification of the soul meant disidentification with the body and its sinful indulgences. Socrates taught that the soul would be judged at death, according to its degree of purification, and that impure souls – those that had overindulged bodily pleasures – would be banished to Tartaros for eternity. Today these ideas form the backbone of Western religious thought about the soul and its fate, especially as preached by fundamentalists of all persuasions.

The Gradual Evolution of a Moral Conception Of the Soul's Journey

At the time they were proposed, Socrates' ideas, passed on through Plato, were considered radical heresy. In Greek thought before Plato, a virtuous life was not rewarded, nor was a sinful life punished. The eternal torment that we now associate with hell was reserved for the handful of mortals who had deeply offended the gods through some uniquely unpardonable sin. According to the mythological tradition handed down by Homer and Hesiod, only three mortals – Titys, Tantalus, and Sisyphus – had ever been banished to Tartaros (Harris 252-256). A fourth serious sinner, Ixion, was bound to a fiery wheel that rolled perpetually through the sky. All four had in some way attempted to compete directly with the gods, or attack, embarrass, or outwit them, and were punished for their audacity. Ordinary mortals, who simply went about their unpretentious mundane lives, went to "a diminished and humiliating post-existence in the underground darkness of Hades, peopled by pallid shadows, without strength and without memory" (Eliade, History 1:260).

As Plato absorbed the Pythagorean concept of life as imprisonment in the body, and the Socratic belief that souls would be judged according to their degree of disidentification with the body, the journey of the soul became understood in increasingly moralistic terms. Within this paradigm shift, Tartaros became the final destination for those who refused to conform to the moral code. Plato then passed on this moralistic conception of the soul's journey to the Judeo-Christian tradition, which began to distort the teachings of Christ with a judgmental denigration of the body that Christ himself never taught. Platonic teachings were found in the apocryphal text known as the Wisdom of Solomon, for example, which declares, "God created man imperishable, and made him in the image of his own eternal self; it was the devil's spite that brought death into the world, and the experience of it is reserved for those who take his side" (2:23-24 – Pelikan 2:77). This view contrasts starkly with more traditional Jewish teachings, which previously held our universal fate to be a dismal eternity in *Sheol*, regardless of whose side we were on.

Christianity was also influenced through Augustine's embrace of Manichaeism, as discussed in Chapter Two. Like the Orphic, Socratic and Pythagorean traditions, Mani preached that the world is the creation of both a good power and an evil one, and that the soul's essential goodness was severely compromised by its imprisonment in the body. During the fertile Hellenistic period, the Manichaean tradition blended with Gnosticism, and the cult of the Persian god, Mithra, both of which reinforced a judgmental attitude toward the body. Through the integration of these ideas in the thoughts of Saint Augustine, moralistic judgment gradually came to predominate in the Judeo-Christian tradition.

The Reinterpretation of Scripture in Moralistic Terms

Under this influence, Biblical scripture began to be interpreted and translated differently. According to the original meaning of the word *nefesh*, roughly translated as soul in the Hebrew language, a man did not *have* a soul, but rather *was* a soul. Genesis 2:7 says, "The Lord God formed man from the dust of the earth. He blew into his nostrils the breath of life and the man became a living being" (Pelikan, The Tanakh 5). The Hebrew word for "living being" is also *nefesh* implying that when God gave man the gift of bodily life, man became a soul. As dualistic notions of soul and body arose within the Jewish tradition, through these other influences, a subtle shift in thinking about the word, *nefesh*, took place, which separated the concept of soul from the concept of being.

During the Hellenistic period, original Hebrew texts were translated into Aramaic, a more prosaic language that evolved as Jewish, Greek and Arabic cultures intermingled. Under this influence, rabbinical scholars began to conceive of man as *having* a soul, which could be lost through sinful behavior (Judaism, EB 22:416). The soul was still subject to dissolution at death, along with the body. But man – who now stood apart from the soul – could save it from this fate through moral rectitude and disidentification with the body. After death, the soul had previously been banished to eat clay and dwell in terminal boredom in *Sheol*, where nothing happened, regardless of how good or bad it was. Now, according to these new translations, the soul reached a crossroads at death, where its fate would be decided according to the choices it had made while living.

The Biblical prophet, Isaiah announced that the "dead will come to life, their corpses will rise," and that "all you who lie in the dust" will be enjoined to "awake (and) exult" (Isaiah 26:19 - Jones 1007). Both the good and the wicked would be resurrected according to their moral deserts. Those who had managed to disidentify with the body and chose a life aligned with Spirit, would be granted "everlasting life." Those who had chosen the body were consigned to an existence of "shame and everlasting disgrace" (Daniel 12:2-3 - Jones 1251). The real Ge Hinnom (valley of Hinnom), historically the place where the Israelites were said to have sacrificed their children to the false god, Moloch, became mythologized as Gehenna, an early conception of hell where the wicked were tortured by fire (Death, EB 16:988).

Within rabbinical tradition, the ethical dilemma that led to either everlasting life, or banishment to the fires of Gehenna, became a matter of choosing between two contrary impulses. One, considered good, was aligned with Spirit; the other, considered evil, was aligned with the flesh, worldly desires, and material interests. Originally, there was no judgment placed upon this choice, the unspoken implication being that in the course of normal life, human beings would have to make both kinds of choices. Being a *nefesh* meant learning how to negotiate the realm of the body with spiritual awareness, and the impulse that guided this process was neither good nor bad. It was not until Hebrew scripture was revised to reflect its absorption of Platonic thought that this viewpoint began to change.

The Hebrew word for impulse is *yetzer*, which literally means "a plan which is formulated in the mind." Where the word appears in the Bible, it is sometimes modified by the adjective, *ra*, which has been translated as "evil," but also means "disorderly," "undisciplined," or "confused" (Judaism, <u>EB</u> 22:417). In Genesis 8:21, in the wake of the Flood, for example, the Lord tells Noah:

> *Never again will I doom the earth because of man, since the devisings of man's mind (yetzer) are "ra" from his youth, nor will I ever again destroy every living being, as I have done.*
>> *So long as the earth endures,*
>> *Seedtime and harvest,*
>> *Cold and heat,*
>> *Summer and winter,*
>> *Day and night*
>> *Shall not cease.*

This is a profound acceptance on the part of God that man partakes of a dual nature. If we translate *yetzer ra* in this passage as "disorderly," "undisciplined," or "confused," God's statement can be understood as one of deep compassion for the ambivalence of the human soul He has created. If we translate *yetzer ra* as "evil," then the passage makes less sense, for if "the devisings of man's mind" were inherently evil, why would God not want to destroy the monster that He had unleashed? This is the ever-present threat brandished by the moralistic religions. Yet here God is promising *not* to destroy man, just because he is *yetzer-ra*.

If we understand the inherent difficulty in fusing matter with Spirit through the exercise of consciousness - which is after all, the task of the soul - then the use of the modifier *ra* cannot be construed as a condemnation. Instead it must be understood as a simple affirmation of the difficulty of the human predicament. Life on earth for most people is in fact, a matter of trial and error that is often "disorderly," "undisciplined," and "confused." The confusion is not inherently evil; it is simply a necessary attribute of the learning process.

Nonetheless, the Aramaic translations of this term, dominated as they were by dualistic notions separating the soul from the body, invariably modified the word *yetzer* with the term *ra*, and translated it is as "evil" wherever it occurred. Rabbinical literature coined the term, *yetzer ha-ra* (the evil impulse) to describe the sinful nature of the choice to indulge the body, while the term, *yetzer ha-tov* (the good impulse) denoted the virtuous nature of the choice to obey God's laws (Judaism, EB 22:417). How man navigated between these two impulses, and how aligned he became with body or Spirit, would determine his fate as a soul after death.

The Evolution of a Moral Code in Islam

This became the prototype, not just for the Judeo-Christian concept of judgment, but also for the Islamic tradition. Islam arose in the 7th century CE, largely as a consequence of the teachings of Mohammed, but was also influenced by the Jewish and Christian traditions that preceded it. Islam honors the same major prophets as Judaism – Noah, Abraham, Moses, and Jesus – and considers Mohammed to be the "seal of the prophets," bringing culmination to the groundwork laid by the preceding four. The Aramaic language, in which Jewish rabbinical texts and commentaries are written, has similarities to Arabic languages. Many of the beliefs about the soul, the afterlife, and the relationship between the soul and the body are also similar.

In traditional Islam, when someone dies, the angel of death (Malah Al-Nawi) judges the soul according to its moral virtue. Souls are then sent either to "the wrath of God" or "the mercy of God," depending upon Malah Al-Nawi's assessment. After the judgment is recorded, the soul is returned to the body for additional questioning by two angels, known as Munkar and Nakir. These angels quiz the soul about Islamic moral doctrine, and then evaluate it according to how religiously it had adhered to the moral code while alive. To this day, as witnessed in theocratic societies throughout the Arab world, a strict sense of morality polarizing the spirit and the flesh serves as the basis for this judgment, which is faced by the soul in both life and death.

As with Greek and Judeo-Christian tradition, such moralistic understanding of the soul's fate was not always the case. In Arabian society before Mohammed, the prevailing belief was that the life of the soul ended with death. The only meaning to be found in existence within the pre-Islamic world was through the pleasure experienced while alive. These sentiments were expounded in a rich body of poetry, praising the man who gave himself to wine, women and song, and who left good stories behind for his fellow tribesmen to tell. Needless to say, there was no moral judgment placed on the enjoyment of the body, nor was it expected that excess would be punished in the hereafter. Such ideas only began percolating within the Arab mindset when traditional Arab attitudes were challenged by an influx of Greek and Judeo-Christian philosophies with which they intermingled for nearly a millennium.

Long before the birth of Mohammed in 570 CE, Jewish and Christian settlements existed throughout the Arab world, asserting their philosophical and moral influence. Makkah, the city where Mohammed was born, was a caravan station on a well-traveled trade route that connected the Mediterranean world with the Far East. It was also a fertile environment for the cross-breeding of cultures, and the likely source of the moral sensibilities that Mohammed brought to his role as founder of Islam. It is believed that Mohammed may have belonged to a group of Makkan Arabs known as *hafnifs* (pious ones), who accepted the ethical monotheism of Judeo-Christian tradition, but maintained their distinctly Arab identity (Oxtoby, <u>Western</u> 343-344). Tradition reports that Mohammed loathed the amoral lifestyle and the idolatry of his reckless tribesmen, and after a series of visitations by the angel, Gabriel (*Jibril* in Arabic), began to conceive his mission as parallel to that of Moses, historically the bringer of laws and a moral code to the Jewish people.

When Mohammed began preaching morality and judgment to the Arab world, he was not well received. At first, he was accepted only among slaves and disenfranchised poor people with nothing to lose by giving up a good life they had never known. He and his followers were often ridiculed and persecuted, except within small pockets of support and protection. Gradually, the moral rectitude and egalitarianism practiced among this small band of disciples began to attract men of greater social standing. Eventually, in 622, Mohammed was invited to mediate a dispute between two warring tribes in the city of Yathrib, where he established the first theocratic Muslim state bound by a strict moral code.

Mohammed soon developed a vision of uniting all of Arabia under this same Islamic banner. Through a series of early caravan raids and later more serious military campaigns, he largely accomplished his goal before his death ten years later. Within 80 years of his death, his followers continued to expand the Islamic empire to encompass an area stretching from the southern borders of France through northern Africa, and from the Middle East into central Asia, and on to India (Oxtoby, <u>Western</u> 348). The result was the rapid spread of a culture in which the plight of the soul was mitigated by a strict moral code, and the previous Arab tradition of celebrating the body was considered the primary source of moral decrepitude.

The Shift Toward a Moral Interpretation Of the Soul's Journey in the East

The drift toward a moralistic interpretation of the soul's journey in Eastern religious culture is less obvious than in the Judeo-Christian-Islamic tradition, but no less damaging to the soul. The transition appears to have taken place during the years preceding the Indo-European invasion of the Indian subcontinent, the same period in which the matriarchal embrace of the cycle of life and death and the Aryan quest for conquest of death merged into a desire for liberation from the cycle of rebirth. As mentioned in Chapter Two, there was not much discussion in the Vedas of an afterlife, and most prayers to the gods were for fulfillment in this life. Nor was there any judgment implied as a consequence of the actions in this life, as there would be in later Hindu scripture. There was in fact, as Joseph Campbell notes, not much to suggest the origin of the religious tradition known today as Hinduism, though the Vedas are generally acknowledged as the source of this tradition. The word, "Hinduism" itself came into popular usage during British colonial rule of India in the 18ᵗʰ and 19ᵗʰ century. It was coined to encompass the various indigenous religious practices that had prevailed since the Indo-European invasion before the Vedas were written.

In the Vedas, there was "no idea of reincarnation; no yearning for release from the vortex of rebirth; no yoga; no mythology of salvation; no vegetarianism, non-violence, or caste" (Oriental 183-184). Other scholars suggest that the caste system was already firmly in place by the time the Vedas were written, imposed by the Indo-European invaders upon the indigenous Harrapan culture (Oxtoby, Eastern 27). But caste was originally construed as a political system of domination, and was not interpreted in moral terms until much later. Nor did the Vedas interpret the concept of *karma* in the same way that we do today, as essentially the Eastern equivalent of sin.

The word, *karma*, which means "action," originally referred to ritual actions performed by priests to appease and supplicate the deities (Oxtoby, Eastern 28). It was only through the reinterpretation of Vedic texts in the Upanishads, that *karma* became the universal system of consequences associated with any action that we understand it to be today. While the Vedas concerned themselves with life in the here and now, the Upanishads spoke of a series of lives, precipitated by the accumulation of unresolved *karma*. This new doctrine declared that the goal of any seeker of truth should not be a harmonious existence, as it had been in the Vedic world, but rather the quest for liberation from the wheel of birth and death. The Upanishads are also referred to as the Vedanta, or as part of larger system of thought called Vedanta. Vedanta means "the end of the Vedas," and it is clear that these new texts and the understanding of the soul that they promoted were a radical departure from the earlier religious tradition they replaced.

The increasingly moralistic conception of the soul's journey, framed in terms of *karma*, *samsara* (*karma* carried from one lifetime to the next), and reincarnation was no small part of this silent revolution.

This emerging sense of morality was spelled out more explicitly in a later series of scripture, called the *dharmasastras*, written in the 1st century CE. The most famous of these scriptures is the *Manava Dharmasastra*, or Laws of Manu, which contains such ironically amoral injunctions as "a virtuous wife should constantly serve her husband like a god, even if he behaves badly, freely indulges his lust, and is devoid of good qualities" (qtd. in Oxtoby, Eastern 49). One might rightly wonder whether this moral code was meant to serve the needs of the evolving soul, or of a patriarchal society that sought to institutionalize its fear of the Feminine, and to keep its women under control. Hindu morality came under serious scrutiny during British colonial rule. Meanwhile, the *dharmasastras* defined virtue in an elaborate list of commandments, and interpreted the civil law of the caste system as religious duty, or *dharma*. Infidelity between husband and wife, for example, became an infraction of *dharma* with karmic consequences – more severe for women than for men – as well as a violation of the social code.

The Trend Toward Moralistic Judgment in Buddhist Thought

Buddhism arose In the 6th century BCE out of the same philosophical ferment that produced this shift in Hindu thought. Buddhism seems to have embraced the concept of *karma* and reincarnation from its origin, although the entire cycle of birth, death and rebirth was conceived in much more impersonal terms than in the Hindu tradition. The Buddha saw there was no self to be reincarnated, and taught that ignorance of this fact led to suffering. He further taught that ignorance was to be treated with compassion, since all sentient beings – whether practicing Buddhists or not – were on their way to enlightenment and liberation. The soul's journey, illusory though it was to the Buddha, was nonetheless conceived as a learning process upon which he placed no moral judgment.

When the Buddha started teaching, after his enlightenment under the Bodhi tree, he taught that shunning the body, as the ascetics of his day did, was wrong, and would not lead to enlightenment. He himself had been an ascetic for six years, wandering from teacher to teacher, learning all that he could of yogic disciplines, standing for hours in hot sun and cold rain, fasting for long periods on only one palm full of water and one of food per day. He became extremely emaciated and weak with hunger, and one day realized that this torturous effort to castigate and purify his body had not taken him one step closer to the state of inner peace he sought. Only when he resumed eating and drinking, and attending to his body's needs with compassion, did he start making progress. Though his previous life as a pampered prince had not brought him any closer to enlightenment, neither had vigorously renouncing all those worldly pleasures for a life of asceticism. After experiencing both extremes, he concluded that the soul's optimal journey was to pursue the "Middle Way," neither feverishly seeking the indulgence of every desire, nor automatically rejecting the body and its needs. In the wake of this realization he chose a pleasant spot beside a cooling river beneath a large shady tree and meditated until he reached nirvana.

The Buddha continued to teach the Middle Way for another 45 years after his enlightenment, until one day an enemy masquerading as a gracious host served him rotten mushrooms for dinner. When his disciples asked him on his deathbed who they should follow after he was gone, he told them to follow the *dharma*. *Dharma* had two meanings in classic Indian thought. The first, and more common was as adherence to law and moral virtue, as mentioned earlier in relation to the Hindu teachings of the *dharmasastras*. *Dharma* in this sense was one of four sources of potential motivation from which the soul could derive its impetus, the others being *kama* (love and pleasure), *artha* (power and success), and *moksa* (release from delusion and ignorance). There was also a more metaphysical and ultimately more fundamental meaning to the word, which derived from the Sanskrit root verb, *dhr*, literally translated as "to hold up, support, carry, bear, sustain, or maintain" (Campbell, Oriental 23). In this sense, *dharma* meant the natural order that supports the universe, a concept related to the Chinese *Tao*.

Though during his lifetime Buddha had outlined an Eightfold Path for alignment with *dharma* – including right view, right thought, right speech, right conduct, right livelihood, right effort, right mindfulness, and right meditation – it is not likely that he promoted this strategy in a moralistic sense. Wrong view, wrong thought, and wrong speech were not the appropriate target of moralistic judgments, but rather of compassion. Wrong anything would lead to more suffering, but suffering itself was the mark of ignorance, not of evil worthy of punishment. The latter association evolved only when less enlightened beings who followed in the Buddha's footsteps attempted to turn living truth into religious dogma.

The *dharma* Buddha spoke of when he taught the Eightfold Path was probably not intended to be a moral code, as it was later interpreted, but rather a prescription for a life of harmony with the natural order, or *dharma* in the more metaphysical sense. One who did not follow *dharma*, according to Buddhist teaching, was not necessarily morally corrupt, nor would they need to be punished. They would simply experience the consequences of their actions, according to the law of *karma*, and suffer or flourish accordingly. This was not a system of reward and punishment with judgmental moralistic overtones, but an ingenious feedback mechanism, built into the fabric of the embodied world, designed to lead all sentient beings toward alignment with *dharma* in the more metaphysical sense. Complete alignment with *dharma* then naturally led to a release from the necessity for suffering, and from the cycle of birth, death, and rebirth.

It is also likely that what Buddha meant on his deathbed by admonishing his followers to follow the *dharma* was that they were not to be beholden to external authorities – moral or otherwise – but to the natural order existing within them and throughout the universe. They were to follow the path toward alignment with the natural order that he had laid out for them (Oxtoby, Eastern 211), and experience *dharma* for themselves. Nonetheless, it was perhaps inevitable that Buddha's teachings would become institutionalized, and spread through the auspice of an external religious authority, as seems to be true for most spiritual teachers that have ever walked the planet. In the case of Buddhism, which spawned many local versions, this authority was relatively decentralized compared to most Western traditions. But immediately following Buddha's death, it began to arrange itself hierarchically and to intervene between practicing Buddhists and their *dharma*.

Buddha taught orally, and did not assign anyone the task of recording his words. They were instead memorized in bits and pieces by various members of the *sangha*, or spiritual community of disciples that surrounded Buddha, and recited in their entirety, whenever the group assembled to study and practice. They were written down only in the 1st century CE, a good seven centuries after Buddha's death, by the Theravada monks of Sri Lanka, after a famine had reduced the *sangha* so drastically that there was a danger the oral tradition would be lost. Through the gradual process of memorization, recitation, and finally written codification of Buddhist teachings, Buddhism became increasingly institutionalized, and the Buddha's original teachings about *dharma* became increasingly arbitrated by religious authority.

No doubt, even with the best of intentions, the Buddha's original teachings were also distorted after seven centuries of transmission by imperfect human memory, and hastily written reconstruction in a time of crisis. As with the Vedic teachings, Buddhist teachings about *dharma* were interpreted in increasingly moralistic tones through subsequent commentary, and institutionalized as the moral authority of the Buddhist priesthood. One of the Theravada Buddhist monks from Sri Lanka named Buddhaghosa, for example, wrote an exegesis on *dharma* called *The Path of Purity*, which asserted that following the moral precepts of *dharma* were an essential foundation to further progress on the spiritual path. Buddha himself apparently accepted disciples into the full range of his teachings, including *dharma*, but later institutionalized Buddhism required mastery of *dharma* by its monks as a prerequisite to a higher order of ordination.

Other Influences on the Tendency Toward Moral Judgment In Eastern Religious Thought

Buddhism remains one of the least moralistic religious traditions on the planet, despite increasing emphasis on a moral interpretation of *dharma*, Yet other influences in the east were not so benign. Though today the Jains represent a tiny minority of India's population, during the Buddha's day, they were a formidable force of great influence. Mahavira, the primary figure in Jain history, was a contemporary and rival of the Buddha, who taught a radical form of asceticism in stark contrast to the Buddha's Middle Way. According to Mahavira's teachings, Spirit and matter were absolutely opposed, and their fusion in the human body was an abhorrent condition to be transcended through a course of detachment from the world, denunciation of the body, and strict moral virtue.

The Jains outlined an elaborate system of heavens and hells, to which souls were resigned at various stages of their evolutionary development, depending upon how well they had upheld the moral code in their last incarnation. In the lowest of these hells, "all being subject to the four cardinal passions of pride, wrath, delusion, and desire," the inmates "torment and mangle one another horribly with arrows, javelins and tridents, clubs and axes, knives and razors, tossing one another to beasts and birds endowed with claws and beaks of iron or into rivers of corrosive liquid or of fire; some are hung head downward into boiling vats of blood and filth, others are being roasted alive; more, pinned through the head to great moaning trees, are having their bodies sliced to ribbons. And the food of this company is poison, sizzling grease and ordure, while for drink they have molten metal" (Campbell, Oriental 228).

Like the visions of Dante, these images were conjured to evoke a fear of straying from the path laid out by the Jain moral code. A similar attitude governed the followers of Zoroaster, who was also actively teaching throughout the Persian empire in the 6th century BCE, at the same time as Buddha and Mahavira. Zoroaster taught not only that this world was a battlefield between the forces of good and evil, but that each individual had a pressing moral obligation to take sides in the battle. The ultimate triumph of good was guaranteed, but not without an immense struggle, and each individual would be judged in the end according to the extent to which he or she had contributed to the final victory. Unlike Jainism, Zoroaster's moral code was not primarily ascetic, stressing instead good thoughts, good words, and good deeds. The final judgment would nonetheless be a physical ordeal by fire in which molten metal was poured into each body, and only the morally pure would survive.

Both Zoroastrianism and Jainism asserted a profound influence upon the subsequent development of Asian religious tradition, including Hinduism and Buddhism, in a way similar to the influence of Egyptian and Orphic influences within the Hellenistic world of the Mediterranean. The result, fermented over the course of centuries, was a tendency away from original concepts of *dharma*, in which the journey of the soul was one that was lived in harmony with natural forces, to a moralistic interpretation in which *dharma* (and its equivalent in other religious traditions) became interpreted according to explicit codes of behavior. The difference is subtle, but important, for where the previous understanding of *dharma* required conscious attention to the balance of forces at play in the moment, the latter merely required obedience to rules set by external authority. Along with the evolution of moral codes that carried the weight of religious law came increasing judgment upon behavior in violation of the code, and increasing emphasis on punishment for transgression.

The Transition From Natural Law to Moral Code In Chinese Religious Thought

The Chinese classic, the *Tao Te Ching*, begins by warning us that "the way that can be spoken of is not the constant way; the name that can be named is not the constant name" (Lau 57). The explicit moral codes adopted by most Eastern religions over the course of the millennium preceding the birth of Christ did attempt to speak of the way, and name the name. In doing so, they departed from the constant way, or *Tao*, which requires ongoing attention to the process of life unfolding anew in each moment. It is not possible to live in accordance with the *Tao* by following a strict set of rules that will apply universally in every situation. One must instead discern the balance between yin and yang at play in the moment, and find one's center within that shifting balance. Yin and yang are Chinese words, roughly translated as "feminine" and "masculine" respectively, but actually encompassing all pairs of opposites juxtaposed throughout the embodied world.

This understanding of *Tao* constitutes an art of living from moment to moment that requires a certain spontaneity of instinct that cannot be bound by rules. Originally taught as an oral teaching, primarily shamanic in origin, the *Tao* was passed on from teacher to student, as much by example as by verbal instruction. The first written teachings about the *Tao*, the *Tao Te Ching*, attempts to outline basic principles, which then must be applied from moment to moment. These teachings are attributed to Lao Tzu, although scholars argue about whether Lao Tzu was a real person. The name, Lao Tzu, simply means "Old Master." It is not unlikely that the historical person, Lao Tzu, was a mythic composite of itinerant teachers wandering through China circa 650-350 BCE, and that the *Tao Te Ching* was a collection of wisdom teachings about the *Tao* that had previously been passed along as part of an informal oral tradition (Mair 120). Others argue that because the teachings of the *Tao Te Ching* show great consistency, they are probably attributable to one man, possibly Lao Tan, who was a contemporary of Confucius (Eliade, <u>History</u> 2:25-26). Whether Lao Tzu actually lived or not, it is clear that the *Tao Te Ching* represents the first steps from a living oral tradition to one that is more formalized in writing.

The principles espoused in the *Tao Te Ching* were elaborated in The Book of Changes, or *I Ching*, which is also likely a composite work, written during the late Chou period of Chinese history (480-221 BCE). The ideas that form the philosophical basis for the system presented by the *I Ching* are said to have been devised by the first of the legendary Ten Emperors, Fu Hsi. Fu Hsi assigned an unbroken line to the masculine principle, yang, and a broken line to the feminine principle, yin, then arranged these two lines into groups of three, in eight possible combinations called *trigrams*. He and other subsequent commentators assigned various attributes, images, and family analogies to each of the eight *trigrams*. King Wen, the father of the Chou dynasty, further combined the *trigrams* to form 64 *hexagrams*. His younger son, the Duke of Chou, is credited with composing the text analyzing each of the 64 *hexagrams*. This text has since been written and rewritten, translated and retranslated, and added to in multiple layers of commentary over the course of the centuries following, a process that continues to this day.

As with the Old Testament, the Vedas, and the teachings of Buddha about *dharma*, subsequent elaboration on the original shamanic teachings of the *Tao* became increasingly moralistic in tone, in part through the commentaries that were added to the *I Ching*. Although this shift can be understood as an historical trend, perhaps no one person was more responsible for the reinterpretation of Taoist principles in moralistic terms than Confucius. Confucius is said to have lived circa 551-479 BCE, which would make him a contemporary of Plato, Mahavira, and Zoroaster. Each was responsible within their sphere of influence for a similar philosophical shift from natural law to moral code.

The Role of Confucius as a Moralistic Interpreter of the Tao

Confucius interpreted Taoist principles within the context of duty to the state, and moral obligation to one's family of origin. Unlike Lao Tzu, whose teaching was oriented toward individuals – including kings and military leaders – who sought to live in harmony with *Tao*, Confucius was concerned primarily with stemming what he felt was the breakdown of moral authority, and the decay of the political system in China. The internal harmony of the individual soul was not his concern so much as the assurance that individuals would play their part in an ordered and harmonious society. In a legendary meeting between Confucius and the older Lao Tzu, Lao Tzu reputedly admonished Confucius to "get rid of your arrogant attitude and all these desires, this self-satisfaction and this overflowing zeal" (Eliade, <u>History</u> 2:25) but Confucius persisted in redefining Lao Tzu's *superior man* (one who lived in harmony with *Tao*) as one who correctly fulfilled all of his social and political obligations.

After his death, Confucius' disciples continued to promulgate his teachings until the 2nd century CE, at which time the sovereign of the Han dynasty decided to entrust the administration of the Chinese empire to the Confucianists, and reorder society according to their principles. These principles – teachings about the *Tao* reinterpreted in moralistic terms – have ever since served as the underlying philosophical basis for the evolution of Chinese culture. In theory, Confucianism stresses the virtue of benevolence in dealing with infractions of cosmic law, and neither Taoism nor Confucianism provide for judgment or punishment for violations of the moral code. In practice, however, the exercise of this moral code has been quite repressive, as witnessed in modern times from the days of Maoism, to the massacre at Tianneman Square, to the current violent ban on the practice of Falun Dafa (a modern version of original Taoist teachings).

Passing Through Inanna's Second Gate Into Realignment with the Tao

Regardless of which religious tradition we study, there appears to have been a radical shift away from organic principles governing human choice – such as *yetzer*, *dhr*, and *tao* – that took place somewhere between 600 BCE and 700 CE. This trend, seen in nascent form in Egyptian culture, became increasingly tangible from the 6th – the 4th century BCE, through the teachings of moralistic religious figures such as Plato, Mahavira, Zoroaster and Confucius. The trend intensified and accelerated from the 1st – the 7th centuries CE, when Egyptian teachings became popular throughout the Hellenistic world, Buddha's oral teachings were written down, Taoist teachings became politicized by the Confucianists, and Mohammed introduced a more formalized morality to the Arab world. As these moral teachings took root, the soul was discouraged from attempting to find its own internal balance in relation to life and death, masculine and feminine, light and dark, and all the other polarities of the embodied world. Instead, it was admonished to obey the code, and substitute the judgments of religious institutions for its own trial-by-error learning process.

Before we can pass through Inanna's second gate, we must shed these religious moral teachings, and find our way back into a more organic relationship with the *Tao*. The fusion of Spirit and matter that gives rise to the embodied soul is a dynamic state of balance between opposites, which reverberates throughout the embodied world on every level on which yin and yang interact. In order for the soul to understand and make optimal use of the spiritual opportunity at the heart of its embodiment, it must find its own way to a state of internal balance between the opposites from which it springs. In Chapter Four, we will explore in more detail why religious moral codes are inadequate in guiding the soul toward the fulfillment of this task, and how we might conceive of the soul's process in terms that are more conducive to its spiritual evolution.

Chapter Four
Through Inanna's Second Gate
Into the Dance of Polarities

In most traditions where judgment is based on moral behavior, it is telling to note that this was often measured largely by one's identification with the body's sexual nature. The imagery used to account for the involvement of the soul in matter and the origin of its corruption was often sexual in tone, and sex itself was seen to be not just a source of corruption, but the ultimate triumph of body over spirit. Within the context of a dualistic worldview that considered Spirit and body to be diametrically opposed, this triumph was construed in moralistic terms as evil, controlling and dominating good. To the extent that the soul was judged to have allowed this to happen, it was consigned to some form of hell. To the extent that the soul had resisted the body's vulnerability to sexual and sensual temptations, then it was allowed to ascend into heaven. Although sex was less overtly repressed in the East than in the West, Hindu yogic practices, later Taoist shamanic teachings, and Jain moral prescriptions are all quite clear in their teaching that the path to enlightenment or proper alignment with Spirit lie in the repression or transmutation of sexual desires.

The Sexual Dilemma Faced By Moralistic Religions

Since the soul and body are inherently and inextricably bound to one another, this prescription was a recipe for psychological schizoid behavior. Under this prescription, every mortal – sons of God, prophets and founding fathers of predominantly patriarchal religions included – was consigned to endlessly wrestle with demons against which he was ultimately powerless.

We see this struggle, for example, in Saint Augustine's embrace of Manichaeism in his youth. As mentioned earlier, Manichaeism was an extremely dualistic doctrine, envisioning the Earth as a battlefield between forces of light and darkness, and prescribing a strict life of asceticism and celibacy for its followers. Augustine, however, was only allowed to participate as a "hearer," a member of the lowest order, to whom marriage was permitted as a concession to human weakness. This concession was necessary in Augustine's case, because at the time he was sexually involved with a woman of low birth, with whom he had an illegitimate son. When it came down to a choice between his sexuality and his religion, Augustine adamantly refused to give up this relationship, and was consequently relegated to the back of the Manichaean Church. Origen, patriarch of the Greek Orthodox Church, took a more radical approach to this same dilemma, when he reputedly had himself castrated, so that he could provide religious instruction to women without the burden of sexual temptation (Origen, EB 8:997). Although the story may or may not be a rumor perpetrated by Origen's enemies, it illustrates the fundamental dilemma of the religious attitude toward sexuality.

This conflict between a religious faith that identifies the body as a source of evil, and a human nature to whom sexuality is an intrinsic and vital expression of being continues to plague Christianity to this day. As I write this (mid April, 2002) the Catholic Church is being scandalized by the story of a priest in the Boston diocese who is being sued by parishioners claiming their children have been sexually abused by him for 25 years with full knowledge of the cardinal supervising his career (Leo, "The Sins of the Fathers"). What is worse is that this is hardly an isolated incident, as numerous subsequent revelations of parishioners nationwide have since confirmed ("177 Priests Resigned or Removed..."). Scandals involving Church leaders supposedly sworn to vows of celibacy, who are found in compromising positions with parishioners, are in fact so common that we can only assume they are intrinsic to an institutionalized attitude toward the body and sex that is repressive, unnatural, and unhealthy.

The Catholic faith is not the only venue that reveals the futility and neurotic hypocrisy of a dualistic attitude toward the body and its sexual nature. A recent newscast on National Public Radio intimated that the Mormon Church could be next in line for the revelation of equally damaging sexual scandals ("Mormon Scandal"). Eastern gurus, ministers, rabbis, fundamentalist preachers, and spiritual teachers of all persuasions have been caught with their pants down, while embracing a doctrine that is not only untenable, but that can only be maintained through a strenuous denial of the very soul that religion supposedly wants to save. As pointed out by Jung and others, that which is repressed and denied so vehemently can and will, according to the laws of human nature, re-emerge in hideous, distorted, and perverted forms, and this is exactly what has happened throughout religious history.

Reclaiming the Sexual Nature of the Soul

To the extent that the soul is inextricably bound to the body in this life, then it is also inextricably bound to its sexual nature. The body comes into being through a sexual act, although sex is obviously much more than just a vehicle for procreation. Sex produces the most intense pleasure possible in human form. It creates an emotional, psychological and energetic bond between two people who share it, and infuses world culture with an erotic charge that permeates on every level, from the crassest form of manipulative advertising to the highest, most sublime art treasured in the world's most esteemed museums. It is a powerful, irresistible force that has not only brought us into this world, but has also at times brought the world to its knees – through war, through political scandal, and through infectious diseases such as syphilis, gonorrhea, and AIDS. As Freud observed, perhaps overzealously, sex permeates human psychology, and reverberates at the core of every action in which energy, subjective information, and feelings are exchanged. It also permeates the plant and animal kingdoms, and the more poetic of physicists might even concede that it permeates the atomic realm in which protons and electrons are bound to one another in a spiraling dance of attraction, intercourse, and interchange of vital energies.

Can it be denied that sex is a core feature of existence on this physical planet that we occupy? To the extent that this is so, then it seems obvious that sex must be recognized as a central concept in any language of soul, capable of illuminating the human spirit. Yet, as with our discussion of death and the body in which death is experienced, sex also has metaphorical implications that extend far beyond the act itself. For what is sex, after all, but the supreme acknowledgement that we live in a soulful universe in which light and dark, pleasure and pain, good and evil, male and female, spirit and body, and every other pair of opposites are intimately bound?

The moment of orgasm is so powerful and compelling, precisely because in that brief moment, the opposites cease to exist. Pleasure becomes so intense, it is often actually painful; the boundary between yin and yang becomes irrelevant to an obliterating embrace in which both merge. Though our religious and cultural conditioning can induce all manner of self-judgments, feelings of guilt and shame, and other tumultuous moral considerations after the fact, in the moment itself, all distinctions between good and evil are irrelevant[1].

Ironically, it is the experience of union between the opposites that most religions seek in their pursuit of transcendence, since opposites are necessary to the existence of the embodied world from which liberation is desired. Despite the official objections of religious authorities, this goal is implicit in a vast body of mystical literature from nearly every tradition, where the imagery is often overtly sexual. Transcendence of the opposites does not come through a systematic denial of one half of the equation, but through bringing together both halves in a union Jung referred to as the *hieros gamos*, or sacred marriage. The *Tao* is not embraced as a life principle when either yin or yang is denied, but rather when both are granted their place in an eternal dance that is essentially sexual in nature. Likewise, in the Vedic system, *rta* (translated roughly as "course" or "way," and similar to the *Tao* in its meaning) was conceived as a force in nature, which was "particularly visible where any surprising, apparently contradictory circumstance becomes an ever-renewed occurrence" (Campbell, Oriental 178). Contradiction is not possible unless both yin and yang are present in relationship to one another. Though *rta* implies a tension that is resolved in the *hieros gamos*, yin and yang exist on a continuum of possibilities that imply an eternal interaction between forces of equal and opposite potency.

Reclaiming Darkness as a Spiritual Force

As long as the physical plane exists, the dance of yin and yang will pervade every aspect of the life of the embodied soul. Salvation of the soul, if such a concept has any meaning, will not be a matter of Spirit dominating flesh, nor good triumphing over evil. It will be a *hieros gamos* in which both halves of every polarity come into a dynamic harmony that is neither good nor evil but an expression of balance, creative fertility, and spiritual vitality. Light will not triumph over darkness, as the moralistic religions insist. It will instead forever dance with and be drawn to it, despite its proclaimed revulsion. Out of darkness comes a depth of being, a humbling identification with the fallibility, inherent vulnerability, and essential flaws that characterize every embodied soul just as surely as our aspiration to moral goodness, enlightenment, and transcendence of mortal limitations. In this rich, fertile darkness, we are forced to acknowledge our broken imperfection, and it is this acknowledgment that makes us fully human.

The story of Inanna's descent into the underworld and countless other variations of this myth, propagated by nearly every culture, speaks to the process of reclaiming the dark side of one's being. The underworld represents not just the realm of the soul, but also everything that is feared, shunned, rejected, disowned and denied within oneself. Paradoxically, through the underworld lies the soul's path to wholeness, for no one can claim to have attained full spiritual enlightenment who has not faced and integrated its apparent opposite. Inanna's sister, Ereshkigal, represented everything that Inanna believed she was not, but she had to go through an encounter with her sister to claim what she envisioned as her full potential. What she did not envision was that in seeking to usurp Ereshkigal's place, she would come face to face with a power that was equal to her own. She was also forced to confront her own mortality, her fallibility and the limitations of her earthly power. Whether she was able to fully absorb these potent lessons may be open to debate, but her descent into the dark, forbidding underworld was necessary to her education.

Even saints and mystics must pass through a "dark night of the soul" before their spiritual initiation is complete. In her classic work on the subject, Evelyn Underhill describes this rite of passage as "a deeply human process, in which the self which thought itself so spiritual, so firmly established upon the supersensual plane, is forced to turn back, to leave the Light, and pick up those qualities which it had left behind" (388).

If this is true for even the most overtly spiritual among us, then perhaps the religious belief that light is good and dark is evil must be reinterpreted in terms of a dual universe where opposites naturally shape-shift into each other. As Jung suggests, "[T]he grand plan on which the unconscious life of the psyche is constructed is so inaccessible to our understanding that we can never know what evil may not be necessary in order to produce good by enantiodromia, and what good may very possibly lead to evil" (Archetypes 215).

Traditional religion admonishes us to be good, but fails to recognize that "good" is a relative term that takes its meaning only through reference to that which is considered "bad." If we admire those we consider saints and masters for their triumph in the face of temptations, then we must also acknowledge that they would not be who they are, were it not for those very temptations that religion has labeled "bad." If the concept of spiritual evolution has any meaning for the soul at all, that meaning must stem from the fact that both ends of the spectrum are engaged simultaneously. Indeed, within a dualistic universe, we cannot attain the good without engaging – wrestling with, seeking to come to terms with, establishing ourselves in relationship to – everything we consider bad. To the extent that facing all we have labeled "bad" leads to our becoming "good," then the bad is necessary to our growth as souls. Any truly useful language of soul must necessarily embrace the duality of human life without judgment, and recognize that every polarity is essential to working through processes that can be facilitated in no other way.

Reclaiming the Feminine

The irony in the Christian tradition is that the connection between moralistic judgment and the fall of the soul is a cornerstone of its mythology. The act that led to God's banishment of Adam and Eve from the Garden of Eden was their audacity in eating the fruit of the Tree of the Knowledge of Good and Evil. This knowledge, in turn, became the catalyst dividing all polarities into armed camps, one with white hats, and the other demonized as the moral enemy. Christianity seems to acknowledge the problem, but then institutionalizes it by choosing sides and entrenching the polarization of opposites into dogma.

Since it was Eve who tempted Adam with the apple, then all women and everything feminine – sensuality, feeling, intuition, imagination, and an immanent concept of divinity, governed by relationship, community and interconnectedness – becomes suspect, while everything masculine – self-control in denying the senses, rationality, a linear and literal interpretation of reality, and a hierarchical concept of divinity, governed by isolated individuality, separation, and competition – becomes conceptually aligned with the Good. Yet as Teilhard de Chardin realized in a moment of spiritual epiphany, "[T]here can be for man... no road to spiritual maturity or plenitude except through some 'emotional' influence, whose function is to sensitize his understanding and stimulate, at least initially, his capacity for love. Every day supplies more irrefutable evidence that no man at all can dispense with the Feminine, any more than he can dispense with light, or oxygen, or vitamins" (59).

Ironically, within the Christian culture out of which Teilhard de Chardin emerged, embrace of the Feminine is not readily acknowledged as a pathway to spiritual attainment[2]. Quite the contrary. Original sin is conceived as a deception of man by the Feminine, and a primal fact that seriously inhibits the integration of this basic polarity within the human psyche. Sexuality, the lifeblood of a soul fed by the interplay of opposites, especially masculine and feminine, instead becomes a source of embarrassment, guilt and shame, as Adam and Eve cover their nakedness with fig leaves. If, according to the Christian myth, it is the Knowledge of Good and Evil that leads to the fall, however, then perhaps the way back to paradise is paved by stones free of the judgments that arise in the face of this knowledge.

Despite fundamentalist protestations to the contrary, the gates of heaven only swing open for those souls within whom the false dichotomy between good and evil has collapsed. For coming to terms with everything deemed evil is the pathway to a less encumbered embrace of the Good, while attempting to *be* good, according to some rigid moral code is ultimately bad for the soul. Such a strategy precipitates fragmentation, psychological schism, and a perpetual state of internal conflict, none of which can be construed as good by anyone.

The Psychological Price to Be Paid For the Knowledge of Good and Evil

Where one side of any polarity is denied, the soul will become obsessed by the necessity to restore balance. Within the unconscious, an internal pressure will arise that is equal to the force of repression, and that embraces everything the conscious mind rejects. As any good Jungian psychologist will attest, the harder you suppress any aspect of your being, the more fiercely it emerges despite these efforts, as an irrational shadow force, governing behavior outside of the conscious control of will or intention.

Chronic dieters struggle endlessly with overwhelming cravings for food; priests sworn to celibacy perpetually wrestle with repressed sexual desires; well-intentioned religious people become angry, irritable, neurotic sinners the moment they leave their place of worship. Anti-abortionists, claiming to be pro-life, bomb abortion clinics and terrorize those who work there. Environmentalists drive gas-guzzling vehicles to protest corporate policies at distant locations. Conservatives, pushing away liberal ideology, readily sacrifice the basic freedoms they claim to want to conserve, in the name of national security.

Republicans who rail at "tax-and-spend" Democrats, swiftly wipe out an historic budget surplus and plunge the country back into massive debt. Ordinary people, in every walk of life, quickly point the finger at those who most blatantly express qualities they have repressed in themselves.

For a time, pushing away that which one considers bad, dark, or evil can seem to justify the claim to moral high ground. Ultimately, repression or denial can only result in a more destructive form of darkness. Freed of moral judgment, darkness is merely that which takes us down into the mortal body, or to the buried depths of our own unconsciousness, or into the churning chaos at the heart of any creative process. Darkness is the point of entry into a relationship with death, both literally and metaphorically. Darkness itself is not bad or evil, but darkness is often feared, because it plunges us into situations that are beyond our control. Just as death in its many guises is kept at bay as long as possible by those that fear it, darkness is repressed or denied by those who resist the surrender of control that it requires. Those who resist are forced to relinquish control anyway, because darkness repressed or denied becomes damaging to the body and the embodied world, which depend upon the interplay between all polarities for their well-being – and their very existence. When we dishonor this dependency through a moral code that seeks to annihilate darkness – which has been labeled evil – then evil will inevitably prevail.

One need only look back as far as the recent World Trade Center bombings, in September of 2001, perpetuated by Islamic fundamentalists intent on obliterating the darkness they perceived to be embodied by the United States, to see that this is so. Conversely, we point the finger at evil terrorists who have plunged us into a dark reality over which we have little control, and impose repressive legislation on ourselves in a pathetic attempt to fight an elusive enemy out there somewhere that we have demonized. But this finger pointing is nothing new. European Christians, whose role model preached loving one's neighbor as oneself, mounted crusades to torture, maim and mutilate hundreds of thousands of women, heathen pagans, and heretics, all in the name of obliterating darkness. In this country and throughout the Americas, native peoples were persecuted, subdued and culturally annihilated by Christian missionaries convinced they possessed the moral high ground in their battle against evil and ignorance. By a similar twisted logic of repression, Jews and Muslims have engaged in dark battle for thousands of years, while Hindus, Sikhs and Muslims have vied for control of India at least as long. And on and on the deadly ironies go.

Wherever moral codes exist (and those who do not subscribe to them are perceived as the enemy) death, destruction and an inadvertent embrace of evil is the inevitable result. Polarity denied is polarity armed with the destructive capacity to reintroduce death into the equation as an equalizer. For when one side of a polarity is denied, then the polarity itself becomes a source of tension, conflict, and eventually war. From a psychological perspective, war is merely a desperate last-ditch effort to reconcile opposites, when more peaceful attempts at reconciliation are blocked by attitudes that prohibit interaction. If sex is the reigning metaphor when the soul is free to celebrate the coming together of both sides of its nature, then war is the metaphor for what happens when one side attempts to live in denial of, dominate or repress the other. At the root of any war – whether an internal psychological war, or an external war between nations – is a fundamental unconscious denial that the soul is conditioned by the neutral dance of polarities.

The Soul's Journey as a Quest for the Embrace of Opposites

To the extent that sex (on all its levels) is an expression of the hieros gamos, or union of opposites, life is marked by love, joyful courage, and co-creative synergy. To the extent that the sexual impulse is blocked, and the union of opposites prohibited, then the resulting internal conflict is marked by hatred (of both self and others), debilitating fear, and psychological entropy or breakdown. Within any life, there will be an ever-shifting balance between the polarities of love and hatred, courage and fear, synergy and entropy, and the soul will invariably negotiate its journey by seeking to integrate all its internal polarities, while stepping through a minefield of unresolved inner tensions. The soul that is bound by a strict interpretation of religious moral codes that deny or repress the sexual impulse is compelled to function in a chronic state of war with itself. In any war, there are casualties, and in the religious war of self-denial, the soul literally lives in danger of its life.

As the Taoists understood and encoded in their famous yin-yang symbol, both sides of each polarity constantly flow in and out of each other. At the very heart of yang is a small seed of yin, and vice versa, which ensures that the two polarities will always be in relationship to each other. This relationship, in fact, defines the polarity, for neither side exists without reference to the other. Without night, day ceases to have meaning. Without the cool, moist, darkness, the hot, dry, light would sear the earth in its unrelenting intensity, and life as we know it would cease to exist. Without the demons that torment us with forbidden desires, the angels would cease to concern themselves with human affairs. Without the Devil, the God of religion would be unemployed.

Dancing between every polarity it encounters is the soul's lot in life, as long as Spirit and body come together to produce it. This truth is so is not something to be cursed or kept in check by a moral code, but rather a cosmic opportunity for growth toward a greater, more fulfilling, more vibrant wholeness of being. Just as the certainty of death lends the embodied soul a heightened intensity of purpose, so does the conscious acceptance of everything denied allow the soul a richer, more honest and more balanced existence.

As Nietzsche so poetically challenged the moralists of his day (154):

> In man, creature and creator are united; in man there is material, fragment, excess, clay, dirt, nonsense, chaos; but in man there is also creator, formgiver, hammer hardness, spectator divinity, and seventh day; do you understand this contrast? And that your pity is for the 'creature in man,' for that which must be formed, broken, forged, torn, burnt, made incandescent, and purified - that which necessarily must and should suffer? And our pity - do you not comprehend for whom our converse pity is when it resists your pity as the worst of all pamperings and weaknesses?

Being "formed, broken, forged, torn, burnt, made incandescent, and purified" is not necessarily a bad thing, if the soul opens itself to these lessons, takes them to heart and assimilates them. For it is only through the incandescent integration of opposites that the embodied soul can achieve a successful fusion of Spirit and matter and fulfill its evolutionary agenda.

The Institutionalized Negation of Polarity Through Monotheism

Before we explore this enticing possibility in more depth, let us address one last implication of the alignment with moral codes that must be shed before we can speak about the soul in a truly useful way. Closely related to the adoption of moral codes is the trend toward monotheism, embraced by most of the major world religions, particularly in the west. Monotheism insists there is one true God, and all other psychic currents in which it is possible to be swept away are the temptations of the Devil, to be resisted and denied at all costs. This worldview is generally considered to have originated with the Hebrews, whose Old Testament prophets were constantly warning of the wrath of Yahweh that would be unleashed by those "whoring" after the false foreign gods of Astarte or Baal. Meanwhile, many ancient cultures - early Greeks; Druids, Celts, Vikings and other pagan traditions widespread throughout Europe; early Vedic and Indo-European cultures of India and Central Asia; Native America; Tibet; Mithraic culture in Persia before Zoroaster; and the Arab world before Mohammed, among them - knew the soul not as a monotheistic experience, but an interplay of competing and contradictory forces, requiring a complex pantheon of gods and goddesses.

Probably, as pioneer in the study of consciousness, Ralph Metzner, suggests, polytheism arose as a consequence of the clash of cultures, in which the sky, Sun, mountain and storm gods of the Indo-Europeans met the ancient Earth, water, Moon and animal goddesses of the matriarchal cultures they attempted to conquer, from about 4300

- 1500 BCE (43). The invaders found – as most conquering cultures do – that they had to assimilate what was foreign to their nature in order to dominate and subdue. Spirit is not just a deity of the skies, they were forced to acknowledge, but also of rocks, trees, oceans, rivers, animals and plants. Each of these, they discovered, has its own psychic correlates, and is fully capable of "possessing" and dominating any soul at a given time. This rich interplay of psychic forces shapes the soul, and for at least six thousand years, before and after the birth of Christ, a polytheistic culture highly conducive to the evolution of soul flourished throughout most of the pre-civilized world (13).

In Europe, the pagan worldview was preserved and passed on to successive generations by the Neoplatonists, a group of philosophers in the 2nd - 6th century CE, who amazingly enough appealed to both Christian monotheists and non-Christian polytheists alike. Early Neoplatonists, led by Plotinus (201-270 CE), taught that there was only one God, but that the universe existed as a series of successively less pure emanations from absolute unity. From the transcendent One arose the mind, and from mind came soul. Soul, in turn was the intermediary between the realm of spirit and matter, the last and most degenerate level of the hierarchy. Through the intellect, it was possible for the soul to swim upstream, back toward the One from which it emanated. These concepts appealed to Christian thinkers of the same era – such as Justin Marytyr, Gregory of Nyssa, and most importantly Saint Augustine – who used Neoplatonic philosophy to add intellectual weight to their beliefs in immortality and the inferior, sinful nature of the body.

Later Neoplatonists, such as Iamblichus (c 250-330 CE) and Proclus (410-485 CE) greatly expanded the original hierarchy of emanation from the One to encompass not just intellect, but also the old pagan gods. They further taught that the soul could only return to the One through the intervention of these gods, whom they called *henads*. The One was removed to a state of transcendence, all but inaccessible to the individual soul, while the henads were immanent within the material world, where they asserted their compassionate influence through sympathetic resonance with various herbs, stones, and other elements of nature. Knowledge of these patterns of resonance – which was thoroughly integrated with the practice of astrology, and a form of ritual magic called *theurgy* – enabled the soul to cultivate a meaningful relationship and eventually reunite with the One.

While some of the most influential of the early Christian thinkers embraced the teachings of Plotinus, this later more overtly pagan form of Neoplatonism was clearly antithetical to Christian teaching, and rabidly opposed by it. So powerful were these ideas, however, that not only did they survive four centuries of persecution by the Church, but they flourished throughout Europe in numerous academies – in Athens, Gaza, Pergamum in western Asia Minor, and Alexandria – where polytheistic pagan philosophy formed the intellectual backbone of serious academic pursuits. These academies were shut down by the Christian emperor, Justinian, in the early 6th century CE, but the pagan ideas espoused by the Neoplatonists have since achieved a certain immortality of their own, resurfacing regularly in slightly altered form.

In the 15th century, for example, Marsilio Ficino translated all of Plato and Plotinus into Latin, and founded a new academy at Florence. The influence of this Neoplatonic/neopagan school was extensive throughout the Italian Renaissance (Philosophical Schools and Doctrines, EB 25:905). It left its mark on Italian painting and poetry, as well as French literature, the English Romantic poets – including Blake, Coleridge and Shelley, and later, William Butler Yeats – and English, French and German philosophers such as G. W. F. Hegel (1770-1831), Henri Bergson (1859-1941), and Maurice Blondel (1861-1949). Many of the ideas of this omnipresent pagan culture also found their way into the Hermetic and European magical traditions, alchemy, and the Theosophical movement of the 19th century.

Much current New Age thinking can also be traced to Neoplatonic and later theosophical roots, although many practitioners may know little if anything about this history. But if Plato was right, and learning is really a process of remembering, then the truth encoded in the polytheistic worldview of paganism cannot be suppressed, even if all the heretics in the world were to be rounded up and shot tomorrow. However commercialized the New Age has become, the ideas within it that reflect the truth hungered for by the soul will survive, and be remembered again and again, by successive generations. Meanwhile, in order to understand the working of the soul, we must restore a bit of pagan polytheism to the language we use to discuss the soul's experience.

If we are to evolve a truly useful language of soul, then we must work to undo the religious stigma attached to the innate plurality within the human psyche. Monotheistic religions consider worship of multiple deities to be sinful, and impose an unnatural assumption of a psychic uniformity the soul simply does not possess. By elevating the multiplicity of psychic forces tugging upon the soul to a level of divinity worthy of sanctity and respect, polytheistic cultures attempted to understand the complex workings of the soul without the psychologically debilitating and unnecessary burden of moral judgment. A useful language of soul must both celebrate and articulate this intrapsychic diversity, replacing judgment with an attitude that understands and appreciates the need to creatively engage both sides of every spectrum of possibilities it encounters.

Astrology's Potential Contribution to the Learning Process

Astrology can potentially provide the template for such a language. Astrology is intimately connected to a rich polytheistic tradition, as espoused by Greek and Roman

⬦⬦⬦

mythology. Each of the planets - representing a diverse constellation of psychic forces at work within the individual and the universe at large - is named for a god or a goddess, and it is the interaction of these various planetary forces that describe the essential dynamic of the birthchart. The pattern of relationships between the planets of a birthchart mirror the divine intercourse of the deities at work throughout the manifest world. This mirroring – which is the essence of the astrological language –provides a language of polymorphous complexity with which to understand the soul's process.

Within this polytheistic framework, the astrological birthchart presents a neutral map of the interplay of opposites within the individual. Every symbol in the birthchart can be understood as part of a natural polarity, which expresses itself simultaneously in opposite directions. Houses oppose other houses; signs oppose other signs; each planet is counterbalanced by other planets expressing contradictory tendencies; each cycle is composed of a waxing and a waning hemicycle. It is impossible to interpret anything astrological without reference to these polarities, and the best interpretations are those that point the way toward a potential integration of the opposites.

The birthchart is a signature unique to the person owning it. It presumes that the pathway to integration of the opposites must also be unique, and thus not automatically subject to judgment according to universal moral codes. The birthchart is an arrangement of universal symbols - the same signs, houses, and planets being common to everyone - in a highly individual way, which recognizes the potentially unique essence of the individual soul. Through an exploration of the pattern formed by the symbols of a birthchart, a deeply personal path is discovered within the universal, archetypal patterns of collective human experience. Or put another way, the birthchart is a depiction of how an individual might become more aligned with *dharma* in the metaphysical sense - not by adhering to an external set of rules, but by learning to live in accordance with his or her own nature.

The birthchart is rendered as a statement of individuality by being calculated for the time and place of birth, thereby acknowledging the soul's intimate connection to the material realm of the body, time, and space as perceived from planet Earth. It can be interpreted as a practical strategy for negotiating the demands of daily life, and as a prescription for soul growth within the context of the everyday experience. As a language of soul, astrology does not distinguish between spiritual process and mundane circumstances, but rather understands life circumstances to be the vehicle through which spiritual growth is made possible. There is no universally right or wrong way to negotiate this opportunity, just ways that work in harmony with one's individual nature, as revealed by the birthchart, and ways that produce disharmony.

Lastly, through various techniques of timing - by *progression*, *direction*, and *transit* - referenced to the natal birthchart, the schedule by which events, experiences and processes unfold is highly individualized, and mapped to the comings and goings of the gods and goddesses both without and within. Within a cyclical understanding of time, astrology outlines the seasons of life, each with its own challenges and opportunities for integration of the various polarities an individual can expect to encounter. Provided that astrology is practiced free of moral judgments about good and evil superimposed upon the birthchart, the birthchart can be read as a timetable to the soul's evolutionary process that maps out the process of integration in cyclical time. Through contemplation of symbol in relation to experience, anyone versed in the language of astrology can more skillfully plumb their lives for a deeper, guilt-free appreciation of the gradual movement of the soul, over the course of a lifetime. Following this timetable leads to the understanding that all is part of the plan by which the soul evolves, and this understanding in turn can gradually lead to a full acceptance of the wholeness of being, in all of its multifaceted, sometimes contradictory glory.

This promise inherent within the language of astrology itself, also depends upon the sensibilities and consciousness of those who practice it. Unfortunately, there has long been a strong pattern of moralistic conditioning within the astrological tradition that must be purged before its full potential as a language of soul can be realized. Though astrology historically took a radical stance in opposition to the culture of religious dominance, with which it was perpetually at odds throughout the history of its evolution, it also apparently absorbed the dualistic attitude of its foe. Many astrologers still fall into a moralistic trap, making judgments about various planets, signs, house positions, aspects, and transits. Certain planets, planetary placements and aspects between planets are considered *benefic*, or good, while others are considered *malefic*, or bad. These assessments persist despite the admonitions of numerous humanistic astrologers, following in the wake of Dane Rudhyar, to take our collective understanding of astrology to a higher, less judgmental level. This moralistic streak has recently been strengthened through a concerted effort to rediscover astrology's roots in antiquity, which are thoroughly intertwined with judgments about good and bad indications, and overly fatalistic delineations of these indications. Before we can evolve a useful astrological language of soul, we will have to shed these judgmental and moralistic overtones.

As a pure system of symbolic logic, however, astrology's recognition and embrace of duality and polymorphic complexity are already there, woven into the very fabric of the language itself. This as a hopeful sign, because one cannot expect to approach the mystery posed by the soul when that mystery has been reduced to simplistic formulas. This is as true for the practice of astrology as it is for a moralistic, monotheistic religious tradition. But at least within the astrological language, the potential exists for discussion of complex psychic processes outside of the context of proscribed moral codes. Each soul must thread its way through the tricky shoals of an intimately personal life, played out upon the complex stage of a dualistic universe, in which the inevitability of death on many levels creates the psychic pressure toward change and growth. This is not a process that is served by a judgmental, one-size-fits-all mentality, and in its emphasis on the uniqueness of the individual, astrology offers a promising path beyond the dilemma posed by monotheistic moralism.

Passing Through the Gate of Religious Morality On the Way to the Underworld

To pass through Inanna's second gate on the way to the underworld, aside from any astrological template we might impose upon this process, the soul must be freed in general from dogmatic judgments of religious morality. These judgments denigrate the sexual interplay of polar opposites that characterizes the psychic reality in which the soul dwells. The soul must be embraced in its inherently ambivalent and self-contradictory complexity. It must be freed to pursue a path that is uniquely individual, bound by collective codes of behavior designed to control rather than enlighten only when it is necessary to protect the rights of others. Any language of soul worth speaking must illuminate the journey of the individual soul, within the larger context of sacred, sexual polarity that transcends traditional religious mores. It must further show how this context provides a fertile field, which when properly tended can bear a rich harvest of meaning and purpose - not in relation to reward and punishment in some postmortem afterlife, but as a learning experience vital to the soul in the here and now.

This is not to say there are not a handful of universal injunctions - against killing, theft or destruction of property belonging to another, violation of the sanctity of committed relationship, perhaps among them - which can serve as guideposts on the path of any soul, for it makes theoretical sense that my right to self-determination as a soul should end where it interferes with your right to the same privilege. And yet, in the course of a life conditioned by duality, it seems inevitable that part of the process by which any soul will find itself broken, torn and burnt on the way to Nietzsche's incandescence will involve learning lessons related to the transgression of these very boundaries that are held sacred by most moral codes. Indeed, most religions have broken every one of their own commandments in the quest to establish themselves within the societies in which they have evolved.

Though society must make judgments which protect souls from each other and society as a whole from the actions of souls acting *in extremis*, it is also important to note that from the soul's perspective, learning may well entail becoming extreme for a time, in order to experience the pull toward center and eventually find a place of balance. The Buddha followed this path, as did many saints and sages before and since. From the perspective of the soul, which is destined to undergo a slow, sometimes painful discovery of balance between the opposites, it is not particularly helpful if this process is steeped in judgment, for it adds an unnecessary and often debilitating burden to an already daunting task.

Any language of soul capable of facilitating soul growth, therefore, must recognize that each soul is on a highly personal path, even though it will entail experiences that are universal to the human predicament. How the individual soul responds to the various challenges it faces is a learning process that is ultimately beyond judgment. This is not to say that judgments will not be imposed, both from within and without. But working through these judgments to a place of self-acceptance, peace and ownership of the judged attributes, qualities and/or behaviors is also part of a learning process that will eventually lead to soul growth.

I would go so far as to say that soul growth is not possible until we unconditionally accept our process, whatever it is, without moralistic judgment. For many of us, this will undoubtedly mean freeing ourselves from religious or societal conditioning, and its attendant definitions of good and bad. Within a dualistic universe, the very intent to free ourselves from our prejudices will invariably bring those prejudices to our awareness, where we can more easily see them for what they are. When they do come up, if we are able to stand back and allow them to move through us with some degree of detachment, then we have already taken the first step toward releasing ourselves from them.

This approach to a gradual transcendence of self-judgment is not a new concept, but comes out of a rich tradition popularized by humanistic psychologists, but rooted in Buddhist spiritual tradition. As described by American Buddhist nun, Pema Chödrön, "both *shamatha-vipashyana* and *tonglen* (Buddhist meditation techniques) are meant to support a softer, more gentle approach to the whole show, the whole catastrophe. We begin to let opposites co-exist, not trying to get rid of anything but just training and opening our eyes, ears, nostrils, taste buds, hearts and minds wider and wider, nurturing the habit of opening to whatever is occurring, including our shutting down" (25).

Or as William Butler Yeats succinctly described the same attitude from a more secular perspective:

> I am content to follow to its source
> Every event in action or in thought;
> Measure the lot; forgive myself the lot!
> When such as I cast out remorse
> So great a sweetness flows into the breast
> We must laugh and we must sing,
> We are blest by every thing,
> Every thing we look upon is blest.

◇◇

Endnotes

[1] Religious judgments are especially heavy in relation to homosexual and lesbian relationships, in which the dance of yin and yang is no less genuine than in heterosexual relationships, although it takes place between souls in bodies of the same sex. In fact, given the fact that gay sexuality entails the reconciliation of a psyche that is often polarized with the body in which it is housed (i.e. as a male spirit living in a female body, or vice versa), the opportunity for spiritual growth within such relationships often encompasses an additional level of complexity and intensity not experienced quite so poignantly by heterosexuals.

[2] Nor is Christianity the only religion where the Feminine is feared and kept at bay. Obviously, the same is true of Judaism, Islam, Hinduism, Confucianism, and every other patriarchal tradition in which a moral code has come to replace the natural balance between the opposites as the criteria for behavior.

PART TWO

THROUGH
THE GATES
OF SCIENCE

Chapter Five
Shedding the Rational Literalism of Science

If religion has erred in divorcing the soul from the body and identifying it with Spirit, then science has erred largely in the opposite direction. Science has completely severed the soul from Spirit, and explained it away as a mere by-product of neurochemistry, or as a figment of the imagination, taking place largely in the brain. Through its influence as the dominant paradigm of the world in which we live, science has essentially declared discussion of the soul's experience irrelevant to the human condition, and defines our collective truth without any reference to it whatsoever. Along the way, it has attempted to confine itself to a rational, analytical mode of processing information which (as I hope to demonstrate in this chapter and the next) is antithetical to the soul's own way of functioning. As we shall see in later chapters, the qualitative, internal, subjective perspective though which soul derives a sense of meaning that is intimately personal to each individual, has also been systematically discounted.

Ironically, many of science's own discoveries contribute toward the implication of conscious, creative intelligence at the heart of the inner workings of the material universe – particularly since the advent of quantum mechanics, chaos theory and the work of pioneers such as Rupert Sheldrake, Jeremy Narby, James Lovelock, Larry Dossey and others on the fringe of orthodoxy. Once you are able to acknowledge that matter is, in some way, infused with consciousness, it is but a small step to recognize the fusion of Spirit and body that gives birth to the embodied soul. Consciousness can easily be understood as the evidence for Spirit's presence in the body, which otherwise would be as aware as a lump of clay. Most revolutionary discoveries that hint at the omnipresence of consciousness throughout creation have yet to be integrated into the mainstream scientific worldview. Therefore, in this, and the following seven chapters, I will be mostly concerned with the tenacious hold of scientific orthodoxy on our collective attitude and understanding of soul.

Questions About Soul
At the Heart of the Early Scientific Debate

Before we explore the various misconceptions that science brings to our discussion of soul, it is helpful to look backward and sketch in broad outline the early philosophical history of science's evolution as a way of processing truth. It is fascinating to note that the earliest pre-scientific thinkers, housed in ancient Greece in the 6th century BCE, were compelled to articulate their ideas within a polytheistic religious culture in which soul, as we are defining it here, was an integral part of everyday life (Tarnas 16-18). Indeed, the first Greek philosophers were called cosmologists, suggesting that questions about soul, the meaning and purpose of life, and the nature of reality lie at the very heart of their intellectual agenda.

Pre-Socratic cosmologists asked their questions at a time when western culture was thoroughly marinated in the mythopoetic tradition espoused by Homer and Hesiod, as familiar to the average person as *Lord of the Rings*, *Harry Potter* and popular television shows are today. A pagan mythology rendered through the poetic imagination, and steeped in astrological lore informed the prevalent mindset against which the scientific paradigm sought to define itself. This mindset was as concerned with the evolution of soul as the later religious traditions which replaced it, and as discussed in Chapter Four, were better equipped to discuss it. Though scientists often conveniently forget their philosophical roots, it is important to note that science gradually emerged in counterpoint as a rational response to the prevalence of a soul-based culture.

Later, as the Christian Church became a more dominant player within the culture and polytheistic pagan mythology gave way to monotheistic religious dogma, it was often deeply religious men, struggling to reconcile their faith with a more rational analysis of the tenets of religious thought, that furthered the evolution of science. European philosophers such as Saint Augustine, Thomas Aquinas, Marsilio Ficino, René Descartes, and George Berkeley provided an intellectual bridge between the dominant religious paradigm of their day and what would eventually become the upstart scientific worldview that replaced it. Some of the most influential philosophers at the heart of the debate about soul were affiliated with the Church. Others sought to use reason in order to explain God's handiwork in creating the miraculous universe that was the object of their study, whether or not the Church was comfortable with their explanations. Regardless of affiliation, all were obliged to wage their intellectual campaigns in acute awareness of, if not strict allegiance to the prevailing religious point of view.

Early philosopher/scientists were not free to simply dismiss the soul as irrelevant to a discussion of truth, but were obliged to articulate their views in contrast to a then dominant paradigm that held the soul to be the pivot point around which reality arranged itself. Thus, it should come as no surprise that over the course of the last 2,500 years, science would come to represent a worldview that is generally considered to be intentionally irreligious, and as will be argued in Part Two, inherently antithetical to an understanding of soul. This is not to say, as some scientists arrogantly claim, that the soul is irrelevant to a discussion of the nature of reality, but its voice has been all but obliterated by a way of conceptualizing truth that systematically precludes any acknowledgment of the soul whatsoever.

The Birth of Scientific Literalism

While most historians date the advent of the scientific revolution with the Renaissance of the 15th and 16th centuries, it actually began much farther back in antiquity at 2:13 PM GMT, May 28, 585 BCE. How can I pinpoint this moment so exactly, you ask? This was the precise time of an eclipse predicted by Thales, a mathematician from the seaport town of Miletus (Espenak). While we take such predictions for granted today as a routine by-product of scientific observation, prior to Thales' purely intellectual feat, the ability to foretell and explain eclipses and other celestial phenomena was the domain of astrologer-priests. These early sky watchers attributed all heavenly events to the movement of gods and goddesses, and understood them to be, on some level, an outer manifestation of the inner workings of soul. Thales showed that such events could be calculated mathematically and predicted without the necessity for metaphysical fanfare.

There is much evidence to suggest that early astronomer-priests had their own methods of calculation, long before the advent of the scientific age, involving the elaborate and amazingly sophisticated construction of large astronomical observatories made of stone[1]. Be that as it may, what was different about Thales' prediction was that he extracted it from the realm of mythology and symbolic connotation in which it was previously rooted. He postulated instead that celestial events (and by extension, all natural phenomena) had rational causes, which could be understood without any reference to gods or goddesses, or mythological underpinnings. As a corollary to this assumption, he also suggested that human beings were rational creatures capable, as he had done, of unraveling the apparent mysteries of the cosmos in purely logical terms.

This was a big first step on the long and winding trail that would eventually lead to the scientific dismissal of the soul as irrelevant to the workings of a strictly material cosmos. In Thales' day, however, it is important to note that the viability of reason as a tool for understanding reality did not preclude approaching that same reality from a mythological or soul-based perspective. By some accounts, Thales himself was a practicing astrologer (Hunt 14), albeit one who apparently discounted his astrological knowledge in denying the symbolic implications of the literal, rational truth he was attempting to articulate.

Beyond predicting eclipses, Thales and his colleagues sought a principle substance, or *arché*, that governed nature and composed its essence. They were determined to use reason as a tool with which to arrive at their conclusions and articulate their discoveries. Yet at the same time, they drew their inspiration and their metaphors out of the very worldview from which they were attempting to distance themselves. At the conclusion of their rational process, Thales reputedly said, "All is water (which he believed to be that principle substance), and the world is full of gods" (qtd. in Tarnas 19) – an amazingly poetic statement to be uttered by one so intent on taking the world literally. Despite its rational pretensions, this conclusion was no different in tone or substance than any that might have been uttered by the astrologer-priests whose worldview Thales challenged. For they too understood the world they studied to be moved by factual, measurable events, even as they ascribed a more metaphorical or soul-based meaning to them.

The Mythopoetry of the Moment in Which Science Was Born

It is quite telling to move to the supposedly more rational side of Thales' statement and consider his choice of *arché* from a mythopoetic perspective. In Thales day, there were generally considered to be four elements: earth, air, fire and water. Water is the most soul-like in its association with the vast underground of the unconscious; the realm of emotions, imagination and fantasy; sexuality; and creative and procreative fertility; the mystical web of interconnection which ties us to this earth and to each other; and a distinctly feminine worldview rooted in an attitude of surrender to mysterious forces beyond the reach of will or reason. To be sure, when Thales declared that all is water, he probably literally meant the wet material substance covering two-thirds of this planet's surface, which was of paramount importance to the seaport culture of Miletus where he lived. Yet, even as he consciously sought to gain a rational foothold against what he considered to be too much mystery and metaphysical mumbo jumbo, he simultaneously proclaimed the very omnipresence of soul that he tried to rationalize away.

An astrologer-priest of Thales' day, looking at a horoscope for the exact moment of the eclipse he predicted, would have noted certain other symbolic features of the arrangement of planets marking the moment (see Figure 1). These features would have been inaccessible to a purely rational mind, but quite telling nonetheless. Perhaps Thales himself took a peek – although since he was attempting to establish a beachhead against the mythopoetic worldview, he did not mention astrology in the same breath in which he made his prediction. While a full interpretation of this chart would be too much of a tangent to take here, it is worth noting a few salient points that illustrate the kind of information available to a soul that has been freed from the straightjacket of literal reason.

The first thing to note about this horoscope, is that Saturn, or Kronus – generally considered to be the god of time, measurement, and a rational, factual, literal approach to life – was culminating just past the Midheaven, or highest point in the chart. The intuitive suggestion here is that the very mindset Thales had employed to make his prediction was peaking at this critical moment. Venus, or Aphrodite – the goddess of sensuality, eroticism, and romantic love, as well as the arts, including poetry, and in Thales day,

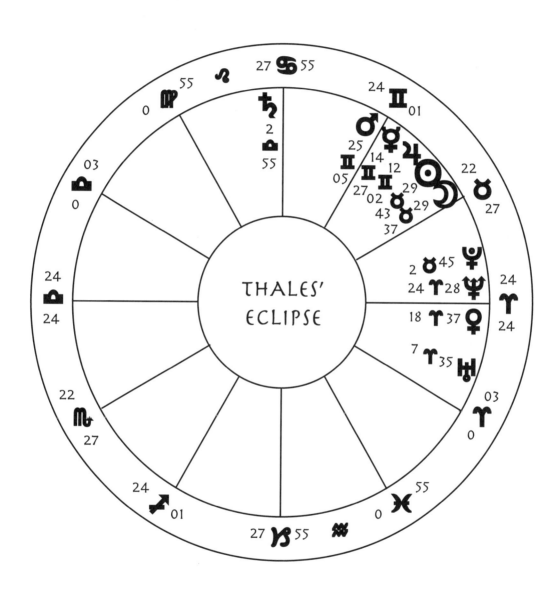

FIGURE 1

the entire essentially feminine, mythopoetic culture - was just below the Descendant, or westernmost angle of the horoscope (see Figure 2). If Saturn represented the forces of reason, logic, and mathematical deduction, then Venus also represented the supremacy of the body, and the sensory awareness that Thales and successive philosophers declared to be inferior.

It should be noted here, that in astrological practice, Venus would be considered to *rule* this chart through its association with both the sign on the Ascendant (easternmost angle) and the Sun sign. This rulership reflects the dominance of mythopoetic culture in Thales day. The fact that Venus was placed just below the Descendant in this chart, however, suggests that this dominance was about to shift. Since the Descendant is the place in any birthchart where planets set below the horizon, and enter an invisible underworld, the symbolic implication encoded in this chart is that the moment Thales' prediction came true heralded the setting of the mythopoetic worldview. This possibility is echoed by the fact that the eclipse itself took place in the last degree of Taurus (ruled by Venus), which is the most sensory of all the signs, poised on the cusp of Gemini, where the mind reigns supreme[2].

Though the planet Neptune had not yet been discovered in Thales' day, a modern astrologer would have noted a conjunction between Venus and Neptune, which was just setting at the moment of the eclipse (see Figure 3). Neptune is the planet most contemporary astrologers would associate, more specifically than Venus, with poetry, myth, and a symbolic approach to the understanding of reality. This set of associations makes the arrangement of gods and goddesses on the stage at the time of Thales' prediction all the more striking and suggestive. Neptune can also represent the realm of illusion, where nothing is as it appears to be. Within the context of this connotation, the Venus-Neptune conjunction aptly describes the attitude of mistrust that the rationalists had toward any understanding derived through sensory awareness and the faculties of imagination.

Perhaps more telling still is the observation that Pluto (discovered in 1930) - the planet that most astrologers today associate with death and rebirth, and therefore with soul - was close on the heels of Venus (sensory awareness) and Neptune (the poetic imagination), just about to set. In addition, Pluto forms a tight *square* with Saturn (see Figure 4), the *square* being an *aspect* (or angular relationship between planets) associated with conflict, suggesting that the scientific world view, represented here by Saturn, would invariably come into conflict with the very concept of the embodied mortal soul, which sat at the heart of the mythopoetic tradition.

Lastly, we might note that the planet Uranus, also undiscovered in Thales' day, was below Venus/Neptune, beginning its descent into the underworld. Most astrologers

FIGURE 2

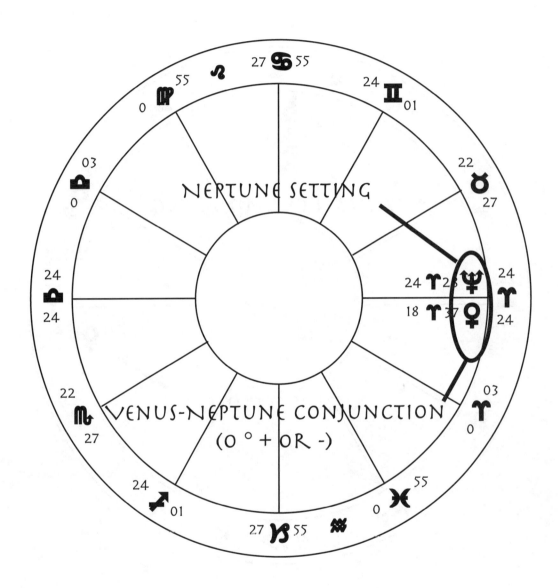

FIGURE 3

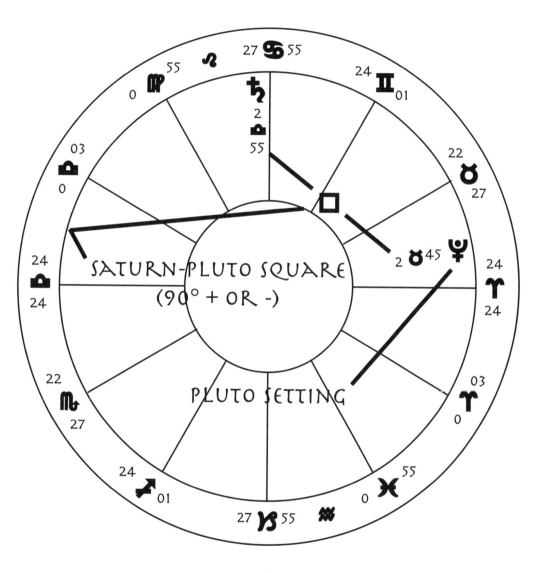

FIGURE 4

today would associate Uranus with the scientific mindset, particularly as it is harnessed to empirical processes of discovery and technological innovation. Uranus is also associated with ceremonial magic, a much more potent manifestation of the same energy within the mindset that Thales was challenging. Uranus has just set in this chart for Thales' eclipse, suggesting on the one hand that the magical worldview was, like the mythopoetic imagination, on the descent - or at least about to go underground, where it would transmute slowly beyond the reach of conscious awareness.

Given this dual meaning we have outlined for Uranus, this placement may also reflect the way that the practice of magic would, after a period of gestation, rise again to become the province of scientists. Certainly to the philosophers of Thales day, all the modern technological wonders that science has wrought - the cellphone, satellite TV, fiber optics, computers and the Internet, air travel and rocket science, modern pharmaceuticals and genetic engineering, nanotechnology and robotics - would all appear to be magic. It is interesting to note that our scientific attitude toward the soul - though infinitely more sophisticated in the magic we use to keep death at bay - is not much different from attitudes widespread throughout hunting cultures in which magic had its pre-historical origin. In any case, in the chart for Thales' eclipse, Saturn is *trine* to (120 degrees from) Uranus (see Figure 5), an *aspect* of creative cooperation, suggesting that the cultivation of Thales' rational approach to knowledge would eventually contribute a great deal to the transmutation of magic into science, through the turning of the cycle that bound these two planets together.

To an astrologer-priest reading these signs, the handwriting would have potentially been on the wall. I say potentially, because these planetary placements can elicit a multiplicity of possible interpretations, and even the most astute astrologer might not have had enough perspective to predict the scientific revolution that would span the next millennium on the basis of these few indications alone. Undoubtedly, Thales had only limited conscious knowledge of his own mission. Had Thales consulted an astrologer-priest at the time, or applied his own astrological knowledge to this eclipse he was predicting, he would have nonetheless gained additional tools with which to contemplate the symbolic meaning behind the literal event. Using these tools, he would have access not just to the external, objective facts surrounding this eclipse and its prediction, but the metaphorical implications of the event, understood from the soul's perspective. This perspective does not easily lend itself to rational analysis, but instead must be approached intuitively with the projective imagination. Of course, this was the very perspective that Thales and his followers hoped to eclipse (pun intended).

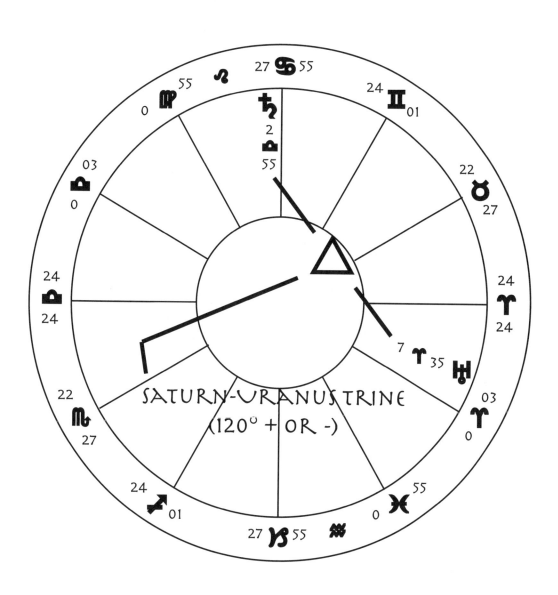

FIGURE 5

The Intermingling of Worlds

Despite the paradox inherent in this position, the Milesians launched a revolution that slowly began shaking the prevalent polytheistic worldview to its roots. They began to champion the use of reason at the expense of the metaphorical approach to reality that is more natural to soul. Other early philosophers, like Pythagoras, rejected the concept of the *arché*, seeking instead to explain reality in purely mathematical terms. Plato, influenced in part by Pythagoras, hypothesized the existence of eternal Ideals – absolute Good, Truth, Beauty, and so on – that in some ways echoed the polytheistic gods and goddesses of his day, but also effectively replaced them with clinical abstractions. He believed the truth that had been symbolized by these gods and goddesses could be more accurately represented by geometric forms than by living archetypes with messy, self-contradictory personalities. In *The Republic, Book II*, Plato insists that children of his ideal state not be taught the Homeric and Hesiodic myths, which he felt to be corrupting influences. Like the Milesians, Plato believed that the gods and goddesses portrayed by these pre-philosophical writers were unworthy role models (Melchert 15).

As discussed in Chapter Two, much in Plato's doctrine appealed to early Church fathers. After being recycled and repackaged for a new generation by Plotinus and the Neoplatonists of the 3rd century CE, Plato's ideas were absorbed by Saint Augustine, who fused the religious teachings of the New Testament with the Platonic tradition and passed it on to the Roman Catholic and Renaissance Protestant churches. Augustine was not quite as enamored of mathematics as was Plato, instead favoring the supreme monotheistic God over the multiplicity of Plato's Forms, or Ideals, but he was no less certain than Plato and the early Greek rationalists that it was through reason that God revealed His Will, and set it into motion. Despite other philosophical differences that would gradually widen the gap between them, both the Church and the slowly emerging pre-scientific worldview were united in their determination to usurp the power of the mythopoetic imagination, and keep both the senses and the emotions in check through the use of the rational mind.

These early pre-scientific thinkers, however, were not prepared to abandon the mythopoetic worldview entirely. Even Augustine was raised by a pagan father, who undoubtedly influenced some of his receptivity to Neoplatonic teachings. These teachings encompassed and preserved much of the pagan worldview, even as they began reinterpreting pagan ideas in monotheistic, rational and anti-corporeal terms. Despite his objections, Plato's *Dialogues* were thoroughly permeated by references to the ancient myths and the esoteric truths of the Greek mystery religions. Thales could not have made his statement about the world being full of gods, if on some level, he did not feel that to be true. While today we might place reason and metaphorical imagination on opposite sides of a polarity, most of the early philosophers of Thales' day straddled what must have been an intensely exciting and soulful razor's edge, with one foot in both worlds.

As philosophical historian, Richard Tarnas, describes the spirit of mystical reverence with which these early philosophers went about their work, it is easy to imagine them not so much abandoning the mythopoetic imagination for reason, as attempting to bridge a gradually widening gap (46).

> For Pythagoreans, as later for Platonists, the mathematical patterns discoverable in the natural world secreted, as it were, a deeper meaning that led the philosopher beyond the material level of reality. To uncover the regulative mathematical forms in nature was to reveal the divine intelligence itself, governing its creation with transcendent perfection and order. The Pythagorean discovery that the harmonics of music were mathematical, that harmonious tones were produced by strings, whose measurements were determined by single numerical ratios, was regarded as a religious revelation.

Despite this more mystical thread that wound through early Greek proto-science, the trend launched by Thales and the Milesians, and continued through the Platonic tradition, was toward a contemplation of the mystery posed by soul through a narrow lens of reason and intellect. Aristotle had little use for Plato's brand of mathematical metaphysics and rejected his doctrine of eternal Forms altogether, launching an alternative approach to truth that would eventually come to exert an equally profound influence on the emerging scientific world view. Despite these important differences, which we will return to later, Aristotle agreed with Plato that the reality of anything must be rendered comprehensible and defined by reason.

The Triumph of Reason Over the Mythopoetic Imagination

This shift from the mythopoetic imagination championed during the pagan era of antiquity, to the elevation of reason as the primary mechanism for exploring the secrets of soul, is the single most important barrier to formulating a true language of soul posed by the proto-scientific philosophy evolving from 600 BCE to 1800 CE. Whether we travel the road paved by Plato, Augustine, or Aristotle, the rational mind became increasingly dominant throughout this period. Our collective journey, as led by these rationalists, was toward an understanding of soul that had largely severed its ties to death, the body, the senses, the emotions and the imagination, and existed only within a narrow band of the mental spectrum.

There were and continue to be important collective reactions to this trend, such as the Humanist movement of the early Renaissance, the Romantic movement of the 18th century, the Symbolist movement of the 19th century, and the Beat/Hippie/New Age cultures of the latter half of the 20th century. But as the center of power within our collective discussion of soul has shifted from religion to philosophy to science, soul has become increasingly conceptualized, within the dominant paradigm, as revolving around a rational focus. It is telling in this regard to consider that the above-mentioned movements were a rebellion against an obsession with rationality, while only two short millennia ago, science began to emerge as a rebellion against the "irrational" dominance of mythopoetic culture.

Ironically, during the Age of Reason, philosophers like Bacon, Locke, Hume and Kant began questioning the limits of reason in addressing the truth of either soul or substance. But when the dust of this intellectual revolt began to settle by the mid 19th century, science emerged as a *rational* method for processing empirical information, including psychological information about the nature of the human being, the self and the soul. In the early days of the scientific revolution, from the 6th century BCE to the mid 17th century, the focus of philosophical discussion was articulating the link between the soul and the rational mind. But by the time Descartes made his famous statement, "*Cogito ergo sum* - I think, therefore I am," in 1641, the mind had already effectively replaced the soul in mainstream thought as the governing principle within a human being, and mathematics and logic had replaced the mythopoetic imagination as the primary languages through which the mind-soul was allowed to speak and be interpreted.

Descartes' role in establishing reason as the faculty of choice, of course, was critical, and is not to be glossed over lightly. Descartes was educated as a Jesuit, and sought to understand soul in a way that would reconcile his religious faith with his intellectual doubts. With one foot still firmly rooted in religious doctrine, he gravitated toward a redefinition of soul that followed Church teachings about the separation of soul and body, but increasingly spoke of the soul strictly in terms of its rational faculties. Like Plato before him, Descartes employed reason to verify and strengthen Church teachings about immortality. Since it was impossible to conceive of survival after death, without a mind to verify the fact of continued existence, he reasoned that the soul – which was now separated from the body and identified exclusively with the mind – had to exist as a mental force after death. Descartes admitted that sensation, emotion and imagination could be understood as an interaction between mind and body, but in keeping with his religious temperament, believed these modes of processing information to be inferior to pure intellect and will, both the primary functions of the soul/mind.

As part of his famous Cogito argument, Descartes went so far as to suggest that while the existence of mind was self-evident, the existence of the body was something that required an elaborate proof he was not sure it was possible to give. In the Cartesian worldview, the soul's intrinsic relationship to the body was negated in favor of a purely mental concept of the soul; and sensation, emotion and imagination were declared untrustworthy as a way of processing information, and inferior to reason. The empirical movement of the 17th, 18th and 19th centuries brought sensory and experiential information back into favor. But this information was still subject to the interpretive authority of reason and the Cartesian mindset – which increasingly became the sole arbiter of truth about what used to be called the soul, and an essential philosophical building block in the scientific worldview.

The Further Deification of the Rational Mind In the 20th Century

The soul and the mind were further entwined as synonyms by the late 18th - early 19th century German philosopher, Georg Wilhelm Friederich Hegel, who used the word *Geist*, translated both as the mind distinct from a body, and as Spirit, to describe the essence of the human being. A small army of philosophers, critics, and devotees have since argued endlessly whether Hegel was talking about mind or Spirit, but the upshot of his monumental, densely inscrutable body of work, was nonetheless an elevation of the mind to a status formerly reserved for deity. Hegel also attacked the value of sensory information, which he called *sense-certainty*, because it could not be conveyed without reference to universal categories of experience, which in turn, could only be discerned by a rational mind.

The larger point that Hegel was making, throughout his prodigious body of work, was that without the rational mind, knowledge of anything was impossible, including what he called *self-consciousness*, or what we might call knowledge of the soul. In fact, Hegel went so far as to suggest that reality was nothing more than a creation of the mind. In making this leap, he not only replaced soul with mind, but he also essentially replaced Spirit, as the central creative force of the universe, by Mind. Though Hegel's arguments were inscrutable and ambivalent enough to influence existentialists, phenomenologists, Prussian Protestants, Marxists, and logical positivists (Christian 2:176) - all of whom would have been somewhat uncomfortable in each other's company – his main contribution to the philosophical trend of the 19th and 20th centuries has been to dismiss anything inaccessible to reason - including the soul - as unworthy of consideration on its own terms.

In the 20th century, renowned British philosopher, Bertrand Russell, and his Austrian protégé, Ludwig Wittgenstein, took the rationalist viewpoint to its logical conclusion by postulating that ordinary language was incapable of articulating truth. Russell was an adamant and articulate foe of the mythopoetic worldview, mysticism and all metaphysical speculation about the nature of reality. In a book entitled *Principles of Mathematics*, co-written with Alfred North Whitehead in 1903, he proposed that reality could better be described by a purely abstract language that would mirror the logical structure of the mind. This worldview, elaborated by Wittgenstein and others, became known as logical analysis. Logical analysis was later combined with the empirical leanings of science to form the philosophical backbone of one of the most dogmatic philosophical schools – logical positivism.

Logical positivism denied the validity of any truth, except what could be extracted from a literal, rational interpretation of reality, verified by replicable empirical observation. Logical positivism influenced many of the early psychologists, who carried the conversation about soul into the latter half of the 20th century. Logical positivism also marked the virtual death of philosophy as a viable language of metaphysical speculation, turning it into primarily a linguistic methodology for clarifying the vocabulary of science. The impact of logical positivism on psychology is discussed in more detail in Part Three. Meanwhile, I wish only to note here that this persistent philosophical thread – launched by Plato and Aristotle, given practical momentum by Descartes, brought into the modern era by Hegel, and established as scientific dogma by Russell and the logical positivists – has effectively replaced the concept of soul with the paltry substitute of the rational mind.

I do not mean to imply, in bemoaning this development, that we must abandon reason in order to understand the soul. Obviously the mind will be involved in any interpretation of reality that we might choose to make, regardless of our philosophical orientation. Rational analysis can be useful, especially when one is attempting to understand consensus reality from an objective standpoint. But without the complementary contribution of sensation, emotion, and projected imagination that flourished in Europe before the scientific age, reason alone cannot provide a complete, or even accurate picture of the soul's experience. Sensation, emotion, and projected imagination *are* the necessary mechanisms by which soul processes information. Despite the need for reason in conducting the everyday business of life, any point of view that systematically negates and denies the validity of these other irrational ways of knowing – as science does – must be antithetical to the language of soul we are hoping to cultivate. Before we can pass through Inanna's third gate on a way to the underworld, we must free the soul from this obsession with rationality.

Kant's Refutation of Reason as A Tool With Which to Understand the Soul

I am hardly the first to point out the inadequacy of reason alone in discussing matters related to the soul. As the scientific perspective was rapidly becoming the dominant paradigm of the western world, Immanuel Kant suggested, in *Critique of Pure Reason* (1781) that reason was incapable of grasping metaphysical truths, such as the nature of God or the human soul. He demonstrated far more extensively than I could ever hope to do here that reason could neither prove nor disprove the existence of the interior, subjective world. He also suggested that reason could be used to argue either side of any metaphysical speculation, and was therefore useless at getting to the heart of subjective truth. Reason could look out into the world and order its perceptions as a reflection of the structure of the mind, but it could not turn inward upon itself and know who it was that was thinking. Whereas the rationalist Descartes could conclude, "I think, therefore I am," Kant in so many words was asking, "I think, but who am I?"

This question, considered in combination with Kant's third critique, *Critique of Judgment* (1790), paved the way for the cultivation of a more intuitive, sensual and imaginative form of epistemology in the Romantic movement of the 19th century. As pointed out by contemporary philosopher, Ken Wilbur, it also paved the way for the death of scientific speculation about metaphysical truths, and freed scientists to go their own way without regard to the impact of subsequent discoveries on the well-being of the soul. "If you focus (solely) on *Critique of Pure Reason*," Wilbur argues, "you could readily become a dedicated positivist and behaviorist: science alone gives cognitive knowledge, 'real' knowledge, and all else is nonsensical metaphysics" (88). This was exactly the path taken by Johann Fichte, who argued against Kant's assertion that there were things the mind could not know, by countering that what the mind could not know did not exist (Singer 118). This view eventually became the rallying cry for successive generations of logical positivists, who infused science with the arrogance it needed to dismiss discussion of the soul – which could not be known by the mind – altogether.

Artists (of every media) throughout the ages have given the soul a more sensory, emotional and imaginative voice, and any art is an excellent medium through which the soul can discover itself and articulate its identity. But how we think and talk about the soul in the wake of science's abandonment of it tends to marginalize art as a fringe activity, or else commercialize it, and few of us without marketable talent are encouraged to approach life artistically. Though individual artists have given us many wonderful collective points of entry to our own souls, the lack of a coherent language with which to embrace the soul in all of its irrational glory has relegated art to the entertainment page of our culture, or in some cases, made it the exclusive province of the cultural elite. From within the dominant paradigm dictated by science, art is what we do to escape reality, not what we do to define it. Meanwhile, the abandonment of the soul by science, in the face of reason's incapacity to address it has left a vacuum in our collective ability to understand and articulate the interior life of individual human beings.

This vacuum has been only partially filled by the proliferation of metaphysical teachings throughout the 19th and 20th centuries. Like the more traditional religions that preceded them, these teachings largely confuse soul with Spirit, and pay less positive attention to soul's connection to the body, the senses, emotions, and the realm of paradoxical imagery. As we will explore in more detail in Part Three, the vacuum has also only partially been filled by psychology, which for the most part is rooted in the scientific world view. Like science, psychology tends to address the more problematic dimensions of the soul's experience without acknowledging the vital contribution that Spirit makes to its existence. Some within the humanistic and transpersonal psychology movements of the last quarter century have acknowledged this deficiency, although for the most part, they still struggle to articulate their message in terms that science can validate. Meanwhile, we are still without a cogent language to parallel the rational language of science with which to speak about and understand the soul, much less fully address the question Kant left hanging: "I think, but who am I?"

The Soul's Quest for an Understanding of the Whole

This is the very question that propels the soul on its journey, and if we had the answer to it before we started, the journey and the entire embodied life that encompasses it would be unnecessary. Most of us begin the journey without a clue that we are even asking the question. We simply respond to circumstances as they present themselves to us, beginning with our parents' expectations, continuing through school, work and social obligations. Gradually, we discover our preferences, our capabilities and our limitations, and out of these cumulative experiences, a sense of self begins to emerge that is able to stand apart from its experience and interpret it. Most of the time, our interpretation of experience confirms and strengthens our definition of self, and the world around us begins to gel into a pattern of familiarity.

Every so often, however, a crack appears in this pattern, and the expected order breaks down. We lose something or someone we care about; we fail to reach some goal that is important to us; we fall off the edge of some unforeseen cliff and long for a return to balance. These experiences of death in the metaphorical sense require a definition of self that is larger than that which has sustained us thus far, and in the face of death, we begin to ask deeper questions about who we are. Who is this "I" in the ultimate scheme of things? Who will "I" be when this embodied life breaks down completely in the face of a death which is no longer metaphorical? Is this fragile, broken "I" with which I identify all there is, or there something more that connects us to a more sustainable reality?

While there are many ways in which we might approach these deeper questions, most of us find that these questions fail to be adequately addressed by the rational explanations that work when life is flowing as we expect it to. There is a reason for this, which we will explore in a moment. First, however, I would like to suggest that a more useful approach to these questions can be found in the very nature of the embodied soul. For if the soul is born of the fusion of Spirit and matter, as I propose, then the soul's quest to know itself on this deeper level must be a journey to discover the true nature of this fusion.

Fortunately for the soul, the coming together of Spirit and matter is not just a freak accident unique to the soul seeking to understand it. It is an omnipresent miracle, permeating the embodied world. As mystical traditions the world over have affirmed, there is absolutely no separation between Spirit and the embodied world it inhabits, nor is there anywhere within the embodied world that Spirit is not. The same sacred breath that quickened the body to consciousness, has infused the entire Creation with Life, creating an intimately interconnected Whole, bound together by the presence of Spirit everywhere within it. It is out of the Whole that the soul is born, and in relation to which it evolves as a living holographic reflection of Spirit. In seeking to know itself, therefore, each soul will necessarily gravitate in its own way toward a vision of wholeness and interconnectedness. It is ultimately this vision that the soul is seeking far more earnestly than a rational explanation for the human predicament in which the soul finds itself.

By a supremely benevolent gift of divine grace, the embodied world is a most accommodating mirror, ready to reveal the omnipresence of Spirit throughout the Whole to anyone who is earnestly looking for it. The catch is that one must be earnestly looking for it, before it can be seen. Just as any mirror reflects back the face that is presented before it without discrimination, what the embodied world reveals will depend upon who is looking into it and how it is approached. The mirror is accessible to scientists and mystics alike, and to anyone else who approaches it. But what one sees in the mirror will be a reflection of the assumptions and expectations that are brought to it. If the soul is intuitively seeking a vision of its place within the Whole, then that is what it will eventually find. If the soul is seeking a rational explanation for its existence and the nature of the embodied world, then what is reflected back will satisfy only the mind, and any possible vision of wholeness will be blocked by reason's inherent inability to encompass it.

Reason's Inability to Comprehend Wholeness

The rational mind, by its nature, is an analytical faculty. Reason automatically attempts to deconstruct wholeness through analysis, under the illusion that by breaking anything down into its component parts, an understanding will emerge that the mind can grasp. The analytical mind, in fact, is only capable of contemplating reality – as scientists have routinely done for hundreds of years now – by exaggerating separation between the seemingly separate bodies in the world. So when the embodied world is approached from a purely rational perspective, the world appears to be a fragmented, disconnected place of separation, and the soul feels itself to stand apart, alone and isolated within that world. Instead of helping the soul to know itself as part of a larger Whole, the rational mind takes the soul farther away from the vision of wholeness and interconnectedness that it seeks.

This vision is only possible when the heart pierces the veil of illusion posed by the appearance of separation. The embodied world reveals itself as an interconnected Whole only when the soul stands before the mirror of the embodied world with its whole being – using not just its thoughts, but also its sensations, its feelings, its imagination, and every other faculty available to it. The soul sees and recognizes itself as a whole being within the mirror of the embodied world not by distancing itself from the world, as the rational mind inevitably does, but by entering more deeply into it with all faculties alive and functioning at full capacity. The soul must feel its experience with the senses and with the heart, and learn to see everything intuitively as part of a living web through which loving, creative awareness (or Spirit) perpetually flows. The rational mind – which detaches itself from the world and seeks to know it by a process of mental dissection – is incapable of providing the soul with this experience.

Astrology's Potential As a Language Of Wholeness and Interconnectedness

Astrology can potentially provide what reason cannot, but only if the birthchart is approached intuitively - not as a analytical tool, but as a point of entry into a more integrated and wholistic perspective. Like the embodied world, the birthchart is also a mirror that can be approached in any number of ways. In order to see a reflection of wholeness and interconnectedness in the birthchart, the astrologer must bring all his faculties – sensory awareness, feeling, imagination, memory, fantasy, instinct, and intuition, as well as reason – to bear upon the birthchart's symbolism. The astrologer must also attempt to sense the birthchart as a whole, rather than merely pick apart and analyze the many pieces it contains. In practice, this is rarely done, and to the extent that it is not, astrology will be no better equipped than rational science to understand the soul.

Having said this, it is worth noting that the birthchart itself is a representation of wholeness and integration, which cannot help but extend an invitation to approach it in this way, for anyone with a true understanding of its symbolism. If we step back from all the inscrutable symbols inside the chart, what we have is a circle - the ultimate symbol of wholeness, of that all-encompassing reality that has no beginning and no end. Filling in the circle with houses, signs and planets - the symbols of the astrological language - we have a complex image of circles within circles within circles. Everything astrological moves in relation to one or more circles and in relation to everything else, and this fact alone makes astrology essentially the study of the interconnected whole. The interconnected whole reflected in the birthchart of any individual soul is also understood astrologically as a microcosmic reflection of the Greater Whole or macrocosm, out of which it evolves. When astrology is approached as an attempt to understand the full implications of this image, it cannot help but be the point of entry into a deeper awareness of wholeness and interconnectedness that the soul is seeking.

Exploring the interconnectedness within a birthchart is relatively easy, since the patterns of interconnection are inherent in its cyclical nature. A planet in a sign is always moving in relation to an entire circle of signs, while simultaneously sitting in a house that is always in relation to an entire circle of houses. Each planet is also always moving in relation to every other planet with whom it shares a cycle of interaction. Planets, signs, and houses are also connected to each other through patterns of rulership (or association by similarity), which resonate in less immediately obvious ways, but which also have a circular origin. Provided that the astrologer attempts to understand the birthchart within the context of these interpenetrating relationships, he or she cannot help but evolve a fairly sophisticated sense of the interconnectedness within the whole.

Perceiving the wholeness of the birthchart itself is a little trickier, though not beyond the reach of any astrologer who makes the effort. An understanding of wholeness comes through the perception of the overall shape of the birthchart taken as a whole, as well as through patterns of distribution that emphasize or de-emphasize certain symbolic categories. If a majority of planets sit on one side of a chart or the other, form an identifiable pattern of *aspects* (angular relationships) with each other, or are placed predominantly in signs related to specific elements or houses of a particular type, then this is all valuable information pointing toward that which ties the chart together as an integrated whole. Not all astrologers take the time to discern these meta-patterns, but to the extent that they do, the wholeness at the heart of the birthchart will slowly begin to reveal itself.

There is also a certain intangible factor that has less to do with astrological technique, and more to do with the awareness that a given astrologer brings to the birthchart. If as Yeats has said, "God is a circle, whose centre is everywhere, the saint goes to the centre, the poet and the artist to the rim where everything comes round again" (Discoveries 287-288), then the astropoet must go to both the center and the rim in order to understand the soul. The rim is a symbol of embodiment, while the center harbors the mystery through which Spirit infuses matter with life, with consciousness, and with the spiritual opportunity to evolve toward wholeness.

Going to the rim is relatively easy; all the astrologer has to do is to track the many cycles that give the birthchart its meaning. Understanding the whole pattern of the chart will also help to bring the rim into clearer focus. Going to the center is harder to do, since it is not entirely an astrological process. It requires a more meditative approach – not just to the birthchart, but to the embodied life that is reflected in the birthchart. If the birthchart can be approached in this meditative way, once the rim has been thoroughly explored, it will yield information that is unavailable to either the rational or the strictly astrological mind.

Using the Breath as a Point of Entry Into an Awareness of the Whole

The soul gains ready access to the center of the circle, and to a more intuitive source of understanding, when we put reason aside, and return to a quieter, more receptive space free from thought and analytical interpretation. The key to making this shift lies in the earliest association of Spirit with breath at the heart of most spiritual traditions. Most religions have repackaged their teachings in rational language, largely because of the influence of Plato in the West, and the influence of European (primarily British) intellectual tradition upon Eastern religions during the age of colonialism. As soon as you look beyond the rational teachings of religion, and seek a genuine spiritual practice, however, your quest will take you right back to your breath.

Despite the infinity of options available to the spiritual seeker today, the essence of all spiritual practice is conscious breath meditation. Meditation is a simple, but profound spiritual practice, common to most religious traditions. In essence, it involves simultaneously quieting and focusing the mind, while remaining alert in a heightened state of receptivity. In this heightened state, the soul is able to commune with Spirit directly, feel and absorb its Presence, without the intermediary of thought or interpretation. While there are many meditation techniques (Leshan), focusing attention on the involuntary rhythm of the breath is one of the most basic and widespread.

In the ancient teaching of the *Malina Vijaya Tantra*, said to be about 5,000 years old (Rep 160), the god Shiva enumerates 112 ways to open to the omnipresence of Spirit within the embodied world. The first four of these, and the foundation of the entire system, involve the breath. Many others involve focusing attention on various sensory experiences, and few of them require thought. Number 83 on his list is "Thinking no thing, will limited self unlimit" (171).

A similar acknowledgment of the importance of breath is given by Saint John of the Cross in his commentary on the mystical poem, *The Spiritual Canticle* (written 1585-1587), when he states (558):

This breathing of the air is an ability which the soul states God will give her there in the communication of the Holy Spirit. By His divine breath-like spiration (sic), the Holy Spirit elevates the soul sublimely and informs her and makes her capable of breathing in the Son and the Son in the Father, which is the Holy Spirit Himself, Who in the Father and the Son breathes out to her in this transformation, in order to Unite her to Himself... And this kind of spiration (sic) of the Holy Spirit in the soul, by which God transforms her into Himself, is so sublime, delicate, and deep a delight that mortal tongue finds it indescribable, nor can the human intellect, as such, in any way grasp it.

Though the concept of breathing as a pathway to self-realization seems deceptively simple, the practice is designed to accomplish a number of essential preliminaries to a recognition of the true nature of the soul.

- First, by focusing on the breath, the practitioner aspires to a state of being that is free of rational thought[3].

- Second, by bringing what is normally an unconscious process into the foreground of consciousness, the practitioner enters the present moment, which is the only place the presence of Spirit can be felt.

- Third, focusing attention within the present moment in turn allows the sensory or emotional awareness, as described in many of Shiva's 112 ways, to become gateways to an experience of Wholeness.

- Lastly, by attuning to the breath, and its rhythmical cycle of inhalation and exhalation, the practitioner also attunes himself to the Great Cycle through which Spirit reveals Itself on the physical plane as It weaves the Whole of the embodied world together.

While the rational scientist emphasizes that the truth can be known only through the mind, the journey of the soul back to a sense of integration with Spirit only begins when the mind is quieted. While both science and religion claim their authority from a tradition extending back into the past, and religion promises its reward in the future, the soul reclaims its spiritual essence by returning to the present moment. As you breathe consciously in this moment, you feel Spirit and body fusing in a timeless rhythm of inhalation and exhalation. As you fill your lungs with oxygen and surrender into the exhale, a simple awareness of Self comes into consciousness, and you understand in a way that your rational mind cannot, who You are. As you focus on the place between the in-breath and the out-breath, you become still enough to understand what lies beneath the comings and goings that seem to define the embodied life in a more superficial sense. Returning to your body through your breath, you begin to understand who you are within the context of all the earthly cycles and polarities you experience within the soul space you call your life.

As important as the breath is, it is really just a horse upon which it is possible to ride into the heart of Life's deepest and most ineffable mysteries and touch the very origin of Being. For the breath connects us to the very Force that first breathed the embodied world and the soul into existence. As the esteemed 19th century yoga master, Swami Vivekananada reveals to us, "*Pranayama* (usually translated as 'breath control) is not, as many think, ...about the breath; breath indeed has very little to do with it.... Breathing is only one of the many exercises through which we get to the real *pranayama*, (which) means control of *prana*" (29). Vivekananda goes on to explain that *prana* is the original creative power of Being that propels the entire embodied world, including the soul, into existence.

The breath is the vehicle through which Spirit enters manifest Creation, but *prana* is the numinous vitality that moves Spirit to breathe, and that ultimately inspires Spirit to want to create in the first place. By following the breath back to its Source, you open a wider conduit through which this same creative energy can enter more deeply into you, quicken you to new life at a higher level of spiritual potency, and synchronize your heartbeat with the ancient pulse at the invisible core of the embodied world. It is in this place, and only in this place, that it is possible to fully understand Who and What the soul is, and why It exists. And this understanding cannot be put into words, or even encompassed by thought, It must instead be experienced in a place that is free of thought, of concepts, or of anything that the rational mind has to offer.

In *The Essence Gospel of Peace*, translated by Edmond Bordeaux Szekely from original Hebrew and Aramaic texts written in the 3rd century CE, it says (37-39):

> *We worship the Holy Breath*
> *Which is placed higher*
> *Than all the other things created.*
> *For, lo, the eternal and sovereign*
> *Luminous space,*
> *Where rule the unnumbered stars,*
> *Is the air we breathe in*
> *And the air we breathe out.*
> *And in the moment betwixt the breathing in*
> *And the breathing out*
> *Is hidden all the mysteries*
> *Of the Infinite Garden.*

After meditation, you will inevitably forget the breath again, and return to a relatively unconscious relationship to the cycles in which your existence constructs and deconstructs itself. Having felt the creative power that sets these cycles in motion, however, you will begin to vibrate in resonant sympathy with that power. You will automatically begin to process your experience in a way that is more naturally aligned with the ebb and flow of Spirit through the embodied world. Through your conscious breathing you have merged with the original, still beating pulse at the heart of this rhythm, and your life will automatically begin to synchronize itself with it. To the extent that you can stay in touch with this pulse, as you go about your life, you will not have to try to figure out who you are or why you are here, nor will you have to think a great deal about what you are doing or why. Instead, you need only remember the *prana* moving through you, and then step into the flow. Having touched the spiritual Source of your being, and indeed of All Being, you are free to simply be, without having to think yourself into existence. The answer to the question "Who am I?" ultimately has nothing to do with thought, but everything to do with breathing your way into alignment, and then opening yourself to experience everything it is possible to experience while you are there.

This is naturally a difficult concept for the rational mind to grasp. It is difficult because the experience of unity with Spirit, and with the original impulse that brought Spirit into the embodied world, is one that is unavailable to the mind. The embodied world is at heart a web of relationships, and only through opening of heart does the soul find itself and its place within this web. The breath facilitates an attunement to the pulse at the heart of Creation, and the heart automatically opens to feel this pulse the way a flower opens to drink in the sun. Spirit enters more deeply into the embodied world through this opening of the heart, only when the endless agitation of the mind is quieted. We cannot reason our way into an understanding of the Whole any more than we can think the world into being. But we can align ourselves with the original forces that brought the world into being, because they also exist within us, as intimately a part of us as the breath that gives us life.

Endnotes

[1] See, for example, Grossinger or Krupp.

[2] Contemporary astrologers used to associating a date in late May with the early degrees of the zodiacal sign of Gemini should note that prior to the adoption of the Julian calendar in 45 BCE, the calendar was a chaotic affair. Ancient Greeks generally accepted a calendar year of twelve 30-day months, followed by five leap days, added at the end of the year, a system modeled after that of the Egyptians and Babylonians. Politicians, however, were known to occasionally add extra days, or even extra months, to extend their term of office. As a consequence of these and other variables,

◇◇◇

when dates prior to 45 BCE are converted to the Julian calendar for purposes of calculation, they do not always coincide with our expectation based on the relatively stable correlation of dates with degrees of the zodiac that we take for granted today. The calculation was performed on the Astro-Dienst web site at www.astro.com, using the moment of greatest eclipse (14:12:16) at Söke, Turkey, the modern location closest to Miletus.

3   Such focus can be attained in countless ways – through the use of a *mantra* (sacred sound), *yantra* (sacred diagram), *tantra* (sensual experiences approached with loving, meditative attention), candle flame, picture of some enlightened being, or koan (imponderable riddle) – to name just a few of the most common non-rational tools to free the soul from its identification with the mind. The astrological birthchart can also be used as a point of focus, but this is more easily done when the art of meditation has already been mastered.

Chapter Six
Through Inanna's Third Gate
Into a Personal Learning Process

Reason fails, not just in its inability to comprehend wholeness. Reason is also of limited use to the soul, because it fails to adequately encompass the soul's experience of the embodied world. The use of reason is primarily based upon simplistic rules of logic, as developed by Aristotle[1], which are incapable of handling the paradoxical fusion at the heart of Creation that brings Spirit and matter and all the opposites together in perpetual relationship to one another. Central to Aristotle's approach to logic are the principle of non-contradiction (the object of analysis cannot be both P and not P); and the law of the excluded middle (the object must be either P or not P). Taken together, these rules governing the exercise of reason insist that a statement is either true *or* false, but cannot be both true *and* false at the same time.

Meanwhile, in a dualistic universe, which is the dwelling place of the embodied soul, we cannot have hot without cold, male without female, pleasure without pain. Quite in contrast to the laws of logic, our actual experience is not a digital affair in which everything is either on or off, black or white, yin or yang, true or false. Instead it is an exquisite and at times agonizingly complex continuum of possibilities spanning an infinite spectrum of gradations. Within the face of this complexity, the "laws" of logic and reason must be understood to have limited utility. In fact, if they have any purpose at all it is to reduce the complex reality of the soul to something simple enough for the mind to understand.

According to Aristotle, and to the early science that was built upon his system of logic, reality is either yin or yang, but not both; whereas from the perspective of the soul, in which all polarities are defined by their relationship to each other, reality is a perpetual and ever-changing matter of yin becoming yang, and vice versa. In the Taoist model, which more accurately reflects the soul's experience, a small seed of each polarity exists at the core of its opposite, and sets up a dynamic in which everything that exists is simultaneously both P and not P. Or as Lao Tzu himself is reputed to have put it (Feng 41):

> *The bright path seems dim;*
> *Going forward seems like retreat;*
> *The easy way seems hard;*
> *The highest Virtue seems empty;*
> *Great purity seems sullied;*

〰〰〰〰〰〰〰〰〰〰〰〰〰〰〰〰〰〰〰〰〰〰〰〰〰〰〰〰〰〰〰〰〰〰〰〰

A wealth of Virtue seems frail;
Real Virtue seems unreal;
The perfect square has no corners;
Great talents ripen late;
The highest notes are hard to hear;
The greatest form has no shape;
The Tao is hidden and without name.
The Tao alone nourishes and brings everything to fulfillment.

Lao Tzu presents a worldview that flies in the face of Aristotelian logic, giving voice to a set of paradoxes which cannot be reconciled with the mind, but which are nonetheless vital clues that the soul can use to negotiate its way through a dualistic universe. To the rationalist, paradox is cause for mental meltdown; to the Taoist, it is simply the Way It is. The Tao is not a binary system, but a description of the eternal dance of opposites, which exist in continuous relationship, constantly shape-shifting across the line between P and not P. The rationalist clings to this line with blind tenacity, and considers the shape-shifting to be an illusion. The Taoist understands it is the line that is illusory, and celebrates the shape-shifting as the dance of Life. To the rationalist, Lao Tzu might say, as he does in the same verse quoted above:

The wise student hears of the Tao and practices it diligently.
The average student hears of the Tao and gives it thought now and again.
The foolish student hears of the Tao and laughs aloud.
If there were no laughter, the Tao would not be what it is.

The Rationalist Ambivalence Toward Sensory Information

From the Taoist perspective, this dance of life is inclusive enough to accommodate the irrational mind capable of contemplating paradox, as well as the rational mind that is not – even though the rationalist would probably not accord the Taoist the same benefit of the doubt. It is not the mind that is at stake in the rationalist's dismissal of the paradox at the heart of duality, however, but the body, and its sensory way of knowing. The unreliability of knowledge derived from the senses caused Thales, Parmenides, Pythagoras, Plato, Descartes and many other early philosophers to seek refuge in reason. Never mind that Thales and the Milesians had used reason to conclude that the Earth was flat, and that successive generations of rationalists have been led to equally ludicrous conclusions. Sensory perception was believed to contribute only to an understanding of appearances, while reason was considered necessary to discover the truth. The senses could not be trusted, because they were attuned to the ever-changing dance of paradoxical information that arose as a natural consequence of the interplay of opposites.

Although Aristotle was very much a part of the rationalist tradition, seeking to transcend the ambiguity of paradox through logic, he broke rank with his lineage in accepting the validity of sensory information. He questioned whether reality could be understood by the mind alone, and brought the senses that had been dismissed by the rational cosmologists back into the process of scientific inquiry. He also made an important distinction between categories of being, which would allow sensory impressions to be placed in their proper perspective.

As rudimentary as these ideas were, they set in motion a third epistemological stream, complementing mathematical proposition and logic in the consideration of truth, and forming the basis of what has since become known as empiricism. Galileo, Kepler, Hobbes and Newton would later dismiss Aristotelian logic in favor of a mathematical approach to the ordering of sensory information. But the movement within the scientific revolution of the 17th century to restore the senses to their rightful place within the empirical process owes a philosophical debt to Aristotle, who had argued nearly two thousand years earlier for a consideration of sensory data, during an era when most of his contemporaries dismissed it as unreliable. On the other hand, it took longer than two thousand years for the rationalist tradition to resolve its ambivalence about the role that sensory information could legitimately play in the quest for truth.

The argument against the validity of sensory information was a cornerstone of the Cartesian mindset that came to epitomize the rational worldview. To test the reliability of his senses, Descartes took a piece of fresh beeswax from a beehive, and heated it in a candle flame (501-502). He noted that everything about the beeswax appeared to change from the perspective of his senses - its taste, smell, texture, color, shape and size, and the sound that it made when he tapped on it with his finger. Yet despite these changes in appearance, he knew from a rational standpoint that he was still dealing with beeswax. From this, he concluded that his senses provided unreliable information, while his reason was a more direct pathway to the truth. In order to make such an assertion, however, Descartes had to discount the validity of his own sensory experience. From the perspective of the soul, this is too high a price to be paid, since it cuts off a primary channel of communication between Spirit and the body.

Sensory Information as a Conduit to an Awareness of Soul

If the soul is defined as Spirit dwelling within the body, then sensory experience can be understood as a catalyst to an expanded awareness of this connection. Because of the need for constant adjustment in relation to the sensory information coming from the body, the senses effectively extend an ongoing invitation to us to bring our awareness into the present moment, which is where all religious traditions say Spirit dwells. As we encounter Spirit through sensory awareness in the present moment, the connection between Spirit and body is deepened, and the soul takes more definite shape. From the mythopoetic worldview, the senses are an essential mechanism through which Spirit awakens within the body, and communicates through the body to the soul.

The rational mind alone cannot produce this deepening, because it rattles on indefinitely without ever making a connection to body that is essential to the alchemical fusion of Spirit and body that is soul. Sensory awareness, on the other hand, cannot occur without making this connection in a very tangible way, thus quickening the soul to life. To say that sense perceptions are unreliable, as Descartes did, because they change from moment to moment, may be accurate from a strictly rational standpoint, but within the world that soul inhabits, it is beside the point, since it is this same variability that provides the soul with its primary call to awareness.

Within the embodied world, the soul also relies upon its sensory awareness in order to navigate, and to find its place within the larger scheme of things. What the soul most deeply wants to know is who it is in relation to the body that contains it, the animating life force within it, and the world that surrounds it in this moment. Not coincidentally, these are the very questions that attune the soul to the Tao, where living in harmony with Spirit becomes a matter of paying constant attention to the ever-shifting balance of yin and yang. The soul learns to align itself with the Tao, or with dharma in the metaphysical sense – not through allegiance to a moral code that makes rational sense, but through the willingness to monitor its own process from moment to moment to moment. The senses are the most basic opening to this kind of awareness.

Through our awareness of sensory information, Spirit enters more deeply into the body that houses it, and the soul enters the moment. Focused in the moment, the senses become a gateway through which the soul connects with the rest of the embodied universe, and to the Spirit that inhabits it. The rational mind may not be able to grasp this experience of connection, since the fluctuation of information coming through the senses is illogical. But the soul will be nourished by the mere act of paying attention to sensory information, which provides an ever-present opportunity for Spirit to anchor itself and become more alive within the body.

The Power of Sensory Awakening

I once had a spontaneous experience of the power of sensory awareness when I was twelve years old. I was walking down the street, on my way to spend my allowance at the corner store, when the idle chatter of my mind was suddenly quieted by an unexpected turn of my attention to the soles of my sneakers touching the pavement. Because the sudden shift from thought to sensation was so startling, I stopped to more completely experience it. Once I stopped walking, and focused on the soles of my feet, I also became aware of the gentle spring wind caressing my face, the fragrance of freshly mowed lawn wafting on the breeze, the sounds of birds singing in nearby trees, and the various shades of green beginning to articulate themselves among the surrounding vegetation of a late New England spring.

As all these sensations converged to fill my awareness in that moment, an utterly strange thing happened. Suddenly, everything became more intense: colors were more vivid, sounds were layered in ways I had never noticed before, textures appeared to have a language of nuance I hadn't previously observed. Most significant of all, I felt more intensely alive than I could ever remember feeling. I felt intimately connected to everything around me. What I can only describe years later as a mystical experience, was my first encounter with the soul of the embodied world, or the *animus mundi*, as the ancient Greeks called it. This experience was precipitated not by some act of reason, but through sensory awareness.

Through this and other experiences, I have come to believe that the senses are designed as a learning device through which the soul orients itself to time and space and to the larger questions of identity and purpose. Far more adequately than reason, the senses can help the soul discover who it is within the shifting interplay of yin and yang that composes the embodied world. To the extent that the soul is born of its relationship with the mortal body, it must necessarily seek answers within the context of the material, sensory world of form, structure and content. This is not to say that the mind cannot also seek a sense of purpose rooted in its ideas or beliefs, but whatever sense of purpose the mind is capable of producing must also be anchored in something it can see, hear, taste, smell and touch, in order to be accessible to soul.

The Soul's Natural Inclination To Pursue Pleasure and Avoid Pain

While the mind believes, the soul gropes toward understanding in part through exploring its sensory relationship to the world around it. To the extent that the soul can free itself from concepts imposed upon it by the mind, it will naturally gravitate toward sensory experiences that bring pleasure, and away from those that trigger pain. Together, pleasure and pain constitute an innate feedback mechanism that is specifically rooted in the body. Stripping the concept of pleasure from its association with sin by religious tradition – in both Western puritanism and Eastern asceticism - it merely becomes a measure of the degree to which we are aligned with what the soul desires. Or put another way, to the extent that the soul is fulfilled through the choices that we make about our lives, we will experience pleasure. To the extent that the soul is wounded, or compromised, or limited by repressive beliefs, we will experience pain - not as punishment for sin, but as a reflection of our lack of alignment with ourselves and as a catalyst to growth. Within the context of most religious teachings, this is heresy, but as we saw in Chapter Four, the dismissal of sensory information by religious teachings can be just as detrimental to the health of the soul as by scientists, though for different reasons.

Among the early Greek philosophers, Epicurus was unique in suggesting that what the soul desired was inherently pleasurable. In his *Letter to Menoeceus*, Epicurus wrote: "Pleasure (is) the beginning and end of the blessed life. For we recognize pleasure as the first good innate in us, and from pleasure we begin every act of choice and avoidance, and to pleasure we return again, using the feeling as the standard by which we judge every good" (359). Epicurus postulated that it was the fear of death that caused all the passions that pained the soul and disordered lives. If we could but relinquish our desire for immortality, and enjoy the perfect pleasure available in each moment, he argued, the soul would be freed from the tyranny of death, and would flourish.

Epicurus' philosophy was misconstrued as hedonism[2], when what Epicurus meant by pleasure was a simple life, filled by the company of good friends, the enjoyment of each moment, and intellectual contemplation. In contrast to Aristotle, who dismissed pleasure as a valid measure of what was good in life because it was a capacity we shared with animals, and in contrast to religious teachings that considered stoic endurance of suffering to be the ideal, Epicurus dared to cut to the chase in suggesting that the soul was nourished through what it happened to enjoy. As the 15th century humanist, Lorenzo Valla, pointed out in *De Voluptate* (1431), defending Epicurus to his peers, even the Bible called heaven "paradisum vulptatis," intimating that the supreme attainment possible for human beings having lived a good life would be exquisitely pleasurable (EB 25:575). Epicurus' unpardonable sin, in the eyes of those who condemned or dismissed him, was to strip soul of its immortal pretensions and suggest that there was nothing wrong with pursuit of pleasure in *this* life. In fact, it was an orientation intrinsic to the very nature of the soul.

Pursuit of Pleasure and Avoidance of Pain As a Catalyst to Soul Growth

Epicurus also taught that the pursuit of pleasure is a learning process that requires constant vigilance, although this part of his teaching is seldom remembered. Pursuit of pleasure is a learning process because within this dualistic universe, pleasure and pain are part of the same continuum, and one cannot be experienced without setting in motion a movement toward the other end of the polarity. Too much pleasure invariably leads to pain, while any amount of pain will generally send us scurrying for its alleviation. It is not possible for the soul to engage the embodied world with the wholeness of its being, without feeling pleasure or pain or some combination of the two, and without cycling around the continuum that encompasses them both. This is not a reality to be transcended through moral behavior or rational detachment, but a learning opportunity to be welcomed, for it teaches the soul who it is and where it fits within the Whole.

Any heroin addict will tell you that the first fix triggers an experience of unparalleled pleasure – better than a gourmet meal, better than sex, better than any less extreme brand of ecstasy available anywhere on Earth. Yet, we all know what happens to the wayward soul that allows herself to be drawn into a more intimate relationship with the needle. She is shot directly through the dark seed at the core of her pleasure into the painful side of the polarity. If she survives this slide down the fast track of the pleasure-pain continuum, and conquers her addiction, there is no doubt but that she will have learned something extremely valuable.

So it is with each of us, most in far less extreme fashion, as we heed the call of soul toward that which provides pleasure, and away from that which provokes pain. Unbridled movement toward either end of the spectrum elicits an instinctual response that invariably draws us back toward the place of balance. Balance is not a static ideal, but an elusive shifting center that moves as we move in relation to it. As we orient ourselves to this center, and circle in upon it, learning to negotiate the balance between pleasure and pain becomes a primary catalyst to soul growth in this life. It is perhaps not the only catalyst, as Freud suggested, but one quite basic to the human experience, and a central feature of the interface between body and Spirit.

Just as any child learns by touching a hot stove, we all learn by experience to moderate our desires according to an increasingly conscious awareness of the sensory entanglement of pleasure and pain. Religious and rational thinkers alike believed that the unbridled indulgence of what they called the animal passions would lead to delusion and damnation. But this is only so when the soul refuses to pay attention to the feedback returning through the process, which would invariably become increasingly painful the more one pushed toward imbalance. In a world where pleasure and pain often trigger each other along the continuum they share, the opportunity for learning and soul growth is ever-present. As the soul experiences pain amidst its pursuit of pleasure, it discovers something about its true nature, which can eventually lead to a more reliable and maintainable state of internal balance.

As the soul finds its center, it evolves toward a deeper, more abiding though less dramatic sense of pleasure that transcends the waxing and waning of the cycle that brings both pleasure and pain. The lows are not so devastating; the highs are not cause for giddy derailment. The capacity to sit at the fulcrum between pleasure and pain, and take both in stride increases as one grows in mastery of sensory awareness. There are also resources,

◇◇

insights, and creative possibilities that reveal themselves only in this place of balance, and that form the basis for a higher level of functioning. This is the level on which the soul exists as a fusion of opposites, and to taste this experience while still in a body is the holy grail of human existence.

Sufi master Pir Vilayat Khan once taught that a saint is someone who is no longer affected by the circumstances of his life[3], suggesting that such a being would be beyond the duality posed by pleasure and pain, or for that matter any other polarity experienced in the embodied state. In a similar vein, Shiva admonishes Devi in the teachings of the *Malini Vijaya Tantra* that the ultimate goal "in moods of extreme desire, (is to) be undisturbed" (Rep 170). But this is not a state of being that can be assumed by an act of will, or a Jedi mind trick, and on the way to sainthood, all souls will bootstrap themselves up the ladder of spiritual possibility by negotiating a series of rungs spanning both ends of every possible spectrum on which pleasure and pain are possible. We don't transcend the realm of polarity by pretending it doesn't exist, but by entering more deeply into it, and learning where the place of balance is for us.

Along the journey to this place of balance, any experience that takes us to either end of the pain-pleasure continuum becomes a fertile opportunity for learning and soul growth. The experience of sexual pleasure and the pain associated with illness, especially life-threatening illness, are two of the most intense openings to a relationship with soul that most people will experience in this life, and both are profoundly sensory experiences. Any experience which evokes a strong sense of either pleasure or pain will necessarily be one that quickens us to life and/or reminds us of our fragile mortality. In either case, it is the sensory and emotional information that we process in the midst of these experiences that awakens the soul to the possibility for growth and deepening. If we define soul as the experience of Spirit, or consciousness dwelling within the body, then it is not implausible to assume that awareness of the body and its sensory messages must be one of the most important soul-making processes available to us.

The rationalist may ultimately be right, in categorically stating that there is not much absolute, certifiable truth available in the dance between pleasure and pain, or along the continuum of any polarity which engages the senses. But it is not absolute, certifiable truth that the soul is seeking. Like a surfer riding the crest of a wave that is just about to break, the soul wants to learn how to live inside a body with awareness of the edge between the opposites and a to achieve a certain level of skill in balancing on that edge. From the soul's perspective, the perpetual flux of information coming through the senses is not a problem, but a tremendous opportunity. For it is in learning how to negotiate this flux that the most meaningful learning will take place. The senses provide the soul with an intimate feedback mechanism that will guide it toward a gradually evolving recognition of itself to the extent that we are willing to pay attention to the messages, subtle and not so subtle, coming to us from our bodies. Any true language of soul must incorporate and accommodate an articulation of these messages.

Or as Rumi once put it ("Sheikh" 46):

> *All day and night, music,*
> *a quiet, bright*
> *reedsong. If it*
> *fades, we fade.*

Emotion as a Catalyst to Soul Growth

The soul's learning process is intensified by the fact that pleasure and pain are not only sensory experiences, but also often points of entry into an emotional dimension encompassing all the core issues that the soul has, in part, taken a body to resolve. These issues cannot be addressed anywhere except within the dualistic universe, because they involve working through illusions about separation, the possibility of abandonment or rejection, and perceived limitations placed upon Spirit by the finitude of flesh, space, and time. If we move toward either side of the spectrum of any polarity the soul is drawn to explore, we will have an emotional response to that movement that is useful to the soul as a navigational aid. Just as the soul seeks pleasure on the sensory level, it seeks happiness on the emotional level, though the pathway to fulfillment of the soul's desire for happiness is not any more straightforward. In fact, the quest for what we think will make us happy in the moment, often triggers the very issues – the sense of unworthiness, fear of rejection, feelings of inadequacy, sense of failure, insecurities, guilt and shame, loneliness and so on – that push us over the edge of the abyss of misery. The good news is that it is not the attainment of happiness that provides the soul with a primary catalyst to its growth, but the learning process that striving toward happiness involves.

This understanding was not foreign to early Greek philosophers, most of whom considered happiness to be the *summum bonum* (Aristotle's term, roughly translated as "highest good") and primary motivation behind all questing by the human soul. Except for the Epicureans, the early Greeks also felt uneasy in the face of the mixed results that inevitably met the quest for happiness. Instead of recognizing this to be the valuable trial and error learning process that it is for soul, they suggested that reason was necessary to keep in check a vast repertoire of untrustworthy impulses that would inevitably lead the soul astray. Meanwhile from the soul's perspective, it is precisely this propensity for going astray – and the emotional feedback that going astray produces – that has the capacity to teach the soul and lead it gradually toward genuine wisdom.

Though Plato taught that the Forms or Ideas that governed the life of the soul were mathematical in nature, he also suggested that a primary avenue through which the soul could indirectly perceive and participate in the Forms, especially the Form of Beauty, was through falling in love. As we saw in Chapter Five, Plato championed the use of reason as a primary vehicle through which the soul could come to know itself. But he also ironically believed that the temporary loss of reason by the lover could be taken to mean that the wings of her soul were beginning to emerge. As anyone who has ever been in love knows, however, the experience is not one of unmitigated bliss at finally being ushered into the radiant presence of Truth or Beauty. It is a learning process, not unlike riding a roller coaster, precipitated through the triggering of emotions that lie along a number of dualistic continuums.

Most relationships are fraught with emotional and psychological complexity, and an interpenetrating web of conflicting emotions is the norm. Love and hate, trust and vulnerability, contradictory needs for surrender and control, and both halves of other similar polarities often coexist side by side – both within each partner and played out in a dance of shifting roles between partners. The rational mind may be perfectly content to regard its experience dispassionately in terms that neatly resolve themselves into measurable units of certainty. But whenever the emotions are engaged, we automatically enter a realm where the opposites mutate into each other with disconcerting lack of regard for the truth that logic might dictate. The experiences of the soul are emotional by definition, because they are thoroughly rooted in death, considered metaphorically. The soul naturally gravitates to love, joy, peace, and pleasure, but it is life's difficulties that invite the soul to grow, and compel it to sink its roots more deeply. The soul cannot seek love, joy, peace, and pleasure without also activating the polarities to which they are connected, igniting a plethora of emotions, whose range is proportional to the capacity of the experience to precipitate soul growth.

When my father died a few years ago, I felt deeply saddened by my loss, as one might rationally expect. But my experience of his death was hardly rational or one-dimensional, for I also felt relieved that his was a relatively short illness; glad that I had gotten to be with him as he was dying; regretful about all the things that we didn't and couldn't say to each other; guilty for not being a better son; angry that the medical establishment seemed to be so indifferent to his plight; happy that he spent his last days in a hospice program staffed by loving people who cared for him; frustrated that he had to struggle with embarrassment at his loss of independence in the final days; and so on.

Not only were both the P and not P of Aristotelian logic present within my experience, but also L, M, N, O and every other letter of the alphabet. The soul lives in a polymorphous universe, where the options posed by the principle of non-contradiction and the excluded middle are far too limiting to adequately describe the internal nature of experience. Reason is often contrasted with emotion by the rationalists, who make the mistake of vehemently insisting that the one is valid and the other is not. Yet the very passion with which they press their arguments underscores the importance of the emotional information they are attempting to deny.

The rationalists of early Greece dismissed strong emotion as sinful, hedonistic, and untrustworthy, in much the same way that they dismissed indulgence of the senses. Though we are more sophisticated and often more ambivalent in our tolerance of emotion today, the same rationalist dismissals are evoked, for example, when environmentalists raise issues of concern about the capacity of cold scientific logic to threaten the very web of life upon which the soul depends. Despite our vicarious cultural preoccupation with emotion in movies, television shows, books, and one political soap opera after another, to tell someone they are being emotional today is just as much a dismissal of what they have to say as it was 2,500 years ago, when the early rationalists began their crusade. Because emotional information often introduces a sense of ambivalence into any discussion of complex issues, whether societal or personal, it is regarded with deep suspicion by those who cling to reason with irrational tenacity. Meanwhile, to process any truth strictly through the use of logic, without taking into account the often contradictory emotional component of that truth, is to render the information useless, if not downright dangerous to the soul.

I loved my father, and at the same time, I was incapable of loving him as honestly or as cleanly as I would have liked. At times – especially growing up – I hated him, and this love that I profess to be irrefutably true, regularly appeared to be the very antithesis of love. According to the tenets of Aristotelian logic, my experience of my father would not be possible. Yet, this was not only my experience, but hardly unique to me, it appears to be the human condition. How then do we talk about the experiences of the soul without extricating ourselves from the logical straightjacket by which the rational mind is bound?

The Craving of the Soul for a Polytheistic Language Of Emotional Complexity

Xenophanes, a contemporary of Thales, the Milesian eclipse predictor, railed against Homer and Hesiod for giving us images of the gods that reflected "all those things which in men are a matter for reproach and censure: stealing, adultery, and mutual deception" (qtd. in Melchert 15). His criticism was the first overtly expressed dissatisfaction of the mythopoetic worldview among the Greeks of his day, but it was certainly not the last. The imperfection of any god – polytheistic or monotheistic – who allows suffering and cruelty, inhumanity and stubborn stupidity, and all the other ugly traits that plague the human race, has become a quick and easy rallying point for successive generations of rationalists, atheists, and agnostics, who complained that the gods and goddesses did not make man in their image, but instead were made by us in ours.

◇◇◇

From the perspective of soul, this is exactly true. For the soul projects itself, emotional warts and all, onto every available screen, including the heavens. Far from being a measure of the inadequacy of the language by which matters of soul are discussed, however, the imperfection of these images provides an accurate reflection our true nature. We mere mortals are not simple clones of a divine and perfect Creator. We are also inherently flawed, vulnerable, torn by contradictory animal urges, and tossed about in the rhythmical dance of complexity posed by a universe in which yin and yang are constantly evolving into one another. While Xenophanes might assert that there is "one god, greatest among gods and men, in no way similar to mortals, either in body or mind" (qtd. in Melchert 16), that is not how the soul recognizes or nourishes itself. What it needs that the rationalists cannot provide are images that embody the innate contradictions that color the human experience at every level. We need images that reflect the complexity of our emotional essence as we actually experience it, not some whitewashed abstraction that makes rational sense.

The soul does not need Plato's Truth, nearly as much as it needs Hermes, who is not only the herald of the gods, whispering their messages and divine admonitions in our ears, but also the patron saint of liars, wandering con artists and thieves. The soul is not nourished by Love and Beauty, nearly as much it delights and agonizes in the seductions of Aphrodite, who not only embodied the very essence of love and beauty, but also routinely precipitated all the dysfunctional patterns of jealousy, betrayal, vanity, and romantic delusion to which human love is subject in the face of that which it desires. For all its genuine spiritual aspirations, the soul identifies less with a remote and perfect God than it does Zeus, who is seduced by all the perks and vulnerable to all the abuses of his position, just as any of us would be if we were in his shoes.

Why? Because these imperfect, dysfunctional, paradoxical pagan gods are a more accurate mirror to real life than the mathematical, logical icons of unattainable perfection produced by reason. Not that there is any virtue in dysfunction, but whatever dysfunction we experience in our lives is a catalyst to a learning process that feeds the soul, if we are courageous enough to see it that way. Acknowledging the dualistic, often ambivalent, and at times downright dysfunctional nature of human emotion up front, as James Hillman has done (70-72), is preferable to expecting the soul to conform to rational ideals of perfection. We anthropomorphize our gods, not because we fail to see the truth of things as they are, which is what the rationalists would claim, but because we seek to know ourselves through projected images that are more accessible to us than our own internal process. The gods and goddesses are not absolute truths unto themselves, but convenient mirrors in which we can see our own evolving truth, as it changes before our eyes. For this we need gods and goddesses that are malleable, and we need many more images of divinity than the One reason is equipped to provide.

I do not believe, by the way, that the ancient gods and goddesses of Mount Olympus are necessarily the most appropriate embodiments of the living forces meandering through the 21st century human soul. But they do provide a well-developed model of archetypal dynamics for the evolution of a more contemporary pantheon, clothed in images better suited to our age. One advantage of living in a postmodern world is that we get to eclectically pick and choose the best of all that has gone before. With access to world mythology not just from ancient Greece, but from a smorgasbord of cultures, both Eastern and Western – not to mention a vast heritage of literature, art, film and history – we have an abundant wealth of images from which to choose any array of symbolic images for our gods and goddesses that happen to strike our fancy.

These archetypal forces are recycled endlessly from one generation to the next, and are also playing currently on a stage near you. They appear regularly in more contemporary guises through our movies, urban legends, and the public arena of political intrigue. Instead of Hermes, for example, we have recently had the highly intelligent prevaricator, Bill Clinton, holding us spellbound with a brilliant analysis of foreign policy options in one minute, and leaving us aghast with his capacity for deception and subterfuge in the next. Instead of Aphrodite and Adonis, we have Bogie and Bacall, Richard Burton and Elizabeth Taylor, Nicole Kidman and Tom Cruise, Brittany Spears and Justin Timberlake. Instead of Prometheus, we have Bill Gates, bringing the fiery gift of computer power to the masses, but chained to the rock of anti-trust litigation for his audacity.

As Jung noted, though the outer manifestations of the polytheistic archetypes governing the psyche may shift from culture to culture and age to age, the themes recycle themselves in dramatic terms that engage the contradictions in our nature. The rationalist and the rationally-conditioned fundamentalist religious thinkers of any age might insist that their God be pure, that is to say, stripped of all human weakness and emotional inconsistency. But the soul in their care is left longing for a more accurate, albeit more complex set of images with depth, in which to see itself reflected. Fortunately, there is no end of suitable images – not just from within the external world of news and pop culture – but from our own lives as well, from which to draw this vital form of soul nourishment. It is not reason that makes these images useful, but rather the power of our projective imagination. It matters less, from this perspective, that you and I can rationally agree on what it is we see, than it does that my images speak to me on a sensory and emotional level, and that yours speak to you, for that is how our souls will find out who they are and get to know each other.

The Importance of Images, Symbols and Metaphors

We don't have to abandon reason in order to embrace these images. Reason and imagination are not mutually exclusive uses of the mind. In fact, both are needed to negotiate the material realms. Scientists themselves routinely move back and forth between the two in making important discoveries. In order to open the mind enough for the soul to breathe, however, we must free the mind from the rationalist insistence on literal interpretation of everything it encounters. To train our minds to process information in a way that is useful to the soul, we must give ourselves permission to see the world, not as a literal fact amenable only to reason, but as a mirror, exquisitely receptive to our image of it. While the mind thinks in ideas and concepts, the soul "thinks" in terms of images, symbols, and metaphors, and it is from these that any truly useful language of soul must be constructed.

Images and symbols are succinct embodiments of a deeply resonant truth, capable of evoking sensory and emotional recognition on some level normally not accessible to the conscious mind. They are partly conscious and largely unconscious. They evoke memories of the past and trigger a subliminal sense of possible futures. They are what they are - the literal snake, mother, or shooting star - but they are also somehow more than that. Like rational facts, images and symbols engage the mind, but they also invite the soul to explore information it can't rationally comprehend that might nonetheless be useful in the soul's quest to know and become itself more completely.

The rational mind is intent on taking the world literally; the soul is more interested in the world's capacity to reflect its own process back to it, as a catalyst to self-understanding. To the soul, the world is not a literal experience, but a collage of images in which to discover subjective meaning. The world that the rationalist believes in is, from the soul's perspective, merely the neutral network of templates into which you and I will project unique sets of images. These images in turn, will trigger insights that are potentially useful to us as souls.

We do this at night, as a matter of course, in our dreams, because in the dream state, the rational mind has been suspended, and a more imaginative faculty takes over. This same imaginative faculty also functions throughout the waking dream that is our life within the embodied world. In daylight, it tends to function largely below the threshold of awareness and at the periphery of our conscious focus - as daydreams, fantasies, sudden intrusions of memory, moments of synchronicity and fleeting insights. All of these experiences can be a valuable source of information relevant to the soul, provided that we pay attention to them. More proactively, we can also choose to cultivate the art of living soulfully by training ourselves to see the embodied world as a mirror of images.

Whenever your soul moves into the present moment, sensations, feelings, and thoughts coalesce around images that mirror the essence of who you are. This mirroring process is intuitive, to the extent that you are willing to let go of your need for rational explanations, and open yourself to the Great Mystery, vibrating within and around you, in each moment. Intuition, as defined here, is an attunement to the essential subjective truth of any situation. It is available in this or any moment in which you can let go of rational thought, and just be here now – alive to your senses, in touch with your feelings, and open to the suggestive power of the symbolic implications of everything around you. The world is not only a literal place; it is a screen upon which your soul projects the information it needs to extract from the world in order to experience itself more clearly. The world can only be seen in this light, however, when image, feeling, and sensory experience fuse in the present moment and speak to an intuitive mind that is free of thought. In this way the soul comes face to face with the Great Mystery, and feeds upon it, even as the rational mind struggles to understand what the intuitive mind has effortlessly grasped.

Many images also point beyond themselves and speak to the wholeness of the entire web of life in which they participate – the interconnectedness, the potential for integration, for finding a vital place within the larger scheme of things – in a way that purely rational information cannot. The complex polymorphous universe that the soul inhabits comes alive, not as the gods and goddesses that inhabit it are dissected and explained away by reason, but rather as they interact with one another and continually surprise us with yet another kaleidoscopic turning of the wheel our mind could not have anticipated. In this constant turning, we see mirrored the mysterious wholeness that encompasses the world, and we see an image of our own wholeness, even in the midst of the melodramas that infuse our lives with sensory and emotional complexity.

The revolution launched by Thales and carried forward by the rationalists of the early scientific revolution sought to explain away the mysteries of the cosmos through the use of mathematical formulas and logical explanations. In doing so, it has stripped the world of images, and tried to demystify it. The soul, however, derives its power not through resolution of mystery, but through the courage to remain in relationship to questions that never quite resolve, once and for all. It finds both its courage and its challenge through projecting its imagination into the world, and then engaging the images that are mirrored back to it. The world taken literally as a collection of facts holds little interest to the soul. The soul is nourished instead by the personal metaphors those facts are capable of triggering.

The Unfortunate Embrace of Rationalism Within the Astrological Community

Many astrologers are also enamored of the rationalist's quest, pursuing their practice of the art as though every symbol has a definitive meaning, which can be articulated in generic terms. Through centuries of observation, and cataloging of collective experience, astrology has become less a matter of contemplating images, symbols and metaphors with the intuition, and more often a matter of intellectually decoding shorthand notation through the simple application of a linear, cookbook knowledge. There is tremendous pressure within the astrological community to conform to the scientific paradigm, in order to gain professional credibility in the eyes of the world, and in the face of this pressure, astrology is becoming increasingly driven by the quest for statistical validation, the logical construction of generic profiles, and a kind of interpretation by formula that can just as easily be applied by computer as by a living human being. It is my contention that to the extent that we want to use astrology as a language of soul, this is a mistake. It ignores the soul's need for living images that speak to it in sensory and emotional ways, and for the fertility of paradox beyond the reach of rational explanation.

Through its symbolic association with a polytheistic pantheon of gods and goddesses, all fraught with irreconcilable paradoxes, astrology is potentially a useful language of soul. Before it can actualize this potential, however, it must divorce itself from its attachment to prepackaged definitions and reopen itself to the power of image, symbol, and metaphor. It must find a way to correlate its own symbolic language with soul experiences steeped in sensory and emotional content, and capable of evoking a more conscious relationship with the living paradox at the heart of each individual's life process. It must rely upon the accumulated body of symbolic information that forms its tradition lightly, so that it can instead focus on the art of processing symbolic information in the moment.

Like the rationalist tradition of the early Greek philosophers, astrology has become a largely intellectual pursuit, an imposition of theory on experience. Since astrology co-evolved with the rational tradition, it is not surprising that as a discipline, it has absorbed many of rationalism's bad habits. So thoroughly infused have these habits become, in fact, that many contemporary astrologers would argue that we need to become more rigorous in our embrace of rational principles. Before astrology can become truly useful as a language of soul, however, it must move out of the head down into the body, the senses, the emotional realms, and the heart, where the soul actually lives, while providing images and symbols that retain their power to evoke in the soul a vital sense of recognition.

Approaching Astrological Images Through the Senses and Emotions

The planet Mars, for example, is associated by astrologers with the experience of war, because of its mythological relationship to the Greek warrior god, Ares, and his Roman equivalent, from which it derives its name. This association is not rational, because there can be no literal connection between the movement of a planet in outer space and any war taking place millions of miles away on earth. The association between Mars and war is better understood in terms of image, symbol and metaphor – faculties which derive their potency from actual sensory and emotional experiences. This is often forgotten by astrologers who have intellectualized their craft, but for anyone willing to reconnect with the roots of the symbols themselves, a deeper, more visceral level of information is readily available.

If I simply close my eyes and "think" of war in sensory terms, I automatically begin to feel certain sensations in my body: I see the colors red, as in the shedding of blood, and black as in the cover of night that provides the stealth and element of surprise that war requires. I hear sounds that are loud, staccato, piercing, as in the sound of gunfire; and other sounds that are deep, booming, palpable as in the trembling of the earth under the explosion of artillery shells, or missiles. I feel the tactile sensation of sharpness, as in the feeling of shrapnel flying; roughness, as in the uncertain terrain beneath my feet as I imagine myself a soldier; and heat, as fire lights up the sky, and bullets pierce my skin. I smell a burnt smell, a pungent, irritating odor that hangs in the air and makes it feel heavy. I taste a bitter, metallic taste in my mouth, and a certain dryness. From this exercise of the imagination, I conclude that on the sensory level, for me, Mars is red, black, loud, staccato, piercing, deep, booming, palpable, sharp, rough, hot, pungent, irritating, heavy, bitter, metallic, and dry. This description makes no sense to my rational mind, but in my body, I can feel it. It makes sense to me, as a pattern of resonance that I can identify and experience, and that I can also associate with Mars, through the principles of a kind of sensory logic that is not rational, but rather astro-logical.

To take this process one step further, I can also explore my feelings in relation to this imagined sensory experience of war. If I close my eyes again, and imagine something red, hot, piercing and metallic, I feel vulnerable, under attack, and in need of protection. If I imagine something loud, rough, and irritating, I feel anger rising to the surface. If I imagine something deep, heavy and bitter, I feel a mounting sense of despair, tinged with panic. These are all feeling states I can associate with Mars. Again, these conclusions are not rational in the Aristotelian sense, but they are astro-logical within the pattern of association that links Mars to my experience, real or imagined, of war. They are also obtained through a process that speaks directly to my soul through the awareness that it elicits in my body, effectively linking Spirit and body in soul space.

To be sure, this is not the way astrology is traditionally practiced. It would, in fact, seem rather foreign to most astrologers. To the extent that this is so, however, I would suggest that astrology has become too rational, too burdened by ideas and concepts that speak to the rational mind, and too lacking in visceral and emotional correlates. Astrology has also become too wedded to interpretations that represent an imposition of rational ideas upon experience. A true astrology of soul would work instead in the opposite direction, to draw understanding from the symbolic implications of sensory and emotional experience. Through such a process, an astro-logic would gradually emerge that was rooted not in a rational interpretation of the birthc ndividual owning it.

Later in this book, I will begin to outline and demonstrate a process for using astrology to draw living images from real life that can then serve as the basis for a symbolic exploration of core issues and potentials. For now, in the context of this present discussion, I wish merely to point out the inadequacy of a rational, literal approach to soul, that is devoid of sensory input and divorced from the emotional dimension of the reality it is measuring. A strictly rational approach to the questions the soul poses is incapable of handling paradox or providing a suitable screen for projection of images. It is incapable of grasping the Wholeness out of which each soul emerges and to which it returns. To the extent that astrology has assumed rationalist pretensions, it will need to be relieved of these, along with science, before we can pass through Inanna's third gate into the underworld of soul. Or, as the problem has been described by poet, Wallace Stevens:

> *Rationalists, wearing square hats,*
> *Think in square rooms,*
> *Looking at the floor,*
> *Looking at the ceiling,*
> *They confine themselves*
> *To right-angled triangles.*
> *If they tried rhomboids,*
> *Cones, waving lines, ellipses -*
> *As for example, the ellipse of the half-moon -*
> *Rationalists would wear sombreros.*

Endnotes

[1] Aristotle did not invent logic, drawing heavily from the previous work of Socrates, Plato and Xenocrates. But more than any other philosopher, he can be credited with laying the intellectual foundation for the growing confidence in the supremacy of the rational mind that came to increasingly characterize the scientific revolution. Descartes, and other pre-empirical scientists used Aristotelian logic to articulate their points of view. Aristotle himself did not use the word "logic," but spoke instead of "analytics," while his followers considered his analytical system, the *organon*, or "instrument" of choice for attaining knowledge.

[2] The Greek word for pleasure is *hedone*.

[3] A comment made in a lecture at Unity Church in Kansas City, MO on March 8, 1985.

Chapter Seven
Shedding the Scientific Insistence on Objectivity

A second major defect in a scientifically driven approach to soul is in the insistence that truth be objective and verifiable by external validation. Science depends on the ability to consistently demonstrate the objective validity of the truth that it discovers, and this works well when the object of scrutiny is external, consensus reality. Consensus reality matters less to the soul than personal reality, however, since it is the specific nature of an individual's personal experiences that make the soul's journey what it is. To the extent that these experiences are capable of triggering pleasure or pain, an emotional response, and/or the spontaneous projection of imagery that are unique to the individual, then this process is not one that can be objectified.

This is especially true when the experience is one of death in the metaphoric sense, since death is what shapes the embodied soul, and keeps it from being identical with Spirit. I would remind the reader here that death in the metaphoric sense encompasses not just the literal fact of mortality, but also the entire range of experiences in which an individual might experience the waning, dissipation, or devolution of life process. It matters not to your soul, within the throes of such experiences, that the unemployment rate is at an all time low or high; what matters is whether or not you have a job. It matters not what percentage of marriages end in divorce; what matters to you is the health of *your* marriage. It matters not what statisticians say about the genetic probability of inheriting a disease your parents had; what matters is whether or not you are sick. Your soul is an intimately personal affair. To speak about it in a language that is designed to delineate an objective, external consensus reality is to miss the point of its existence entirely. It is no wonder that scientists gradually came to dismiss the soul as illusory, since they were looking for it in all the wrong places. It is not out there in some statistical average. It is inside of you, as intimately yours as the beating of your heart.

As the famous Swiss doctor of soul, Carl Jung wrote (Symbols 231-232):

> Though we do not possess a physics of the soul, and are not even able to observe it and judge it from some Archimedean point 'outside' ourselves, and can therefore know nothing objective about it since all knowledge of the psyche is itself psychic, in spite of all this, the soul is the only experient of life and existence. It is, in fact, the only immediate experience we can have and the sine qua non of the subjective reality of the world.

〈〉

If this is so, then we must not approach the soul by external standards of measurement, nor attempt to classify the soul's experiences according to objective criteria. Instead, we must embrace it on its own terms, in a language that is largely personal to it.

Science is incapable of providing that language, because it is intentionally designed to sacrifice the personal in order to delineate the parameters of objective consensus reality. To the extent that the soul lives in the embodied world, then scientific information about consensus reality can be useful. The soul discovers itself not by conforming to consensus reality, however, but by differentiating itself from it through a *subjective* process that Jung called *individuation*. I will talk more about this process later. Meanwhile, in this chapter, I will trace the development of the objective orientation, pointing out along the way various would-be champions of subjective truth, who struggled – often against great odds – to take the conversation in a more useful direction.

The Sophist's Contribution to a Language of Subjectivity

During the first 2,300 years or so of the scientific revolution, from Thales' prediction of an eclipse in the 6th century BCE to the flowering of empiricism as a cornerstone of the scientific mindset in the 17th century, the evolving science based on rational thought, mathematics and Aristotelian logic, was largely theoretical. Early on in the process, the field became littered with competing theories, each claiming to explain the true nature of the external world. The development of logic by Aristotle and others was one response to this profusion of theoretical speculation. The intent behind the development of logic was to articulate the laws of rational discourse, by which the truth or falsity of an hypothesis might be determined. The adoption of mathematical models postulated by thinkers such as Pythagoras and Plato was another response, since mathematics was an objective standard that could be applied equitably to test the validity of emerging theories.

A third approach to the same problem was pioneered by the Sophists, a group of itinerant teachers and secular humanists led by Protagoras. Unlike his peers, who insisted that objectivity was the criteria by which truth should be evaluated, Protagoras suggested that "man was the measure of all things," and that each person had his own subjective perspective. This was actually a rather refreshing view at a time when most philosophers were discounting subjective information as unreliable. Because the Sophists charged money for their teachings, and sold their services to clients of questionable, self-serving intent, their attempt at elevating subjective truth to an equal footing with objectivity was not particularly well received.

Their teachings nonetheless hold some value for us in our attempt to construct a useful language of soul, since they did champion the subjective primacy of the individual. According to the Sophists, the rational mind was incapable of producing anything but opinion, and true objectivity was impossible. All we could ever know through the use of the mind was our own internal thoughts, which the Sophists considered to be mere conjecture about the appearance that reality posed, and not an accurate understanding of reality itself. Metaphysical speculations about the true nature of reality were a waste of time, and there was no such thing as objective truth. Each of us had to decide for ourselves what was true and what was not, and act accordingly.

Because the same rationalist perspective that limited their more speculative peers also conditioned the Sophists, they failed to fully appreciate the freedom that a subjective understanding of the soul might facilitate. Like the other rationalists of their day, the Sophists mistrusted the senses and the information that came through them. Though they railed at reason's capacity to discern ultimate truth, they would not have thought of suggesting anything but reason as the faculty of choice for the individual soul to use in turning to its own affairs. Unlike their more dogmatic peers who insisted that reason would eventually lead every rational person to the same conclusion about the nature of reality, the Sophists were bold enough to suggest that reason was no antidote to the inescapably subjective nature of truth.

The Sophists came close to affirming the value of a subjective approach to understanding reality, but they did not know how to cultivate such an approach in a way that would actually nourish the soul. Instead they taught the art of logical manipulation, or what is more commonly called *rhetoric* - that is to say, the ability to use reason on either side of any argument, in pursuit of "enlightened self-interest." Modern day con-artists, public relation hacks, advertising flunkies, used car salesmen, politicians, spin doctors, lawyers and telemarketers all owe the Sophists a huge debt for paving the way for their professions, and the Sophists were largely mistrusted during their day, principally by Socrates and Plato, for the same reasons we remain wary of their more modern cousins now.

Distinguishing Subjective Truth From Relative Truth

To this day, subjective truth is confused with sophism, and dismissed for the same reasons, when the two are actually quite different. To say that the soul's truth is subjective is not to say that everything subjective reflects the soul's truth. Subjective information is only useful when you have the intention to know yourself more clearly and cultivate a more genuine expression of your being. Without this intention, subjective information - especially when directed outward into the world - can become delusional, or be used to manipulate others. The art of manipulation was, in fact, what the Sophists taught their clients, which is why they were eventually discredited. Just as objective information can be misused to rationalize questionable behavior, so can subjective information be misused to spread a distorted view of reality.

Objective information is valid when used to understand the external world; subjective information is valid when used to process experience internally. When subjective arguments are incorrectly made to try to convince others of the objective nature of reality, they commit a logical fallacy called *relativism*. Relativism is illustrated by the famous anecdote of the blind men exploring the elephant, one the sinuous trunk, another the wispy tail, and still another the thick, immovable leg, each arrogantly claiming they knew what an elephant was on the basis of their subjective experience. Since the Sophists were attempting to employ a subjective perspective to gain advantage within the world, they were essentially teaching a form of applied relativism with the intent to manipulate opinion, and were justifiable chastised because of it. In their own way, they were just as confused as the early philosopher-scientists who attempted to objectify the soul, though their confusion lay in the opposite direction.

One story - probably an "urban legend" - about Protagoras, illustrates the absurdity of this confusion (Melchert 43-44). Protagoras once offered to teach a young law student how to use rhetoric to win his cases, with the stipulation that the student could pay for his lessons after he had won his first case. When some time went by and the student had not yet paid, Protagoras himself sued the student, arguing that whether the student won or lost the case, he would have to pay. If he won, he would have won his first case, and by their agreement, would be liable for Protagoras' fee. If he lost, the court would make him pay. The student, having been trained well, however, argued just the opposite - that whether he won or lost the case, he would not be liable for Protagoras' fee. If he won, the court would relieve him of his obligation to pay. If he lost, he would not yet have won his first case, and by his agreement with Protagoras, would not yet owe him any money. Obviously both were right from their own subjective perspective, but their arguments were not useful in resolving the external differences between them. Both were arguing relative points of view.

The fact that relative truth is of little value in the quest for objective truth matter little to the soul. The soul is not an elephant wandering around out there somewhere in consensus reality. It is an intimately personal and internal reality, accessible only to the individual. In the same way that my body identifies me as an individual, distinct from you in your body, so too are the souls housed in our bodies unique to each of us. Some would say that the separation is an illusion, and if we are talking about the soul in its spiritual dimension only, I would agree. But the soul is not just Spirit. It is the fusion of Spirit and a body, and must be understood as belonging in a subjective way to each of us, individually. The soul is what makes me who I am and you who you are.

If I make a statement about myself, and attempt to articulate my own experience, then I can only do so from a subjective point of view. If I speak only of my experience in objective terms, describing myself as an American of German ancestry, raised a Catholic in a lower middle class working family, with a liberal arts degree from a small New England college, this does not really tell you who I am as a soul. More to the point, it does not provide me with much useful information with which I can really understand my own internal process. For that I must process these same experiences and others – which will be far less tangible in an external way – from a subjective perspective. As I do this, it matters not in the least, whether my subjective experience is relative to yours. What matters is that it gives me a point of entry to a deeper relationship with my own soul.

Socrates' Affirmation of Personal Objectivity

Though Socrates was one of the most outspoken opponents of the Sophists, he was also accused by some of his enemies of being one, in part because of this confusion between relativism and subjective truth. Socrates dismissed the Sophists' relativistic notion that the only knowledge possible was a matter of mere opinion, but he shared their focus on the personal nature of truth. Socrates was intellectually honest enough to admit that he did not know what was universally true or not true, only what was true for him. Unlike the cosmologists that had preceded him, he did not insist that his point of view was The Truth, but sought instead to cultivate methods of inquiry to discern the truth. In this regard, he shared the Sophists' dislike of the cosmologists' arrogance, as well as the Sophists' shift in focus from questions about the cosmos "out there" and the nature of objective reality, to a more personal concern with the life of the individual and the ethical considerations that revolved around personal choice.

It is interesting to note in passing that the charge against Socrates that led to his death was corrupting the youth of his day by encouraging them to look within for answers, instead of to some external authority. The unspoken suggestion within this charge is that subjective knowledge is dangerous to the external powers that be because it undermines their authority, and threatens them with loss of control over those who dare to think for themselves. The fear, from a societal perspective – both then and now – is that if everyone were to rely upon their own internal compass for guidance, instead of seeking to conform to the consensual norm, there would be anarchy and social chaos. Subjective truth, however, is not necessarily anarchistic, especially when the intent of the one seeking it is to know and live the *dharma* of soul.

Since the embodied soul is in relationship to everything and everyone else within the embodied world, cultivation of subjective truth that is truly useful to the soul can only evolve within a context that takes the needs and rights of others into account. To the extent that subjective truth is confused with the relativistic notion of "everyman for himself," then it will be misconstrued as anarchistic and dangerous to those with a vested interest in maintaining social order. Apparently, it was this confusion, in part, that led to the fatal misinterpretation of Socrates' views by the authorities of his day. Socrates was not promoting anarchy. Quite the contrary. He encouraged self-understanding that he believed would ultimately lead to behavior which would be of benefit not only to the self, but also to others, and to society at large.

Socrates is famous for affirming the Delphic oracle's admonition to "Know thyself," and he believed that through self-understanding, it was possible to cultivate a relationship to the soul that would bring happiness. His well-known quotation, taken from Plato's *Apology*, "life without . . . examination is not worth living" (72), is an invitation to look within for information useful to the soul. Unlike the Sophists, who believed that it was up to each person to decide what was true and right, Socrates believed that there were certain universal truths that each soul could discern for itself, were it provided with the proper guidance. Socrates dismissed the mythopoetic worldview as the mere invention of poets, preferring instead a rational dialectic, or method of asking questions. But he also believed that guidance could come to the soul through non-rational avenues such as revelations experienced in dreams, signs and oracles. He himself was noted by Plato to hear an inner voice, and to occasionally go into trance, while pondering some question posed by a pupil (Fieser 68).

Socrates also clearly parted company with the Sophists and their backhanded affirmation of the subjectivity of the soul in his firm belief that by whatever method, the soul's quest was for a universal, essentially objective truth – principally about the right way to live. Like the Sophists, he believed that the pursuit of truth was an individual process, although he drew entirely different moral conclusions from this assumption. Unlike the Sophists, he never doubted that knowledge of the truth would lead the individual soul to right action. Indulgence of a subjective learning process, which would necessarily revolve around making mistakes, he labeled ignorance. He appeared to create a philosophical opening for a subjective processing of personal experience, a radical notion that proved a fatal departure from the conventional wisdom of his day. Ironically, he was really on a quest for the same objective truth that was sought by those who convicted him, although by a more internal and personal route.

Through Plato's articulation and embellishment of Socrates' ideas, he affirmed the supremacy of objectivity as a quest for absolute truth. Subjective understanding, and by extension, the individual soul that was the subject of such understanding, became of secondary importance to an objective truth, universally applicable to everyone. Though other philosopher-scientists were later to question Plato's assumption that absolute truth could be determined using reason alone, the die was cast. From this point forward, the philosophical quest for truth was assumed *a priori* to be a quest for objective truth. Though the methods for attaining truth were widely and hotly disputed, it was rarely questioned that the truth each of us was seeking was out there somewhere, and would be as true for me as it was for you.

Augustine's Quest For Internal Objectivity

Saint Augustine, influenced by Plato, and indirectly by Socrates, also argued for the value of the introspective life as a pathway to objective truth. Whereas for Socrates, introspection would lead to knowledge about the right way to live in the world, for Augustine, introspection would lead directly to God, and the soul's deeper identification with Spirit. God was necessary in order to illuminate objective moral truth, and God was to be found within. More importantly, God was the embodiment of Truth that was unchanging and eternal, and so for Augustine, it was the source of the only truth worth seeking. Augustine did not deny the validity of an objective truth found within the external world. But it was the interior life of the soul that interested him, because it was the presence of God or Spirit at the heart of each individual soul that provided the only real opportunity for lasting happiness in a world of transitory appearances. Unlike the rational cosmologists, who applied the mind to understand the external world, Augustine directed his quest for answers to ultimate questions about the nature of reality to the internal world of the soul.

Even though Augustine was looking in the right direction, what he was looking for was not subjective truth, but internal certainty. He had learned the hard way that subjective truth (derived through the senses, the emotions, and the imagination driven by desire) did not always lead to happiness, and as such, could not be relied upon as a guide for the soul's journey through life. The only reliable guide was unchanging truth, which, according to Augustine, could only be found in God. As he described the human predicament, speaking to God in his philosophical manifesto, *Confessions*, "You alone have perfect knowledge; for your being, your knowledge and your will are immutable . . . . And therefore, for you my soul thirsts like a land parched with drought, for just as it cannot give light to itself, neither can it quench its own thirst. In you is the source of all life; your brightness breaks on our eyes like dawn" (323). The soul moves inward, in other words, not to find its own subjective truth, but to find the unchanging truth that is God, which to Augustine represented internal objectivity.

Aristotle's Potential Contribution To a Truly Subjective Language of Soul

Among the early Greek philosophers, the most promising forbearer of a truly subjective approach to truth was Aristotle. Aristotle argued that the particular was more important than the universal. He also affirmed many of the subjective mechanisms by which truth is obtained. Aristotle disagreed with Plato's assessment that the soul was imprisoned in the body, instead considering the soul to provide form, function, and purpose to a body with which it was inseparable. He refused to dismiss information derived from the senses, and contended that knowledge of the natural world derived from the sensory perception of patterns could be formulated into general principles through the use of reason. He understood that feeling could be a barometer of truth, provided one were willing to seek the emotional balance found between extremes of excess passion and lack of sufficient emotional investment in life. Finally, Aristotle gave his allegiance to the mythopoetic gods, whose movement by astrological association in the sky he considered a reflection of the perfect order in the heavens. Within this overall orientation to the world – very different from that of his former teacher, Plato and the other rational cosmologists – he believed that each individual soul sought to fulfill its purpose, and grow toward a realization of its full potential, along its own unique path.

Needless to say, Aristotle's ideas came into major conflict with the Christian Church, which was rising in dominance throughout Europe just as Aristotle's teachings were becoming institutionalized in Western academia. The Church was adamantly opposed to Aristotle's embrace of the polytheistic worldview, and considered his idea that the soul was inseparable from the body to be heresy. Moreover, Aristotle's definition of the soul as the form and function of a *particular* body – a view highly conducive to our quest for subjective truth – made the Church fathers extremely uncomfortable, since it implied the soul's journey was unique to each individual. This challenged the Christian belief that only through the universal pathway embodied by Christ, could the individual soul could attain salvation, and left too much of the soul's fate open to subjective process. The Church fathers also absorbed Plato's confusion of subjective truth with relative truth, and adopted his obsessive determination to actively discredit both. Within the context of this mindset, Aristotle became a dangerous source of potential subversion of Church teachings.

In the first part of the 13th century, the ecclesiastical authorities at the University of Paris attempted to impose a ban on lectures teaching the physics, the metaphysics, and the psychology of Aristotle and his commentators. As with anything censored, this ban ultimately succeeded in arousing curiosity, and increased demand for greater exposure to his work. When the Dominican friar, Albertus Magnus made Aristotle's works an indispensable part of philosophical and scientific literature in the Latin world curiosity about Aristotle extended beyond academia to the very Church circles where his work was supposedly suspect. Thomas Aquinas, who was Albertus Magnus' pupil, drew heavily on Aristotle's thought in composing his own masterwork, the *Summa Theolociae*, as did the German mystic, Meister Eckhart. Similarly, the Spanish Arab, Averroës, spread a distorted version of the Aristotelian heresy throughout the Islamic world.

Despite an earnest attempt on the part of both Christian and Muslim religious traditions to squelch Aristotle's radical teachings about the mortality of the soul, the importance of the senses, the primacy of the particular, and the validity of the astrological worldview, Aristotle's ideas became the intellectual bedrock of most major European universities through the 17th century. As a result of successive ecclesiastical condemnations of Aristotle and Averroës in Paris and Oxford throughout the latter half of the 13th century, philosophical truth was increasingly conceptualized to be distinct from religious truth, and both were studied side by side. Thomas Aquinas, in particular, argued that each type of truth was valid in its own domain, and through his influence, the Church - unable to unseat Aristotle entirely - chose to accept this intellectual segregation as a reasonable compromise.

While the full account of this fertile period in the evolution of human culture is fascinating, what is important to note is that Aristotle was pioneering a concept of soul that was very different than the immortalist religious traditions and the rational cosmologists that preceded him. At first blush, in fact, Aristotle would seem to be outlining a philosophy in which the individual's subjective relationship to the embodied soul was acknowledged. There are important caveats in relation to his thought and those who followed in his footsteps that should be noted, however, so we can further differentiate the scientific tradition - which took shape largely in response to Aristotle's worldview - from the soul-based astropoetic perspective I am promoting here.

Aristotle's Confirmation of the Objective World View

First, it is critical to note that Aristotle's focus was not upon the evolution of the individual soul as it existed in its own right, but upon the objective world in which that soul took its shape and momentum. In Aristotle's view, the soul's relationship to the body was not an equal partnership between Spirit and matter, but a convenient way of talking about the soul, in terms of form and function, that would allow it to be more easily observed. The value of sensory perception was not to provide information to the soul, but to allow the mind to test its rational hypotheses about the external world. Aristotle's understanding of purpose and potential was rooted in biological necessity, not in an appreciation for the paradox of Spirit evolving within matter. The soul was not the subject at the heart of subjective inquiry, but a point of entry into an objective understanding of human nature.

God, for Aristotle, was not a spiritual reality, but rather an impersonal causal force conjured intellectually as a logical explanation for the process of observable change within the manifest universe. God was a Pure Mind undisturbed by participation within the manifest creation, including the embodied souls He set in motion. Aristotle's involvement with the mythopoetic gods of antiquity was not as a set of images conducive to self-reflection by individual souls, but a confirmation of Pure Mind at work in the ordering of natural phenomena.

Aristotle's openness to sensory information, emotions, and the mythopoetic imagination could have served as the basis for a form of subjective empiricism as useful to the soul as its more rational cousin was to the scientific exploration of external reality. But Aristotle never took his ideas in this direction, and what has come of these ideas in the wake of his enormous influence has helped nail the coffin in which science has buried subjective truth. What began with the cosmologists as an investigation into questions of relevance to soul, became quickly transmuted into a discussion of external reality as it could be understood by the rational mind, and Aristotle was very much a part of this tradition.

Despite his willingness to accommodate non-rational sources of information, Aristotle never suggested using this information to enter the subjective realm in which the soul resides. His focus, like the rationalists who came before him and the empirical scientists who came after him, was the external objective world. The later empiricists of the 17th and 18th centuries would seriously question the role of the mind in processing sensory information, but the line of inquiry pursued by Aristotle and brought into focus by the scientific revolution, recoiled from the embarrassing inconsistency of the subjective realm and moved toward a strictly objective definition of truth.

Dancing on the Edge of the Subjective Abyss With Descartes

As discussed in Chapter Five, the rationalist point of view probably reached an important peak with Descartes, who was instrumental in facilitating the final transition from a serious philosophical discussion of soul, to one in which the soul was understood as an antiquated synonym for mind. Yet when Descartes questioned whether or not all he could really ever know was the contents of his own mind, he came dangerously close to the prior teachings of the Sophists – a precipice referred to by philosophers as *solipsism*. If Descartes had gone over this edge, he would not have concluded that "I think, therefore I am," but instead, "I think I am the only being that actually exists."

This would have been a statement of extreme subjectivity, which can be just as delusional as extreme objectivity. On the other hand, it is also a statement that could be, and has been made, in a more enlightened context by many mystics. When enlightenment is attained, by whatever pathway, there is no longer any separation between the individual soul and Spirit. Everything is identified as part of a larger all-inclusive sense of Identity, for which the statement, "I am . . ." extends far beyond the skin. The process is necessarily subjective, since it takes place within the awareness of the individual experiencing it, and not in the external world. The external world as measured by an outside observer does not change, but the one perceiving it changes profoundly in ways that cannot be measured objectively. This kind of mystical experience is only misunderstood as extreme subjectivity or delusional by a mindset anchored at the opposite extreme, where reality is defined as a strictly objective affair, accessible only to the rational mind, and measurable only by external criteria.

Descartes backed away from both extremes, suggesting that mind and body were utterly distinct from each other. While the body was subject to the same mechanistic laws of nature that governed all of objective reality, he argued, the soul/mind was not. In staking out this middle ground, he laid a logical foundation for the mechanistic theories being championed by Copernicus, Kepler and Galileo, in which the world was like a giant clock, running in predictable fashion according to immutable principles that could be discovered empirically. At the same time, he did not entirely abandon the validity of subjective truth, though like the rationalists that preceded him, he conceived of the subjective realm as one that must be governed by reason. Descartes believed in the subjective reality of a rational soul, but he understood the world inhabited by that soul to be mechanistic, material, and objective.

The Systematic Denial of Purpose By Hobbes and Bacon

Those who came after Descartes, questioned why the soul/mind should be exempt from the objective view of nature he had espoused. Why should the soul be any different than the rest of the material universe? Thomas Hobbes, in particular, proposed that the mind was nothing more than a derivative of the senses, which in turn were a physical response of the body to the external world. Taking Descartes' reduction of soul to mind one step further, Hobbes concluded that the entire life of the mind was nothing more than a bodily function, which could be measured objectively like any other material process. This, of course, was the philosophical foundation of modern materialism, and a major stepping stone to the current notion that soul, mind, psyche and consciousness are all just a matter of brain chemistry.

It is interesting to note that although Hobbes was quite critical of Aristotle, as were many of his 17th century peers, his conceptual leap had brought the Aristotelian notion of the soul as the function and form of the body full circle. For in equating soul with form and function, Aristotle implied that soul was knowable, at least in part, through the observable behavior of the body. Like Aristotle, Hobbes was concerned with what could be observed externally by an objective observer. Unlike Aristotle, he did not see any need to assume the existence of a soul in order to make his observation.

When Aristotle asked himself what moved the body to behave in certain ways, he concluded that it was not just the mind that Hobbes considered to be a bodily function, but also appetite, imagination, and a sense of purpose (46) – all of which were rooted

◇◇◇

in a subjective, internal dimension of soul that lie beyond the reach of observation or measurement. Because the soul was driven by internal forces and had a sense of purpose, Aristotle could not simply equate soul and body or dismiss the soul altogether as Hobbes was prepared to do. For Aristotle, the soul was what endowed the body with purpose, and that purpose was ultimately spiritual in nature. For Hobbes, all discussion of purpose was idle speculation. The soul (now understood as mind) was simply a body in motion, and it was the motion itself that was of interest.

Once Aristotle's metaphysical assumption of purpose was deemed superfluous, the soul simply disappeared from the scientific understanding of what it meant to be a human being. What we were left with was a mere body without a soul, governed not by an evolutionary spiritual agenda, but by the same objective laws as the rest of the material universe. According to the Encyclopedia Britannica, the *Anatome Corporis Humani* (published in 1672) was the last textbook of anatomy that discussed the soul within a routine description of the human body (Death, 16:992)[1]. Hobbes died in 1679, and with him and his contemporaries, so too did serious scientific speculation about the nature of the soul. This was a major development in the widening schism between religion and science, which left soul neglected on both sides of the chasm.

While Hobbes was dismissing Aristotle's insistence on the purposeful nature of the mind, Francis Bacon decided that any possible explanation of the world that spoke of purpose would also be superfluous. Like Hobbes and many of his peers, Bacon was skeptical of all metaphysical assumptions about the nature of reality. Governed by that sense of skepticism, he sought to reformulate the empirical basis of science with reference to nothing but the data itself. The purpose of gathering data, he postulated was not to understand the soul's journey toward the fulfillment of purpose, but rather to understand the material world – which included human beings – in strictly materialistic terms. All notions of metaphysical function, or purpose, should be treated as a mere fiction of the mind, unless they could be substantiated by empirical evidence. Better yet, he insisted, science ought to divorce itself from the messy business of metaphysics altogether and stick to what it could do best. The goal of science, according to Bacon, ought to be to describe nature as an interplay of strictly impersonal, material forces. Within the scientific worldview, he argued, all considerations of soul were unnecessary and misleading.

Thus what had started out with Aristotle as a promising beginning to a subjective language of soul, became, in the hands of Hobbes and Bacon, a mere methodology for rationally organizing empirical data into an objective body of knowledge. Once the data was stripped of its subjective associations, and its purposeful nature, the information became useless to soul. Whatever could not be identified as having physical substance, was illusory according to the dictates of materialism. Instead of asking how the nature of the soul might be reflected in the world that surrounded it, philosopher-scientists after

Hobbes and Bacon became increasingly distracted by the world itself. Leaving soul out of the discussion, they turned their collective intention to understanding how forces within the world impinged upon and influenced each other. Maintaining this focus to the present day, scientists summarily dismiss any subjective context that would be meaningful to the soul.

Unlike the rational cosmologists who had placed soul at the center of this world, the world of the newly emerging scientific paradigm increasingly left the center unoccupied. When the soul/mind, was considered at all, it became but another billiard ball on the mechanistic table of cause and effect, subject to the same objective forces that moved the rest of the material universe. Though science has been forced to re-evaluate its mechanistic view of the world in the wake of Einstein's discovery of relativity and quantum mechanics, it has clung tenaciously to its *a priori* assumption that the universe – including the internal realm encompassed by the human soul – is an objective reality devoid of purpose.

As Nobel Prize winning molecular biologist, Jacques Monod said, in his essay, *Chance and Necessity* (21), "The cornerstone of the scientific method is the postulate that nature is objective. In other words, the systematic denial that 'true' knowledge can be got at by interpreting phenomena in terms of final causes – that is to say, of 'purpose' . . ." This pure postulate cannot be verified or refuted,

> . . . *for it is obviously impossible to imagine an experiment proving the nonexistence anywhere in nature of a purpose, or a pursued end. But the postulate of objectivity is consubstantial with science, and has guided the whole of its prodigious development for three centuries. There is no way to be rid of it, even tentatively or in a limited area, without departing from the domain of science itself.*

If this is so, then we must "depart from the domain of science," to develop a subjective language of soul, in which a sense of purpose is central.

Endnotes

1   Philosophers before Hobbes had long debated the location of the soul in the body. Some early theorists thought the soul was to be found in the liver, since that organ did not appear to have a physical function. Empedocles, Democritus, Aristotle, the Stoics, and the Epicureans all argued that the seat of the soul was the physical heart. Pythagoras, Plato, and Galen, an early Greek anatomist and physician, opted for the brain. Herophilus, a famous physician of the Greek medical school of Alexandria (circa 300 BCE) assigned the soul more specifically to the fourth ventricle of the brain, a small area immediately above the brain stem. The debate raged furiously on

◇◇◇

into the 17th century, when Descartes declared the soul to be located in the pineal gland. After Descartes, the quest for the location of the soul in the body largely became an effort to understand the physiological infrastructure of the mind. Interest in the location of soul within the body resurfaced briefly in the early 18th century, after experiments by English clergyman, Stephen Hale, who concluded that the soul must reside in the spinal cord. The "spinal cord soul" stirred great controversy, until further experimentation showed that what Hale was calling a soul could be explained scientifically, without metaphysical implications.

Chapter Eight
Through Inanna's Fourth Gate
Into a Sense of Purpose

Even though science dismisses the idea of a purposeful universe, the concept of purpose is central to the soul's quest for self-understanding. At its most basic level, the soul's purpose is a direct consequence of the polarity between Spirit and matter, out of which it comes into existence. If purpose is defined as that toward which one is moving, then any polarity involves a natural attraction and instinctual movement of each pole toward the other. The symbol for the Tao, which depicts this interaction most succinctly, is not a symbol of stasis. There is a constant flow of yin into and through yang, and vice versa, and it is the dynamic relationship between the two polarities that gives birth to their very identity. Since soul mediates the opposites, the soul's purpose can likewise be understood in terms of this two-way flow. In the broadest sense, the soul's purpose revolves around the movement of Spirit into matter, and conversely, around the movement of matter back toward Spirit.

Understanding The Soul's Purpose
As the Movement of Spirit Into Matter

According to most mythological accounts of creation, known as "creation myths," Spirit creates the myriad forms of the manifest world - including individual souls. In some accounts, Spirit is anthropomorphized – that is, given human attributes; in others, Spirit is understood in more abstract terms as light or concentrated energy, i.e. the scientific theory of the Big Bang. In nearly every account, there is a flowing outward, dissipation or distribution of energy, consciousness, and/or substance from the One to the Many, that results in the formation of the embodied world, as we know it.

Many of these creation myths describe the process in literal terms as a dismemberment and redistribution of body parts, originally belonging to the Creator. Noted Jungian psychologist, Marie-Louise von Franz, relates several of these in her seminal book, *Creation Myths*. In the Hindu cosmology, for example, creation emanates from the body of Purusha, whose "head becomes the sky, his navel the air, his feet the earth, from his mind springs the moon, from his eye the sun, and from his breath the wind" (96). Likewise in the Chinese myth of P'an Ku, whose corpse fell into five pieces to form the five sacred mountains of China; and in the Germanic myth of Ymir, out of whose brow came Midgarth, the realm of human beings, whose brain shaped the angry

~~~~~~

clouds, and whose blood formed the boisterous sea of the harsh Nordic landscape. Even in Jewish mystical tradition, while Adam's head was in the Garden of Eden, the rest of his body was laid out across the Earth (99).

The implication in all of these myths is that Spirit permeates creation and infuses it with its essence. In the creation of this world, there is a movement from Spirit into the embodied world, including each individual soul, that gives meaning and purpose to existence. Part of the purpose of any soul, then, becomes opening the heart, the mind, and the senses to this movement, so that the soul might align itself with and receive the incoming energies. As the soul is able to receive, Spirit in turn becomes more consciously embodied by the soul. Through an increased awareness of Spirit's presence within it, the soul will discover the spiritual nature of its embodiment, and the spiritual essence of everything it encounters within the embodied world. The more receptive the soul becomes, the more the embodied world will mirror the movement of Spirit into matter, and more the soul will feel itself to be defined by this movement.

This movement is of course not recognized by science, because it can't be measured objectively or understood rationally with the tools that science has to offer. Science acknowledges the body, but fails to see the embodiment by Spirit that brings the body to life. The denial of embodiment by science both parallels and compounds the predicament posed by the transcendent, monotheistic God of religion, who no longer participates in the creation He once set in motion. Both deny the ongoing movement of Spirit into matter, and the capacity of the human soul for recognizing, and more consciously identifying with this movement. Obviously, to speak about the soul's purpose in a meaningful way, a language of soul must do what neither science nor religion seem able or willing to do. It must articulate the immanence of Spirit within the embodied world, and encourage the soul to discover itself through a more conscious recognition of this immanence.

Understanding Purpose As the Movement of Matter Toward Spirit

The movement that gives soul purpose also flows in the opposite direction - that is to say, from soul to Spirit. Most spiritual traditions speak not only of Creation, but also of a reciprocal process by which the innumerable manifestations of the Many gradually return to the One. As discussed in Chapter Two, this return is generally conceived as an act of transcendence through which the soul is liberated from the burden of embodiment. If we understand embodiment to be a good thing - essential, in fact, to the spiritual life of the embodied soul - then we must think about the return in a different way. Within the perspective of embodiment itself, the return of soul to Spirit must take place right here on

Earth, while the soul is still alive within a body.

As the embodied soul awakens to the presence of Spirit within, it is not suddenly catapulted into a higher, more ethereal realm. It is instead empowered to function at its highest capacity in *this* realm, so that it might further the creative evolution of consciousness within the embodied world. If the movement of Spirit into matter is what gives the embodied soul the gift of life, then the movement of soul back to Spirit must necessarily involve giving something back to the Whole of which one is part. This converse movement requires us to use the gifts of Spirit we have been given – including consciousness and creativity – to make a contribution to the embodied world, and to leave the world a better place for having lived within it.

Many indigenous peoples considered this contribution to be the essence of soul's purpose. The Pueblo Indians of the American Southwest, for example, believed that every soul had a contribution to make to the cosmic order (Native American Peoples, EB 13:378). Without the full cooperation of every creature (human, animal, and plant) serving the function they were meant to fulfill, they believed that the Sun would not be able to complete its annual journey, the rain would cease to fall, and the crops would fail. In fact, without the active, intentional involvement of individuals fulfilling their soul's purpose, the divine order inherent in the embodied world would collapse. Conversely, by creating social structures and support systems to encourage finding the soul's purpose and making a unique individual contribution, the cosmic order continued evolving in a positive direction with beneficial consequences to the group.

This idea has been popularized in recent years by visionary New Age author, Ken Carey, who describes the further evolution of the human species as a process of fully awakening to the presence of Spirit within us, and then consciously and deliberately assisting Spirit as co-creators. Speaking from the perspective of the Creator, Carey says (144-145):

> *Every creature is capable of knowing my   in spirit, but most life forms are able to translate only a portion of that wholeness into biological expression . . . . Only human beings possess the systems of generalized biocircuitry that can translate the full range of my awareness into comprehensive forms of physical plane communication and creation . . . . The ultimate human purpose is to share with me in the enjoyment of these dimensional realms, and to assist me – by being the body or family in which I am incarnate - in the creation . . .*

It is worth noting here that Carey's idea of co-creativity depends upon an awakening of Spirit within the body, or an activation of what we are discussing here as embodied soul.

Because science dismisses the possibility of a purposeful universe, science would have no comment to make about Carey's vision, although Carey implies that enlightened scientists could very well become contributors to this co-evolutionary process. Enlightened scientists are proving this to be true, as they touch in various ways upon a creative intelligence at work at the very heart of the inanimate, purposeless universe they are studying. Most of these scientists are faced with a dilemma in such moments of revelation. They can either step outside of the orthodoxy, embrace the idea of purpose, and risk being ostracized by the mainstream scientific community. Or they can deny the metaphysical implications of their discoveries in order to make a contribution to their field that is more readily accepted by their peers.

If science is, in fact, a quest for truth, then its empirical discovery of patterns in the objective world can ultimately only be attributed to a Creative Intelligence at work, and will eventually lead to an acknowledgment that this same Intelligence is at work within us. Perhaps this will then lead to curiosity about the possibility of a sense of purpose behind that Intelligence. Even then, since science is conditioned to speak about anything it discovers in objective terms, we will be left without a language to articulate the soul's experience, and science will remain irrelevant to our quest for subjective understanding. Meanwhile, our discovery of the presence of Spirit within us, and our effort to more consciously and creatively participate in the ongoing evolution of the embodied world, will infuse our soul with its deepest and most vital sense of purpose.

The Potential Value of a Subjective Quest for Knowledge

It should be noted that the empirical process by which science discovers the objective truth of a universe devoid of purpose is not, in and of itself, antithetical to a language of soul. The soul's process of discovering its relationship to Spirit, and learning how to more effectively embody Spirit, is also an empirical process. Every life proceeds, consciously or not, through trial and error, and whether or not we articulate it to ourselves, we are constantly evolving and refining a working hypothesis about who we are in relation to ourselves and the world around us. A true language of soul would not discourage an empirical approach to the discovery of truth. It would make such an approach more conscious and deliberate, but also turn the process inward, and legitimize the subjective nature of its focus.

Stripped of its scientific orientation, empiricism is actually a useful concept. In so far as it promotes the systematic exploration of recognizable patterns of experience, it can be applied not just to sensory data about the external world, but also to the interior world of sense perception, emotion, and projected imagery that is intrinsic to an understanding of soul. To be relevant to the soul, however, an empirical methodology must be developed that recognizes the primacy of subjective understanding, It must further acknowledge that the goal of subjective understanding is ultimately a sense of spiritual purpose and place within the larger cosmic scheme of things. Science denies the possibility that the world it measures is purposeful, while demanding that the world and everything in it – including human beings – be understood objectively. In so doing, scientists have produced a methodology that is useless to the soul seeking subjective understanding of purpose, as a critical focal point of its journey.

Religion acknowledges a purpose at the heart of the soul's quest, but lacks an empirical process for approaching an understanding of that purpose[1]. Religion also makes the same mistake as science in assuming the necessity for an objective approach to understanding, even though it takes this assumption in an entirely different direction. Most religions assume that the return to union with Spirit is a universal, generic process, and that the animating purpose behind the movement of soul is the same for each of us. In a purely metaphysical sense, this may be true, since as spiritual beings, we are ultimately not separate from the Creator to whom we are trying to return, and the return itself is incidental to a fate that can be understood as universal and generic. But the soul's journey is not just a spiritual one, nor is our quest purely metaphysical, and what a return to Spirit means and looks like on the subjective level varies greatly from individual to individual.

A true language of soul must recognize both the universal human yearnings, and those that are highly personal to each of us. The desire to love and be loved, the quest for a sense of place and belonging, the drive to make a creative contribution to the world in which we live, and the need to maintain reasonable health are all desires that we generally hold in common. There are, however, an infinity of ways it is possible to prioritize these desires, and an even greater infinity of complications that can arise in our quest to satisfy them. Though we can catalog motivations and recognize a certain universality of purpose within them, in the end, these motivations must be approached subjectively, in order to understand where the soul is going and why it is trying to get there in a particular way. We can use an empirical methodology to explore these issues – as I will demonstrate doing later. But we must adapt our empirical method to a process that honors the subjective truth of each individual soul, in a way that neither religion nor science seems willing or able to do.

The Subjective Nature of the Soul's Experience

Science looks out into the world and measures what is true for everyone, while each individual soul looks out into the world and sees a reflection of itself, which it must understand in a uniquely subjective way. An objective empiricist observes a kitchen table, takes out a tape measure and dutifully notes its dimensions; considers the kind

◇◇

of wood used in its construction, the method of assembly, the color of its finish, and its other physical attributes. If he is concerned at all with function or purpose – which most empiricists after Bacon were not – he would assume that a kitchen table was an object that facilitated the eating of food. Putting together this empirical data, using the cataloguing and deductive functions of the rational mind, the empiricist would arrive at a standard definition for a table, which could then be applied in every subsequent situation in which the concept of table had relevance. Empirical science would quickly close the book on tables, and move on to the next unsolved mystery begging for rational, objective explanation.

Each individual soul, meanwhile, would approach its understanding of the concept "kitchen table" in a radically different way. One soul might remember mealtimes during her childhood when she was forced to eat her broccoli before she could go out to play, thus becoming visibly agitated though nothing but a table sat before her. A second soul might remember sweeping away a table full of dishes in a moment of passion in order to make love to his wife in the early days of their marriage, and feel a wave of nostalgia and sadness that the relationship had changed. A third might remember late nights in graduate school studying for her bar exam at the kitchen table, and shudder with relief that she had finally put that hurdle behind her. Still another soul might become mesmerized by the grain on the surface of the table and get carried away to a place of peaceful reverie that reminded him of ocean waves. And so on. The same table is experienced in endless subjective variations that never enter into an objective discussion of truth.

From a subjective perspective, the same table would essentially become an entirely different table each time it were observed by a different subject. This is not to say that we can't all objectively agree a table is a table, but from the perspective of the soul, there is so much more to an understanding of a table – or anything in the embodied world, for that matter. The objective empiricist misses at least 90% of the data, and at best comes to a partial, superficial understanding of reality. The soul needs that missing 90% and the more intimately personal data it contains far more than it needs objective quantifiable measurements, because it is through an articulation of the personal dimensions of its experience that the soul will arrive at a subjective understanding of its purpose.

Aristotle's Contribution to a Language of Quality

The emphasis our culture places on the pursuit of objective truth is damaging to the soul, not just because the soul seeks to know its purpose subjectively, but also because objective information must be measured by quantity, while the soul seeks to describe its experience in terms of quality. The objective empiricist is uncomfortable with the idea of quality, because it can't be measured by the tools that science has to offer, and thus places our actual experience of reality beyond the reach of science. We can devise ways to measure some qualities objectively – noting the actual temperature of the room, for example, or correlating emotional states with brain waves, or correlating images and symbols with discrete definitions, which reduce them to a form of shorthand notation. But we can't consider reality in a way that is meaningful to soul without exploring the subjective quality of its experience. Subjective qualities cannot be measured mathematically; they must be felt, and then described in words – the more personal the language, the better.

From the soul's perspective, the qualities that make a table what it is have less to do with the objective table itself, and everything to do with the subjective associations that are brought to its perception. The experience of quality is necessarily subjective, because it depends upon a previous history of experiences which are intimately personal to the soul, and which must be understood within the context of the soul's journey. To understand the true meaning of sensory data, emotion, or the imagery that suggests itself to the individual, we must also understand something about the nature of the soul having the experience, where it has been, and where it is trying to go. Conversely, the way an individual describes his experience – through identifying the subjective qualities that he projects into it – is an attempt by soul to understand itself.

This point of view is consistent with Aristotle's understanding of the nature of quality, although he would not have put it in quite these terms. While Plato believed that qualities existed apart from the object that expressed them, Aristotle argued that a quality such as beauty existed only when something beautiful was encountered. For Aristotle, quality was something that had to be understood within the context of individual experience, on the subjective level, before it could be articulated. Though Aristotle did not come right out and say that a qualitative understanding of sensory information could lead the soul to a deeper understanding of its purpose, his approach to the empirical processing of sensory data by a soul with purpose did not exclude that possibility.

Aristotle did say that every soul was evolving toward a fulfillment of its purpose. He also said that observable change within the world of sensory information was evidence of an evolutionary process, and that quality was a legitimate category of observation. Putting these ideas together in a way that Aristotle probably would not have, it follows that observing the quality of sensory experience could potentially help the observer know the purpose toward which her soul was evolving. By taking the projections of the soul into the world of sensory objects seriously, anything could become a source of valuable subjective information. If empiricism had developed on the basis of this understanding, we would have a far different understanding of the soul today.

The Systematic Denial of Quality by Science

Unfortunately, this is not the direction the scientific revolution was heading, nor was it how the empirical method evolved. Instead, the empirical process became impervious to the subjective experiences that can and must be described through reference to quality. The individual became just another material body, subject to the same objective, mathematical measurements that described the rest of the material world. Because this worldview depended upon a systematic denial of subjective truth, then science had no choice but to categorically deny the value of quality as a source of information.

This denial became an important component of the agenda of the early empiricists. Galileo made a clear distinction between qualities that were absolute, objective, immutable and measurable, and those that were relative, subjective, changeable, and derived from sensory experience. He called those qualities in the first group primary, while those in the second group he labeled secondary. Primary qualities were essentially those that could be described mathematically – like weight, and temperature, and motion – while secondary qualities were those that could not be measured. While I agree with Galileo on the inadequacy of science to evaluate secondary qualities, he considered only primary qualities to be worthy of consideration as a source of empirical knowledge, and dismissed secondary qualities altogether as illusory and subject to the flux of opinion.

Galileo took great pains to explain how the senses could be attributed to the action of particles, or atoms, of a particular number, weight, figure, velocity or other measurable property, and those sensory experiences that he could not explain in this way, he simply dismissed as unreal. For Galileo and the scientists who followed eagerly in his footsteps, reality was that which could be measured mathematically. Secondary qualities – which fell outside of the scope of measurement – simply ceased to exist as a factor worthy of consideration. This represented a profound shift from the philosophy of Aristotle, in which human beings were central to an understanding of the universe, and an assessment of quality was essential to an understanding of human experience. Now, according to the early empirical scientists, human beings were effectively banished from participation in the real world, except through their capacity to know it as outside, objective observers.

As noted philosopher of science, E. A. Burtt states (90):

> The features of the world now classed as secondary, unreal, ignoble and regarded as dependent on the deceitfulness of sense, are just those features which are most intense to man in all but his purely theoretical activity, and even in that, except where he confines himself strictly to the mathematical method. It was inevitable that in these circumstances man should now appear to be outside of the real world; man is hardly more than a bundle of secondary

qualities . . . . Man begins to appear for the first time in the history of thought as an irrelevant spectator and insignificant effect of the great mathematical system which is the substance of reality.

Though many philosopher-scientists played a role in facilitating this development, few were more instrumental in marginalizing the qualitative, subjective experiences of human beings than Galileo. Galileo also had a profound influence on other empiricists of his day - including Kepler, Hobbes, Bacon and Locke - and set the tone for the evolution of the scientific paradigm over the course of the next three centuries. To this day, scientists are defined as empiricists who measure the material universe quantitatively using mathematics as their primary language. In retrospect, Galileo's attitude toward quality can be considered a transitional perspective. It lies midway between the Aristotelian worldview that placed the human soul at the center of the observable universe and Hobbes' view (and science's current mainstream stance) that considers human beings soulless lumps of matter, no different in essence from the external world they observed. As long as the soul remained a viable metaphysical concept, and metaphysics still played a part in philosophical speculation about the nature of reality, quality could not be dismissed as a measure of the soul's experience. Conversely, as long as quality remained a legitimate category of experience, the human soul maintained a toehold in the emerging scientific worldview.

The Empirical Dismissal of Quality

In Galileo's day, the Church was still enough of a player on the world stage to impact the debate about soul that was taking place in secular circles. With the memory of Copernicus' fate still fresh, empiricists were forced to continue paying lip service to the existence of a soul and the quality of its experiences, even though for all intents and purposes, the radical shift toward a soulless, strictly mathematical worldview was well under way. As a consequence of the cultural climate in which the early empiricists attempted to stage their revolution, Galileo was forced to maintain the concept of quality as a nod to the part of the soul that lies beyond the reach of objective science. As the 17th century shaded into the 18th, however, other empiricists were ready to complete the job that Galileo had started. While many philosophers contributed bits and pieces to the overall task, it fell to Bishop George Berkeley to finish stripping the scientific lexicon of all reference to quality. Why should primary qualities be exempt from suspicion, he wondered, since no information coming to the senses could be guaranteed to accurately represent the reality it was apprehending?

Ironically, Bishop Berkeley was reacting to what he considered to be the "atheistic materialism" toward which he felt science was heading. His dismissal of quality as a valid category of experience was a futile attempt to restore spiritual order to the old universe the empiricists had dismantled, for if no sensory data could be trusted, then what could be trusted in his estimation was revelation through the senses from the mind of God. God revealed the natural laws of his kingdom through the senses so that scientists could "discover" the nature of reality. Berkeley had no problem with scientists going about their business, as long as they were clear that sensory data and everything they encountered in the so-called material world was really of the mind, and ultimately rooted in the mind of God. Berkeley was really more of a rationalist than an empiricist, but he inadvertently galvanized the empiricists in their determination to dismiss anything they could not measure mathematically as unreal.

The final step toward removal of quality from the scientific lexicon was taken by a younger secular contemporary of Berkeley named David Hume, a bona fide empiricist, in the tradition of Galileo, Hobbes, Bacon and Locke. Hume agreed with Berkeley's questioning of the value of secondary qualities, but disagreed with his religious, rationalist solution. In fact, he inverted Berkeley's reasoning and declared that all ideas about the nature of reality must derive from sense perceptions. When he went looking for the mind, he could find nothing but a hodgepodge of sense impressions. When he went looking for God, much to the consternation of Berkeley, he found no sense impressions at all. He had the same experience looking for the soul, and concluded that all metaphysical assertions about the nature of reality were meaningless.

Hume also had a few choice observations about the limitations of the emerging scientific method being developed by his peers, to which we will return later. For now, it is sufficient to note that with the soul's displacement from the center of the sensory universe, the systematic denial of purpose, and the dismissal of qualitative information by the 17th and 18th century empiricists, not only did the emerging scientific paradigm level the subjective universe to what Ken Wilbur calls a "flatland" of mathematical propositions, but it also fostered a cultural atmosphere in which it was impossible to talk about the subjective experiences of the soul in a meaningful way. In describing this collapse of the soul's language, Wilbur observes that "[A]ll interiors were reduced to exteriors. All subjects were reduced to objects; all depth was reduced to surfaces; all I's and we's were reduced to its; all quality was reduced to quantity; levels of significance were reduced to levels of size; value was reduced to veneer..." (61).

In many ways, the empiricists' insistence on booting God off the seat of honor in the hall of scientific knowledge was a development whose time had come. As Descartes, Kant and others had declared, and as was becoming glaringly obvious even to diehard religious thinkers, the existence of God and the soul could not be proven or disproven by the emerging language of science. This did not mean – as the more secular of the empiricists tried to assert – that the soul did not exist, though it did mean that from this point forward it would prove difficult to talk about soul, as we are defining it here, in a way that either science or religion could accept. Speaking about soul required a qualitative language, yet neither side was comfortable with the notion of quality. Religion accepted quality on the light or positive end of the dualistic spectrum, but held heavy moral judgments about quality at the dark end. After Hume, science dismissed quality altogether.

The Necessity for Evolving a Language of Soul Capable of Qualitative Nuance

Without a recognition of quality, science lost its ability to talk about the human experience in a way that would be meaningful to the soul. Though subjective experiences can be described in both quantitative and qualitative terms, it is an awareness of quality that will best describe the unique experience of each individual. Quantity – which is actually well suited to a description of the external, objective world – does not communicate nearly as much information useful to a subjective quest for understanding. If experience is defined only in terms of objective, externally measurable quantities, there is no language in which to talk about individual differences, except as deviations from a statistical norm. In the subjective reality of the soul, the norm is meaningless, since within it there can be no reference to the actual experience of individuals, nor of the context in which that experience takes place. This is obviously true when individual experience tends toward some personal sense of purpose, but it is also true on the most basic level on which experience can be interpreted.

Two people side by side in the same room may have contradictory experiences say, of the temperature of the room, even though from an objective, quantitative perspective, the actual temperature of the room is the same for both people. One who has just been out jogging on a warm day, for example, might suddenly feel cold upon entering an air-conditioned room, while someone else who has been there all day, sitting at a desk, drinking coffee and struggling to meet a deadline, might be working up a sweat. Measured quantitatively, the sensory data would be the same for both people, but measured qualitatively, it is processed differently by each individual, since each individual is functioning within an entirely different subjective context.

A subjective language of soul must be flexible enough to articulate the nature of individual experiences in a broad variety of qualitative terms. Within the example described above, it may not even be sufficient to simply say that one person was hot while the other was cold. To explore the actual experience from the soul's perspective, we must consider a wide range of nuances in terminology, say from sweltering to feverish to sweaty to flushed to lukewarm at the hot end of the spectrum, to cool to shivering to clammy to hypothermic to frigid at the cool end. As discussed earlier in considering the inadequacy of the digital nature of Aristotelian logic, so too must we broaden the range of words we use to discuss subjective experience along any qualitative sensory continuum. Or put it in a way that is perhaps more relevant to the subject of this book, we must stretch our latent capacities as poets.

The same is true when considering emotional information. Just as two people might experience temperature or other sensory experiences differently, so too will they process the same event differently on an emotional level. Two siblings present at the death of a parent, for example, might have an entirely different emotional response. The one who felt tormented by the parent's constant criticism might feel guilty relief at being released from the bondage of the relationship; while the other sibling, having placed the parent on a pedestal and sought to please them, might suddenly be plunged into inconsolable grief, anger at being abandoned, and a profound sense of loss. With emotional information, as with sensory information, it is necessary to broaden the range of words we use to describe these emotional experiences. For even the category called grief can encompass an exquisitely poetic range of subjective flavors. One person's grief might be inconsolable and a debilitating source of chronic depression; another's might be an irritating distraction; a third person might experience grief in intermittent waves that throw her into an irrational tailspin of tearful rage.

The Qualitative Nature of Images That Feed the Soul

As any good poet will attest, images that contain the essential paradoxes that feed the soul, are also rendered as a description of quality, and with careful attention to nuance. Images are attractive to the soul, because they evoke a sensory, visceral response, rekindle dormant emotions, and point toward a constellation of possible meanings, some of which only make partial sense to the rational mind. As Jung defined it, "a symbol is an indefinite expression with many meanings, pointing to something not easily defined and therefore not fully known" (Symbols 124). The soul must feel its way toward understanding through the creative use of the imagination, which "thinks" in terms of quality. To really get to the heart of any subjective experience, we must speak poetically in terms that are intimately personal to each individual, and open to liberal subjective interpretation. This is not what science offers.

Instead, science rushes in to codify qualities in the same way that quantity is codified – that is to say, according to standardized definitions. Senses are stripped of their individual nuances, and redefined in terms of predictable responses to external stimuli. Emotions are eventually divorced from the palpable impact of individual life stories, and assigned to measurable and increasingly manipulable endocrine functions. Images, whether arising spontaneously in dreams, embodied in myth, or interpreted astrologically, are objectified and given generic definitions that are derived through statistical analysis of large numbers of observations. In all of these developments, individual experience has been increasingly subsumed under a collective umbrella, where it is catalogued, classified, and profiled. By the time the scientific revolution entered its second century, empiricism essentially meant the quest for measurable, objective truth, and the subjective realm of quality and nuance was increasingly discounted.

Within the subjective realm of imagery, it is my headache, my depression, and my dream about snakes that my soul is interested in articulating, not a quantified template designed to provide a one-size-fits-all explanation. To the extent that this is so, then all the cataloguing, categorization, and rational definition in the world cannot take me past the threshold of my soul's experience. Codified explanations can at best be helpful in getting me oriented to a range of possibilities, but they cannot substitute for the much more difficult task of discovering what is true for me. If I make no effort to move beyond them, they will merely provide a convenient default position that precludes asking the more difficult questions that might potentially lead to answers that are meaningful to me on the subjective level. Far more useful, from the soul's perspective, is the empirical effort to systematically track subjective experiences and discern the patterns and themes that emerge through their cumulative impact. Any true language of soul must leave standardized definitions behind and make room for a subjective empirical process that can lend poetic perspective to the irrational, sensory, emotional, and imagistic meanderings by which the soul circles in on itself.

Contemporary Astrology's Contamination By Objective Empiricism

Because astrology deals in symbolic images that are capable of triggering a recognition of subjective quality, astrology can be a useful foundation on which we might build a viable language of soul. However, astrology has not been exempt from the empirical passion for standardized definitions. Because early empiricists, including Aristotle, assumed that the rational mind was necessary to order all information, they sought to catalogue not just the sensory data derived through observation of the external world, but also the images of the mythopoetic world they were hoping to leave behind. Since these images were intimately entwined with the astrological worldview, empirically-minded astrologers, influenced by Aristotle's passion for cataloguing, sought standardized definitions for astrological symbols that could be readily accessible to the ordering principle of reason.

⋄⋄⋄⋄⋄⋄⋄⋄⋄⋄⋄⋄⋄⋄⋄⋄⋄⋄⋄⋄⋄⋄⋄⋄⋄⋄⋄⋄⋄⋄⋄⋄⋄⋄⋄⋄

The Egyptian astronomer Ptolemy, in particular, undertook the monumental task in the 2nd century CE, of ordering astrological principles along rational lines, which could be empirically verified. As a result of this prodigious effort astrological symbols were quickly rendered less useful to the soul, and cast in dogmatic terms that they would be interpreted according to set definitions. Ptolemy felt that because astrology attempted to describe the realm of human affairs in terms of quality, it was necessarily a less exact science than physics or astronomy. He also believed, however, that it was possible to understand the qualities suggested by astrological symbols in an objective way, and set the tone for future astrological investigations up to the present day.

As considerations of quality became discredited in empirical circles of the 17th and 18th century, astrology – which relied on qualitative analysis - was also dismissed as meaningless. There are other reasons for this dismissal, which we will discuss later, but most of them revolve around astrology's inability to prove its validity in quantitative terms. Astrologers since then have taken the scientific challenge seriously, scrambling to verify astrology's assessments through statistical analysis and other objective measures that are inadequate criteria by which to assess a subjective language of quality. Despite the proliferation of individual astrologers practicing a blatantly qualitative art, contemporary astrology as a whole has yet to recover from Ptolemy's influence, which drives many sincere practitioners out of the realm of symbolism altogether and into a soulless quest for empirical objectivity.

Before astrology can become truly useful as a language of soul, we must strip it of its pretensions toward quantifiable objectivity. The assumption of most astrologers is that if they gather enough evidence for the way in which a particular symbol or symbolic pattern works, that evidence will gain authority as an objective definition which they can then use to interpret the chart of someone else with a similar symbol or pattern in their chart. This is an assumption based upon unconscious scientific conditioning, which confuses objectivity for truth. If the goal is to articulate a collective consensus reality, then scientific empiricism is entirely appropriate. If the goal, however, is to chart the interior life of an individual soul, then what matters is not how a given symbol has manifested across the board for other people, but how it is manifesting within the context of a particular life process. To make this kind of assessment, we need empirical data – not from others outside this context, but from within the context itself. We must evolve a methodology for exploring the symbol or symbolic pattern subjectively, in relation to the individual life story to which it refers.

Any true language of soul must be subjective, must restore a sense of purpose to the discussion of the soul's process, and must pay careful attention to the quality of the soul's experience - especially on the sensory, emotional and imagistic levels on which that experience registers. This experience cannot be adequately articulated with reference to standardized definitions or categories of explanation. Instead, our evolving understanding of a given soul's process must be rendered poetically, through words marinated in subjective nuance and intimately personal associations that may or may not be meaningful to anyone but the individual making them.

In order to pass through Inanna's fourth gate, then, we must relieve the soul of any requirement that it define itself in measurable terms. In its insistence on objective, mathematical empiricism, devoid of considerations of quality or purpose, science is an inadequate paradigm through which to provide such a language. Though its empirical approach to gathering information can be useful to an exploration of soul, it must first be turned inward, refocused on the quality of the soul's experience, and given expression through an intimately personal language of poetic nuance. With some modification in attitude and approach, astrology can provide a model for this path of subjective empiricism, and a conceptual platform on which this poetic language of soul can be built.

Endnotes

[1] I am speaking here of orthodox mainstream religion. The mystical and esoteric traditions within most religions do have an empirical process for understanding the flow of Spirit into the body – through meditation, yoga, fasting, silent retreat, trance work, ecstatic dancing, and other spiritual disciplines. To the extent that these experiential schools also encourage participation within the embodied world through good works, compassion, karma yoga, *seva* (or service), spiritual community, and other forms of giving back, then they also encourage an understanding of the movement of the soul back to Spirit. Outside of the context of these experiential traditions, however, mainstream religions do not encourage an activation of the immanent spirit within, but rather an allegiance to the transcendent Spirit that exists beyond the embodied world, and to the religious authority that mediates between Spirit and the soul. Neither mainstream religion nor experiential traditions stress the subjective nature of the process, since both promote a one-size-fits-all approach to spiritual experience.

Chapter Nine
Shedding the Scientific Concept of Causality

Once science had divorced itself from all discussion of purpose and subjective quality of experience, it was reduced to a consideration of simple mechanics – the *how* of natural phenomena. Implied in this narrow focus was the principle of causality, which states that if any change occurs within the observable world, something must have set that change in motion. This idea was also endemic to Western religious tradition, and to many early philosophers who considered God or Spirit to be the First Cause, as well as to Eastern religions who subscribed to the causal laws of *karma*. But since religious and philosophical causes could not be measured objectively, they quickly became purged from the scientific lexicon. Science postulated that reality could be defined as a complex interplay of cause and effect that was inherently measurable. Conversely, anything that could not be described in terms of this more limited concept of cause and effect was considered to be outside of the scope of science. After the empiricists demonstrated that the embodied world was amenable to the measurement of causes, science began to conduct itself increasingly within the strict context of this assumption.

Lost in this conceptual revolution were all metaphysical questions that addressed the *why* of phenomena, the purpose for which they occurred, and the spiritual dimensions of existence. But as philosopher of science, E. A. Burtt points out, those who deny the metaphysical underpinnings of reality, will nonetheless operate within a metaphysical framework chosen unconsciously and by default (229). Typically, they will assume that their own methodology dictates the nature of whatever it is they are investigating. When science began distancing itself from religion and philosophy, this is exactly what happened. While science was still establishing itself, from the 17th through the mid 18th centuries, it was humble enough to admit its limitations in asking metaphysical questions about meaning and purpose. In these matters, it deferred to religious authorities, who themselves were gradually becoming confined to smaller circles of credibility and influence. As the theory of cause and effect proved its validity through countless experiments in a wide range of applications, and the intellectual authority of religious thinkers shrank, the scientific mindset became increasingly intolerant of these troublesome metaphysical questions.

By the dawn of the 19th century, most scientists took for granted that metaphysical considerations were irrelevant to an understanding of reality. Anything that was outside the range of causal explanation was either not real, not worthy of investigation, or both.

◇◇

The fact that the Church had actively persecuted or condemned many seminal scientists during preceding centuries for their beliefs only served to widen the schism between science and religion, and create a deeper sympathy for the emerging scientific viewpoint within secular society. Meanwhile, as the Church lost its political authority and its power to influence society outside of its immediate circle of believers, and science refused to address the soul's metaphysical "why" questions about purpose, such questions were increasingly left without a language with which to address them.

Questions about "how" – ostensibly the domain of science – are also of interest to the soul, particularly when the soul becomes concerned with the logistics of actualizing its potential. The soul will want to know not just why it came into being, but how it can best fulfill the purpose for which it exists. Since science does not recognize the reality of soul as the cause, or effect, of anything, nor the concept of purpose as a legitimate framework in which to ask meaningful questions, it can offer very little to the soul, even within this secondary realm of logistics. Before we present an alternative to what science has to offer, it may be enlightening to explore causality's evolution as a conceptual cornerstone of the scientific worldview in more depth. When we then remove it from the foundation of our language of soul, we can more fully appreciate the ways in which this action liberates us to speak about soul in a more meaningful way.

Aristotle's Distinction of Types of Cause

Aristotle was the first thinker to discuss the idea of causality as a scientific concept. As part of his effort to clarify the discussion of the rational cosmologists through the use of logic, Aristotle observed that the possible answers to the question of why things are the way they are fell into four different categories. One could say that something was the way it was, because it was made of a particular material, which would then describe its *material cause*. One could say that something was what it was because it fit the formal definition for that thing, which would be an expression of *formal cause*. One could say that something was what it was because of the forces, conditions, or experiences that shaped it, a designation of what Aristotle called *efficient cause*. Or one could say that something was what it was because it was striving to fulfill a given purpose, as a consequence of *final* or *teleological cause*.

To the extent that science is oriented to "why" questions at all, it is concerned strictly with material causes and efficient causes – the stuff of which something is made and the forces that bring it into being. What are most relevant to the soul's understanding of itself, on the other hand, are final causes, and perhaps to a lesser extent, formal causes. The soul wants to know where it is going, and what purpose this life serves – a process that can be understood with reference to final causes. Because an answer to these questions depends on an understanding of the soul's essential nature, and is a matter of actualizing its potential, as Aristotle believed to be true, the soul's most pressing questions can also be answered through reference to formal causes.

"Who am I?" asks the soul, and "What is my purpose?"

"You are a carbon-based life from composed of skin and bones and various internal organs," answers science, "and you are a product of genetic conditioning passed on from your parents and the external sociocultural forces that shaped your personality."

The soul is only partially satisfied at best with these answers, since they do not acknowledge its relationship to Spirit and thus cannot penetrate to the core of its spiritual essence. Nor can they explain why this essence has chosen to manifest in the unique way that it has, within the context of its subjective life process. But material and efficient causes suit science's purpose, because they easily lend themselves to objective, quantitative measurement. They affirm the methodology, and reinforce the use of it to explain the nature of reality in terms that continue to affirm it. Reality is material and causal in nature because the methodology scientists use to measure it does not register evidence pointing to other possibilities. There is no final cause or purpose underlying the measurable universe, because science cannot measure it. The soul does not exist because it does not show up, in science's exclusive focus upon efficient and material causes. This circular reasoning then becomes the basis for science's unconscious metaphysics, which leaves the soul's most pressing questions unanswered.

Formal causes, though strictly speaking outside the range of science, can be bent to fit a scientific paradigm, as they often are in the widespread practice of psychological profiling, standardized typologies, and diagnoses. This can only be accomplished if subjective differences are reinterpreted as deviation from a statistical norm. The very concept of deviation implies that it is the norm that is important here, while from the soul's perspective, it is the deviation that makes the soul what it is. Formal causes can also be a legitimate focus of a soul's inquiry into its own nature, but only if the inquiry is based upon qualitative evaluation of subjective information that is unique to the individual. While formal causes are treated objectively by science, the soul understands them subjectively, since it is *your* soul that propels you on a quest for answers about the meaning and purpose of *your* life – not the idealized life of some hypothetical statistically average person.

Meanwhile, this subjective information is routinely and systematically discounted by science, since it does not lend itself to a methodical quest for efficient causes. Sensory impressions, emotions, and imagery are all perpetually in flux, and as such, cannot be understood to be the efficient cause of anything. They are, according to science, the effects of causes that are material in nature – biological, biochemical, neurological, genetic,

◇◇

or some combination of the four. Lost altogether is any sense at all of how subjective experiences can potentially lead the soul to a recognition of the formal and final causes which contribute to its sense of identity or purpose.

Science can perhaps explain how the senses are triggered neurologically, or biochemically, but it has nothing to say about what these sensations are trying to communicate to the soul that is bound to the body in which they are experienced. Science can empirically test hypotheses about the correlation of emotions with endocrine imbalances, or genetic predispositions, but it cannot articulate the ways in which these emotional experiences can be used by a soul struggling to understand and actualize its spiritual potential. Science will one day likely begin to understand how specific projected images are hardwired into the neurochemistry of the brain, but unless it broadens its *a priori* assumptions, it will never understand the purposes for which these images are projected, because it will never even ask the relevant questions. It will instead, content itself with explanations limited to material and efficient cause. It will tolerate discussion of formal causes, but only within strict categories that it standardizes, and it will dismiss all concerns with final causes as unworthy of consideration.

The Implications of a World Devoid of Final Cause

A language of soul must not only address these concerns, but also reaffirm their central importance to the human experience. In a postmodern world in which science provides the dominant language, we expect questions about why we are here to be answered, once and for all, shortly after the onset of puberty, and to be narrowly focused in terms of career aspirations. This limiting focus produces an educational system that measures its effectiveness primarily by how well students perform on standardized tests, rather than how well it prepares each individual student to fulfill the purpose for which they were born. Rare indeed would be the school that even bothered to ask such a question. Instead, most schools strive to prepare their students to take a functional place within the job market, but never address the soul's need to know and actualize itself. A scientific culture stresses preparation for contributing to an agenda set by others, rather than guiding each individual toward the fulfillment of a vision of self-actualization arising from within. It serves powerful economic, political and military masters well, but leaves the individual soul stranded in an environment hostile to the evolution of a more intimately personal and more deeply spiritual sense of identity and purpose. It measures the worth of a human being by salary, social status, and external achievements, rather than by the more subtle assessment of whether or not an individual has been true to his inner calling.

Any sense of purpose not identified with productivity, defined in terms of the collective agenda, is at best marginalized within a scientific culture, and often dismissed as a waste of human potential. Relationships become utilitarian vehicles for satisfying needs or furthering societal agendas. The individual gets squeezed between a set of media images designed to promote a saleable brand of individuality with mass appeal, and a social code that is secretly terrified of true individuality. True individuals – who are actively attempting to actualize their soul's agenda with only incidental reference to objective, consensual standards of behavior – are likely to find themselves perpetually at odds with a control-oriented educational system, a corporate job environment, a natural world which is sacrificed to the march of progress, and an homogenized consumer culture defined by a consolidated media that punishes in subtle, and sometimes not so subtle ways, any serious deviation from the norm.

An activated soul questions its motives and its agenda at every meaningful juncture, and to the extent that it participates in society, it will also want to know why we are collectively doing what we are doing. A society whose unspoken assumptions are tacitly dictated by a scientific mindset concerned only with questions of "how," will find the questions of soul embarrassing, ludicrous, distracting, threatening, and at times, all of the above. Individuals who ask such questions – those who are actively attempting to attune themselves to soul – will be marginalized, discredited and/or ostracized, if not thrown in jail for threatening the status quo through their refusal to play by rules that do not serve their best interest. In the current political climate, as we crank up the war on terrorism, those who intentionally stand apart from the consensual mindset in order to think for themselves and cultivate a more personal sense of identity and purpose become increasingly suspect, even though they are doing nothing wrong.

A scientific culture that asks only "how," but not "why," will inevitably outstrip its ability to process the consequences of the policies it pursues until after measurable damage has been done. It will shoot first and ask the harder questions later, if at all, simply because it has the technology to accomplish its objectives. Humans will likely be cloned by other humans sometime in the 21st century, for example, despite the moral objections of the few, simply because one day in the not too distant future, we will know how to do it. Questions about the rights of these individuals, their relationship to the rest of society and to those who are responsible for bringing them into this world, and many other questions we won't even have the foresight to ask before it happens, will be left for future generations to resolve. Questions about soul and about who or what these beings are in a spiritual sense may never even be addressed, although surely an embodied soul created in a laboratory from genetic material belonging to another will be different than one that is simply born. But the scientific mindset does not concern itself with metaphysical implications. For the scientist, and for the culture that revolves around the scientific mindset, knowing how is all it takes to trigger the march of progress.

Meanwhile, it is tragically ironic that a scientific culture predicated on an assessment of efficient causes is apparently so disinterested in measuring the consequences of collective actions on the quality of individual experience. Instead, it uses statistics to justify collective actions that leave significant numbers of individuals out in the cold, in precarious circumstances, or at risk. If something can be done, if there are measurable amounts of money to be made doing it, if "collateral damage" can be kept below the radar screen of measurable detection, if discovery of undesirable effects can be postponed and passed on to future generations, then questions of final cause – "Why we are doing what we do?" and "Is it really in our best interest to be doing it?" – can be dismissed. We may pay lip service to these questions, but they are not the driving engine for change.

Certainly, not all scientists are so shortsighted, or cynically self-motivated. But in a scientific culture with no language of soul for addressing final causes, or subjectively determined formal causes, this will become our default attitude toward what we do as a society. Since science refuses any metaphysical context that would require it to question its own purpose or limit its capabilities, or even ask which course of action is in our best interest as a society, its resources are often easily co-opted by those with little interest in the truth that science is capable of revealing. Science is, to some extent, regulated by government, but government – especially a government increasingly controlled by corporate interests and harnessed to an agenda based on control of information – also easily bends science to its own purposes with the skillful sophistry of political spin doctors. Operating from within this co-opted scientific mindset, we have and will continue to collectively act in ways that leave future generations wondering what we could possibly have been thinking when we did the foolish things that we did. Perhaps the fault rests more squarely in the political arena, but science provides a soulless language of justification to those all too ready to abuse it, and cannot be excused from complicity in the outcome.

The Limitations of Efficient Cause As An Explanation For Subjective Behavior

But I digress. Despite the fact that a sense of final cause or purpose is necessary to the soul, and is missing in science, we might – instead of dismissing science altogether – keep the scientific idea of cause and effect and simply add the notion of final cause to the mix. Efficient cause is, after all, a useful concept in helping to explain how we got to be the way we are. It is used all the time, for example, in discussions of developmental psychology. Your mother neglected you, and now you feel insecure. Your first three marriages failed, and now you are convinced that marriage is not for you. Because there is a history of heart attacks in your family, you assume that it is wise for you to pay special attention to the condition of your own heart, as you grow older. We routinely make these kinds of correlations, based on efficient causes, and often they are valid and helpful.

The idea of efficient cause and effect is also thoroughly integrated into the Eastern mindset through the concept of *karma*. If we choose to be mean-spirited, hurtful, and abusive in this life, then our actions will eventually come back to haunt us. Conversely, if we choose to express the most positive qualities within us, do good deeds, and live a righteous life, we will be rewarded – if not in this life – then presumably the next. In a spiritual sense, our actions cause ripples in the pond of our existence, which in turn manifest effects that condition our experience. Whether we look to Western science or Eastern religion, the message is the same: regardless of the ultimate purpose for which we exist, there are rules and consequences on the way to the fulfillment of that purpose that we can understand in terms of efficient causes. And on a practical level, this is obviously true.

If our goal, however, is to understand the soul in subjective terms, as the standard by which its own truth must be measured, then the notion of efficient cause is an inadequate measure of our relationship to the embodied world. To conceive of our relationship to the world in terms of efficient causes is to entertain one of two possibilities: a) that the objective world is the cause of our subjective state of being; or b) that our subjective state of being is the cause of the state of the world. While these assertions may appear to be true in a limited sense, they are rather misleading. What happens in the world can definitely have an effect on us, and trigger something subjective within us, but the world is not ultimately the cause of who we are. In fact, in stepping back from the world's impact on us, we are likely to discover our most essential identity. Tribal cultures routinely encouraged, and in some cases required their young people to undergo a rite of passage called the vision quest, in which they sought a personal understanding of formal cause, and perhaps final cause, in solitude away from the tribe. They understood that these causes came not from the objective world, but from the presence of Spirit within us.

Considering the second possibility, we must acknowledge that it is possible to have an impact on the world, and hopefully as we find our purpose, we will have a powerful positive impact. But regardless of how significant that impact is, we are not ultimately responsible for the world being as it is. Nor is our subjective state of being the cause of anything outside ourselves. New Agers like to say that we create our own reality, which is true on a subjective level, but makes no sense if what we mean by this is that if we get our act together, it will change the essential nature of the world. From the soul's perspective, the world remains what it is, while our projections onto it evolve to reflect our internal process. At best, we can temporarily shift the drama generated by the interplay of opposites in one direction or another, within our own world and within our sphere of influence. But because we live in a cyclical world where the opposites are constantly evolving into each other, pressure in any direction produces an equal and opposite pressure to counterbalance it, and the pendulum eventually swings back the other way. This is the nature of the embodied world, conditioned by polarity, and no amount of subjective effort will ever dismantle the pendulum, or cause the world to be fundamentally different.

If human beings were capable of changing the world itself, then surely Christ's brief sojourn on the planet ought to have ushered in a golden age of kindness, tolerance, compassion, and all the other noble sentiments that he taught. Instead, it was followed by a long slow painful pendulum swing through a history of religious intolerance, narrow-mindedness, violence, institutionalized abuse, and spiritual divisiveness that continues to this day. By a similar argument, the lives of Gandhi, Martin Luther King, John Kennedy, Mother Teresa, Albert Einstein and countless other light beings who made a significant difference while they were here, ought to have changed the nature of the world in positive, recognizable ways, but they did not. Instead, each evoked a response in equal measure from the dark end of the spectrum.

Gandhi watched the beloved freedom he sought for India from the oppression of British colonialism degenerate into civil war, when the British left the country. Martin Luther King worked tirelessly for the civil rights of black Americans, only to be shot at the height of his power. Had he lived, he would be appalled at the current practice of racial profiling, the disproportionate numbers of young black males in prison today, and the dismantling of affirmative action by a reverse discrimination backlash. Albert Einstein, who was perhaps one of the most enlightened scientists to ever walk the planet, and a truly peace-loving man, suffered the bitter disgrace of watching his revolutionary theoretical breakthroughs harnessed to the machinery of war, and the creation of the atomic bomb.

The World as a Mirror for the Interplay of Light and Dark

Though individual souls have undoubtedly grown to live better lives because these great beings showed the way, the world per se is every bit the same battleground between light and dark today that it was 2,000 years ago, or indeed since creation set all the polarities that define our world in motion. In fact, we could reasonably argue that given our increased technological capacity to destroy ourselves, the entire battle has intensified. The faces of the protagonists change endlessly, we occasionally shift arenas, the challenges evolve, and from time to time the forces of both light and darkness will appear to wax and wane, but as long as the embodied world exists, the battle will rage on, beyond the reach of cause and effect. It's not that the efforts of these brave souls were in vain, but the world is hardwired for reflex action, and there is nothing that any of us can do to change that.

Some would call this reflex action, cause and effect, as Newton did in his Second Law of Thermodynamics. But my sense is that this movement from light to dark and back again is really just a reflection of the endless Cycle of Life and Death turning, of yin changing into yang, of day changing into night. One day, the Great Chief of Death shows the beautiful side of his face; the next day, he shows the side that is crawling with maggots. We don't cause the Cycle of Life and Death, nor all of the smaller cycles of which the Great Cycle is composed, nor do they cause us to be who we are. We merely participate in them. How we participate reflects who we are as embodied souls, and who we become as we either grow into the Wholeness of our Being or fragment with the passing of the body. The cycles play themselves out endlessly within the embodied world and within us, and the world itself simply mirrors this process. We who encounter the world, respond to it, and our response in turn, shows us who we are, and what we have entered a body to do. The more clearly and fearlessly we embody this knowledge, the more apparent it becomes that it is *we* who are changing in relation to the world, not the *world* that is changing in relation to us.

In most esoteric traditions, it is the illusion that the world is in need of changing, and that the individual can cause the world to change, that characterizes the immature soul. As Siddha guru, Swami Muktananda once advised his students, "As long as a saint is aware of the world as the world, he is not a saint. He becomes a saint only when the world has vanished completely" (255). If we define the world as the arena in which the endless dance of polarities plays itself out, then from this perspective, the only way to change the world is to make an internal shift in consciousness beyond the reach of duality. This shift, however, does not cause the world to change for anyone other than the one making the shift. In an objective sense, the world will continue to be what it always has been – a mirror to the state of being we bring to it, whatever that might be, both collectively and as individuals. I can change *my* world by changing my consciousness of who I am in relation to it. But the world itself is only the ongoing reflection of my state of being, not the result of my effort, nor the effect of anything I am capable of causing to happen.

The more mystical among us might argue that Spirit is ultimately the cause of everything, and that as the individual soul realizes its identity with Spirit, it participates more directly in the ongoing creation of the world. But this too, is more a matter of being than of doing. If I experience myself to be one with Spirit, then I experience the embodied world as an extension of Myself. The notion of cause and effect has no meaning, since everything simply emanates from and returns to the One that I am. Until I reach that blessed state, movement toward this liberating realization is only possible through a shift in consciousness that I cannot will or cause to happen. Quite the contrary, it is only as I relinquish my sense of myself as "the doer" or cause of anything outside myself, that I am capable of opening to the state of being in which this shift in consciousness becomes possible. As mystical poet, Kabir, says:

> The spiritual athlete often changes the color of his clothes,
> And his mind remains gray and loveless.
>
> Or he sits inside a shrine room all day,
> so that God has to go out and praise the rocks.
>
> He drills holes in his ears, his beard grows enormous and matted,
> People mistake him for a goat...
> He goes out into wilderness areas, strangles his impulses,
> Makes himself neither male nor female...
>
> He shaves his skull, puts his robe in an orange vat,
> Reads the Bhagavad Gita, and becomes a terrific talker.
>
> Kabir says: Actually, you are going in a hearse to the country of death,
> Bound hand and foot.

Yaqui brujo, Don Juan, states the human predicament just as bluntly when he says, "we must know first that our acts are useless and yet we must proceed as if we didn't know it. That is a sorcerer's controlled folly" (Castenada, Separate Reality 97). Controlled folly is the relatively enlightened realization that our participation in the embodied world is not the cause or effect of anything, but a statement of being. Everything we do makes a statement of being that resonates throughout the web that weaves the embodied world into a seamless whole. The world in turn reflects back to us the statement we have made, and appears to shift in subtle ways to accommodate the being that we have become as a consequence of our doing. But the world is just a mirror, in which Spirit knows itself through us, and the mirror remains a mirror, untouched in its essence by the reflections that move like clouds across its face.

According to Don Juan, a spiritual warrior (the conscious doer in each of us) relates to the world most effectively by following a path with heart. The spiritual warrior does this not to change or benefit the world, but in response to the calling of her own soul, which longs to become whole and experience the full vibrancy of Spirit within her. If a path has heart, it creates an opening to this experience of Spirit; if it doesn't, life becomes empty and mechanical. As Don Juan states, "Both paths lead nowhere, but one has a heart, the other doesn't. One makes for a joyful journey; as long as you follow it, you are one with it. The other will make you curse your life. One makes you strong; the other weakens you" (Castenada, Teachings 122). The object of following a path with heart is not to change the world, but to experience the presence of Spirit within us more consciously and to give clear expression to this awareness through our being in the world.

This does not mean our actions do not matter, but they matter much more to us than they do to the world. Obviously, we can and do have impact within the range of effective motion that management consultant, Steven Covey, calls our personal "circle of influence" (82). But even within this relatively limited reach, as embodied souls, we are not the cause of what other people do or don't do because of our presence in their lives. Nor are we the cause of how the world responds to our presence within it, any more than sun and rain cause the seeds that bloom under their attention to become what they become. If this is true, there must be some way other than cause and effect to understand our relationship to the embodied world. Cause and effect is useful in understanding how the external objects of the physical world work, but it doesn't help us much when we want to know who we are in relation to the rest of creation, and why we are here.

Hume's Critique of Causality

This is hardly the first time the value of causality has been called into question. The 18th century empirical philosopher, David Hume pointed out the limiting nature of cause and effect as a conceptual paradigm in great detail. While his contemporary, Kant was outlining the limitations of reason as a tool for exploring metaphysical truth, Hume was questioning the limitations of causality on similar grounds. Earlier empiricists had dismissed Aristotle's notion of final cause two centuries earlier, but Hume questioned the very notion of cause itself. Hume believed that human experience was rooted in sensory perception, and that what we could not actually experience, we could not know for certain. Since the mind never actually experiences cause happening, he argued, there is nothing within human experience to confirm causality as an organizing principle of reality.

Instead the mind experiences a juxtaposition of events, and interprets their relationship to be causal. Since B consistently *follows* A, the assumption is made that A *causes* B. But we never actually perceive this happening; we merely infer it, and then we grow to expect it, as a habit of thought. Science infers cause as an explanation for what it can't observe, in other words, and then interprets what it does see as evidence of cause. The explanation seems reasonable, especially if the experienced juxtaposition of A and B is consistent and universal – as it would be in a scientific experiment sufficiently replicated. This is the basis of inductive reasoning, and has been a cornerstone of objective knowledge, ever since empiricists began documenting the consistency of the relationship between A and B. According to Hume, however, it is an assumption about the nature of that relationship, and not an actual fact, verifiable by observation.

The assumption is not an actual description of reality, but an intellectual sleight of hand that allows us to speak about what we can't actually confirm by direct experience. Science actually does this in every arena in which it exercises its empirical capacity. No one has ever actually seen an atom, or the genetic code, or a black hole, or radioactivity. These ideas about the nature of reality are all inferred from observations that *can* be made. Given sufficient repetition, the inferences are then taken to be fact. Science derives its immense intellectual power through the brilliant fusion of observation and inference. As reasonable as this approach to understanding of objective reality appears to us today, it is important to note that the evolution of inductive reasoning was actually a gradual and at times painful fusion of two radically divergent schools of philosophical thought,

The Birth of Modern Empiricism

The rationalist school, first championed by Socrates and Plato, and brought to its most convincing expression in Descartes, had thoroughly mistrusted information derived from the senses. The rationalists argued that the mind could only understand reality through a process of logic and deductive reasoning. The empiricists, beginning with Aristotle and flowering into full bloom with Bacon, Locke and Hobbes, argued conversely that sensory information was primary. Reason was perhaps useful in bringing order to sensory information. But if the sensory data did not demonstrate a verifiable fact, then reason alone could not legitimately jump to any deductive conclusions. Reason alone, they argued, was incapable of discerning truth, and empirical data was necessary to anchor reason to the objective world.

As unlikely as it would have been in the days when the rational cosmologists held court, it was the gradual fusion of sensory observation with the deductive power of reason that gave science the intellectual authority that it wields today. It can be argued, in fact, that this was the essence of the empirical revolution that took place from the 16th through the 19th centuries. It took the better part of three centuries for these two schools of thought to merge seamlessly, because for at least two millennia prior to that reason and sensory awareness were considered to be antithetical to one another. It was this synthesis of opposites nonetheless that gave science the tool of inductive reasoning, which in turn allowed it to claim, among other things, that we live in a causal world.

Despite their general mistrust of reason, empiricists would typically begin their observation with a rational hypothesis - a philosophical speculation, which they then sought to confirm or refute by experiment. Aristotle had framed all of his biological studies within a metaphysical context that postulated God as the Final Cause of everything that could possibly happen within the natural world. Kepler began his scientific explorations of planetary orbits only after convincing himself that the universe was fundamentally mathematical in nature, and that God was a master mathematician. Galileo invented the telescope, not to empirically determine the structure of the solar system, but so he could confirm his belief in the theories of Copernicus and the Neoplatonists about the mathematical ordering of the planetary spheres. For these early empiricists, metaphysical theory came first, and empirical experimentation was a means of testing that theory.

It was Francis Bacon who first suggested that perhaps this approach to science was putting the cart before the horse. He did not dispute the notion that reason was necessary to order the information derived from the senses, but he argued that empirical research ought to come first, and conclusions only later, after enough data had been gathered to warrant them. With Bacon, the metaphysics underlying the scientific method began to slip into the unconscious, as Burtt warned it would, making methodology the primary determinant of truth. When Newton took Bacon's suggestion to heart, he effectively launched the modern scientific method – a process without preconceived ideas about the outcome of experiments, predicated on an a deductive assumption of a causal model, confirmed by careful empirical observation, and drawn to a conclusion through cautious inductive reasoning. Unlike scientists before him, Newton came to his research relatively free of metaphysical speculations. He dispensed with the notion of hypothesis, and vowed to stay close to the phenomena under study, only gradually coaxing an explanation from the actual data. It was largely through his example, that the pattern for subsequent scientific investigation was set.

The persistent problem, however, as Hume pointed out, was that there was still a gap between what could be observed and what could be concluded about what was observed. No matter how many times A followed B, it was still a leap of faith to conclude that A would always follow B as an irrefutable fact or law of nature. The more often A was observed following B, the less risky the leap would seem, but there was still no empirical basis for assuming a causal explanation without this leap. Inductive reasoning allowed scientists to bridge the gap between empirical observation and rational conclusion and stake their claim to a confirmation of causality. Hume refused to accept this artful little device as a legitimate mechanism for the derivation of human knowledge. He stood instead in a long thin line of skeptics stretching back 2,000+ years to the Sophists, by declaring that the only possible knowledge of the world was inherently subjective.

This stance is all the more profound given the fact that Hume had actually set out to apply the principles of objective, inductive, causal science to the human mind, but found that he could not. Instead, he concluded that the mind was a bundle of disjointed sense impressions that could not be ordered in any reliable way, and all scientific pretensions to objective knowledge were unfounded. Kant later sidestepped Hume's dilemma by suggesting that the world was unknowable except through organization of sense impressions by the mind. Objective knowledge was, by definition, a reflection of the way in which the mind interpreted reality in its own image. Since the mind naturally wants to make the leap from direct observation to inductive conclusion, Kant argued that inductive conclusions are a legitimate basis – indeed the only possible basis – for objective knowledge. If, on this basis, we form the inductive conclusion that A following B implies causality, then causality must also be an *a priori* organizing principle of objective knowledge.

Kant agreed with Hume that a leap must be made to get from what could be observed to what could be known. As pointed out in Chapter Five, he also made a clear distinction between the objective realm in which science had some legitimate authority, and the metaphysical realm in which ultimate truths had their roots. But as he watched Newton make the leap from sensory data to inductive conclusion quite convincingly – both in his study of optics, and in his articulation of the laws of gravity – Kant parted company with Hume, concluding that causality was a legitimate way to explain what science observed about objective reality. As also previously pointed out, he then dismissed scientists from Sunday school classes, freeing them to go their own way without philosophical remorse. They took their assumption of causality with them, and Hume's protest was left in the dust of history, still largely unanswered.

Toward an Acausal Principle of Soul

If Hume is right, however, then the whole notion of causality is arbitrary, and we might just as well identify a different kind of relationship between A and B that better suits the soul's needs. Within a cyclical universe, A's relationship to B need not be understood as causal. Instead, A and B could be part of a cycle unfolding. Day follows night, and night follows day, but neither causes the other. A scientist would say that both are caused by the rotation of the Earth about its axis, within the context of its relationship to the Sun. But this begs the question, "What causes the Earth to turn about its axis?" Science, of course, has an explanation for this, as well. But the Earth turning about its axis and the alternation of day with night could just as easily be part of a larger invisible process, which is acausal in nature.

For every cause induced from empirical data, a larger conceptual framework can be imagined, in which causality need not be the only possible explanation. Take this process back far enough, and we arrive at a consideration of First Cause, construed by Aristotle and other early philosophers, as God. Here the inductive gap gleefully leaped by scientists suddenly widens to become the impassable chasm between modern science and metaphysics. Take the process one step beyond that, however, and we arrive at something that has no cause. If we ask the question, "What causes God?" the only answer possible, without dismissing the idea of God altogether, is "Nothing. God just is." If soul is the participation of God, or Spirit, in matter, then discussion of the soul is an arena in which the principle of causality also breaks down.

If we deny human existence its origin in Spirit, as scientists do, then we can understand it in purely causal terms. The embodied soul divorced from Spirit is just another ball on the billiard table of space and time. Bring Spirit back into the equation, however, and the basis of the soul's subjective reality becomes its participation in the Great Cycle of Life and Death - which is acausal in nature. Within the Cycle, the flow of life will still appear to be causal. B will still follow A with predictable regularity. But the Cycle itself is beyond cause. The Cycle is without beginning or end, is self-perpetuating, immortal and eternal, and like Spirit, nothing causes it. It just is. If the soul's purpose is to open to its Wholeness, and return to God, while bringing Spirit more consciously into the embodied world, then a full experience of the Cycle is the mechanism for doing this. Since both Spirit and the Cycle exist beyond cause, then the soul's journey cannot be understood in terms of causality. Some other explanation must be found that better suits its purpose.

In fairness, it should be noted that although hardcore science has marched toward a soulless future with metaphysical impunity, not all important thinkers since Hume have been able to dismiss his question about the arbitrary nature of causal explanations, nor Aristotle's concern with purpose. A long tradition of philosophers, writers and scientists – stretching from Hume through the German thinkers Goethe, Hegel, Heidegger and Jaspers to Einstein, Jung, Bergson, and Teilhard de Chardin – has sought to bring soul back into an understanding of reality, both internal and external. As suggested in Chapter One, the soul's questions are perennial, and durable enough to persist, despite mainstream science's dismissal of them. To the extent that science is still at heart a sincere quest for truth, then science must also continue to wrestle unconsciously, if not consciously, with metaphysical questions posed by soul, even though it will insist its interest lies elsewhere. Science will also edge closer to an understanding of reality that is acausal in nature, since it cannot penetrate to the heart of the mystery of life it attempts to study without following all cause back to its origin in no-cause.

Chapter Ten
Toward an Acausal Understanding
Of Soul Process

A major recent contribution to the quest for an acausal understanding of the soul's experience has been made by Rupert Sheldrake. Sheldrake is a cutting edge scientist and former Director of Studies in biochemistry and cell biology at Clare College, Cambridge University in England. Following in the footsteps of Hume, Sheldrake suggests that all the causal regularities in nature that traditional scientists consider as immutable laws are nothing more than habits. To explain the habits of nature, he suggests a mechanism called morphogenetic resonance, through which all of nature – including animate life and even supposedly inanimate objects - have a kind of collective memory, which both conditions how it functions in the short term, and allows for evolution in the long term. Put another way, morphogenetic resonance is the influence of like upon like through space and time. All things that are, in some way, like each other, will share a resonance through which information is transmitted and memory becomes a common resource. Through participation in the same morphogenetic field, habits are cultivated which scientists interpret as causal relationships. These habits, however, are changeable once new information enters the morphogenetic field and begins to influence the behavior of all those who share the resonance of the field.

Sheldrake's theory of morphogenetic resonance is a radical departure from science as usual, and more traditional scientists cling to their habit of explaining everything that happens in terms of causality with fierce tenacity. Sheldrake's ideas have been thoroughly castigated by a handful of vociferous critics within the scientific community, among them Sir John Maddox, Emeritus Editor of the scientific journal, *Nature*. In a review of Sheldrake's first book, *A New Science of Life*, Maddox wrote, "This infuriating tract . . . is the best candidate for burning there has been for many years" (A Book for Burning). In a later interview on BBC television, he said: "Sheldrake is putting forward magic instead of science, and that can be condemned in exactly the language that the Pope used to condemn Galileo, and for the same reason. It is heresy" (Sheldrake Online). The irony here is that condemned though he was, Galileo irrevocably altered the face of science. Perhaps one day, Sheldrake will too. If by "magic," Maddox means that which scientific orthodoxy can't explain, then Sheldrake is guilty as charged – although his accusers are themselves guilty of clinging to their habits of mind with irrational tenacity. Meanwhile, Sheldrake's theories have never been proven or disproven by actual scientific experimentation.

$$\Diamond\!\!\!\times$$

Using Sheldrake's Ideas as the Template For a Theory of Soul Resonance

As Sheldrake himself points out, however, the whole idea of morphogenetic resonance is not new. The concept was first introduced into biology in the 1920s, and elaborated by British biologist, C. H. Waddington. The idea was taken up, and articulated in another context by Carl Jung in his theory of the collective unconscious (Fox and Sheldrake 165). For what is the collective unconscious, but a repository for all the universal habit patterns that form the generic template for the collective memory of the human psyche? Psychotherapist and research scientist, Stanislav Grof, has more recently embraced the notion of the morphogenetic field, in an attempt to articulate an expanded notion of causality that incorporates both morphogenetic resonance and Aristotle's emphasis on purpose (Beyond the Brain). What Sheldrake and Grof add to Jung's work is the notion that the archetypes, or collective habit patterns that guide the evolution of the soul, are rooted not just in the psyche, but also in the cellular biology of the body. This does not mean that the soul (known only as mind) is a strictly biological phenomenon, or that what we call the soul is caused by biology, as a more orthodox scientist might want to believe. It does mean that there is a natural resonance between body and Spirit that makes them part of the same morphogenetic field in which soul comes to know itself.

The relationship between body and Spirit, in other words, can be understood as an interactive mirror capable of yielding useful information to the soul. What happens in the body is a reflection of the habit patterns in which Spirit has been conditioned to operate. The sensations, emotions, and images that spontaneously arise in the course of our embodied experience are a measure of the current state of our relationship to Spirit, because body and Spirit share a morphogenetic field through their convergence in each of us. The soul takes shape, in Sheldrake's terms, within this morphogenetic field.

Within this field, habits are formed which tend to repeat themselves as cyclical processes. These habits, in turn, become amenable to change or reinforcement, as their repetition provokes awareness of the patterns that they represent, and as we experience sensations, emotions, and/or images which bring them to our attention. When this information evokes a sense of pleasure, joy and well-being, the habits of soul that we experience are reinforced. When we experience pain, suffering and the psychic pull of our mortality, then we become motivated to change our habits of soul to create a more harmonious alignment of body and Spirit. If the soul is evolving toward a fulfillment of its potential, and if pleasure and pain can be understood to be a subjective measure of our alignment with purpose, then the Great Cycle of Life and Death and all the smaller cycles within it become mechanisms for transmitting information relevant to the soul's evolutionary process. In this way, the morphogenetic field becomes a catalyst to soul growth. The morphogenetic field does not cause growth, nor is growth guaranteed. Instead, the mere fact that body and Spirit share a morphogenetic field conditioned by an intrinsic sense of purpose, fosters an environment in which learning and growth become possible.

Extending the Morphogenetic Field of the Soul To Encompass the World

Thinking of soul in terms of fields also suggests that the learning process need not be limited to the body. Instead, it takes place within the larger arena of experiential possibility encompassed by the embodied world. As each individual soul participates within the world, it resonates with everything in the world that is in some way like it, or put another way, that reflects back to it, its habits of being. As these reflections register consciously within the body – through sensations, emotions, and the evocation of images – information about the relationship between body and Spirit is imparted to the soul, and the embodied world becomes a complex nexus of opportunities for soul growth. The world does not cause the soul to grow, but to the extent that the world is brought into focus through awareness, it becomes a morphogenetic field in which growth becomes possible.

Because this is a subjective process, the world will be a somewhat different place for each of us. To the extent that my habits of being are those that I have absorbed from the collective culture, then I will live in a world that is generic and universal. To the extent that I have paid attention to the information coming to me from my own experience, however, then the world will tend to become the reflection of a more personal relationship to soul that is more or less unique to me. The objects, people, and images of the world will acquire a symbolic meaning that communicates information that is useful to me, though perhaps not to anyone else. Through a conscious monitoring of the quality of my experiences within the embodied world, I can gradually adjust my relationship to the world to reflect an optimal sense of alignment between body (in the larger extended sense) and Spirit.

In this way, the objective world that is measured through an assessment of causal relationships by science becomes a subjective world measured through an assessment of patterns of resonance. This subjective world must be interpreted not through reference to immutable objective laws, but rather to individual habits of being that are subject to change as I bring my awareness to them. For every change I make in my own habits of being, the world around me will reflect a slightly different pattern of resonance. If I grow in my capacity to embody Spirit, everyone with whom I am in resonance will, on some level, recognize this and experience a nudge toward changing their own habits of mind in a more conscious direction. If I fall out of alignment with myself, then everyone who is in resonance with me, will feel that on some level as well. If enough of us change our individual habits of being, for better or worse, it is not inconceivable to imagine that the collective habit patterns of the larger morphogenetic field we share will also begin to change, and that even the so-called objective world will reflect those changes.

More accurately understood, it is our collective relationship to the objective world that changes - our perception of it, the understanding we bring to it, the images we hold of it - and not the world itself. The embodied world remains an arena in which the interplay of opposites - light and dark, male and female, self and other, and every other polarity - conditions our experience, for better or worse, regardless of how we conceptualize the process. But our collective relationship to the embodied world is also capable of evolving, just as our individual, subjective worldview is. I would not be writing this book, if I did not believe in the possibility of shifting collective attitudes and perceptions. As the history of ideas presented in these pages bears witness, however, our collective attitudes and perceptions are also capable of devolving in directions that make it harder to talk in meaningful ways about the soul. Be that as it may, as collective attitudes and perceptions about the world of consensus reality change in any direction, the world itself, as objectively defined, becomes a different place.

The Power of the Hundredth Monkey

Sheldrake's theories have often been associated with a concept called the hundredth monkey effect, which illustrates this possibility. The concept derives from a story about a colony of monkeys, who were observed in Japan, teaching each other to wash sweet potatoes before eating them. The idea presented by the story is that once a certain critical number of monkeys (set arbitrarily for purposes of illustration at 100) learned to wash their potatoes, all monkeys would automatically begin to wash theirs. If such a thing actually happened, it could offer evidence for the validity of Sheldrake's theories, since they would provide a plausible theoretical explanation for how information was passed from the hundredth monkey to all the others.

The hundredth monkey effect and the story from which it was inferred was originally discussed by zoologist, Lyall Watson, in 1979 in a book called *Lifetide*. Unfortunately for Sheldrake, the story has since been shown to be more metaphor than scientific fact, since Watson had to fabricate some of the details of the phenomenon that he was citing, in order to make his point. Nor has the effect since been scientifically proven. The metaphor was nonetheless adopted by New Age thinker, Marilyn Ferguson, and humanistic psychologist, Carl Rogers, and later expanded by human potential movement pioneer, Ken Keyes. In the early 1980s, Keyes wrote a book about nuclear war called *The Hundredth Monkey*, in which he suggested that if enough of us believe in the possibility of change, we could create a peaceful world.

This became the rallying cry for the next generation of New Agers, who as critics have pointed out, often use it to justify regression to a childlike state in which the magical power of wishful thinking replaces meaningful action and the exercise of political will (Olson). When understood correctly, however, the story of the hundredth monkey is a simple recognition of the impact that we are capable of having on each other and the world in which we live – not by causing each other to do or not do anything, but through the networks of resonance that we share. If I see you washing your sweet potatoes and enjoying them more because they are dirt free, I may well be inspired to do the same, and then in turn, share my newfound discovery with others. In this way, the idea of washing sweet potatoes (or any other idea) spreads and becomes a collective habit of mind. One need not wait for the hundredth monkey to see that information useful to the soul is spreading through the shared power of resonant experiences. This process has accelerated exponentially since the advent of the Internet, but is in play whenever two or more of us get together, by whatever means. The fact that every monkey in a polar world will not ultimately resonate with the idea of washing potatoes does not negate the suggestion that our resonance with ideas and other people within the embodied world is the mechanism not just for individual growth, but for our collective evolution as well.

If you've ever been moved to see a movie that the critics raved about, or join a spa because your friends who were working out inspired you with their healthy glow, or become more sensitive to the potential for sexual harassment in the workplace in the decade since Anita Hill's accusations against Supreme Court Justice, Clarence Thomas, then you have had an experience of the hundredth monkey effect at work. Sheldrake's theories simply describe a biological mechanism by which this effect becomes an intrinsic part of our nature as embodied souls in relationship to one another. It should be noted here, in fairness, that Sheldrake was outlining an alternate theory of biological evolution to challenge the orthodox Darwinian paradigm of natural selection, and the adaptation of his theories to the possibility of social change is largely a revolution staged by others. Ironically, the popularity of this idea can be seen as another example of the very phenomenon the hundredth monkey effect describes, for the idea continues to propagate, despite the fact that it has no scientific basis.

The story has great appeal, in part because it speaks to the way in which we participate in the larger web of life that encompasses the embodied world. This *is* how the soul extends itself into the embodied world, and participates in the evolution of the collective. If enough people resonate with the same idea or experience, it becomes a catalyst toward change within the collective space that we all share. This is not a causal process, but rather a shift in patterns of resonance, necessary to more accurately reflect the habits of being that gradually become the ever-evolving norm. It is a process that proceeds as each individual soul explores and brings its awareness, whatever that might be, into each relationship within its sphere of influence.

In contrast to the scientific paradigm, which suggests that consensus reality determines the experience of individual souls, the idea of the hundredth monkey suggests that the individual soul can also conversely influence the evolution of consensus reality through an embrace of its subjective truth within a resonant field. In a polar world, not every incidence of shared resonance will produce desirable results, although what is desirable and what is not will depend upon your point of view. Anti-abortionists will resonate together on their side of the fence, while pro-choice advocates will resonate with equal intensity on theirs. The process itself is neutral and does not guarantee evolution toward an ideal state. In fact, given the reflex action of the polar world in which we live, there will be equivalent resonances on either side of any polarity that is activated.

Resonance is nonetheless a useful concept for understanding how individual souls come together to form a collective. If enough souls resonate in relation to the same idea, or *meme* as it has been more recently called (Dawkins 192), then the culture as a whole begins to shift in a particular direction. Since ultimately the soul is in relationship to everything within the embodied world, it is not inconceivable to envision even the habits of mind that scientists take for granted and consider to be immutable laws of nature gradually mutating in this way to reflect an evolution in our shared collective patterns of resonance.

If this seems far-fetched, consider the existence of the cell phone, a handy technological device that is rapidly becoming taken for granted in the early days of the 21st century. Imagine telling a scientist of the 17th century that one day we would be able to carry on a conversation with someone 1,000 miles away, as though they were speaking directly into our ear, while traveling in a vehicle moving 70 miles per hour. You would have been told, "That is impossible. It defies the immutable laws of physics, and it can't be done." Creating the first cell phone took many thousands of hours of research and development. Now they are mass produced, and available at any department store. No one had the habit of mind that could encompass the concept of a cell phone 30 years ago; now we all have habits of mind broad enough to include them. Furthermore, our habits of being have changed because of them, and our collective, objective reality is different. Babies born today will take for granted something that didn't even exist when their grandparents were growing up. And so has it been with every invention, impossible a short time ago, but omnipresent now – passenger planes, computers, the Internet, digital cameras, genetically altered soybeans, you name it. Science prides itself on pushing the limits of our objective habit patterns; it just frames what it does according to a different model based on the language of causality.

The Arrogance of Science in Assuming Causality To be the Only Possible Explanation

If Hume was right, however, then it really doesn't matter whether we speak of causality, or morphogenetic resonance, or the invisible workings of the Matrix[1] as an explanation for how the world works, since any concept we could possibly devise would in the end, be yet another habit of mind. We all take our habits of mind seriously, but they are not the truth. They are merely a template that we impose upon the truth in order to better perceive and then explain it. Causality is actually a rather useful template to help explain how the objective world works; so useful in fact, that it is hard to imagine attempting to discuss very much of anything within the objective world without reference to it. But that is exactly what a habit of mind is, and if the adopted habit of mind works, there is no need to change it. It is where it does not work – to put it scientifically, where the data does not support the hypothesis – that we are justified in cultivating new habits of mind.

The problem with the scientific mindset, however, is that it fails to recognize its own insistence on objectivity, causal explanations, and the systematic denial of purpose as habits of mind. Instead science asserts that theirs is the only possible framework in which reality can be understood. The framework then becomes what philosopher of science, Thomas Kuhn called a "paradigm," an overarching intellectual context governing the evolution of ideas. As Kuhn points out in his seminal book, *The Structure of Scientific Revolutions*, the history of science is marked by a succession of paradigm shifts, each caused by an achievement "sufficiently unprecedented to attract an enduring group of adherents away from competing modes of scientific activity . . . (and) sufficiently open-ended to leave all sorts of problems for the redefined group of practitioners to resolve" (10). The work of Aristotle, Descartes, Copernicus, Newton, Einstein, Darwin, Freud and many others have precipitated paradigm shifts, which gradually changed the face of science many times over.

While this progression of paradigm shifts suggests great open-mindedness and flexibility within the scientific community, this has hardly been the case. As Kuhn noted in a postscript, seven years after the publication of the first edition of his work, "a paradigm is what the members of a scientific community share, and conversely, a scientific community consists of men who share a paradigm. Not all circularities are vicious, . . . but this one is a source of real difficulties" (172). Not the least of these difficulties is the insular arrogance of the scientific community in considering ideas that do not fit the current paradigm in which they are working. The revolutions Kuhn spoke of innocently in the first edition of his book happen slowly and against great narrow-minded inertia, if and when they happen at all. This is so despite the fact that most contemporary scientists would scoff at many of the ideas held to be gospel truth by their predecessors who subscribed to an earlier paradigm. Add to this the fact that science has increasingly become a money game tied to corporate interests, which are not just intellectually but also financially invested in the paradigms that fuel their business aspirations, and you have a recipe for institutionalized inertia that vigorously resists habits of mind contrary to its own.

The Difficulty of Stepping Outside the Causal Paradigm

Consider, for example, the plight of anthropologist, Jeremy Narby, who sought to understand the statement made by the *ayahuasceros* (shamans) of the Amazon that the plants of the rainforest communicate their medicinal uses directly to the healers who use them. Traditional anthropology, informed by science, dismisses this claim as preposterous, because there is nothing within a causal paradigm that would allow an orthodox scientist to entertain the possibility of communication with plants, and there was nothing in Narby's scientific training that equipped him to either confirm or refute the claim. Though Narby does not discuss the economic implications of his work, we might also consider the potential impact on an immense scientific research infrastructure, underwritten by a multi-billion-dollar pharmaceutical industry, were word to get out that direct knowledge of the use of medicinal plants was possible without all this research, and that we need not wait for some multinational corporation to "discover," patent, package, and sell it to us before we can benefit from it.

Financial considerations aside, science is unable to explain how a so-called primitive people without electron microscopes or a bona fide knowledge of modern chemistry could discover ayahuasca in the first place. The discovery required the native shamans to choose from among 80,000 Amazonian plant species, one plant containing an hallucinogenic brain hormone, then combine it with a second plant containing substances that deactivate an enzyme of the digestive tract which would block the hormone's action. Science might have arrived at the formula for ayahuasca, or the many other medicinal substances used by the ayahuasceros, given hundreds of years of round-the-clock laboratory research, using the methodology dictated by a causal paradigm. But in light of this amazing discovery, I think it is a bit presumptuous of science to claim epistemological superiority, or dismiss the possibility that the ayahuasceros employed an alternative way of acquiring their knowledge.

Could it be that the ayahuasceros were pursuing knowledge subjectively, by participating in a morphogenetic field of natural resonance that has evolved over thousands of years of contact between themselves and the plant community where they live? This is at least as plausible an explanation as any the scientific community can come up with. Actually, science has by and large dismissed not just the outcome of Narby's exploration of ayahuascero culture, but the very questions he proposed to address. Because the scientific community did not have the tools to consider a phenomenon that fell outside its range, it took the attitude that such phenomenon was unworthy of investigation. Its habits of mind, in other words, have over the course of the last three centuries, become confused with reality itself.

The Importance of Resonant Context In Extracting Subjective Truth

Does this mean that the ayahuasceros are right to pursue medicine their way and traditional medical doctors are wrong? Of course not. Does this mean that allopathic doctors can expect to simply march into the rainforest, ingest ayahuasca, and suddenly know what the native shamans know? Of course not. They do not belong to the same resonant field, evolved through countless generations of healers living in the embodied world that contains these medicinal plants, and it is not likely that the same information will be instantaneously available to them. A transmission of information through patterns of resonance requires first that there actually be a resonant relationship between the one who seeks to know and the context of resonance in which that information is available. Building such a pattern of resonance takes willingness to live within the context and cultivate resonant relationships. While there are pharmaceutical companies eager to capitalize on this knowledge, their quest is as presumptuous as that of a native healer, were he to walk into a modern pharmacy, expecting to make immediate use of the hundred of bottles of pills that sat before him on the shelf.

The mere fact that information is available through resonance within a given context does not mean that anyone who encounters the context will automatically resonate with the information. It does mean that within different resonant contexts, different kinds of relationships may exist, different rules may apply, different pathways to the truth may be followed, and different conclusions may be drawn. It also means that the net cast by science to catch the truth has holes in it that science won't or can't admit are there, because it only resonates within its own context, without even recognizing that its knowledge is context dependent.

If a monkey walks into a bar and asks the bartender for a banana, we all laugh at the joke, because we see that the monkey is making assumptions about the bar, based on its experience of its accustomed resonant context. When a scientist walks into a bar, however, and asks both the monkey and the bartender for DNA samples, nobody laughs because we have all become conditioned to think it is science's prerogative to claim the entire embodied world, and everything in it, as its resonant context. So successful has the scientific revolution been, that science's presuppositions about the nature of reality are automatically assumed to be applicable across the board in all resonant contexts. When the soul walks into that same bar, however, and the scientist doesn't even see it, because it has no DNA sample to give, then the joke is on us, even though it is the scientist who is blindly operating out of context.

According to Narby (139-140):

> The problem is not having presuppositions, but failing to make them explicit. If biology said about the intentionality that nature seems to manifest at all levels, 'we see it sometimes, but cannot discuss it without ceasing to do science according to our own criteria,' things would at least be clear. But biology (and most orthodox science) tends to project its presuppositions onto the reality it observes, claiming that nature itself is devoid of intention.

Science projects these presuppositions not just in relation to intentionality, but also with regard to causality, objectivity, a strictly quantitative approach, and every other component of the paradigm by which science attempts to understand reality. Instead of saying, "These are our preferred habits of mind, and this is what we can learn within this framework," science says, "This is the only framework possible, and anything outside the framework doesn't exist."

Meanwhile, the framework is ill-suited to a subjective language of soul. At the risk of scientific censure and ridicule, we must look beyond causality for an acausal point of entry into an understanding of the soul's experience. The concept of morphogenetic resonance is attractive in this regard, because it preserves the notion of intentionality, and provides a mechanism for intentionality to work itself through the transmission and absorption of information. The morphogenetic field is a learning environment, in which growth takes place through recognition of resonance, or dissonance. If I feel a strong affinity, or a strong aversion, to something within the range of my awareness, and I consent to a relationship with it, then learning will take place that creates an opportunity for me to align more clearly with my soul. I may or may not take full advantage of this opportunity, but the opportunity itself is inherent in the fact that Spirit and body come together to create the morphogenetic field in which my soul exists.

This is not to say that the concept of morphogenetic field is a more accurate description of reality than causality. Both are habits of mind, and thus both can only be mere speculation about the nature of a mystery that neither we, nor the scientists, can access in any ultimately definitive way. But more important than nailing down an absolute definition of how something works, is working with it and seeing what it can teach us. Scientists have worked with causality for hundreds of years, and found it a useful habit of mind through which to understand objective reality. My sense is that the concept of morphogenetic resonance can provide the same framework for an understanding of the subjective reality of the soul.

Applying the Concept of Resonance To the Astrological Model of Soul

Let's take a moment to speculate how this might be so, within the context of an astrological framework. The astrological tradition, cultivated for thousands of years, is nothing if not a cumulative study of patterns of resonance. Each symbol within its domain – particularly the Sun, Moon, and eight known planets of our solar system – is a focal point for resonance of a particular kind, or what Sheldrake's predecessor, Waddington, called an *attractor*. Each attractor serves as a kind of vibrational essence around which various images, feelings, sensations and experiences tend to organize themselves. If the organizing principle within any morphogenetic field can be considered to be purposeful, then each symbolic attractor within a birthchart will tend to crystallize awareness of images, feelings, sensations and experiences that contribute toward the fulfillment of a particular purpose, or psychic function.

In traditional astrology, the planet Mercury is associated with communication (among other possible associations). Within the context of this new model of resonance, we might say instead that Mercury serves as an attractor to all those experiences that facilitate communication. Calling Mercury an attractor does not mean that the physical planet attracts anything, nor that the symbol in the birthchart is the source of attraction. Instead, the symbol reflects a process of attraction by which the soul resonates with and draws to itself experiences designed to teach it the art of communication, and other skills that are symbolically within Mercury's domain. The fulfillment of Mercury's purpose within a birthchart will require clear communication, an effective declaration of identity, and skill at using language to work through differences with others.

Each individual works toward a fulfillment of Mercury's purpose in a highly subjective way that is reflected astrologically by Mercury's placement in the birthchart. This placement will be described by sign and house, as well as by Mercury's relationship to the other planets, and within the overall pattern of the birthchart as a whole. How Mercury functions will also necessarily vary with the consciousness that is brought to bear within Mercury's domain. Consciousness cannot be assessed by reference to the birthchart alone, but nonetheless determines the level of possibility on which the birthchart, and the various patterns of resonance within it, will manifest. To understand what Mercury means within a given life process, we must consider both the birthchart and the consciousness expressed within the life process to which the birthchart refers.

The individual's relationship to Mercury, and the consciousness through which the individual fulfills Mercury's function will shift from time to time, as Mercury moves through periods of activation and deactivation, symbolized by astrological timing techniques called *transits*, *progressions*, and *directions*. Each period of activation will provide an opportunity for the soul to grow in relation to the astrological context in which Mercury participates. As the individual soul evolves in relation to Mercury through its learning experiences, the meaning of the birthchart will gradually change to reflect an evolutionary process of soul growth at work.

A full discussion of this topic is beyond the range of our present focus, but I will pick up this thread again in the second book in this series. Meanwhile, suffice it to say, that within the resonant field represented by a birthchart, Mercury will function as an attractor with a specific focus. It will serve as a symbolic pivot point for experiences that revolve around that focus, but that are highly personal and subjective to the person experiencing them. These experiences, in turn, will take place within a resonant context of meaning that is determined in part through their association with the symbolic attractor, Mercury, and in part through reference to a gradual evolution of consciousness in relation to the lessons to be mastered within Mercury's domain. This evolutionary process will unfold according to a time frame that can be correlated with the various cycles in which Mercury participates, and mapped to a process of soul growth.

The planet Mars, by contrast, serves as a very different kind of attractor, which in turn reflects its own evolutionary process. Symbolically, Mars can be associated with experiences that facilitate action, since the fulfillment of its purpose requires doing, tangible achievements, and the intentional pursuit of an agenda. Again, according to Mars' placement within a given birthchart, and the consciousness brought to its domain, each individual soul will experience a pattern of resonance related to Mars that is highly personal. This pattern will fluctuate and evolve over time, contributing in idiosyncratic ways to the fulfillment of overall soul purpose, as reflected by the birthchart as a whole. As with Mercury and Mars, the other eight major planets in the birthchart will also serve as attractors that crystallize specific life lessons in fulfillment of particular psychic functions.

When the soul functions as an integrated whole, Mercury and Mars will work together to actualize the same sense of purpose, though in different ways. Mercury will want to talk about purpose, in order to more clearly articulate it to self and others. Mars will have little patience with talk, but be anxious to get on with the actualization process itself through hands-on participation, and by following its instincts. Obviously, both a clear vision and the capacity to manifest that vision through focused action are necessary to fulfill any purpose. If the soul is to accomplish its purpose, then it is clear Mercury and Mars will have to learn to cooperate. Each must learn how to work with the other within the resonant context that they share, so that the relationship between them will contribute to the fulfillment of the soul's overall agenda. I speak here of Mercury and Mars as symbols for a constellation of distinct needs, wants, predispositions, innate tendencies, drives, and aspects of being, though I am really talking about the soul, as it can be perceived through an astrological kaleidoscope of resonant attractors.

If the soul can be understood as an arena for the integration and outworking of contradictory forces, then there will also likely be times when Mercury and Mars are at odds with one another. When this happens, they will function as a polarity, pulling in seemingly antithetical directions, each pursuing an agenda that generates a sense of internal tension and stress for the other. Mercury will want to have a plan in place before proceeding with its implementation; Mars will prefer to make up a plan on the fly. Mercury will want to be able to articulate its purpose, whether or not it fully accomplishes what it sets out to do; Mars will want to get as much done as possible, even if it can't put its sense of purpose into words. Mercury will want to talk things out and explain its position to others; Mars will want to push forward, without the patience to explain, even though this may create interpersonal friction. Obviously, if Mercury and Mars are going to cooperate in the fulfillment of the soul's agenda, they will have to find a way to negotiate these differences.

At times, everyone may experience impediments on the winding road to the fulfillment of soul purpose that can be understood symbolically as a discord between Mercury and Mars. For certain individuals, who in astrological parlance have hard aspects (angular relationships generally representing a division of the whole circle by some multiple of two) between Mercury and Mars, the tension between these two planets tends to be chronic, creating a core issue around which a lifelong process of learning and soul growth can potentially take place. Working out the habitual tension between Mercury and Mars, can in fact, be part of an individual's soul's sense of purpose, and provide a pivot point within the morphogenetic field around which some of life's most meaningful experiences will crystallize. Others, who have soft aspects (angular relationships generally representing a division of the whole circle by some multiple of three) between Mars and Mercury, tend to experience less functional tension and more synergistic cooperation.

Toward a Sensory Exploration of Planetary Resonance

Leaving aside for the moment these ideas, derived from traditional astrology, we can also understand the interaction between Mercury and Mars in more basic sensory terms. In Chapter Six, I discussed the mythological association of Mars with war in sensory terms as red, black, loud, staccato, piercing, deep, booming, palpable, sharp, rough, hot, pungent, irritating, heavy, bitter, metallic, and dry. By a similar process of association to the trickster god, Hermes, I might likewise experience Mercury in sensory terms as transparent, blue, luminous, quick, fluttering, syncopated, light, cool, agitating, disorienting, dry, slippery, high, ozonous, and wiry. Putting these associations together with a little imagination, it is not hard to speculate that some of these qualities will combine in naturally synergistic ways, while others will clash.

When Mars is piercing and Mercury is quick, for example, I could find if fairly easy to go directly to the heart of any matter to which I turn my attention. When Mars is booming and piercing and Mercury is agitating, I might have to occasionally deal with migraine headaches. When Mars is heavy and Mercury is light, the potential exists for taking life too seriously one day and avoiding it the next. Or this combination of qualities could also facilitate a life-long learning process of reaching more balanced participation in life that mediates between the extremes. When both Mars and Mercury are feeling dry, I might have a tendency to become too dry, in all the ways that dryness can become a metaphor for the quality of my experience - too intellectual, too wedded to stale routine, or too non-committal and aloof. And so on. The possibilities are endless as various permutations and combinations of these sensory qualities come together in actual experience.

Within the astrological worldview - considered both traditionally and with reference to sensory and emotional correlates - the relationship between Mercury and Mars is qualitatively different for each person, as is the relationship between all 45 possible planetary pairs. The relationship between each pair invariably harbors some combination of cooperative synergy and developmental tension. It will contribute to and at times complicate the soul's quest for actualization of its purpose, to varying degrees of relative importance within the overall life process. Often three or more planetary attractors form a pattern of particularly intense resonance, which in turn, serves as a center around which constellate major life issues and opportunities for soul growth. The birthchart as a whole, in this way, provides a map of the morphogenetic field in which the soul evolves. Read wisely, it describes in great detail the interplay of the polar tensions as well as the archetypal synergies that make any soul the complex, dynamic, uniquely individual integration of Spirit and body that it is. Knowing the birthchart does not preclude the necessity for experiencing the morphogenetic field and living through its lessons, but it does make the patterns of resonance within it more accessible and comprehensible.

Each of the planetary pairs that generate creative synergy and developmental tension are in some identifiable stage of at least three ongoing cycles: 1) planet A is moving In relation to fixed point of reference, natal planet B; 2) planet B is moving in relation to fixed point of reference, natal planet A; and 3) planet A is moving in relation to moving planet B. As all three of these cycles are considered together, the birthchart will also provide an evolutionary clock, indicating when various core issues are likely to be triggered, along with attendant opportunities for growth, and advancement of the soul's agenda. When planet B forms a hard aspect in real time to natal planet A, or vice versa, or when planet A and B form a hard aspect to each other in real time, there will tend to be increased tension in the morphogenetic field. There is also potentially an increased opportunity for learning and growth. When planet B forms a soft aspect in real time to planet A, or vice versa, or when planet A and B form a soft aspect to each other in real time, there tends to be increased harmony in the morphogenetic field, and an increased opportunity to work toward a more natural, less conflicted expression of the relationship between them.

Astrology's Contribution to a Mathematics of Soul

Since both the placement and subsequent movement of planets in relation to each other can be charted with mathematical precision, some within the astrological community assume that this means astrology is innately suited to the causal paradigm - which is articulated through the mathematical language. But this is confusing methodology with metaphysics. Since Newton first formulated the laws of motion, mathematics has been the language of choice with which to describe causal relationships. Mathematics, however, measures only the external, quantitatively measurable, objective movements of material bodies. It does not begin to describe the qualitative patterns of resonance that make the subjective movements of individuals meaningful. It does not provide a qualitative screen upon which individuals might project and then recognize images that help focus those patterns of resonance, nor does it even acknowledge the validity of the attempt to do this.

In the early, pre-scientific days of the 6th century BCE, Pythagoras - in many ways, the father of mathematics - concerned himself with the metaphysical implications of mathematical relationships. For Pythagoras, mathematics was a language through which he could understand the inner workings of Spirit within the realm of matter, or put in our terminology, the fusion of Spirit and matter that creates the embodied world. Drawing from both the ancient mystery religions actively practiced in his day, as well as the newly emerging science of Thales and Anaximander, Pythagoras sought to bridge the gap between number and soul. He was, however, swimming against the philosophical tide, and as all the cornerstones of science - including rational literalism, objectivity, quantitative materialism, and causality - were wedged into place over the course of the next two-plus millennia, numbers were severed from any possible association with soul and the imagistic, qualitative realms of subjective resonance that soul attempts to navigate.

Astrologers, of course, kept this possibility alive through a continuous though marginalized process of development that was embraced through at least the 17th century, by astronomers like Copernicus, Kepler, and Galileo. Though contemporary astronomers vehemently disavow and deny their own history in condemning the practice of astrology, the belief that numbers ought to be capable of revealing quality, even while being used to measure phenomena quantitatively, persists despite two-plus millennia of ridicule by science. Obviously, there must be some truth to the idea – which is distinctly astrological in nature – or it would not have survived such a concentrated and persistent opposition. Meanwhile, stripped of qualitative meaning, numbers become a mere measuring device for causal processes, which is exactly what has happened to them in the hands of mainstream science.

Unfortunately, many contemporary astrologers are determined to earn their way back into the camp of their detractors by articulating a causal mechanism in quantitative terms to explain how astrology works. Arguments comparing the minuscule gravitational pull of the planets to the gravitational pull of the doctor delivering a newborn baby illustrate the futility of this approach, and invariably make astrologers look stupid (Bok 31). Pioneers like Percy Seymour and Bruce Scofield are attempting to reframe these causal arguments in terms more amenable to the astrological worldview, discussing astrological influences in terms of planetary magnetism and biological circuitry respectively. These efforts may one day command begrudging respect at the periphery of some scientific circles, and who knows – one day some causal theory may even garner the scientific sanction that has eluded astrologers for thousands of years. However, I believe the efforts of the astrological community could be more usefully applied toward the cultivation of an acausal astrological epistemology, based on a symbolic exploration of patterns of resonance, that does not depend upon conformity to the scientific paradigm for its validation.

Perhaps a causal approach to astrology can be useful to better understand the cycles that govern movement and change within the external, objective world. Not all astrologers are concerned with the fate of the soul. Some attempt to analyze patterns in the stock market, predict earthquakes and other natural disasters, and explore the relationship of planetary alignments with social and political trends. Perhaps these more collective mundane concerns can benefit from a more scientific approach to astrology. If the focus of our astrological attention is the individual human soul, however, and the quest for a sense of meaning and purpose, our efforts would be better spent developing a nonscientific model of astrological resonance, which is designed to help each individual find his or her own way into the heart of an intimately subjective truth.

To pass through Inanna's fifth gate on the way to the underworld of the soul, we must let go of the requirement that the soul explain itself in causal terms. While the soul can be understood according to many possible habits of mind other than causality, I propose that we begin thinking of the soul in terms of patterns of resonance, which are not caused, but rather emanate from Spirit, as expressions of Its Being made manifest through the unfoldment of cycles in the embodied world. In Chapter Eleven, we will look at how this world, which I like to call *soul space*, is constructed, free from the necessity of causal explanations.

Endnotes

[1] The Matrix is a computer-generated world of illusion, created by machines that use human beings as an electrical energy source, while entertaining them with software programs fed directly to their brains. This bizarre, but insightful metaphor was presented in a 1999 futuristic movie of the same name, directed by the Wachowski brothers.

Chapter Eleven
Through Inanna's Fifth Gate
Into Resonant Soul Space

To understand the world the soul inhabits, we must make another circle around the ancient tower, through philosophical history, and reconsider the way we think about space and time. Within the scientific worldview, space and time are largely construed as mathematical abstractions, providing a context in which causal processes can be measured and explained. From the soul's perspective, however, both space and time have huge metaphysical underpinnings, and how we think about them will make a tremendous difference in how we talk about soul, and the world that soul inhabits. In this and the following chapter, I will briefly trace a philosophical history of thought about each concept, and explore a perspective of greater use to the soul.

The Great Debate About Space
Among the Rational Cosmologists

Early debate among the rational cosmologists revolved around the question of whether space was empty or full. Parmenides, a contemporary of Socrates, argued that contrary to the evidence of the senses, empty space was an impossibility. He argued logically that since it was impossible to contemplate nothingness, space could not be empty. There was only Being, and Being filled all of space with Its presence. You and I and everything else that exists are of that Being, and so there is no space between us. Ironically, Parmenides vigorously exercised his intellect to arrive at this conclusion, which is virtually identical to that held by most mystical traditions, whose process requires a quieting of the mind. He was also a precursor to the Neoplatonists, who believed in a complex hierarchy of emanations from the One, which completely filled and encompassed all of space.

Parmenides had no sooner asserted this point of view, than it became hotly contested. "No," argued Parmenides' contemporaries, Anaximander and Heraclitus, "the world is pretty much as it seems, and yes, space is in fact empty."

Out of the dust of this purely theoretical fray came an attempt by two other philosophers, Leucippus and Democritus, to bridge the gap between these polar views, both of which contained attractive features. They liked Parmenides' notion of the omnipresence of Being throughout space, because it upheld cherished metaphysical views, but they could not argue with Heraclitus' observations about the apparent emptiness of space, which confirmed common sense experience. Their idea, which laid the foundation

◇◇

for modern scientific materialism, was that even though space was filled by God, God was not an obstacle to movement in space. For Democritus, despite the omnipresence of Being, empty space was still the arena where bodies in motion interacted with each other and change took place.

Democritus' Contribution To a Scientific Understanding of Space

While such a debate might appear to be purely academic now, it was essential to the scientific notion of space that would evolve later. Motion and measurable change are not possible in space that is occupied, and so before science could establish itself, it had to at least make sure that the omnipresence of Spirit throughout space would not be an obstacle. It would take another 2,200 years or so before God was evicted altogether, but Democritus' ideas reassured the emerging scientific worldview that even an omnipresent God would not interfere with the movement of bodies in the space that He occupied. The gradual acceptance of Democritus' ideas allowed science to derive the causal laws through which the movement and interaction of material bodies in space could be measured. Democritus' arguments about the nature of space were not consciously calculated to make room for science, but they nonetheless laid the foundation upon which a scientific concept of space gradually became the dominant understanding.

Democritus further speculated that the bodies moving through space were composed of indivisible physical atoms, and that it was the concentration of atoms of various shapes, arrangements and positions that gave rise to the apparently separate things of the world. Soul, according to Democritus, was also composed of atoms, although of a more refined type than material bodies. Later scientists would not find these material atoms composing the soul, but they readily embraced the notion of an atomistic, material universe, in which physical bodies composed of atoms moved through empty space. Atomism did not gain immediate widespread acceptance in early Greek thought, largely because of opposition by Plato and Aristotle, who both refused to reduce the whole of reality, including man, to an aggregate of moving atoms.

Though Aristotle rejected the underlying metaphysical assumptions of atomism, he did not question Democritus' assertion that the objective universe was composed of material bodies juxtaposed in empty space. Ultimately, it was through Aristotle's confirmation of his philosophical stance that Democritus' notion of space came to be the accepted understanding passed down through science into contemporary thought. Despite the early unpopularity of atomism, Democritus' ideas were critical, because they emptied space of Spirit, and then refilled it with matter, thus paving the way for the Cartesian mindset that would govern science for the first 300 years of its history.

Aristotle's Concept of Place
And Its Causal Reworking During the Scientific Revolution

It is important to note that although Aristotle supported Democritus in his conception of space, for Aristotle space was not just a mathematical abstraction[1]. Aristotle postulated that space also had a qualitative dimension, which we might translate as a sense of place. Bodies endowed with purpose, or soul, moved through space, according to Aristotle, in order to find their place. Although Aristotle did not understand place in psychological terms, this is nonetheless a concept that is quite useful to a language of soul. Finding one's place – on earth, within the larger community in which one lives, in relation to the culture at large, and in a broader sense, in relation to any experience one might have – is in fact one of the primary tasks for any soul seeking to discover who it is and what it has come here to do. How one goes about that task, and where one tends to wind up will to a great extent determine who the soul is in relation to the space that it occupies, and to the Whole that encompasses that space.

Aristotle's qualitative concept of place continued to influence the philosophical discussion about space for the next two thousand years. During the scientific revolution of the 17th and 18th century, however, space was stripped of its qualitative connotations, and became a strictly quantitative parameter of measurement. This development was part of the general dismissal of quality from the scientific lexicon initiated by Galileo and the empiricists, as discussed in Chapter Eight. By stripping space of all qualitative associations, the empiricists were able to reinterpret motion as a mathematical concept, and redefine space as the context in which motion could be measured. It was largely through Galileo's influence that the more overtly metaphysical discussion of place became an antiquated vestige of an outmoded way of thinking, at least within the minds of the empiricists, and began to quietly disappear from science.

The groundwork for the dismissal of place as a relevant concept actually began with Copernicus, a century earlier. Copernicus is famous for asserting and later proving that the Sun, and not the Earth, is the center of our solar system. Aside from the paradigm shift his work precipitated in the world of astronomy and science in general, his displacement of the Earth from the center of the solar system also psychologically altered our sense of space. For if the Earth were no longer the pivot point around which the heavens revolved, then perhaps the human soul was not the pivot point around which life on Earth revolved. Though the mathematics of planetary motion fell into place with unmistakable elegance, once the Sun was enthroned at the center of the solar system, the soul became a philosophical refugee with a much more marginalized position within the brave new paradigm Copernicus articulated.

This was necessarily so, because in a broader sense – both symbolic and existential – the Earth is the extended body that houses the soul. It is where the embodied soul lives and must ultimately find its place. As the Earth lost its place at the center of the solar system, the embodied soul moved to a more peripheral place in the cosmic scheme of things. Meanwhile, as the Sun – which has been metaphysically associated with Spirit throughout the ages – was enthroned at the center, it essentially paralleled and compounded the religious confusion of soul with Spirit documented in Chapters One and Two. While the soul had already been disembodied by religion four millennia ago, it wasn't until it was displaced by the Copernican revolution that it began to disappear completely as a concept relevant within the dominant scientific paradigm.

Though Protestant religious reformer, Luther called Copernicus an atheist "upstart astrologer," arrogant enough to contradict both the prevailing scientific dogma of his day and the Holy Bible, Copernicus himself was as concerned with the metaphysical implications of his discovery as he was the mathematics. In *De Revolutionibus* (qtd. in Burtt 56), he wrote:

> Then in the middle of all stands the sun. For who, in our most beautiful temple, could get this light in another or better place, than that from which it can at once illuminate the whole? Not to speak of the fact that not unfittingly do some call it the light of the world, others the soul, still others the governor, Tremigistus calls it the visible God; Sophocles' Electra, the All-Seer. And, in fact, does the sun, seated on his royal throne, guide his family of planets as they circle around him.

Despite his metaphysical leanings, Copernicus' work was banned. All those that taught his heliocentric theory (placing the Sun at the center of the solar system) at Church-dominated institutions of learning were fired; and Copernicus was interrogated by the Inquisition, forced to recant, and placed under house arrest. When the censorship of the church eventually backfired, the paradigm shift he initiated became firmly anchored a century later by another upstart astrologer named Kepler. Fired up in equal measure by the mathematical notions of Pythagoras and a vision of the Sun as the central image of God, Kepler worked out the "harmony of the spheres" on a mathematical basis, using the heliocentric model. Galileo then sealed the fate of the heliocentric worldview through the irrefutable empirical evidence provided by his telescope, thus proving to the extended senses the model of the solar system Copernicus and Kepler had worked out mathematically. Ironically, these mystical scientists, standing on a flimsy bridge between science and religion shortly to collapse, ushered in the very displacement of soul they had hoped to centralize. It was Spirit in the guise of the Sun that they elevated, while soul languished with a much less clearly defined sense of place, on the side of the road of progress.

The Symbolic Importance of the Geocentric Perspective

Critics of astrology often point to the fact that most practitioners still study the geocentric system as evidence that they are caught in a bygone, nonscientific, pre-Copernican era. According to the scientific model, if the science or the math underlying a pathway to knowledge is faulty, then no truth worth knowing can come from that system. Thus the derogatory label, pseudoscience, is often used by scientists with no true knowledge of astrology to dismiss a perspective that does not conform to their authoritative habits of mind. What science fails to realize, however, is that it is not mathematical truth that nourishes the soul, but experiential. As pre-eminent astrologer Dane Rudhyar and many others have pointed out, "We do not experience, actually and sensorially, the fact that the Sun is the center of a system of which the Earth is but one planet" (80-81).

We don't experience this life from the perspective of the Sun, nor through the all-knowing eyes of Spirit, dwelling at the center of it all, but from a humbler, and more peripheral station somewhere off-center. We revolve around the Sun, seeing it kaleidoscopically from every possible angle, but we don't see what the Sun sees. Our perspective is necessarily skewed by personal experience, and this is reflected quite accurately by the fact that this experience takes place on a planet that is not at the center of the solar system. Paradoxically, when our concept of space is considered subjectively from this displaced perspective, then soul is given the opportunity to discover and occupy its rightful place in the larger scheme of things. Place is the subjective inhabitation of space, in the same way that soul is the subjective embodiment of Spirit. To be meaningful to the soul, space must be understood from an earth-centered perspective as a subjective sense of place, despite the fact that this is not mathematically or scientifically correct.

The Positivist Denial of Space's Spiritual Dimensions

To complete the scientific definition of space, Newton derived cogent mathematical laws of motion and gravitation, which governed the interaction of bodies in space. In so doing, he evolved the methodology by which the function of space as an arena for the measurement of causal forces was made more explicit. While a causal understanding of space had been implied in the concept of motion, it did not crystallize into a working definition until Newton showed how this could be so, through rigorous empirically derived laws rendered with mathematical precision.

Ironically, Newton was as much a theologian as he was a scientist, who echoed Parmenides in conceiving of absolute space as equivalent to the omnipresence of God. In response to religious criticism of his *Principia*, in which he presented his scientific understanding of space, he added an addendum, called the *General Scholium*, to the second edition. In the *General Scholium* (qtd. in Burtt 258-259), he affirmed his belief in God, and his conviction that

> (God) *endures for ever, and is everywhere present; and by existing always and everywhere, he constitutes duration and space . . . He is omnipresent, not virtually only, but also substantially, for virtue cannot subsist without substance. In him are all things contained and moved; yet neither affects the other; God suffers nothing from the motion of bodies; bodies find no resistance from the omnipresence of God. It is allowed by all that the Supreme God exists necessarily; and by the same necessity, he exists always and everywhere.*

This is quite a statement from a man remembered for expressing an ultimately irreligious, scientific point of view, but it also demonstrates just how vital religious concerns about God's role in space still were two thousand years after the original argument between Parmenides and Heraclitus.

Despite Newton's religious sensibilities, his theories were quickly stripped of their metaphysical implications by those who came after him, and embraced as the work of mathematical and empirical genius that they were. In retrospect, Newton can be seen to have paved the way for logical positivism, although he conducted his own science within the context of a personal awareness of the Final Cause that would put his work into a metaphysical perspective. Positivists who came after Newton saw no need for metaphysical explanations at all. What remained in their minds, and in their boundless estimation of Newton, were the causal laws that he rigorously defined, while the spiritual underpinnings of those laws were lost to all but a few diehard philosophers of science. Within this shift toward positivism that followed in the wake of Newton's gargantuan achievements, space became the empty, mathematical playground of causal forces, devoid of soul or Spirit that most of us, weaned on the dominant scientific paradigm, unquestioningly accept it to be.

From Empty Space to Field Theory

A final fly in the ointment of this conception of space was by introduced by William Gilbert, who wrote *On the Lodestone and Magnetic Bodies* in 1600. Magnetism and gravity were a bit of a conundrum to those who subscribed to a mechanistic view of space. According to this view, bodies could only act directly on each other through motion, but magnetism and gravity appeared to act at a distance. To explain how this could be, Gilbert suggested that the magnetic body emitted an effluvium. This effluvium was immaterial in nature, like a breath or vapor that awakened a responding vapor in the attracted body. Clearly no positivist, Gilbert believed that magnetism was an animate soul force that attracted bodies to each other. Since he believed the Earth to be a giant magnet, he went so far as to suggest that the Earth had a soul, a theory that would be echoed later, and elaborated by James Lovelock in his Gaia hypothesis. His ideas were not that farfetched within the context of a soul-based theory of morphogenetic resonance, in which the Earth is the classroom where learning takes place through resonance with various attractors. But they did not sit well with Gilbert's more positivist peers.

The immaterial nature of magnetism, and the metaphysical implications of his theory galvanized the positivists of Gilbert's day to search for a more suitable explanation. By the middle of the 17th century, the notion of magnetic effluvium had evolved to become *ether*, and magnetism was redefined as a causal force. Ether was conceived as a homogenous fluid, filling all uspace that was not occupied by other bodies, but devoid of properties except for its ability to provide a continuum through which magnetism could proceed. Until Newton, scientists were still not sure about gravity – whether it operated like magnetism through the ether, or as a mechanical force. They were more comfortable with the idea of a diffuse substance filling space than something immaterial, since it fit both the theory of a mechanistic universe, and preserved the causal nature of space, without resorting to teleological explanations. These ideas were expressed most succinctly by the older contemporary of Newton, British chemist, Robert Boyle (1627-1691), who greatly elaborated the theory of ether, and prepared the way for Newton's theories about gravity, which took the notion of ether for granted.

The concept of ether was gradually replaced by field theory through two centuries of post-Newtonian experimentation that included Faraday's discovery of electromagnetic induction in 1831, Maxwell's work with electromagnetic fields in the 1870s, and Becquerel's discovery of radioactivity in 1896. Field theory allowed scientists to return to the concept of empty space, with which they were more comfortable, while preserving causal explanations for what happened within space. Electricity, magnetism, gravity, radioactivity, and cohesion were conceived as forces operating within fields, and this conception maintained the basic model of space as a neutral abstract container for predictable causal processes.

The Quantum Revolution's Deconstruction Of Cartesian-Newtonian Space

After Einstein's discovery that mass and energy were equivalent, science underwent another yet serious paradigm shift, and the whole Cartesian-Newtonian conception of space as an arena in which causal forces acted on material bodies began to break down. For it was no longer clear where bodies ended and forces began, and whether the intervening space was filled with forces acting on bodies, forces acting on other forces, bodies acting on other bodies, or all of the above. New insights into the atomic structure of matter were beginning to suggest that matter was constantly breaking down, releasing energy, and reformulating itself, so rapidly it could scarcely be documented. Einstein's discovery that gravity affected not only *space*, but also *time* meant that the old school scientists could no longer be sure where space ended and time began. To explain how this could be so, Einstein theorized that space curved in the vicinity of large bodies, but flattened out at a distance. This is why, for example, the trajectory of a comet would appear to enter a steeply curved path near the Sun, but straighten out in space.

These discoveries shattered the old model of space as homogenous inert media. Space was no longer empty, except for the discrete material bodies that interacted within it, and were acted upon. It was now conceived as a space-time continuum, literally teeming with quantum-mechanical activity, in which virtual particles were created and destroyed in the blink of an eye, and energy and matter shape-shifted back and forth through cycles of endless transformation. After experiments conducted by Einstein, Planck, Bohr and others, the solid bodies occupying space no longer seemed so solid, nor their motion quite so predictable. According to Heisenberg's Principle of Uncertainty, it was possible to know either the location of a body in space, or its momentum, but not both simultaneously. Schrödinger, who speculated that his cat was both dead and alive (or anything in the material universe both existed and didn't exist) until actually observed, seemed to imply that space was more a continuum of possibilities than a containment of measurable certainties. Indeed, as Richard Tarnas points out (356):

> By the end of the third decade of the twentieth century, virtually every major postulate of the earlier scientific conception had been controverted: the atoms as solid, indestructible, and separate building blocks of nature; space and time as independent absolutes, the strict mechanistic causality of all phenomena; the possibility of objective observation of nature. Such a fundamental transformation in the scientific world picture was staggering . . .

Yet despite these remarkable developments, what is even more remarkable is that the work of Einstein, Planck, Bohr, Heisenberg and other quantum mechanical theorists only seemed to reinforce the notion of an impersonal universe, devoid of Spirit or soul, in which human beings were at the mercy of strictly material forces beyond their control. Though popular writers such as Fritjof Capra, Gary Zukov and Fred Alan Wolf have written intriguing books outlining the philosophical and metaphysical implications of quantum theory, by and large, quantum theory has had little impact on the way we understand who we are as embodied souls. Where these ideas have filtered down to the masses, they have reinforced the notion that life is inherently unpredictable, and that even science can no longer be trusted to supply definitive answers in the face of life's uncertainty. For the most part, quantum theory is simply too inaccessible to the layperson, and too arcane even for most scientists to assimilate. Even after 70-plus years of consideration and study, there is no comprehensive treatise comparable to Newton's *Principia* that would tie quantum theory together into a coherent worldview capable of altering the everyday practice of science. No one disputes the significance of these discoveries, but in practice, scientists and laypersons alike tend to cling to the more reassuring Newtonian worldview, where space is understood as an arena in which causal forces impact moving bodies (including people) and can still be measured objectively by science.

Though several generations of scientists have lived intimately with quantum theory, science as a whole remains relatively impervious to the fact that the philosophical rug has been pulled out from under it. Scientists have gravitated to the practical applications of these new ideas, spawning a host of technological inventions ranging from smart bombs and robotic nanotechnology to digital consumer electronics, fiber optics, semiconductors, and CT scans. But the deeper metaphysical implications of quantum theory are simply not within the scope or interest of science to address. As science writer, John Horgan has observed, "if the theory can foretell the performance of a doped gallium arsenide semiconductor, why worry about its epistemological implications?" Scientists are, in fact, systematically trained not to consider the epistemological or metaphysical implications of their work.

Scientists are also trained to consider only the external, objective world and to separate themselves conceptually from that world. They are conditioned to believe that the world is knowable using the empirical methodologies they have evolved over several hundred years of fine-tuning, and they see nothing within the quantum revolution to change that fact. The few scientists attempting to understand the deeper implications of quantum theory for science itself are, for the most part, attempting to reconcile the subatomic chaos discovered by quantum theorists with the fact that the external, objective world still behaves on the macro-scale, very much as scientists conditioned by Newtonian physics expect it to (Semeniuk). Scientists are not suddenly opening to a new way of understanding reality that would make space for the concept of soul, much less trying to provide a language by which the soul could more clearly understand its journey through the embodied world. They are instead scrambling to patch the holes in their leaky, but trusted Newtonian bucket.

As staunch science advocate, John Maddox, summarizes this attitude: "there is nothing in quantum mechanics or chaos theory that puts God back into mechanics. The laws of mechanics, which have been amended once since Newton's time, may have to be amended yet again if people manage to make a bridge between gravitation and quantum mechanics, but there is nothing to suggest they are other than deterministic, one state of affairs following from its precursors" (The Prevalent Distrust). As long as this attitude prevails, the new breed of scientist will be no more capable of helping you or I explore the subjective truth of soul space, or find our place within the cosmic scheme of things, than their predecessors.

Naturally, we can enjoy the technological fruits of these discoveries, but our relationship to the roots of the tree from which all things are made possible remains hidden. Not because it is not there for anyone with a clear intention to see, but because guided by the unspoken rules of positivistic, literal-minded scientists, we are unconsciously conditioned not to look. Most of the pioneers who made the discoveries that upset paradigms and triggered revolutions in our scientific world view - from Aristotle to Descartes to Copernicus to Newton to Einstein and beyond - were deeply religious men, as committed to understanding the soul's place within the cosmic order as they were in mapping that order according to scientific principles of objectivity, rational empiricism, and materialism. Though Spirit and matter came together in the conceptual focus of these great men, what prevailed in their passing was an increasing split between Spirit and matter that left the soul with no place of its own.

The good news is that there is also a great deal of useful information within all of their discoveries, as Capra, Zukov, Wolf, and others have pointed out. When this information is understood symbolically, rather than as literal causal truth, it can yield a great deal of conceptual reinforcement to our emerging language of soul. We need not wait for scientists to embrace the metaphysical implications of their work to make use of these implications ourselves. If space, for example, is understood by quantum physicists as an arena in which matter is constantly breaking down and reformulating, then we can easily understand this as the interplay of life and death at the most basic levels on which manifest reality exists. If energy and matter are interchangeable, then we are faced with a scientific metaphor for the ongoing fusion between Spirit and body that makes soul possible. As energy formulates matter, Spirit takes up residence in a body and the soul is set in motion. As matter reverts to an energetic state, the soul is released from the body and becomes absorbed within the larger oceanic, omnipresent body of Spirit. If space curves in the region of bodies asserting a gravitational pull, then space must be qualitatively different for each individual soul at the center of subjective space. And so on. By considering metaphorically the same information that science takes literally, we gain a point of entry to an understanding of space that is much more useful to a potential language of soul.

Reconceptualizing Space as a Resonant Soul Field

In redefining space, it is helpful to draw upon our previous notion of the soul as a morphogenetic field. Again, though Sheldrake is perhaps not quite ready to make the leap from a biological theory to a liberal, metaphorical application of his ideas to an understanding of soul, he does follow in the metaphysical footsteps of all those aforementioned paradigm shifters, and I cannot help but believe he would not only be open to the idea, but actually encourage it. Though Sheldrake doesn't use the word "soul," he does say at the conclusion of his landmark book, *A New Science of Life* (206-207):

> *The universe as a whole could have a cause and a purpose only if it were itself created by a conscious agent which transcended it . . . . If this transcendent being were the source of the universe and of everything within it, all created things would in some sense participate in its nature. The more or less limited 'wholeness' of organisms at all levels of complexity could then be seen as a reflection of the transcendent unity on which they depended, and from which they were ultimately derived.*

Sheldrake goes on to "affirm . . . the causal efficiency of the conscious self," but not without first giving that self a space to play in that has been refilled with Parmenides' mystical assertion of omnipresent Being. Sheldrake also provides the theoretical basis for a return of the soul to the center of that space. For once we place the soul within a morphogenetic field where it becomes the central attractor for an extended field of resonance, we have the basis for redefining space in terms more relevant to the embodied soul's experience. This is a fairly technical way of saying each of us is the center of our own subjective universe, but the more elaborate description adds a dimension to this simple idea that helps us explore and discuss it more clearly. Let's play with this image a bit, and see how this is so.

As the earliest religious cultures intuitively realized with horror, a body without a living, breathing connection to Spirit is just a dead lump of matter, not worth the chemicals that compose it. Once Spirit enters a body, however, then you have life. Within the language of morphogenetic resonance, you also have an attractor that serves as the center of a resonant field. Since the soul is evolving toward a fulfillment of its purpose – which we might describe in the simplest terms as a fully conscious embodiment of Spirit – the soul's power as an attractor will also be purposeful. The soul will draw to itself all those experiences within its resonant field that can in some way facilitate the actualization of this purpose. These experiences will hold the power to evoke a sensory, emotional and/or imagistic response, and draw into awareness the necessary lessons to be learned on the way to full embodiment. Where the soul creatively integrates these lessons, its experience will be pleasurable; where the soul is unwilling or unable to do so, its experiences will be painful. Through orienting itself between these two basic polarities (and every other polarity within its being), the soul will fine-tune its capacity as an attractor, clarify its understanding of purpose, and hone its capacity to actualize purpose within the morphogenetic field that encompasses its embodied life.

Space, for the soul, will then be defined as a nexus of relationships between the core sense of being that sits as an attractor at the center of the space and everything around it with which it is in resonance. Within the context of this definition, it should be obvious that although you and I may occupy the same world – say as neighbors, or even more poignantly as siblings growing up in the same family – the experience of our respective resonant soul spaces will be qualitatively different for each of us, since who we are and are in the process of becoming, on our way to a full embodiment of Spirit, will necessarily be different. Among the myriad objects, people, ideas, and experiences it is possible to attract, each of us will evolve a different pattern of relationships; and our relationship to each of the myriad objects, people, ideas, and experiences within our shared objective space will be qualitatively different on a subjective level.

Science is ready to supply a causal explanation for the differences between your experience and mine, but can't explain why two people exposed to the same causative factors will respond differently. The answer lies in the fact that as embodied souls, you and I are different beings with different lessons to learn, and consequently will attract a different set of circumstances capable of facilitating those lessons. As attractors, you and I will function differently, and the consequent ordering of soul space will be different for each of us, even though objectively the embodied world we share appears to be the same.

An important corollary to this revitalized concept of space is that the measurement of physical distance emphasized by science becomes largely irrelevant. If I think about you – and especially if my thoughts evoke feelings, a cellular memory of sensory experience, or imagery – then you are in my resonant soul space, though you may physically be thousands of miles away. Conversely, if you are standing next to me, and I am unaware of you, or not in resonance with you, then we inhabit different soul spaces, even though we are physically side by side. Within a language of soul, resonance means being moved to a heightened awareness of relationship through sensory input, emotion, or imagery, and when this happens, physical distance collapses and becomes meaningless. World events, images on television or in movies, dreams of people, places and things that don't exist in the "real" world measured by science, can all become part of the resonant space in which the soul seeks a sense of meaning and purpose.

Defining Soul Space From an Astrological Perspective

Within the language of astrology, soul space is primarily described through the arrangement of planets and signs in relation to houses. Houses are divisions of the space through which the Earth rotates about its axis. If the Earth is understood as the extended body of the soul, as discussed in Chapter One, then the Earth's rotation about its axis becomes analogous to the process by which the embodied life revolves around the soul's internal axis. Within the context of this analogy, the Earth's axis symbolizes the axis of attraction through which Spirit is embodied on Earth, and through which the embodied life of the soul is generated. The divisions of the Earth's rotation around this axis are depicted by the houses of a birthchart, and can likewise be understood to symbolize the resonant soul field that evolves as a consequence of embodiment.

Each house describes an area of life experience – finances, health, intimate relationships and so on – that in turn provides a potential context in which core issues of consequence to the soul play themselves out. Astrologically, these dynamics are indicated by the presence of planets in the houses, or to a lesser extent by planets *ruling* (in resonance with) the signs on the *cusps* (at the beginning of houses), and the *aspects* (angular relationships) between planets that occupy or rule houses. Each planet acts as an attractor within the soul space, as it is defined by the house the planet occupies or rules. Put another way, if a planet occupies or rules a house, then we can safely assume it will attract experiences that facilitate soul growth within the area of life experience associated with the house. When two planets form an aspect between houses, then together they will attract experiences that resonate within the soul space encompassed by the relationship between the two houses.

If, for example, the planet Mercury occupies the 1st house (see Figure 6), then it serves as an attractor for all those experiences that facilitate the evolution of a basic sense of identity, which is the fundamental focus of the soul space encompassed by the 1st house. With Mercury in my 1st house, I have come to learn who I am (experienced the unfolding of a 1st house process) by following my curiosity, attempting to understand my process in words at each step of the way, cultivating the art of communication, exercising and broadening my mobility, learning to be more flexible, adaptable, and spontaneously responsive (all ways of being we can associate astrologically with Mercury).

Through a similar process of astrological association, I can also recognize that with Mars in my 9th house (see Figure 7), it has often been through taking a contrarian position, engaging in heated discussion, and butting heads with those holding different opinions (all ways of being resonant with Mars) that I have gradually broadened my own understanding and hammered out a life philosophy, part of which I am sharing in this book (the 9th house is associated with writing for publication). Evolving a life philosophy is a process that takes place in the 9th house of any birthchart, thus having Mars in my 9th house suggests that my life philosophy will evolve in ways that are resonant with Mars' basic nature.

Through the interplay between Mercury and Mars in my chart (see Figure 8), connected by the *square* (90°) *aspect* between them, my soul space defines itself as an arena in which identity (1st house process) crystallizes through the gradual articulation (exercise

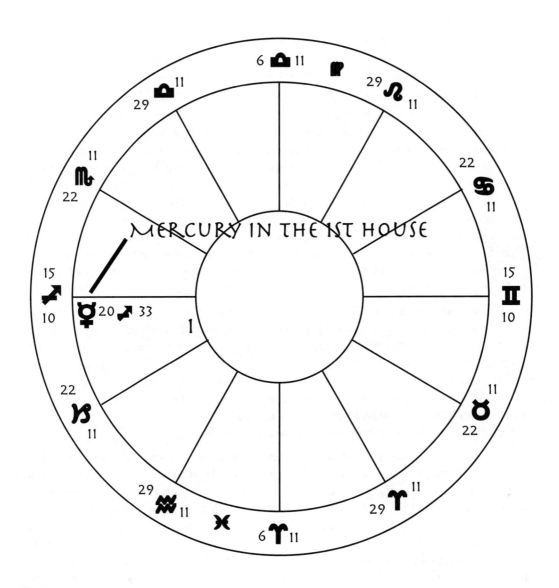

FIGURE 6

FIGURE 7

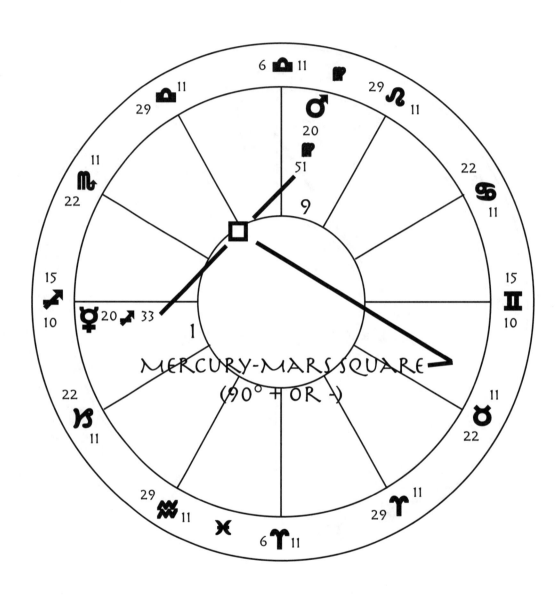

FIGURE 8

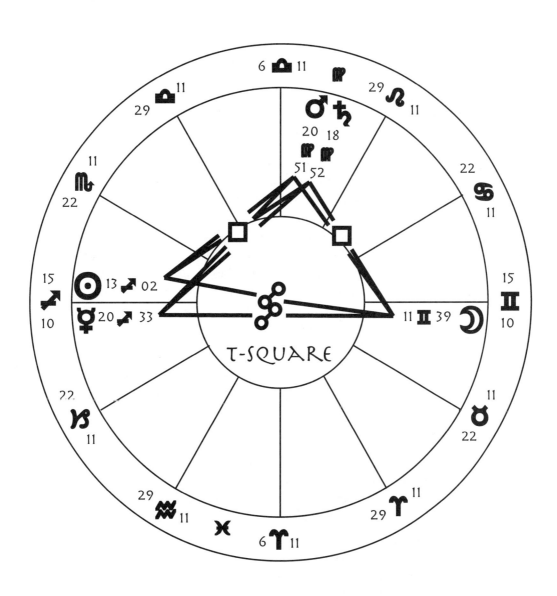

FIGURE 9

of Mercury in the 1ˢᵗ house) of a contrarian (the influence of Mars) philosophy of life (in the 9ᵗʰ house).

Meanwhile, since both Mercury and Mars are part of a larger pattern in my chart – called a *t-square* – involving no less than five of ten major planetary bodies (see Figure 9), it can be considered an important relationship within my birthchart as a whole, and thus a relationship central to outworking my soul's purpose in this life. There is of course far more to this pattern, and to my soul's purpose than can be encompassed by a discussion of this one aspect, and a full exploration of this topic would be far beyond the scope of this book. For our purpose here, suffice it to say, that within the whole pattern of my birthchart, the square between Mercury and Mars provides one important point of entry into a deeper understanding of soul process, and of my soul space. It represents a core attractor within soul space, around which lessons and issues of major importance to my evolution as a soul will revolve.

Soul space is not measured by distance, or motion, or the interplay of objective, causal dynamics, as a scientific approach to space would imply. It is instead measured subjectively by the quality of my evolving relationship to myself and to the embodied world around me. My relationships within the embodied world will, in turn, reflect the relationship within myself between various subjective aspects of my own being. Within my soul space, the square between Mercury and Mars symbolizes a source of attraction that will draw to me experiences designed to teach me how to work with Mercury and Mars, and all that they symbolize, at ever higher levels of integration. The quality of soul space I enjoy at a given point in life will depend upon how well I have managed to integrate these lessons. When I was 7 years old, the dynamic between Mercury and Mars was rather crude, and the fragile identity I was able to cultivate for myself at the time was regularly undone through the verbal abuse of my peers (Mercury) and daily fist fights on the playground at school (Mars), which I invariably lost. Now, at age 53, I am somewhat more skilled at expressing my contrarian point of view, without starting a fight, although I must still remain ever vigilant to that possibility. I like to think I am gradually evolving as a soul in relation to these recurrent resonant lessons, attracted as a reflection of the square between Mercury and Mars in my chart.

The core issues posed by Mercury-Mars provide a pivot point around which soul growth can take place over the course of a lifetime of experience. The part of me that resonates with this square will continue attracting opportunities for growth in relation to the issues that it raises, as long as I have something to learn from them. The space in which I assimilate these lessons will host an ever-changing parade of objects, people, ideas, and experiences resonant with these lessons. The issues will serve as the attractor within the space, and the space will reflect the patterns of resonance that revolve around the lessons. As I learn what I am here to learn, the quality of the soul space in which Mercury and Mars do their perpetual dance will gradually become more refined, more conscious, and more reflective of an harmonious embodiment of Spirit. I am here, in other words, to learn how to communicate my truth without unnecessarily antagonizing others or provoking their anger, and to the extent that I learn to do this, or fail to learn to do this, my resonant soul space will adjust itself accordingly.

This is a very different concept of space than that entertained by science, but to the extent that science insists on defining space strictly in terms of objective, mathematically measurable, causal parameters, it will be inadequate in providing a language with which to discuss the process of human evolution taking place within resonant soul space. The morphogenetic model being developed by Rupert Sheldrake begins to depart from this rigid insistence, and in doing so, becomes a useful template for our purpose.

Endnotes

[1] To explain how change was possible, Aristotle proposed a series of nested celestial spheres moving through space in relation to each other, which had great metaphysical significance as evidence of God's handiwork. Incidentally, this notion of moving celestial spheres had astrological connotations, which Aristotle acknowledged, although since he considered motion in space to be a causal concept, his model has limited utility in helping us to articulate an astrology of soul.

Chapter Twelve
Through Inanna's Sixth Gate
Into Cyclical Soul Time

A s with space, the scientific concept of time will also prove to be of limited use in providing a framework to understand the soul's process, unless it is modified to accommodate the qualitative, subjective, and purposeful nature of the soul's experience. In this chapter I will discuss time as it can be understood both from within the scientific worldview, and from a more useful soul-based understanding. Toward the end of the chapter, I will also demonstrate how a soul-based understanding of time can be articulated astrologically as an empirical point of entry into a deeper understanding of the soul's process.

A Brief History of the Evolution
Of the Scientific Concept of Time

It should not be surprising that the same Greek philosophers who argued over space in our last chapter also argued over time. The central dispute concerned whether or not time even existed. Parmenides, who mistrusted any information coming from the senses, and taught that Being was immutable (not subject to change), argued that contrary to our sensory experience, time was an illusion. At the other extreme, Heraclitus argued that nothing was immutable and everything was subject to perpetual change, just as it appeared to be. Time, for Heraclitus, was the mechanism by which all things came into being and evolved. Heraclitus postulated the existence of *logos*, or a divine fire that set being in motion and ordered its becoming. The concept of *logos*, it seems, predated Aristotle's understanding of teleology, in which time was also a mechanism through which the soul's purpose was realized. Implied in this understanding was the idea that the experience of time is qualitative in nature. We cannot evolve, except through change, and change necessarily implies a change in quality of experience. Heraclitus also recognized the interplay of opposites to be the driving tension that set change in motion, and in this regard was a Western counterpart to (as well as a probable contemporary of) Lao Tzu[1].

As in the debate about space, early scientists tread a middle ground between Parmenides' and Heraclitus' respective theories of time. In theory, they accepted Parmenides' theory of the immutability of Being, but they tried to reconcile this appealing metaphysical concept with the observation that everything around them appeared to be changing all the time. Eventually scientists would reject the idea of immutability, but not without also dismissing the association of time with quality and purpose that Heraclitus brought to the discussion. Also lost was the relationship between time and the cyclical interplay of polar opposites. As remarked by Heraclitus' predecessor, Anaximander, the things of this world "make reparations to one another for their injustice, according to the ordinance of time" (qtd. in Melchert 14), a rather convoluted way of saying that polar opposites tend to balance each other out over time. The mechanism for doing this is the cycle, in which an ascendant waxing half cycle, or *hemicycle*, brings one set of forces into play, while a descending *hemicycle* triggers their opposite.

The rational cosmologists – motivated in part by a desire to extract all metaphysical connotations from the concept of time – dismissed the idea of cycles as the primitive vestige of a pre-scientific, mythopoetic and overtly astrological era. Instrumental to this dismissal was Democritus, who agreed with Parmenides that qualitative change was impossible, but disagreed with him by arguing that quantitative change was not only possible, but the sole basis for all possible observation of change. As mentioned earlier, Democritus theorized the existence of invisible atoms, characterized only by measurable properties - size, shape, and motion. He further suggested that observable changes in quality were actually measurable changes in the arrangement of various combinations of atoms, which remained essentially unchanged. As later empirical scientists, such as Hobbes, Galileo, and Newton increasingly dismissed the notion of quality, scientists then set out to measure these quantitative changes. A casualty of this trend in scientific thinking was that time was dissociated from quality, and became a strictly mathematical context within which changes in quantity – particularly motion of physical bodies – could be measured.

While Hume argued that space, time, and causality were all habits of mind, Kant countered that be that as it may, they were habits of mind that were intrinsic to the functioning of mind itself, and as such, were the only possible basis on which reality could be known. Although they were synthetic – that is, manufactured by the mind – they were still necessary constructs since they enabled the mind to comprehend what apparently existed outside of itself. A mathematical approach to understanding space and time was justifiable, according to Kant, because it successfully mirrored the way the mind worked. "Geometry is based upon the pure intuition of space. Arithmetic attains its concepts of numbers by the successive addition of units in time" (qtd. in Melchert 440). Space and time are thus habits of mind, which naturally give rise to a mathematical interpretation of reality. By telling scientists that it was okay to think of space and time in linear, quantifiable terms, because that was the way the mind worked, Kant effectively dismissed the notion that they could be seriously considered in any other way. From that point forward, a cyclical and qualitative understanding of time – more amenable, as we have seen, to the soul's process – became increasingly dismissed as unscientific.

The Religious Notion of Time as a Destructive Force

It is important to note that scientists are not the only ones who have ravaged time. Religious thinkers such as Augustine, also made a distinction between a sense of time that could be measured and the timelessness of God. To the extent that soul became identified with Spirit, and its goal was conceived as an immortal reunion with Spirit, then time was understood by religious thinkers as something that worked against the soul. Time was an essentially destructive process that culminated in death, while spiritual salvation was widely understood as a liberation from the destructive power of time. This was true not just within the Western Judeo-Christian-Islamic tradition, but also among Eastern religions, where enlightenment, *moksha*, *nirvana*, and other flavors of religious triumph essentially involved freedom from the endlessly agonizing wheel of time – which like Parmenides, many considered to be illusion. Meanwhile, God was widely construed as existing in a timeless place, where He waited for the individual soul to join him.

Thus, while scientists stripped time of its qualitative associations, and the cyclical interplay of polar opposites, religious thinkers gave time a negative connotation that conceptually removed it from its rightful place within the soul's experience. Religious thinkers were right in associating time with the destructive power of death, but wrong in assuming that this was something to be avoided, postponed, or transcended. For the embodied soul is who we are in relationship to the mystery of the *whole* Cycle that encompasses *both* life and death, and time is what allows the soul to cultivate and deepen that relationship. In fact, as the cycle of time waxes and wanes, the soul comes into being, and within this context, we might assume that far from being something that works against the soul, time is what makes the evolution of soul possible.

Heidegger's Contribution to a Philosophy of Soul Time

Time was understood in this constructive way by the 20th century German philosopher, Martin Heidegger, to be the mechanism that allows being, or what he called *Dasein*, to unfold. Truth, for Heidegger, was not something that pre-exists in nature, as it is for most scientists, but rather a knowing that reveals itself only as we open to it. Thus there was for Heidegger an intimate relationship between the knower, the known, and the process of knowing that was inherently subjective in nature. The highest truth was an innate awareness of being, which revealed itself gradually and allowed the realization of its potentialities over time. Time, for Heidegger, was a context in which self-awareness became possible, self-actualization unfolded, and the meaning of life emerged.

Although Heidegger was well aware of the suffering inherent in life, and "the sober anxiety which brings us face to face with our individualized potentiality for Being" (qtd. in Melchert 690), he also considered the process of actualizing this potential to be inherently joyful. This joy Heidegger called "anticipatory resoluteness," suggesting that it is a force that propels us forward through time with determination to be all we can be. Heidegger also understood how the inevitability of death lent an edge to the resoluteness with which we attempted to anticipate our evolution. We are racing against the clock – not as religion suggested, to make the leap into identification with a timeless Spirit before time runs out – but to more authentically become ourselves within our embodied existence, while we have the opportunity. There are many forces pulling us this way and that, away from authenticity, and in order to realize our goal, in the time allotted to us, we must approach the task with care. We must learn to use time consciously in order to discover the subjective truth of our being, and most importantly, to actualize that truth in the living of our lives.

If the embodied soul exists only within the context of this life in this body, then we might legitimately wonder why the soul should be concerned with self-actualization at all. On the other hand, given that the soul's process of self-actualization inevitably requires it to come into what Buddhists would call *right relationship* to everything and everyone within its resonant space, then self-actualization is the path to the very transcendence of time that is necessary to ensure continuity after death. For it is only when the individual soul identifies with the Whole while alive, that its disembodiment at death ceases to be problematic. And it is only when we realize the interconnectedness of all Life and experience our place within the Whole that what happens to the individual speck of life that harbors this body when death reclaims it becomes a moot point.

If we use the time allotted to us to come into right relationship with everything and everyone in our soul space, then what survives our death is the living resonance of those relationships, which our participation in life helped create, and which continues to resonate within the soul space of others after we are gone. The trees we plant will continue to grow; the children we raise will carry our essence forward; the creative contributions we make will serve as the springboard for future generations to make theirs. The more authentic we become, the more authentic will be the world that we leave behind us. To the extent that we have made conscious use of our time, then we transcend the limitations of time as understood from the scientific (and the religious) perspective, because every seed of authenticity we plant will continue to blossom despite the fact that for us personally, time has run out.

We would not be talking about Buddha, or Heidegger, or Plato, or any of the other great beings mentioned in this book if this were not a possibility. To self-actualize is to create a legacy that will live on, after we are dead, and to enhance the quality of all Life as it cycles through us and beyond. We need not attain fame or glory to leave a legacy, but we do need to actualize an authentic self, and cultivate the potentiality of our Being, within the embodied world, as Heidegger and many others have invited us to do. We also need to learn how to love, and how to care for the resonant space in which we live, by paying attention to the quality of our interactions with others, and with the web of life that enfolds us. In short, we must learn to "care for the soul," to borrow a phrase from Thomas Moore (xiv – xx), and to gradually broaden our understanding of what soul is through a caring and conscious exploration of the resonant space in which it exists.

Caring for the soul is a process that involves learning to make conscious use of time. Making conscious use of time is important because the embodied soul evolves in time, and the human lifespan is of limited and uncertain duration. While Plato and the religious immortalists sought to transcend the destructive capacity of time, caring for the soul actually means learning to use time constructively. We must learn to more consciously and deliberately harness the creative opportunities within time, without losing sight of the inextricable relationship between time and death. It is only as we live each moment as though it were our last, as conscious as possible of the opportunities for growth within it, and as willing to take advantage of them as we can, that the soul is able to gradually fulfill its purpose and become what it was meant to be.

The key to being able to use time consciously is to understand the cycle, which contains both creative possibility and an acknowledgment of the laws of entropy to which all creative endeavors are subject. The soul evolves in relation to the cycle of life and death, and the cycle provides a context within which the process of growth can be more clearly understood. As we become aware of the rhythm of the cycle, and the waxing and waning of the life force within it, we become more conscious of the possibilities inherent in each moment, and begin to use time more constructively.

The Qualitative Nature of Soul Time

This implies, of course, that time is qualitative in nature – that each moment in time is different from every other moment in time, and that using time more consciously is a matter of becoming aware of the quality of the moment. This is a radical concept considered within the context of the scientific worldview, but it is common sense for anyone who takes a moment to consider it. Is not the budding of leaves in spring qualitatively different than the falling of leaves in autumn? Is not the moment in which your mother died qualitatively different from the moment in which you got that last raise at your job? Is not the moment of horror in the wake of the terrorist bombing of the Twin Towers qualitatively different than the global sense of elation when the Berlin Wall came down? Each moment in time is qualitatively unique, and in order to use it wisely, we must learn to discern these qualitative differences with greater skill.

The qualitative nature of time has been noted by a few great thinkers, most notably, the French philosopher, Henri Bergson, and by the Chinese in their delineation of the

◇◇

64 hexagrams of the I Ching. The I Ching is useful in describing the interplay of yin and yang within the context of an entire cycle of unfolding possibilities, and understanding a given moment within the context of that cycle. In the West, Bergson argued that time was not simply a quantitative measure of motion in space, but also experiential –a qualitative interaction between consciousness and the resonant field in which it operates. Bergson did not speak of time in terms of resonance, but he clearly understood time, or *duration*, as he referred to it, to be a sensory, emotional and imagistic interaction with the world. To interact with the world in what we would call a soulful way, is to engage a process he called *intuition*. To be intuitive, according to Bergson, is to approach time consciously as we have discussed it above - a process that necessarily implies conscious attention to the quality of one's experience in the moment.

Both Bergson and the Taoists have parted company with the scientific mindset which insists that time is strictly quantitative in nature. To this day, scientists wrestle with Bergson's concept of duration, which implies time is a subjective experience, partially rooted in the past through memory, and partially projected into the future through fantasy. Scientific research about memory largely concerns the biological mechanisms that produce them, their accuracy with respect to objective reality, and the causal factors impacting accuracy (Searleman), As we shall see in more detail in Chapter Fourteen, fantasies are treated in much the same way. This is irrelevant, to a soul seeking to make conscious use of time, since it is the subjective infusion of memory and fantasy with idiosyncrasy, accurate or not, that makes duration what it is for the individual soul.

Paradoxically, memories are created when we pay full attention to our experiences in the moment, and as we consciously register sensory information, feelings, images and impressions, or engage the world intuitively in the sense in which Bergson used that word. Put another way, memories are the registration of moments of soul resonance, in which we attract experiences that are meaningful to the soul. Memories may or may not be accurate in the objective sense, but they are thoroughly infused with subjective significance by our emotional investment in them. In those ordinary moments in which the soul is not resonating, or intuitively engaging soul space, our memories are likely to be of short duration and little consequence. On the other hand, those memories that survive for years, retained as episodes and anecdotes in the perpetually unfolding stories of our lives, are those in which the experience of soul resonance was relatively strong.

Fantasy, or projection of future possibilities, in contrast to memory, tends to occur when we are not resonating in the present moment. This is a more subliminal process, referred to by practitioners of meditation as the activity of *monkey mind*, a racing back and forth between memories, fleeting impressions of the present moment, and anticipation of future possibilities. When we are engaged in this fantasy activity - which for most people constitutes a fairly large percentage of their time - we leave the realm of measured clock time, and enter soul time. In soul time, we move through soul space by a process Freud recognized as "free association," but that we might now label resonant association, in accordance with the current model we are exploring. Resonant association is a process of circling one or more internal attractors, along pathways of resonance that have formed in soul space around those attractors.

Following the Soul Through Soul Time

If, for example, I am walking downtown to buy a book of stamps at a post office in Texas, and encounter, a sandy-colored dog, I might suddenly remember a vision quest I took several years ago on some property owned by a friend from New Mexico, in which I was followed by their sandy-colored dog named Socrates. Remembering the dog, I might then also remember my friend, with whom I have subsequently had a falling out, and begin to feel sad at the loss of our friendship. Feeling sad, I might suddenly notice a homeless person, digging through a dumpster on the street on which I am walking in present time. I might then remember that I was planning to take several boxes of old clothes to the Salvation Army this coming weekend, and briefly imagine doing that. The anticipation would remind me that in the past I have found interesting books at bargain prices, tucked away unnoticed on the book shelf in the back of the Salvation Army Thrift Store. I remember the book I am writing, and begin thinking about how time is not linear at all, but apparently a random circulation of consciousness through soul space. At that moment, I might arrive at the post office, and get in line. While in line, it might occur to me that all this meandering through soul space has purpose, just as my walk in external space to the post office had purpose. And so on, through a similar process of mental meandering all the way back to the computer at which I sit now, writing this sentence, remembering my minor epiphany at the post office.

Most of the time, this is how our mind works. To an objective observer, we are doing whatever we appear to be doing in physical space, moving in chronological time toward goals that appear to be the natural causal consequences of our actions. Meanwhile, we are also meandering internally through soul space, weaving together an ongoing dialogue in soul time that may or may not have anything at all to do with what appears to be happening externally in the outer world. Occasionally, there will be a moment of intersection between inner and outer process, such as my moment of minor epiphany at the post office, when my realization that this internal meandering had purpose coincided with my return to awareness of the external purpose that prompted the errand I was on. In these moments of intersection between inner and outer experience, there is a heightened sense of recognition of information that can in some way be useful to the soul.

These moments of intersection were conceived by the early Greeks as the confluence of two very different kinds of time – *chronos*, which was essentially clock-time, measurable objectively, and the same for everyone; and *kairos*, which was subjective soul time, during which the soul meandered in the fashion described above, oblivious to the passage of time in the outer, objective world. Subject as we are in modern culture to the unconscious metaphysics of science, in which measurable experiences are valued and non-measurable experiences are not, we live lives that largely revolve around and are often oppressively dominated by *chronos*. The wrist watch, adapted from the pocket watches of train conductors, whose trains were expected to run on time, and now necessary for most people to function in the outer world, has become the ubiquitous symbol of enslavement to *chronos*. Yet as the early Greeks recognized, it is *kairos* that affords the opportunity to connect with ourselves in a more meaningful way. Or to put it in the context of our present discussion, it is *kairos* where the soul meanders in search of itself.

From the perspective of *chronos*, a soul in *kairos* might appear to be wasting time, but this is actually where the work of soul gets done. For in *kairos*, we explore the network of resonant connections within soul space that place us in living relationship to the Whole. Then, as we emerge from kairos into the more conscious world of clock-time, as though waking from a dream, we have the opportunity to become more aware of these patterns, and harvest a piece of information potentially of great value to the soul.

Whether or not the soul is conscious enough to take advantage of this opportunity or use the information available in kairos is another matter entirely. Most of the insights that come during the intersection of kairos and chronos are relatively minor, and may not have enough significance in the overall scheme of things to register for more than a fleeting second. Most of the time, the soul will slip right back into its unconscious meandering, and lose whatever insights are potentially available for harvesting. Nonetheless, whenever kairos and chronos come together and soul space in some way resonates with physical space, we have an opportunity to learn something new about who we are, why we are here, where we are and where we are going. To the extent that we take these messages to heart, and intentionally incorporate them into our everyday lives, we experience some measure of soul growth – of embodying Spirit more completely and of coming more fully and more consciously into relationship with the Whole.

Synchronicity and the Opportunity for Soul Growth

Jung called these moments of potential soul growth, in which inner and outer come together through awareness in present time, *synchronicity*. Synchronicity is often understood as "meaningful coincidence," but what makes the experience meaningful is the confluence of soul time and clock time that makes possible a more conscious awareness of the relationship between inner and outer. Whenever our soul process

– this apparently random meandering through soul space in soul time – comes into sufficient alignment with the manifest universe for us to notice it, we create an opening through which Spirit can enter matter more completely. This happens because we are bringing our awareness more completely into the embodied world, and our awareness is the presence of Spirit within us. This is definitely a meaningful event from the soul's perspective, because the soul's purpose *is* to bring Spirit more consciously into the embodied world. Each moment of synchronicity is both a demonstration and an actual experience of embodiment. The more synchronicity we experience in our lives, the more embodied Spirit becomes in us. The more consciously we are able to bring our meandering in kairos into the present moment, the more soul-full our lives become.

When soul space coincides with physical space, and soul time moves into the present moment, the soul has the opportunity to peer into the true nature of the embodied world. What is revealed to us in this moment, however briefly, is a glimpse of the interconnected Whole that permeates soul space, in which Spirit flows endlessly in and out of form, without ever disappearing. Within the synchronistic moment is the opportunity to realize that we are part of the endless recycling of Life that flows from Spirit, according to an evolutionary plan that we are helping to fulfill. There is generally a great deal of soul work to do, before we are capable of fully absorbing the implications of this truth, but from the soul's perspective, that is why we are here. Clearing away whatever obstacles block a full embrace of our true identity and our place within the Whole *is* our soul's purpose. As we spend our time doing this work, *kairos* will coincide with *chronos*, and we will become increasingly aware of the synchronicity that permeates life within the embodied world.

The more aware of synchronicity we are, the greater the opportunity for fulfillment of the soul's purpose will be. Thus, any truly useful language of soul will facilitate an awareness of the intersection of clock time and soul time. Since the soul evolves through its participation in various cycles, awareness of soul time is essentially awareness of where the soul is with regard to the cycles in which it is participating. In telling the stories about our lives that reveal who we are as souls, we generally lay those stories out in linear time. If we could somehow reconstruct these same stories from the perspective of cyclical time, we would begin to understand more clearly how soul time interpenetrates clock time and provides the ongoing opportunity for a more conscious embodiment of Spirit. Any language that could help us understand our life experiences in terms of the cycles that permeate them, would be a useful language of soul indeed.

Astrology as a Language of Soul Time

There is no more sophisticated system for understanding life in terms of cyclical time than astrology. Like the Taoists, astrologers believe that the quality of a given moment can be determined by reference to where the moment is in relation to the larger cycle of which it is part. Unlike the Taoists, who attempted to describe the moment in relation to a universal cycle of 64 phases, astrologers conceive of each moment as the reflection of many intersecting cycles, each symbolized by a planet or a planetary pair, and each a thread in a tapestry of becoming unique to the individual soul. An astrological birthchart is essentially a snapshot of these intersecting cycles, as they are playing themselves out at any given moment. Astrologers further observe that any being born at a given moment bears the quality of that moment, and that this being will evolve toward an actualization of its purpose in a manner that unfolds in accordance with the cycles in play at the time.

The moment of birth is the moment at which Spirit is embodied in matter, and from the astrological perspective, this moment – considered as a nexus of cycles – has deep, lifelong significance for the soul. The soul's evolutionary process, unfolding in soul time, takes place according to a timetable that can be mapped out in relation to the various cycles in play at the moment of birth. Put in a slightly different way, the moment of birth reflects a pattern of resonance with which the individual soul identifies and that serves as the foundation for a lifelong process of learning. The learning takes place through the cyclical activation and deactivation of that pattern. As a template for the formation of identity, the birthchart facilitates an exploration of soul space, and in its function as a complex attractor through which learning takes place, it becomes a tool through to help us make more conscious use of soul time.

These are radical notions within the context of the scientific paradigm, since there is no apparent cause that links a given pattern of resonance to the individual who resonates with it. Yet in the very act of attempting to discern these patterns of resonance between cosmos and the individual soul, we create an opening to a deeper knowledge of soul, because we are setting the intention to observe and become more consciously aware of the intersection between clock time and soul time. We could, as some astrologers have suggested, arbitrarily take any astrological pattern and use it as an intuitive springboard to this kind of self-knowledge. On the other hand, when we choose a pattern specifically related to the precise place and time in which we were born, we place ourselves at the center of a uniquely personal resonant space, where the qualitative nature of time can be experienced as a subjective extension of our being. It is the act of being born – that is to say, embodying Spirit – in a particular space and time that defines us as souls, and so to explore the symbolic implications of the space and time of our birth is to more consciously understand the particular embodiment of Spirit that we are. Looking at the birthchart as a description of various interpenetrating cycles, we can also arrive at a more conscious use of time. We can discern not only what we have come here to do, but when, and within what kind of time frame, we might best attempt to do it.

Applying Astrological Analysis to Soul Time

Perhaps it will be helpful at this point, to illustrate how this process works in actual practice. In discussing the notion of astrological space in Chapter Eleven, I used the example of my 1st house Mercury square to my 9th house Mars. I've identified this as an important pattern of resonance in my chart, out of which a relatively significant opportunity for soul growth might arise. Now let's take a closer look at how we might use astrology to articulate and explore this opportunity in more detail.

First, noting that the relationship between Mercury and Mars is an important feature of my resonant soul space, we can also assume that this relationship will also serve as a template for triggering a rhythmical pattern of resonance between them. Because they are *square* (90 degrees apart) at birth, the rhythm will tend to be composed of resonant beats at 90 degree intervals. In other words, every time Mercury moves to some multiple of 90 degrees from Mars, the pattern of resonance between these two planets will be emphasized somehow within my life experience. Likewise, every time Mars moves to some multiple of 90 degrees from Mercury, the pattern will also be activated. It should be noted here that because Mercury and Mars are in aspect *natally* (at birth), every transit of Mercury to Mars will also be a transit of Mercury to Mercury, and every transit of Mars to Mercury will also be a transit of Mars to Mars (see Figure 10). It is this dual triggering of both planets simultaneously by transit that constitutes an activation of the pattern of resonance between them.

We could track this rhythmical pattern in relation to Mercury's ever-changing relationship to Mars, as it moves through the sky, but because my natal chart establishes the subjective map to my personal soul space, it will be more informative to track moving (*transiting*) Mercury's changing relationship to stationary (*natal*) Mars, or transiting Mars' changing relationship to natal Mercury. While both the Mercury-Mars and the Mars-Mercury cycles will provide useful information about the pattern, the transits of the slower moving planet to the faster moving natal planet will generally reveal the pattern in greater depth. Metaphorically speaking, the slower the motion, the deeper, slower, and more meaningful the pattern of resonance. Thus, if we want to see this pattern of resonance at work in my life, the transiting cycle of Mars to natal Mercury would be the most useful exercise in observation.

Let's see what happens if I actually track this cycle. Looking backwards in the *ephemeris* (table of planetary positions) from today's date, I see that the last time transiting Mars formed some multiple of a 90 degree aspect to Mercury was on May 19, 2002, when these two planets sat in *opposition* (an aspect of 180 degrees) to each other. If I allow a window of observation of a day or so on either side of that date, I should be able to

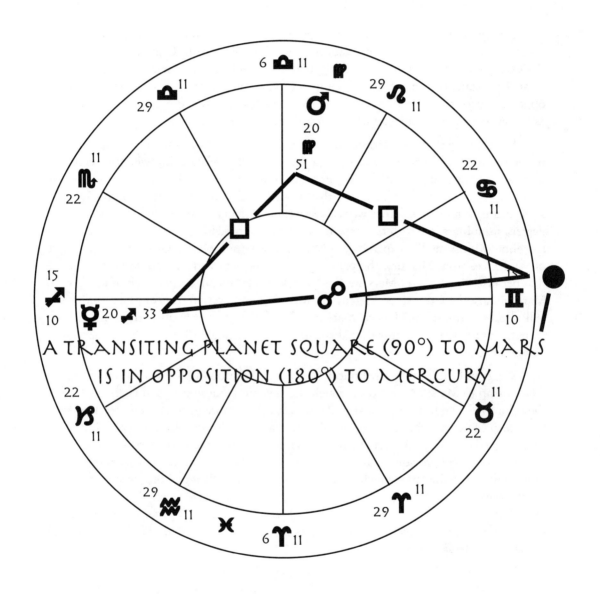

FIGURE 10

note activity related to the pattern of resonance generated between these two planets in my chart. In discussing this pattern of resonance in the section on soul space above, I described it as a process of learning how to communicate my truth without antagonizing others or provoking their anger. This is not the only possible manifestation of this pattern of resonance, but whatever we see when we look through the window should somehow fit the symbolism that is resonating. Let's take a look and see what I was actually experiencing from May 18-20, and see if we can discern the interplay of Mercury and Mars within my process.

According to my journal – which is an invaluable tool in tracking the movement of the soul through cyclical time – I was visiting my sister in Florida on the dates in question. On the evening of the 18th, I got into a potentially controversial conversation with my sister's boyfriend about the imagined difficulties that gay parents must face raising their children. My sister commented to me later how amazed she was that we could have this discussion without getting into a more heated exchange – confirmation, perhaps, of the progress I am making in learning to communicate my truth without antagonizing others. This incident obviously fits the pattern we have been discussing, and provides one example of how the pattern of resonance between Mercury and Mars might play itself out within my soul space, at a particular time when this pattern is being activated. We can see that there is a certain quality about this experience that fits the pattern, and the symbolism used to describe the pattern.

Other events during this period are not so clearly related to the pattern, nor will every transit of Mars to natal Mercury necessarily produce a recognizable manifestation of the pattern. If we continue this process, however, we might begin to get a sense of the value in learning to recognize the pattern through tracking it within these windows of observation. Continuing to move backward through the ephemeris, I would note that from January 5-7, 2002, transiting Mars formed a *waning square* to natal Mercury and an *opposition* to natal Mars. During this period, I experienced a breakdown in communication and increasing feelings of separation from my life partner, Ann. We were not communicating (utilizing Mercury) very well, and it was creating friction (an agitation of Mars) between us. It should be noted here that Ann's Mercury is square my Mercury and conjunct my Mars, so she is one person within my resonant soul space that will tend to activate and at times aggravate this pattern (see Figure 11). Furthermore, the quality of my communication with her will provide an ongoing measure of how well I am doing in the integration of life lessons encompassed by my own Mars-Mercury square.

This breakdown in communication with her during the waning square is a very different manifestation of the pattern of resonance between Mars and Mercury than the potential clash of viewpoints skillfully executed during the preceding phase of the cycle, but I would hope it is still possible to see the pattern in motion, through its changing disguise. The ability to do so, in fact, is an important key to the use of astrology in becoming more conscious in our use of soul time. In this case, we might note that both instances involve the necessity to communicate through a potentially difficult or confrontational situation. Where communication is successful, it produces a deeper sense of intimacy and connection. Where it is not, it can produce increasing friction, separation, and alienation. The more we take the time to observe these patterns, the clearer we can become about what they actually mean, and the more consciously we can begin to approach them.

Continuing the process, I would note the next window of observation to be August 18-20, 2001, when transiting Mars formed a *conjunction* to (occupying the same place in the zodiac as) Mercury, and a *waxing square* to its own natal position. During this period, I was in a car accident with Ann, in which the other driver, who had no license, no insurance, no brakes, and apparently no sense, ran a red light and broadsided us as we were crossing an intersection. Thankfully, no one was hurt, including the small child in the other driver's car. But my anger immediately rose to the surface, and I had all I could do contain myself as I told my side of the story to the investigating officer, and made sure the other driver would receive the multiple tickets she deserved.

During that same period, I also became aware of a crisis situation in a land cooperative where I own property that would require several rounds of intensive communication and radical actions over the course of the next several months – many of which would subsequently lead to misunderstandings, second-guessing, slander, and other forms of angry miscommunication, quite in keeping with the emotional tone of this resonant pattern when it generates soul lessons yet to be mastered. In both incidents, it should not be hard to see (and feel) the resonance between Mercury (the planetary attractor associated with communication) and Mars (the planetary attractor associated with conflict, both potential and actual). I cannot refrain from speculating that the variety of ways in which this pattern of resonance is apparently capable of playing itself out is surely evidence of an infinitely fertile imagination at work, within the fusion of Spirit and body that constitutes soul space.

I would note here that from a linear perspective, there is no direct causal relationship between any of these experiences. The conversation with my sister's boyfriend, the distance between Ann and I, the car accident evoking my anger, and the troublesome situation at the land cooperative, have no obvious connection with each other at all, if I look at them in linear time, and attempt to process the information from a causal perspective. If, however, I move into soul time, and look for patterns of resonance between these experiences, I can begin to see how they share similar themes and reveal certain common issues. All four incidents in this case, for example, revolve around the potential for conflict in the midst of communication. This similarity and

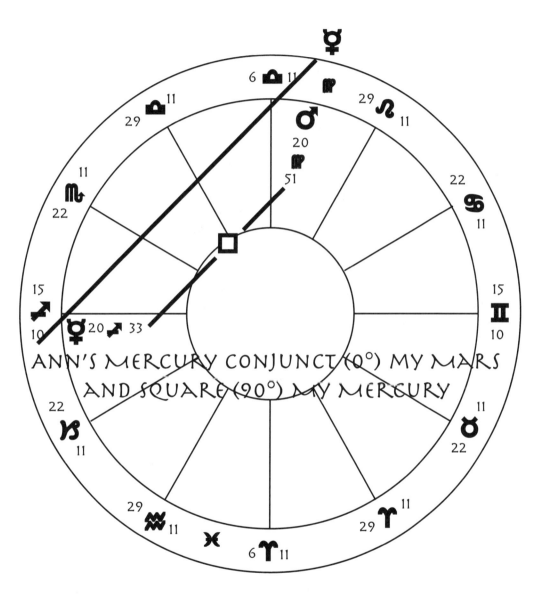

FIGURE 11

235

perhaps others yet to be discovered are symbolized astrologically by the relationship between Mercury and Mars. Given enough observation of the pattern of resonance between Mercury and Mars in cyclical time, I can begin to intuit what purpose this relationship serves within my personal soul space, and how I might approach it more consciously and with greater skill.

With enough information, I would also begin to recognize certain sensory experiences, feelings, and images as belonging to this particular area of soul space, and acquire a personal vocabulary with which to talk about this particular dimension of my soul's experience. Difficulties in communication, for example, might be understood as a dynamic in which Mars has become too sharp while Mercury is agitating, or alternately, when both Mercury and Mars become too dry. The accident in which Ann and I were involved could easily be understood as a piercing Mars triggering a disorienting Mercury. The anger that arose in the wake of the accident can be understood as a quick, agitating Mercury fueling a hot, sharp, heavy Mars, while the antidote to such anger might involve deliberately accessing Mercury's coolness to balance Mars heat, and its lightness to balance Mars' heaviness.

The possibilities for exploration here are endless. But I would hope that these few examples might give the reader some sense of appreciation for how one might use astrology to observe soul process during key moments of the cycle that symbolizes the resonant pattern under observation, and how an astropoetic approach to these observations can suggest a pathway to more conscious embodiment. I will explore this astropoetic process in more detail in Part Four of this book. Before we dive into the deep end of the astrological pool, however, we must circle the ancient tower once more, to explore how the soft science of psychology both contributes to, and in some ways, inhibits our attempt to evolve a genuine language of soul. I would note in conclusion that moving through Inanna's sixth gate on the way to the underworld of the soul will involve leaving behind strictly quantitative notions of space and time. We must take off our watches in order to enter cyclical soul time and feel the network of resonant connections that characterizes soul space.

Endnotes

1   Heraclitus lived c 535-475 BCE. The dates for Lao Tzu are more problematic, since we cannot be sure that he was a real person. If he can be identified with Lao Tan, as suggested as a possibility by Eliade (History 2:25-26), he would have lived sometime during the 6th century BCE and probably been no more than a generation or two removed from Heraclitus.

PART THREE

THROUGH
THE LAST GATE
WITH
PSYCHOLOGY

Chapter Thirteen
Liberating Psychology
From Its Scientific Trappings

Most of the shortcomings of science would be irrelevant to our discussion of the soul had science chosen to confine itself to a study of the external world. Since the emergence of psychology as a scientific discipline in the late 19th century, however, this has not been the case. Science has instead made increasingly bold and authoritative forays into territory it is ill equipped to explore, for reasons explained earlier in this book. In order to understand these developments and their impact upon our current understanding of soul, whether called by that name or not, we must trace the history of science's evolution a bit further, through the psychological landscape.

The Philosophical Underpinnings of Psychology

The Greek word, *psyche*, that forms the root of the word, psychology, derives from the verb, *psuchô*, meaning "to breathe, or blow." As we saw in Chapter One, the words for breath, breathing, wind, spirit, and soul were virtually interchangeable in many languages, suggesting that psychology, at least in its etymological origins, is meant to be a study of soul. A soul-based psychological dimension runs throughout most of the religious traditions of both East and West, and in the primary philosophical discussion in the West, at least up until the scientific revolution dismissed the concept of soul as irrelevant in the 18th century. Though this dimension was often implied rather than stated, the potential was there at least, for the emergence of a modern and more explicit discipline of psychology oriented around a study of soul.

Such a psychology would have philosophical roots dug deep through centuries of implication in a broad range of traditions and disciplines. The Buddha's Eightfold Path of *dharma* and Lao Tzu's teachings around the *Tao* are as much a prescription for psychological well being as a pathway to spiritual attainment. Saint Augustine studied memory, emotion, motivation, and the connection between reason and desire, as an integral part of the process by which he articulated the parameters of Christian theology. Aristotle pondered the nature of the soul in virtually the same breath in which he applied empirical techniques to a study of sensory processes, imagination, intelligence, needs, motivation, will, feeling, memory, sleep, dreams, and other aspects of the human psyche that we would today consider the province of psychology. Indeed, if we track the history of ideas about the human soul, and human beingness, as we have done throughout this book, it is not possible to separate that discussion from a parallel and interpenetrating history of psychology, in the etymological sense of the word. For all intents and purposes, the two are one and the same.

The Emergence of Psychology as a Scientific Discipline

Having said that, it is important to note that the same conceptual baggage that has burdened the discussion about soul, as documented in Part Two, has also affected the development of psychology. By the time it emerged from the general quest for knowledge as a separate field of inquiry in its own right, it was not the study of the soul it might have been, but rather a scientific inquiry into the nature of mind and human behavior. When René Descartes declared in so many words, that soul was mind, the psychological discussion, still underground at that point, began to focus on the nature of the mind. When the rational empiricists of the 17th century insisted on objectifying knowledge through empirical observation, the seeds of an outwardly focused, objective psychology were also planted. When scientists in the wake of Newton established causality as the fundamental basis for all observable phenomena, they also laid the theoretical foundation upon which future psychologists would build, when they turned their observations inward to the workings of the human psyche.

Consequently, when psychologists began to study the senses in earnest in the 19th century, they did not concern themselves with the value of the senses as a primary source of subjective information, but focused instead on their objective etiology within the generic human body. When William James framed the debate for psychological study of the emotions, emotions were assumed *a priori* to function within a causal framework as the connecting link between sensory information, thought, and observable, measurable behavior. By the time Freud began his exploration of soul space, or what he called the unconscious, in the late 19th century, he pursued this all-important mission, never questioning the scientific assumption that whatever happened in soul space must be governed by a generic set of rules that could be scientifically determined. Although the focus of psychological inquiry in these and many other instances was on topics of great interest to an understanding of soul, the method of inquiry and the unconscious metaphysical assumptions that informed that methodology, precluded finding answers that the individual soul could actually use.

Although psychological questions have been around at least as long as questions about the nature and purpose of soul, psychology emerged in the late 19th century as a science, limited in scope and purpose to what science could comment on with legitimate authority. As an early pioneer in the emerging science of psychology, Hermann

Ebbinghaus was prompted to comment, "Psychology has a long past, but a short history" (qtd. In Sdorow 9). That history essentially began when German physiologist, Wilhelm Wundt published his landmark book, *Principles of Physiological Psychology* in 1874, announced his intention to found a new science, and opened the first experimental laboratory at the University of Leipzig the following year. As the title of Wundt's book implies, the study of psychology emerged at the confluence of philosophical speculation about the nature of mind and the scientific study of physiology and biology. By the time Wundt introduced psychology as a field of inquiry in its own right, its focus was on understanding the mind, not in terms of soul, the way Descartes had conceived it, but as a simple physiological matter of brain function.

The history of psychology has since essentially been the effort of scientists to provide rational, objective, external, causal explanations for the experience of soul, which is irrational, subjective, internal, and acausal by nature. This effort proceeded without actual reference to the soul, and in systematic denial of the metaphysical implications of the soul's experience. Like religion and science before it, psychology has edged up to the threshold of the underworld, but ultimately failed to adequately describe what it saw there through the lens provided by its scientific conditioning. There have been and are trends within psychology that are hopeful, and helpful in articulating a more cogent language of soul, but before we discuss these, it might be worthwhile to briefly outline some of the ways in which psychology has created its own obstacles to a more direct encounter with soul.

In Chapter Six, I spoke of the way in which the soul absorbs information primarily through sensory perception, emotion, and projected imagery. These are all areas in which psychology has chosen to focus its attention, albeit through a methodology that impedes understanding what was being observed on a metaphysical level. These phenomena were understood not as avenues of information through which the soul could begin to explore its subjective resonant field, but as mental functions, which were in turn a matter of physiology, brain chemistry, and neuroscience. Perhaps if we look more closely at what was missed in psychology's scientific exploration of each of these areas, we will have a better sense of what must be restored before sensory, emotional and imagistic information can be of genuine use to the soul.

The Psychological Exploration of the Senses

Since the senses are obviously one of the most important ways in which the mind receives information about its environment, they became an early focus of psychological study. The study of the senses was preceded and made possible by important discoveries about the nervous system in the 18th and early 19th centuries. In the early 18th century,

English clergyman, Stephen Hale, sought to repeat an experiment originally conducted by Leonardo da Vinci, in which a frog was decapitated, but continued jerking when stimulated by electricity. The jerking continued until its spinal cord was severed, an observation that led Hale to conclude that the soul must reside in the spinal cord. The "spinal cord soul" subsequently became the subject of much debate and stirred great controversy, until further experimentation showed this phenomenon could be explained scientifically without the necessity for any reference to the soul.

The jerking of the frog remained of interest, since it implied a physiological mechanism within the body that was capable of conducting electrical signals. Another cruel frog experiment was conducted by the Italian physiologist Luigi Galvani, who applied electric charge to a frog's leg and made it kick, thereby confirming that some form of "animal electricity" ran through the nerves. In the early 19th century, English anatomist, Charles Bell and French physiologist, Francois Magendie, independently discovered that the nervous system was composed of sensory nerves through which information flowed from the senses to the brain, and motor nerves through which information flowed in the reverse direction from the brain to the muscles and organs.

Once it was determined that sensory information flowed through the nervous system and that the nervous system could be stimulated, then the direction of research about the senses was established according to a causal model of stimulus and response. Any departure from this method of inquiry was often the subject of ridicule, censure by the scientific community, and potentially irreversible damage to one's reputation and career. When Charles Bell was accused by some of his colleagues of indulging a more metaphysical intent in his study of the senses, he reassured them by stating, "I have found some of my friends so mistaken in their conception of the object of the demonstrations which I have delivered in my lectures, that I wish to vindicate myself at all hazards. They would have it that I am in search of the seat of the soul; but I wish only to investigate the structure of the brain, as we examine the structure of the eye and ear" (qtd. in Herrnstein 23).

Johannes Müller elaborated and expanded Bell's work related to the specificity of sensory nerves a generation later, raising new questions about the ultimate value of the "knife-happy" experiments of his peers (Hunt 110). He echoed Kant in concluding that a strictly empirical approach to the study of the senses was not adequate to account for their metaphysical function in the life of the human being who employed them. His opus, *Handbook of Physiology*, was an awkward mix of experimental findings in the scientific study of the senses, and a philosophical discussion of a "vital force" of a non-physical basis, which temporarily inhabits the body and animates it. This vital force can be understood as the last dying vestige of the concept of soul, rendered in language that an increasingly scientific world would perhaps find more palatable than outright reference to metaphysical principles. Seen in retrospect, however, Müller's insistence on the existence of the vital force is understood mostly as the quaint musings of a disturbed genius, who is remembered and greatly respected for his significant contributions to a physiological understanding of psychological process, while forgiven his wayward philosophical speculations. Müller himself was conflicted, and ultimately unable to reconcile his prodigious scientific accomplishments with his evolving metaphysical sensibility. He suffered from lifelong bouts of depression, and as a sad footnote to his story, committed suicide in 1858.

Müller's own students rebelled against what they felt to be his embarrassing metaphysical indulgences. In 1842, several of them published a manifesto, supposedly signed in blood, pledging the following solemn oath (qtd. in Wertheimer 47):

> No forces other than the common physical-chemical ones are active within the organism. In those cases which cannot at the time be explained by these forces one has either to find the specific way or form of their action by means of the physical-mathematical methods or to assume new forces equal in dignity to the chemical-physical forces inherent in matter, reducible to the forces of attraction and repulsion.

In 1845, these same students formed a club, the Berliner Physikalische Gesellschaft (Berlin Physical Society) to promote their view that all psychological processes could be explained causally through reference to physical principles alone. This club, and all those who sympathized with its basic premise, launched the template for the unholy marriage of psychology and scientific positivism that would dominate the field for the first 120 years or so of its existence.

For the most part, psychologists investigating the senses – including the physicist, Hermann von Helmholtz, a pioneer in the study of vision and hearing; Ernst Heinrich Weber, a physiologist who investigated touch with human subjects; and Max von Frey, who studied the sensations of warmth, cold, pressure, and pain – built their understanding on this template, which became the source for a self-fulfilling proof of its own validity. The more vigorously it was assumed that sensory processes were purely physical in nature, the more experimental evidence was accumulated to "prove" that this was so; and the more evidence amassed, the more the assumption seemed to be justified. Not only were the experiments designed in such a way that no other conclusions could be drawn, but any deviation from the expected outcome was also attributed to physical causes.

Müller himself had concluded that the unreliability of sensory information so vigorously debated in preceding centuries, was due not to the irrational nature of the soul in interpreting such information, but to small but significant variations in the condition of nerves and the efficiency of brain function. While the rational empiricists of the 17th and 18th centuries concerned themselves with the metaphysical implications of sensory unreliability, the physiological psychologists of the 19th century concerned themselves only with psychological effects of purely physiological causes. An entire branch of psychology became devoted to the study of perception, and the ways in which perception was impacted and could be influenced by sensory stimulation.

The methodology for the scientific study of perception was greatly advanced by Gustav Theodor Fechner, a contemporary of Müller, who also subscribed to a similarly unorthodox view of the relationship between sensory information and the soul. Fechner, the son of a village preacher, thought he could prove to his more materialistic peers that human beings were both material and spiritual in nature by demonstrating a mathematical relationship between external sensory stimuli and the resulting internal sensations, which he considered to be the expression of soul. Though he failed to win many converts, in the course of his crusade he developed several important research methods that would later become the foundation for experimental psychology.

Meanwhile, in his obsessive commitment to the process, he also became virtually blind, emotionally and physically exhausted, crippled by severe digestive problems and too unstable to teach. After three years of laxatives, shock treatments, and self-imposed social isolation, holed up in a room he painted completely black, he emerged to have a mystical experience of heightened sensory acuity in a garden. About this experience he wrote, "I had no doubt that I had discovered the soul of the flower, and thought in my strangely enchanted mood: this is the garden that lies behind the boards of this world. The whole earth and its very body is merely a fence around this garden for those who still wait on the outside" (qtd. in Hunt 123).

Ironically, those who were using Fechner's methods to study sensory information from a materialistic, causal perspective had placed themselves, unwittingly or not, outside this garden. Not that the information derived from a physiological study of the senses is invalid, as far as it goes. But questions were rarely asked about the subjective function of sensory process, as one primary source of information through which the soul comes to know itself. By the end of the 19th century, to ask them, in fact, would have been professional suicide. Müller and Fechner could be forgiven their occasional departure from the scientific fold in exchange for the genius of their contributions to science; those who followed in their footsteps, could not. By the late 20th century, not only had the soul been entirely eliminated from the vocabulary in which sensory processes were discussed, but the senses themselves were stripped of any association with actual experience. In the ecological theory of visual perception proposed by James J. Gibson, for example, the brain generates perception directly from information provided through the eyes without the necessity for us to interpret what we see. While this theory is still somewhat controversial, it is possible to see it as the logical conclusion to a process which has systematically sought to eliminate the soul completely from the neurochemical machine that houses it.

Sensory Experience as a Mechanism for Embodying Spirit

If we return to the ancient Jewish concept of the *nefesh*, however, according to which we *are* the soul that scientific psychologists would eliminate from the study of human process, then a neurochemical machine can be of no more interest than an ancient rusting vehicle, stripped of its parts, overgrown with weeds in the corner of the junkyard. The eye that sees without interpreting what it sees is nothing more than a biological camera. The ear that hears without the capacity to take delight in the symphony of life that swirls around it might as well be an ear of corn. The fingers that touch only to feed information to the brain are like the robotic tentacles of some alien life form incapable of being touched where it matters. To *have* a soul is to have something that can be lost in a world where it is systematically denied, but to *be* a soul is to participate in a world that we create, as we perceive it.

Even if sensory perception is only brain chemistry, as the scientific psychologists would have us believe, then as souls, we are the ones generating this chemistry. The fact that scientific psychologists are only concerned with how this chemistry works does not preclude the possibility that we are triggering this chemistry for a purpose, as part of a spiritual agenda. Even if the scientists can explain away the process, as souls it is still no small part of our quest to discover what the nature and purpose of this agenda is, in general, and more specifically, how sensory information can contribute to its fulfillment. These are questions a scientist would never ask, but it is what the soul wants to know. If we *have* a soul, it is easy to put the questions aside. If we are willing to *be* a soul, however, then our life will revolve around them.

Being a soul means being willing to provide a space in which Spirit can explore its relationship to the world of embodied form. From this perspective, the senses are the agency through which this exploration becomes possible. Given that the primary vehicles for our perception of the world are the senses, then it is through the exercise of the senses that we more fully incarnate as the soul that we are. When we sense anything, we become aware of it, and this awareness is Spirit making contact with the world. As Spirit makes contact with the world, the world is infused with Spirit. As the world becomes infused with Spirit, living within the world becomes a spiritual experience. As discussed in Chapter Two, most religious traditions seem to argue that only by denying the senses, not taking too much delight in them, not allowing them to fill us with their sacred numinosity, can we live a spiritual life. From the soul's perspective, however, just the opposite is true. It is only by cultivating the senses, that we invite Spirit to infuse the embodied life with its Holy Presence.

Of course, sensory experience for its own sake can be a source of pain as well as pleasure, as discussed in Chapter Four, and learning to cultivate the senses will necessarily teach us to find balance along the continuum of each polarity they encompass. Enjoying a bath means finding the proper blend of hot and cold water. Cooking a nourishing meal means learning to negotiate the various tastes – sweet, sour, salty, pungent, bitter, and astringent – so that none is excessive and all are in balance with each other. Taking time to smell the roses means cultivating life as a garden in which roses bloom on stems with thorns, weeds compete with flowers for space, and stinging insects pollinate the beauty. Cultivating the senses does not mean seeking pleasure and avoiding pain. It means opening the avenues through which Spirit makes contact with the world so both pleasure and pain, and everything in between can become a vehicle for the embodiment of Spirit that is the making of soul.

As the Kabbalah instructs us, "When you eat and drink, you experience enjoyment and pleasure from the food and drink. Arouse yourself every moment to ask in wonder. 'What is this enjoyment and pleasure? What is it that I am tasting?' Answer yourself, 'This is nothing but the holy sparks from the sublime, holy worlds that are within the food and drink' " (Matt 150). Let the scientific psychologists reduce sensory experience to brain chemistry. The way of the soul is to use the brain chemistry it has been given to elicit holy sparks from its experience, for it is through the experience of these holy sparks that the soul is able to sense the presence of Spirit within the embodied world. To the extent that psychology fails to recognize this, then it will also fail to provide an adequate language of soul capable of encompassing sensory experience as one of its most vital parts of speech.

A true language of soul must also encompass the possibility that each of the senses has metaphorical, as well as literal functions, many of which are utterly subjective in nature. What we see is not just a simple registration of what is "out there" to be seen, but also a projection of what we want, need, expect, or are afraid to see. We embellish the simple physiological act of seeing, in other words, with a secondary agenda, which is born of the soul's need to use the world as a mirror. If I look at you and see a person who reminds me, in some way, of my father, then I am not seeing you as you are. I am seeing you, in part and probably mostly unconsciously as a person with whom I can work through residual father issues. Freud labeled this act of secondary seeing, *projection*, considering it to be pathological, and failing to recognize it as the source of valuable information to the soul that it is. The simple fact that we have a discrepancy between the image produced by brain chemistry alone, and the raw image as it is seen by the soul, however, suggests that the individual soul adds something to the experience that is not present in an objective, scientific interpretation of psychological reality. It is, in fact, this "something added" through the process of projection that makes the individual soul what it is. If, as Gibson proposes, the act of seeing does not depend upon the interpretation of what is seen, then there is no opening for an exploration of this intimately personal dimension of being that is brought to the experience of sight by the individual soul.

The same is true for all the senses. I don't necessarily hear everything that is there to be heard; I hear selectively, and what I hear has more to do with my capacity to process information of use to my soul than it does with a discrimination of pitch, volume, auditory direction, or any of the other physiological dimensions of the hearing process measurable by a scientific approach to psychology. Smells, tastes, textures, various pressures, temperatures, and all sorts of other sensory awarenesses likewise have their personal associations born of cumulative experiences, which are necessarily unique to each soul. Unless these awarenesses are mapped to learning processes that are relevant to the soul's agenda, they might as well be happening to someone else. To the extent that psychology fails to take into account the subjective layers of association and projection that are superimposed upon and blended with the perceptions induced by brain chemistry, it will fail to adequately address the soul's sensory experiences, and fall short as a useful language of soul.

The Psychological Exploration of the Emotions

While there had been a rich discussion of the senses within philosophical tradition for psychologists to draw upon when they began exploring them from the scientific perspective, there was no such foundation for the exploration of emotions. Although the debate had often raged with great passion over the question of how far the senses could be trusted, the senses were nonetheless considered to be part of the function of the mind, and controllable by reason. The relationship between the rational mind and the senses had in fact been debated for at least 2,500 years before psychology became established as a science. Senses also had quantitative dimensions that could be measured by empirical research, and when psychologists turned their attention to investigating the physiological foundation of mental processes, the senses were easily molded to the scientific template as a suitable subject for study.

Emotions were a much trickier matter. As pointed out in Chapter Five, once the rational cosmologists began disputing the validity of the mythopoetic worldview, most philosophers turned their attention to the mind and the power of reason to guide human behavior. When Descartes declared being to be derived from the power to think, any potential discussion of the emotions swirled into a philosophical backwater, where it languished for centuries. Descartes himself identified six primary emotions – admiration, love, hatred, desire, joy and sadness – but then proceeded to describe them in such intellectual terms as functions of the mind, that they became hardly recognizable as the intense volatile states of being anyone who has ever felt one would recognize them to be (Passions, the 69th Article – the 93rd Article). It was, in fact, the volatility of intense emotional states, their capacity to render a rational man irrational, and his inability to control them that kept most philosophers intimidated and tongue-tied in attempting to discuss them.

When an emotion, or passion as it was called, reared what was considered to be its ugly head, most philosophers took refuge in some statement of ethics. Like the morality of religious tradition, the philosophical study of ethics avoids the issue of emotion altogether, by prescribing a behavioral code to be followed, regardless of which emotions happen to be engaging the psyche at any given moment. Strong ethical beliefs allowed the emotions to be safely placed under the control of reason, or at least so the prevailing theory went. In actuality, the emotions often threatened to undermine the dominion of reason, refusing to conform to a rational model of how life ought to be lived, and most philosophers had no clue how to deal with the disturbing psychological wildcard that emotions presented.

The Dutch philosopher and theologian, Baruch Spinoza, one generation past Descartes, was typical in his approach to the emotions, although to his credit, he also attempted to look the problem squarely in the face. In his major work, entitled *Ethics*, he distinguished between active emotions, which he considered to be a pleasurable alignment with one's true nature, conducive to health and well-being, and passive emotions, which are the ones against which most philosophers erect ethical codes. He further argued that we are often the victims of these passive, reactive emotions which hold us in bondage, and that the way to freedom was through the intellectual love of God. By this he meant the use of reason to see the world as God saw it, and then act accordingly. Spinoza did affirm the power of emotion to determine our well being, and in refreshing contrast to his religious contemporaries, saw pleasure as a sign of emotional health. But in the end, he was no less a champion of reason than Descartes, and understood happiness to be a matter of using the mind to keep emotions under control. This is still often the goal of psychological intervention today.

Despite his shortcomings, which were largely a by-product of his rationalist orientation, Spinoza did offer future psychologists a point of entry into the scientific study of emotions, by defining them as "the modifications of the body whereby the active power of said body is increased or diminished, aided or constrained..." (qtd. in Christian 2:77). While this was a formal definition not meant to be experimental, if a way could be found to measure the active power of the body, under the influence of various emotions, then one could study the emotions scientifically. This tantalizing promise went unrealized for two centuries, while the emerging scientific paradigm built a theoretical foundation and a methodology powerful and bold enough to tackle the relationship between physiological and psychological states of being. Spinoza, in retrospect, can be considered an armchair psychologist, at least as far as his discussion of the emotions went. As the science of psychology started gaining momentum toward the end of the 19th century, it is not surprising to find that the discussion of emotions also began taking a more scientific turn. The focus shifted from simply giving them formal definition to quantifying and then measuring them – as a prerequisite to their control.

The Behavioral Approach to Emotion

Actually, the first person to consider the relationship between emotions and behavior from a scientific perspective was not a psychologist, but the renowned naturalist, Charles Darwin. In *The Expression of the Emotions in Man and Animals*, published in 1872, Darwin argued that emotions evolved for their survival value, first within the animal kingdom, and then among humans. Fear, for example, was useful in helping to escape an enemy, anger in mounting a counter-attack, and sexual desire in ensuring the continuity of the species. Though other emotions were not so clearly traced to survival issues, this did not seem to bother Darwin. Since he had already established the validity of the evolutionary paradigm through his landmark publication of *The Origin of Species* more than a dozen years earlier, he felt certain that everything, including the emotions, could justifiably be understood within that conceptual framework.

By the turn of the century, psychologists absorbing Darwin's ideas were apt to say that emotions derived from physiological instincts, which in turn were geared toward the satisfaction of basic needs. But there was still no way to directly measure emotions, which were subjective, internal, qualitative states, and as such, beyond the reach of the objective, external, quantitative tools of science. The instincts could be measured in terms of response to hunger, thirst, or pain, but emotions could only be inferred from behavior and this has proven to be a stumbling block that remains only partially overcome to this day. You could, of course, simply ask each person what they were feeling, as most psychotherapists routinely do, but as far as science is concerned, this is an unreliable source of information. Meanwhile, as psychological historian, Morton Hunt points out, although there are currently about a hundred distinct scientific theories about the emotions, some relating emotions to visceral states, others to the nervous system, still others to higher mental and/or brain function, at present there is no general agreement about what the emotions are, what causes them, or how they can best be measured (483).

◇◇

What science has done instead is to equate emotion with the inferred behavioral consequences of emotions, which are within the realm of measurement. If I behave in a certain way, say by shaking my fist, then it can be deduced – or so a behavioral scientist would say – that I am experiencing the emotion of anger. If I cry, I must be sad; if I laugh, I must be happy, and so on. It's not surprising that the connection between emotion and behavior would be of great interest, since it was the deviation from rational, predictable, and controllable behavior that most disturbed and confounded theologians, philosophers, scientists, and psychologists alike. If the behaviors associated with emotions could be understood and controlled, or so the unconscious theory probably went, then emotions themselves could be brought back within the reach of rational control. This has proven to be a huge "if", because as scientific psychologists were soon forced to acknowledge, different emotions can be associated with the same physiological and behavioral response, and not all emotions are amenable to the same treatment. Before this discovery could even be made, it took a solid half-century for psychologists to find a way to measure the correlation between behavior and emotion postulated by Darwin, and thus make it adaptable to scientific research.

In 1908, the psychologist William McDougall broadened Darwin's assertion that all emotions were related to survival by proposing that the psychological impulse connecting instinct to emotion was motivation. Emotions, in other words, facilitated instinctual movement toward a goal, of which survival was certainly primary, though perhaps not the only goal possible. Ten years later, Robert Woodworth proposed the concept of drive to replace the Darwinian notion of instinct, and by the 1920s, behavioral psychologists finally had something they could measure, for if the goal could be determined, or manufactured in a laboratory, then motivation could be measured in terms of drive toward the goal. Drive was then measured in terms of success in reaching the goal, response time, and the capacity to learn behaviors that would facilitate reaching the goal.

It is interesting to note, at this point, that behavioral psychologists were coming full circle, back to Aristotle's concern with final or teleological causes. If I am moving toward a goal, then as a soul, I have some sense of purpose. There was, however, no discussion of the soul within the work of the behavioral psychologists, and goals were construed only in terms of physiological needs – for oxygen, fluids, food, sex, a comfortable temperature and avoidance of pain. When other drives were discovered that had no immediate or obvious survival value, behavioral scientists labeled these drives, "secondary," or "acquired," suggesting that they were learned behaviors, capable in some way of facilitating the movement toward fulfillment of primary drives. Later psychologists – including Jung, Adler, Horney, Fromm, and Maslow, among many others – cultivated elaborate theories around various "secondary" drives, which in turn became primary to their theories. Throughout all of this discussion, however, the concept of the soul had virtually disappeared, to be replaced by an image of the human animal as a predictable creature, motivated by a set number of identifiable needs, which could be triggered, measured and manipulated in various ways. Emotions themselves were squeezed out of the discussion, since what was being studied was solely in the realm of external movements. Internal, subjective states were of little interest to behavioral psychologists.

The Metaphysical Irony at the Heart of Behavioral Psychology

The great irony here is that behavioral psychologists have outlined the physiological basis of a theory that is potentially useful to the soul, for the soul does move toward the fulfillment of a goal, and the movement is a learning process. The goal is not a mere survival of the body, however, but an increasingly conscious fusion of body with Spirit that is embraceable in living a life of meaning and purpose. The learning that takes place is not limited to the mere satisfaction of physiological needs, but also to the actualization of creative potential in service to a larger evolutionary agenda that the mind can only occasionally begin to fathom. None of this can be measured, or even spoken of, in terms that are objective, or measurable in terms of efficient causes, and so the behaviorists simply pretend the spiritual dimension of what they are so intent on measuring does not exist.

Indeed, most behaviorists - Thorndike, Pavlov, Watson and others - conducted their experiments mostly on rats, chickens, and dogs, avoiding any contact with human subjects, which might possibly provide insight into the human soul. As Hunt points out, "These experiments . . . were part of a bold attempt, beginning at the end of last century, to answer - actually to eliminate from discussion - the most perplexing and intractable problems of psychology: those having to do with the nature of the mind" (243). It is clear from the examples that Hunt provides in the discussion that follows - questions about consciousness, a non-material sense of self, and what happens to that essence after death - that he is really talking about the soul, which has since the time of Descartes, and in the minds of most early psychologists, been replaced by the concept of mind. The behaviorists were attempting to take this devolutionary process one step further by replacing the concept of mind with the notion of a self-regulating body that could be understood purely in terms of measurable physiological processes.

As bizarre as this idea seems to anyone who is the least bit interested in the still unresolved questions that the soul poses, its popularity is not to be underestimated. By the early 20th century, any discipline that fell outside the parameters of the scientific paradigm was automatically suspect, and subject to intellectual ostracism. Witness the vociferous campaign against astrology that rages unrelentingly to this day. To the extent that psychology was still willing to entertain ideas about soul, or even a non-material conceptualization of the mind, it too, began treading on thin intellectual ice. At a time when psychology was still attempting to establish its own credibility, any hint of deviation from the scientific standard was actively discouraged, if not systematically banned. Behaviorism, on the other hand, could legitimately claim to be a truly scientific psychology. As such, it was able to command the respect that the psychological establishment was craving - not to mention, its fair share of university resources, laboratory space, and research grants.

From 1920 to 1960, behaviorism became the dominant force in the American psychological landscape, and by extension throughout most of the rest of the civilized world. As behavioral historian, Greg Kimble points out, "In mid-century American psychology, it would have cost a career to publish on mind, consciousness, volition, or even energy" (qtd. in Hunt 263) since all of these topics were outside of the reach of behaviorism and smacked of an earlier age in which questions about the soul, and the purpose of human existence were not considered frivolous or irrelevant. Nor were the original questions about the role of emotions in human behavior that occupied Darwin ever addressed, much less answered. The very concept of emotion had been replaced in the minds of the behavioral psychologists, by a causal relationship between need and response. In the end, what the behaviorists had attained was not a better understanding of emotions at all, but a practical body of knowledge about how to manipulate laboratory rats, which then inevitably extended to human rats as well. One need look no farther than the nearest commercial break on television to see the result of this soulless foray into the relationship between emotions and behavior.

The James-Lange Theory of Emotions

To be sure, not all early psychologists were enamored of the scientific avoidance of emotion. William James, for example, bemoaned the fact that for most of his colleagues, "feeling constitutes the 'unscientific' half of existence, and any one who enjoys calling himself a 'scientist' will be too happy to purchase an untrammeled homogeneity of terms... at the slight cost of... banish(ing) (feeling) to a limbo of causal inertness, from whence no intrusion or interruption on its part need ever be feared" (487). Though James received funding to open a psychological laboratory at Harvard the same year that Wilhelm Wundt opened his at Leipzig, the two men had very different attitudes toward their research. While Wundt embraced the new scientific psychology with unabashed fervor, James held part of his enthusiasm in reserve.

James saw that the behavioral school was unable to adequately account for most of the attributes and functions of psyche that we associate with being human - consciousness, volition, emotions, identity, creativity, or even the thought process - and increasingly turned his own work in the direction of trying to rectify this imbalance. James agreed with his contemporaries that the concept of soul was unnecessary to account for psychological phenomena. But he also thought that his more scientifically-minded colleagues had gone too far in dismissing the idea that human beings were not just at the mercy of external stimuli, but could also initiate and participate in their own experience. Staking out a middle ground between the wholly unscientific notion of the soul and the unholy notion of a soulless, mindless body, James proposed the "empirical self" as an appropriate subject for scientific scrutiny.

Furthermore, James proposed that the stream of consciousness, which constituted the life of the empirical self, was one in which emotions played a primary role. While the conventional wisdom of the day said that emotions preceded physiological changes that took place in response to perception, James argued that it actually worked the other way around. Emotions were the reaction of the empirical self to these physiological changes, and as such could be measured in direct relation to physiological response. This theory was known as the James-Lange theory, to include a Danish physiologist, Carl Lange who came to the same conclusion independently.

To the theory's credit, it was the first serious attempt to introduce a discussion of subjective states into what had previously been an awkward silence about them within the psychological community. On the other hand, it gave the behaviorists a potent excuse to continue assessing human behavior in terms of physiology alone. In the hands of those who ran with the James-Lange theory, the empirical self sadly became just another rat in the maze. For all its appeal to the scientific community, the James-Lange theory was also counterintuitive. You see a bear; you feel afraid; your heart starts pounding; and you run. This seems simple common sense, but according to the theory, you see a bear; your heart starts pounding; you run; and only then do you feel afraid. Needless to say, the theory has remained quite controversial, even as it rapidly became the accepted premise for the continued behavioral treatment of emotions.

Other psychologists challenged the theory for this and other reasons. Most notable among them was Walter Cannon, who claimed in 1934 that an emotion was produced not by physiological response, but by the thalamus, a portion of the brain conveying information to the cerebral cortex, the skeletal muscles, and the sympathetic nervous system. Later research has refuted the role of the thalamus in producing emotion, but one need not be a research scientist to see where this is going. Whether one accepted or rejected the James-Lange theory, by mid-century the question was firmly anchored by the expectation of an answer that would refer solely to the function of the brain. From this point forward, there would not be any reference whatsoever to the soul, the mind, or even the empirical self that was nonetheless at the center of the experience of emotion, however it might be construed.

Though it has been a long and winding road from Spinoza's association of emotions with the active power of the body to where we are today, the current passion for the use of Prozac and other mood-altering drugs to control emotions can be understood as part of the same historical process, and a direct outcome of the application of scientific principles to the study of behavioral drives. Science has labeled any emotional deviation from the norm as disease, treatable in the same way as physical disease. Beneath this use of drugs, however, is the same fear and desire to control emotions that motivated the armchair psychologists of antiquity to bring the emotions and their behavioral consequences under the control of reason. The difference is that modern science has at last, discovered a mechanism for doing this, launching an entirely new branch of science called behavioral medicine.

While these new psychoactive drugs are undoubtedly viewed as a godsend to those who struggle with chronic, debilitating psychological conditions, from the soul's perspective, the control of behavior is not the goal. Quite the contrary. It is the capacity to fully and more consciously experience the emotional states before and after behavior that leads to a deeper embodiment of Spirit. To the extent that science has biased the psychological study of emotions toward their essential neutralization through reduction to external drives and treatment by drugs, then it has crippled the way that we think about and respond to the needs of the soul.

Freud's Contribution to the Study of Emotions

Psychology's exclusive focus on the physiological machine was to change somewhat through the influence of Sigmund Freud, widely acknowledged to be the father of psychotherapy. Unlike the behavioral psychologists, who often preferred the company of rats to that of other people, Freud's theories evolved directly through contact with patients, who were coming to him with human problems. To be sure, Freud was trained as a physician, and thoroughly cut from the same scientific cloth as his predecessors and contemporaries. He was also a bona fide member of the same rabidly materialistic Berliner Physikalische Gesellschaft that had influenced the students of Johannes Müller to reject all non-scientific explanations for psychological phenomena. Working with people everyday in his practice, however, he could not so easily dismiss the experiences of the empirical self as those who spent their days isolated in a laboratory. Faced with the raw reality of human emotions, Freud had to find a way, beyond simple physiological explanations, to deal with the empirical self at the core of his patients' psychological pain.

Ironically, if fate had not intervened, Freud would have lent his genius to further consolidation of the behavioral school's authority within the nascent psychological community. After meeting and idolizing Ernst Brücke, a co-founder of the Berliner

Physikalische Gesellschaft, Freud became intellectually enamored of the physiological approach to psychology, and wanted to follow Brücke into the research laboratory. In a small piece of guidance that inadvertently changed the course of history, Brücke advised against it. The hard reality of Freud's day was that a poor Jew could not realistically hope to pursue a career in pure science, so Freud toughed it out in medical school, and received his M.D. in 1881. After training with Theodor Meynert, the world's leading brain anatomist, and being exposed to the ideas of Josef Breuer, a physician who experimented with hypnosis and a form of "talking cure" based on a rudimentary form of free association, Freud opened his own private practice five years later, as a specialist in neurological and brain disorders.

At first, Freud treated his patients' neuroses as though they were a neurological disease. But as he began to feel more comfortable in his practice and as he encountered patients whose emotional problems did not respond to standard treatments, he began experimenting with Breuer's techniques. Gradually over the course of the first 15 years or so of his practice, he evolved the therapeutic system of psychoanalysis for which he is known. Though Freud remained convinced throughout his life that the psychological conditions he was treating had a physiological basis, he also came to the conclusion that these conditions had their own reality on a purely psychological level, apart from any physiological underpinnings. Needless to say, within the prevailing atmosphere established by strictly scientific behaviorists, this was heresy, and Freud was often ostracized and castigated for his views. While today, we consider Freud's approach to psychotherapy to be antiquated in light of more recent advances in theory and technique, it is easy to forget that he hacked out a foothold for psyche, in the etymological sense, within the practice of psychology that ironically did not exist until he felt the necessity to create it.

Freud often used the German word, *Seele*, to describe this rediscovery of psyche, and *Seele* is often translated as "soul," although it also has many other meanings. Scholars have argued that what Freud really meant by *Seele* is the internal mental and emotional life of the individual, but even this was a radical assertion within a scientific profession that demanded an objective approach to mental and emotional processes. Despite the fact that Freud was very much a scientist, evolving objective theories inferred from the cumulative observation of his patients, in practice, Freud gave credibility to the idea that the life of the psyche was an intimately personal affair that often defied rational, linear, strictly causal explanations.

Through his practice he found the internal processes that contributed to an individual's psychological condition were subjectively wired in a highly individual way that did not easily lend itself to the emergent behaviorist paradigm. Although this internal wiring had its own logic, often rendered symbolically through dream imagery, patterns of association, and threads of memory, it was not a logic that could be forced to fit a rational, material, scientific model. In order to understand the logic of the individual psyche, Freud and the psychoanalysts who followed in his footsteps had to depart from the realm of purely physiological explanations and enter into the actual experiences, external and especially internal, of a living soul.

Within this dynamic, the emotions played a critical role. No longer strictly bound to their physiological causes, emotions became the point of entry into the subjective realm analyst and patient were attempting to explore. That is to say, whenever a strong emotion was evoked, through the memory of some childhood experience, or through engaging the fantasy material of a dream, the psychoanalyst could be sure that he or she was hot on the trail of something important within the life of the person being analyzed. Freud made the mistake of attempting to impose a generic theory of sexual interpretation onto emotional experience that rendered it less useful as a point of entry to soul, but he was a true pioneer in valuing emotional experience as a source of important psychological information.

It should also be noted that as a *metaphor* for the essential dynamic of the soul negotiating a world of polarities, Freud's pansexual theory is absolutely brilliant. As discussed in Chapter Four, sex provides the enticing symbolism for the soul's attempt to integrate every polarity it encounters within the course of its journey. It is through finding a balance between Spirit and body, male and female, light and dark, hot and cold, and every other pair of opposites that the soul discovers who it is, and learns to embrace the wholeness of its being. This is an emotional process, because it begins when the soul feels the pain associated with its imbalanced identification with one side of a given polarity at the expense of the other, and is motivated to rectify the imbalance and reclaim what it has rejected. Sex is a fitting metaphor for this process, because healing inevitably involves opening to a more fluid psychological intercourse between all the rejected parts of self, and a more joyful union of both sides of every polarity. Understood as a metaphor, Freud's description of the human psychological predicament as a sexual problem is actually quite useful to the soul, but Freud's scientific training apparently did not allow him to consider the broader metaphorical implications of his theory. Instead, he took it literally and evolved a theory that was a caricature of its own metaphysical wisdom.

The symptoms brought to Freud by a steady parade of patients could easily have been understood as the attempt of the soul to negotiate one or more internal polarities. Instead - according to the unconscious scientific metaphysic at the core of Freud's work - they were interpreted as further literal proof of the validity of his pansexual theory. It was not the theory per se that was problematic, but Freud's literal interpretation of it and his inability - born of scientific training - to see nothing but a conformation of his theory in the experiences of his patients. Freud's scientific blindness was compounded to the extent that his patients attempted to conform to Freud's theories in order to win his approval – a common hazard of psychoanalysis that he called *transference*. To successfully undergo Freudian psychotherapy, his patients had to distort their complex, psychological predicaments to fit the system, and much of the subjective nuance that a metaphorical interpretation of these experiences might have elicited, was lost. With this loss of nuance, the opportunity to explore soul space from a truly subjective perspective was also sacrificed on the altar of psychoanalytical dogma. Because of his scientific training, Freud imposed a generic template on the human experience that in retrospect proved as damaging to the soul as the Victorian patterns of sexual repression it challenged.

Social Psychology and Other Post-Freudian Influences On the Understanding of Emotion

Despite these shortcomings, Freud broke the mold of the James-Lange theory of emotions, and proposed an alternate model according to which emotions could be traced not to physiological correlates, but to memories, actual life experiences, and fantasy images – in short, to a subjective soul-based source. This is not to say that post-Freudian psychology has been a return to the unabashed study of the human soul. It has not. Nor have emotional states generally been recognized as the expression of an interior life, exposing itself for exploration, even though at the practical level, this continues to be the case in psychotherapy of almost any persuasion. The fact that actual soul work continues within the auspices of therapy, despite science's ongoing mistrust of it, can be directly attributed to Freud.

Meanwhile, most psychological theorists in Freud's wake have focused on the external causes of emotional behavior. Perhaps in their own way, they were refuting the behaviorist notions of the soul as a physiological machine, but in general, they were also failing to take advantage of Freud's invitation to explore the interior realms on their own terms. After Freud, most psychological theorists sought the cause of emotion within the life of the individual soul, and this was certainly an improvement over a purely physiological or behavioral approach. There was still no recognition, however, of the relationship between emotions and the evolutionary life of the soul experiencing them, much less that this was a legitimate and even necessary mechanism through which the soul could come to know itself. A notable exception to this mindset is found in the work of Carl Jung, to whom we will return in the next two chapters.

Following the example set by Freud, most psychoanalysts sought the causal roots of emotion in childhood experience – particularly in relationships with parents, other significant adults in the child's immediate environment, and siblings. In the 1930s and

◇◇

40s, historical events such as the Great Depression, the rise of fascism and the Holocaust began affecting the emotional life of large numbers of people in ways that transcended their individual stories. This intense climate of external psychological pressures – amplified and broadcast through the emerging power of mass media – spawned conditions ripe for the development of a social psychology. Kurt Lewin, a primary spokesperson for this movement, began conceptualizing the life of the psyche in terms of a field theory, in which the soul sought to find its equilibrium amidst a complex interplay of social, cultural, and environmental forces impinging upon its "life space."

Although behavioral psychology remained king throughout Lewin's lifetime, during the 1950s and 60s, social psychology began to vie with behaviorism for space within the curricula of most major universities. Lewin's ideas, and the social psychology movement in general, provided psychological justification for such important social movements as civil rights, the antiwar protests of the 1960s, and perhaps more indirectly, feminism. Under the influence of the social psychology movement, it became legitimate to think of the psychological development of large groups of people in terms of patterns of social conditioning, which could, and in many cases, deserved, to be changed.

The appeal of this collective approach to psychology is strong, and not entirely misplaced, since a better world creates the opportunity for individual souls to find and actualize themselves. Social, political and cultural factors do play an important part within the resonant soul space of each individual, shaping identity, influencing and conditioning various patterns of resonance, and defining the context within which souls evolve. But there are also internal reasons why individuals respond differently to these influences. Not every black male growing up in an urban ghetto becomes a drug dealer; not every disenfranchised youth in the 1960s protested the Vietnam War; not every affluent white woman, growing up with a liberal, middle-class education becomes a feminist. There is an entire range of emotional and psychological responses to these conditions, and where a given individual falls within the spectrum depends as much upon the individual consciousness brought to bear within the circumstances being experienced as it does upon the circumstances themselves. This is not something social psychologists are any better prepared to assess than behavioral psychologists.

Behaviorists have proven somewhat receptive to social psychologists, who in general share their scientific objectivity, even if their methodology is necessarily somewhat different, and the contemporary trend is toward increasing cross-pollination of the two approaches. Meanwhile, after vociferously attacking the unscientific nature of Freud's approach to the psyche in his day, behaviorists have persisted in their insistence upon physiological causes, though they have graduated from the James-Lange theory to more sophisticated analysis of neurochemistry, brain function, endocrine imbalances, and genetic predispositions. Over the last thirty years or so, their influence has been tempered by the emergence of cognitive psychologists, who believe that thoughts are the precursors to both emotions and physiological states.

The Contribution of Cognitive Psychology To An Understanding of Emotion

In 1958, Joseph Brady demonstrated through experiments with two monkeys, one of whom had the power to shock the other, that the mere anticipation of being shocked was enough to induce ulcers, even when no actual shocks were administered. In 1962, Stanley Schachter and Jerome Singer conducted experiments showing that emotions were virtually interchangeable and depended upon the conceptual perception of the situation in which they were aroused. Subsequent experiments throughout the 1960s and 70s further demonstrated the connection between conceptual perceptions, beliefs, attitudes, and emotional states, all of which point toward the primary role of mental conditions in dictating the life of the psyche.

As with the external sociological factors explored by social psychologists, thought processes obviously play their role in the ordering of soul space. This is especially true of emotions like guilt, shame, or embarrassment, where preconceived ideas about who one ought to be and how one ought to respond create obvious patterns of interference with who one actually is. On the other hand, not everyone exposed to a particular set of beliefs adopts them, nor does everyone attach the same emotional significance to the same thought. Cognitive psychologists have had to resurrect the concepts of will, intentionality, and purpose, in order to explain these individual differences, which in turn suggests that even if mental processes do precede emotional states, they themselves are generated by something more primary within the individual. Cognitive psychologists continue to puzzle over the fact that even when armed with accurate information that is clearly understood by the mind, most individuals will not always make choices that are in their own best interest.

These unanswered questions within the cognitive worldview suggest the existence of something at the core of the individual – why not call it a soul? – that exists before thoughts are generated, and to some extent determines which thoughts will resonate and which will not. If emotions are reflective of the thoughts that trigger them, then both emotions and thoughts can provide clues to nature of the resonant soul space in which they arise. Likewise, when thoughts and/or emotions converge around sensory experiences – or the physiological responses measured by behaviorists – we have a more potent opening to the life of the soul than can be provided by sensations, feelings, or thoughts alone. It is not that cognitive, or social, or even behavioral psychologists are wrong; but each is choosing to focus on one particular position in the larger kaleidoscopic turning by which soul is understood, without acknowledging the central reality around which the kaleidoscope revolves. It is when we bring these factors together within one overarching and all-inclusive inquiry, and reintroduce the connection to Spirit that infuses their convergence with numinous vitality, that we have a language through which the soul can begin to recognize itself.

When thought, emotion, and sensation are evoked in the face of social, cultural and/or political influences which mirror them – especially within the context of an individual life story – we have a fertile field through which images and symbols meaningful to the soul arise. As we will see more clearly in Chapter Nineteen, we also have the basis for an astropoetic language of soul that arises not as an objective theory, but as a direct flowering of each individual's subjective experience. Before we can explore this convergence of sensation, feeling and thought, however, we must first free psychology of the scientific demand that it approach any study of these internal processes objectively.

Meanwhile, if the separate streams of psychic information must be handled subjectively, then this is even truer for their convergence. As these streams come together internally, they invariably fuse into a set of perceptions, images, and attitudes that transform the world into a subjective mirror to the soul that is utterly unique to each individual, despite the fact that the world of consensual reality that science measures is the same for everyone. Through creatively engaging the images the soul projects into this mirror, the soul gradually learns who it is and what it has incarnated to do through its participation in the world.

Before exploring this enticing possibility in more depth, we will continue our discussion of psychology with an eye to understanding the role that imagery and symbolism have played in its development. As with explorations of sensory information and emotion, we will see how psychologists have often stumbled upon ideas relevant to the soul, but were at a loss to make the connection, given the fact that the very concept of soul had long been stripped from the vocabulary. Putting the soul back into the discussion, we will begin to evolve an understanding of the imagination and the image that it produces that not only revitalizes psychology, but also renders it infinitely more useful as a language of soul.

Chapter Fourteen
Toward a Subjective Approach
To the Image-Making Process

Before we trace the evolution of a psychological understanding of the imagination, it will be helpful to explain what I mean by the word, "image." The first entry in my dictionary defines an image as "an optically formed duplicate, counterpart, or other representative reproduction of an object" (American Heritage 642). This is the sense in which a behaviorist would understand the term. But this definition is too outwardly oriented and objective to adequately address the inner, subjective experience of the soul. To get to a definition that is more useful, we must move farther down the list of dictionary entries, until we come to one that defines an image as "a mental picture of something not real or present"; in other words, a product of the imagination. If we then cross reference this definition with that for imagination, we find as the very first entry, "the power of the mind to form a mental image or concept of something that is not real or present." An image, then, in the sense I am using it here is a subjective creation of the imagination.

This is not to say that what the imagination produces has no basis in reality, as the dictionary implies. For the imagination does not work in a vacuum. It perceives the external world, and absorbs information about the world through the senses. But then it modifies that information internally through a complex synergistic process, in which sensory information converges with memories about similar situations experienced in the past, fantasies about the immediate future, feelings colored by memory and fantasy, thoughts about the relationship between past, present, and future, beliefs, instincts that propel one toward habitual patterns of behavioral response, insights into the nature of its experiences, an intuitive sense of meaning and purpose in relation to the present situation, and spontaneous impulses that arise through the interaction between instinct and insight. Out of this complex process, comes an image, or more accurately understood, a nexus of impressions, which together form an evolving image of the world. This image is then projected onto to the world, and forms the basis for the dynamic relationship with the world that is measured and analyzed by behavioral psychologists.

Through an exploration of this image within the embodied life, the soul comes to know itself. The image is almost always at odds with a strictly objective interpretation of reality, and thus with the strictly scientific interpretation of its meaning. But far from being a liability, this discrepancy between image and objective reality is a rich and fertile source of motivation, creativity, and psychological vitality. Where the image is rooted in unresolved issues from the past, it will tend to generate a painful relationship to the world, but out of that pain can also come tremendous incentive toward growth. Where the image is rooted in some vision of future possibility, it will drive the individual to use her imagination creatively in order to maximize pleasure, self-actualization and fulfillment. The world will remain what it is, but the image projected onto the world by the individual will determine who that individual becomes as an embodiment of Spirit, and how that individual relates to the world. It is through the projected image that each of us sets in motion the patterns of resonance that define our personal soul space. The exercise of the imagination – both creatively and pathologically – within this soul space, becomes the process by which the soul reveals itself to itself.

The Scientific Approach to Imagination

According to this perspective, imagination is essentially a subjective response to objective reality. The history of scientific psychology can be understood as an attempt to understand and control this subjective response through measurement, analysis and manipulation of its external effects, but largely with only incidental reference to the image, and the image-making process out of which these effects arise. Since objective reality is posited as the only reality there is by science, science is obviously ill equipped to understand, much less facilitate, the cultivation of a healthy imagination conducive to soul growth.

In fact, if you compare the standard psychiatric definitions for hallucination to the dictionary definition for imagination, it is not hard to discern a thinly veiled contempt for what science considers a suspicious activity beyond its scrutiny or control. Swiss psychiatrist, Eugen Bleuler, who coined the term, "schizophrenia," defined hallucinations as "perceptions without corresponding stimuli from without" – a definition that remains generally accepted to this day. But the imagination, which is fully capable of drawing material from the unconscious without the necessity for outside input, and then projecting it outward, thrives on these "hallucinatory" perceptions. Granted, a schizophrenic hallucinating something that is not there will have a qualitatively different experience than someone who is aware of the difference between image and objective reality. Yet the difference is more of degree than of kind, since the image produced by the inner, unconscious working of the psyche often emerges beyond the range of conscious choice, and in stark contrast to one's conscious orientation to the world.

As the similarity between these definitions implies, imagination must almost by definition, be dismissed as delusional, according to the dominant worldview. Imagination is tolerated in the arts, which today are mostly pursued as escapist entertainment, or as an expensive fetish cult of the wealthy. But, except for a few notable exceptions, which we will explore shortly, it is not honored as the central function of the psyche. Nor is it recognized as central to the soul-making process by a scientific psychology that denies the existence of the soul, and then strives to be objective, dispassionate and impersonal in its observation of internal process.

In most professional circles, mental health is defined in terms of the degree to which one's internal image of the world matches and effects a successful adaptation to consensus reality. As this ideal is approached, however, the imagination collapses, since there is insufficient discrepancy between inner and outer to sustain and motivate the image-making capacity of the soul. As the popular bumper sticker says, "Reality is for those who lack imagination." When all you have is reality, the image that sustains the soul as a source of motivation, creativity, and psychological vitality begins to implode. To the extent that mental health is construed as a process of minimizing the discrepancy between image and reality, then we find ourselves in the paradoxical and untenable situation in which the goal of psychology becomes a recipe for rendering infertile the very soil from which the soul draws its nourishment.

The more alive the soul is, the more it will instinctively rebel against this pressure to conform to consensus reality, by manifesting psychological symptoms. It will do this, as a matter of course, in order to increase the psychic distance between image and reality, so that it can have enough breathing room to cultivate and nurture an internal sense of self. The greater the threat of suffocation, the wider the gap between image and reality will become. When the standard to which the individual is expected to conform does violent disservice to the soul attempting to create itself in imagination, the individual can potentially experience the severe widening of the gap between image and reality that psychologists label as schizophrenia. Normally, the soul thrives on the creative tension between image and reality, just as it does on the interplay between all polar opposites (as discussed in Chapters Two and Three). But when the gap becomes too polarized, the tension can become too much to bear.

Consider, in this regard, the observation of Scottish psychoanalyst, R. D. Laing (95):

> In over 100 cases where we (Dr. Laing and colleagues, Drs. Cooper and Esterson) have studied the actual circumstances around the social event when one person comes to be regarded as schizophrenic, it seems to us that without exception the experience and behavior that gets labeled schizophrenic is a special strategy that a person invents in order to live in an unlivable situation. In his life situation the person has come to feel he is in an untenable position. He cannot make a move, or make no move, without being beset by contradictory and paradoxical pressures and demands, pushes and pulls, from himself, and externally, from those around him. He is, as it were, in a position of checkmate.

The irony implicit in this observation is that true mental health – and the health of the soul – depends not upon attempting to coerce, encourage, or otherwise psychologically orchestrate conformity between image and reality, but to nurture the artful cultivation of the discrepancy between them. Given the systematic denial of the validity of subjective process by a scientific psychology, this essentially means finding ways to nurture a positive relationship with image, as defined above. If we define image in this larger sense, as the convergence of multiple psychic streams in subjective response to objective reality, then we can trace a hopeful, though largely peripheral, track within the history of psychology upon which we might build a more deliberate language of soul.

The Contribution of Early Psychologists to an Imagery of Soul

The first tentative steps on this path were taken by a student of William Wundt by the name of Edward Tichener. While Wundt was laying the foundation for *functionalism*, a precursor to behavioral psychology, Tichener was developing a more internal approach to the study of the mind. This short-lived school of psychology, called *structuralism*, sought to measure the subjective response to external sensory stimuli through an elaborate technique Tichener called *analytic introspection*. Tichener would typically provide some sensory experience – a sound, a color, or an aroma – then interview his subjects about the images, feelings, thoughts, and sensations they had in response to the stimuli. To be sure, Tichener's goal in conducting this laborious research, which could take 20 minutes to record the response to a stimulus lasting a second or two, was an objective assessment of the function of the mind. But his methodology gave credence to the image by which soul comes to know itself, and could potentially have established the emerging science of psychology on a more subjective footing.

Unfortunately, the philosophical bias against the reliability of subjective information was insurmountable. So when introspective reports tended to vary considerably from individual to individual, this was not understood to confirm the subjective potency of the image, but viewed instead as the fatal flaw in Tichener's approach to psyche. It was also argued that the very act of introspection changed the nature of that which one was observing. Of course, this is true, because the soul interacts through the image with the world, which both shapes and is shaped by it within resonant soul space. At the advent of the psychological revolution, however, this disconcerting power of soul made Tichener's subjective approach suspect, since his results did not confirm the scientific paradigm of his day. Despite Tichener's international reputation and tireless activism, structuralism barely survived him as a viable stream within psychological thought.

The goal of the structuralists was to analyze the relationship between discrete stimuli and patterns of internal response. The school of Gestalt psychology, developed by Max

Wertheimer, Kurt Koffka, and Wolfgang Kohler instead promoted the idea that the mind organized stimuli into *gestalts*, or integrated patterns of holistic perception. Their famous dictum, "the whole is more than the sum of its parts" arises from this conviction, as does the idea that mind is active in the ordering of its own internal landscape. Though early Gestalt psychologists did not speak of soul or image, they nonetheless had evolved a concept of mind that was harmonious with the existence of a resonant soul space. They also recognized that the central agent within this space – whether construed as soul or mind – sought a sense of integrity, congruence and integration. Wertheimer was often at odds with the structuralists, whom he called "brick and mortar" psychologists (Sdorow 14), for their painstaking piecemeal approach to psyche. But both Gestalt psychology and structuralism gave credibility, in different ways, to the quest for understanding of the image-making power of the soul.

Freud's Contribution to an Understanding of Image

Though Freud was more influenced by behaviorism than either structuralism or Gestalt psychology, the psychoanalytic approach to psyche that he developed was essentially an attempt to approach an understanding of the image that informed resonant soul space. He called the central organizing principle within soul space the *ego*, distinguishing it from the mind that served as the primary object of study for behaviorists, structuralists and Gestalt psychologists. The ego included the mind, but was also endowed with important additional psychological functions – including identity, will, and the power of choice. The ego was not just a messenger between the external world of sensory information and the brain; it organized and interpreted this information in a way that was relatively unique to the individual. The ego was related to the individual's sense of identity, which was something that never entered into the equation of the behaviorists, and it implied a sense of purpose, which was also intimately personal. In order to understand the ego, and the image that it projected onto the world, Freud found it necessary to enter into the resonant   of each individual patient, in a way no laboratory psychologist would ever think of doing. Of course, we take such interior exploration for granted today, but it is worth reiterating that despite his scientific background, Freud had to be a bit of a contrarian to insist on moving inward toward the psyche, while others were so intent in focusing on the body and its external response to the outer world.

Furthermore, Freud recognized that the essential tension giving rise to the ego's image of the world was between the external forces of collective pressure, largely centered in the world itself, and a more internal, subjective force. This subjective force revolved around the gratification of personal needs, desires, and in general, a purely selfish agenda that given free reign would pay no attention to the world's expectations. The external

265

forces of collective pressure, he called the *superego*; the subjective force of self-gratification, he called the *id*. As a practicing psychoanalyst, Freud felt that his task was to bring the more primitive and unruly id under the control of the ego, with the help of the superego. The ego was understood to be the dike, holding back the raw, instinctual, soul-based impulses of the id – the passions, the desires, the sensory and emotional steams within the unconscious that contribute to the formation of the image – for the sake of social normalization.

When the ego functioned as psychoanalytical theory felt it should, the image was essentially shaped and molded to fit the norms of consensus reality, and meet the expectations of society. But the soul naturally identifies with the id, because it represents a more instinctual, uncensored, less compromised expression of being than either the ego or the superego. As frightening as it can sometimes be in the intensity and seeming unreasonableness of its demands, the id is nonetheless an important source for the generation of the image of soul that is projected, for better or worse, onto the world. The ego must then attempt to negotiate a compromise between the id and the internalized conditioning imposed by the world, which has become the superego.

As we shall see in Chapter Sixteen, the image is formed not only by id, but also by Spirit – an idea that concerned Freud only peripherally through his interest in animism, mythology and pre-religious thought. Nonetheless, within the context of the psychoanalytic theory that he developed, his first great contribution to a language of soul was acknowledging the central tension in the formation of the image. The id is in fact, a psychological expression of the relationship between soul and body, though Freud understood it more as an unconscious psychic repository of infantile desires, which erupted in irrational behavior and pathological symptoms that upset the psychic order. The Victorian world in which Freud lived, marinated for centuries in religious denigration of the body, and philosophical distrust of both the senses and the emotions, insisted that the unconscious impulses of the id be brought under control of the conscious ego, and so that is the direction that Freud felt compelled by his conditioning to take his patients.

Leaving the psychoanalytical agenda aside, however, it is possible to see the id in a less judgmental light. For as the unconscious impulses originating in the id are brought to awareness, acknowledged and allowed their place within resonant soul space, they infuse the image we project onto the world with primal desires that arise directly out of the soul's connection to the body. Within the context of the polarity between id and superego, it would be just as imbalanced for the ego to identify completely with the id, as it would for the id to be entirely repressed. But this is something that each soul must work out for itself. Meanwhile, to the extent that the id was not given enough space in which to allow the soul its expression within the body in Victorian Europe, Freud was compelled to deal with the endless parade of pathological symptoms that found their way to his couch.

The Unconscious Roots of the Image

Freud's second great contribution to a language of soul was the recognition that the formation of the image and the symptoms associated with its projection are largely an unconscious process. Before the advent of psychoanalytic theory, psychology was concerned solely with the function of the conscious mind, and the impact of conscious mental processes on behavior. To really understand behavior, Freud suggested, we must dive beneath the surface to identify the real psychic forces at play in the unconscious depths of soul space. The ego might have its head above water, but the id and the superego had roots that were identifiable only through reference to processes that took place below the surface flow of the conscious mind.

In dealing with a steady stream of patients for whom the resources available to the conscious mind could shed little light on their problems, Freud had come to the conclusion that "the material for (psychoanalytic) observations is usually provided by the inconsiderable events which have been put aside by the other sciences as being too unimportant" (qtd. in Hunt 195) among them slips of the tongue (which revealed motivations at odds with the conscious agenda of the patient), dreams (which made no rational sense from the externally oriented scientific perspective), and patterns of free association (in which the mental pathways through soul space were often mapped with no reference whatsoever to immediately obvious conscious connections). It was in accounting for the source of this information – foreign to the conscious mind apprehending it – that Freud inferred the existence of the unconscious.

If it is the discrepancy between the image and consensus reality that feeds the soul, as I suggested earlier, then it is out of the unconscious that any image useful to the soul must arise. The conscious mind is too closely aligned with consensus reality to make sufficient space for an image to exist in contrast with it. The conscious mind is content to understand consensus reality as objective fact, while consensus reality is merely the portal through which the soul makes contact with a deeper, more intimately personal level of being. The conscious mind can take the soul to the portal, but the soul can only move *through* the portal into the more subjective sense of self-awareness that it seeks by allowing the unconscious to speak to it. The unconscious is constantly attempting to engage the soul, as Freud pointed out, through subliminal dialogue that frequently erupts into consciousness through dreams, slips of the tongue, and the other mechanisms of unconscious communication that he studied.

These eruptions of the unconscious become necessary because the conscious ego is identified too strongly with one side or another of any given polarity, forcing the soul into an unnatural state of imbalance. Meanwhile, the id, which represents a more instinctual if unconscious identification of the soul with its wholeness, tends to resonate with the opposite polarity, thereby creating an internal pressure within the psyche toward balance. This pressure charges the soul with an explosive numinosity that in turn, erupts into consciousness as part of the image that is projected into the world.

If I am unable or unwilling to access the assertive side of my nature, for example, and consciously identify myself as a peaceful person, aggressive bullies who insist upon intruding into my personal space and provoking me may suddenly populate my world. These bullies will represent an exaggerated image of the part of myself I have yet to claim. The intrusion of this image will be uncomfortable to the ego, but it will also assert powerful pressure upon me to embrace a larger sense of self – one that is not only peaceful, but also capable of taking a more assertive stance and fighting back when the situation warrants. If I am unable or unwilling to do this, the projected aggression may move to a deeper level, perhaps manifesting as an actual assault, or the aggression of cancer cells invading my body.

When the conscious mind is unwilling or unable to assimilate the image projected into the embodied world by the unconscious, the unconscious begins to speak more loudly through the manifestation of psychosomatic symptoms and psychological pathologies. If the soul continues to ignore the unconscious pressure toward balance, it will become increasingly imbalanced, until the symptoms and pathologies it manifests become life-threatening.

Freud considered pathology to be sexual in origin, which as we discussed in Chapter Two, is metaphorically speaking, not that far off the mark. As a scientist, however, he took his metaphors literally, and failed to see the deeper, more spiritual implications of sex as the natural interplay of polar opposites giving rise to the soul's image of the embodied world, and impelling it toward wholeness. Though his patients, being human, undoubtedly struggled to find a point of balance between many intertwined and overlapping sets of opposites, Freud became a one-trick pony in a circus with rings too numerous to count. The image, which draws its potency through an attempt to integrate the various streams of sensation, memory, fantasy, feeling, thought, instinct, insight, and spontaneous impulse that flow through a broad multiplicity of polarities, was collapsed into a literal sexual drama, played out according to the archetypal pattern of the myth of Oedipus.

The Myth of Oedipus
As a Template for the Image-Making Process

According to Freud's interpretation of this myth, the generic template governing the formation and subsequent development of the psyche was a forbidden desire on the part of every man for sexual union with his mother. This desire in turn required him to kill his father, who was his primary rival, and an obvious obstacle between him and the fulfillment of his fantasy. Freud also conceived a converse fantasy for women, which he related to the myth of Elektra. In Greek mythology, Elektra was Clytemnestra's daughter, who hated her mother for the murder of her father, Agamemnon, whom she adored. Since polite society would not allow such outrageous emotions to play themselves out without serious consequences, the psyche had to find ways to repress, deny, rationalize, sublimate, displace, project, or otherwise transmute the energy invested in these fantasies of incest, murder and revenge. The psyche did this through a number of defense mechanisms, putting the raw, primal energy of the id to more productive and socially acceptable use. In discussing the various ways in which the psyche could process the unacceptable primal fantasy, Freud was essentially mapping out some of the more dysfunctional strategy options available to the soul in creating and projecting its image onto the world.

As pointed out by Liz Greene, Jungian psychologist and astrologer, however, Freud misconstrued the meaning and purpose of the myth of Oedipus in order to make his point. For in the myth, Oedipus does not kill his father in order to possess his mother; he kills his father before he ever meets his mother, and he marries his mother without knowing they are related. The killing is the fulfillment of a curse that was placed upon his father, King Laius, in exchange for abusing the hospitality of King Pelops, by abducting and raping his son[1]. As Greene points out, this is not primarily a myth about incestuous desire, but about the expiation of ancestral sins passed down from fathers to their sons, who must somehow free themselves from the curse before they can live their own life. Making allowances for the patriarchal culture in which this myth originated, we might safely assume that Oedipus is the representative of every soul, male and female. Oedipus killed Laius, not because he wanted to have sex with his mother, but because the old man was standing in his way – both literally and figuratively. According to Greene, "...the point of the battle is not so much the possession of the parent of the opposite sex. It is the overthrowing of the old order and the assertion of the independent, individual spirit...." (181).

This is, in fact, what every soul must do, before it can call its resonant soul space its own. Many of the patterns of resonance which create tension between the image projected by the soul onto the world and the world itself arise from the psychic inheritance we absorbed by osmosis from our parents, from our schools, from our religious authorities and from the culture at large. One of the primary tasks for any soul – a task that Jung would later label *individuation* – is separating out what is truly ours, that is to say resonant with our essential nature as a soul, and what we have unconsciously absorbed that doesn't really belong to us. This is what the first part of the Oedipal myth is about, at least according to Greene, with whom I agree. It is not the control of the id that is important to the soul, but the reclaiming of the id from the tyranny of the superego.

Freud would argue that the superego encompasses the collective morals, values, and traditions of the society in which we live. As such, it holds a legitimate place within the psyche and is as necessary to psychic balance as the ego or the id. When the voice of the collective rises up in fear of the unbridled irrational power of the id, however – which it did in Freud's day, and which it apparently also did among Oedipus' ancestors[2] – it becomes a tyrannical source of repression to the individual soul, seeking to discover its own voice. Breaking free of this tyranny, wherever it exists, is thus one major evolutionary task in the process that gives rise to the image.

A second major evolutionary task facing every soul correlates to the second part of the myth, in which Oedipus unwittingly marries his mother. After killing Laius, Oedipus travels on to Thebes, where Hera had just cursed the city with a beast called the Sphinx, a creature with the face of a woman, the body of a lion, and the wings of a bird. The Sphinx was apparently an educated monster, since it asked its victims a riddle before devouring them. If they could answer the riddle correctly, they would be spared. The riddle was this: "What is it that has one name that is four-footed, two-footed, and three-footed?" The answer, which everybody now knows, is man at various stages of life: the infant, crawling on all fours; the adult, walking on two feet; and the elder, limping along with a cane. No one at the time in Thebes, however, seemed able to figure this out, so the Sphinx was terrorizing the city and killing lots of people. In despair, the regent Creon offered his throne and his sister, Jocasta (Oedipus' mother) as wife, to anyone who could answer the Sphinx' riddle, and end its reign of tyranny. Of course, our man Oedipus did, and the rest, as they say, is history.

Undoubtedly, there are many ways to interpret this half of the myth, just as Freud and Greene and many others differ in their interpretation of the first half. What makes the story a myth, in fact, is its capacity to serve as a psychic mirror for the image of large groups of people. It carries this capacity, in part, because it contains a universal truth with which we all resonate. But not everyone will resonate in exactly the same way to the same myth. The best myths will simultaneously speak to our collective quest as a culture, and to each individual in a way that is relatively unique to them. This leaves a wide range of latitude for subjective interpretations, the best of which speak to our universal predicament as human beings.

In any case, for what it might be worth, what I see in the second half of this myth is a recognition that the way we evolve as souls is through assimilation of everything that seems opposite to that with which we identify. The Sphinx is a multidimensional being – an irrational juxtaposition of seemingly disparate parts – and an imagistic mirror to the unintegrated soul, the monster that is each of us, when the polar tensions within us are at war. The word Sphinx means "strangler," suggesting that this narrow identification with one side of a polarity at the expense of the other strangles the soul, cutting it off from its Wholeness in Spirit. The riddle that the Sphinx poses is an invitation to us to realize that we are not only multidimensional beings in quest of integration, but that we will change our shape and our mode of transportation, so to speak, many times in the course of that quest, in order to claim the various "lost" parts of our being. The object of the quest is two-fold: union with every aspect of every polarity with which we do not identify, and a return to the Source of our Being. Both processes are symbolized by Oedipus' union with his own mother – who represents all that he is not, and is also the biological source of his embodiment as a soul.

It is interesting to note that there are three endings to this story – two by Homer, and one by Sophocles. In the first Homeric version, Oedipus lives and rules Thebes with the full weight of his father's curse upon his shoulders for the rest of his life, while Jocasta commits suicide and goes down to Hades. In the second Homeric version, related in the *Illiad*, Oedipus leaves Jocasta after he discovers the truth, remarries, and then goes out and gets himself killed in battle. In the third version, by Sophocles, which is the most widely accepted of the three (Morford 325), Oedipus and Jocasta and their four children live happily together for awhile, and only learn the truth many years later, at which point, Jocasta commits suicide, and Oedipus blinds himself with the brooches from her robe, then goes into exile.

These unhappy endings suggest a number of truths about the soul and its image-making process. First, the psychic inheritance that is passed down from generation to generation is not that easily released, and separating the id from the superego is a task that generally takes the better part of a lifetime, if it is accomplished at all. This is a matter discussed at length by Greene in her book, *The Astrology of Fate*, which is about that aspect of the soul's experience that is inescapable, rooted in mortality, and known by the Greeks as Moira. Secondly, whether the soul is conscious of its ancestral inheritance (1st ending), in denial of it (2nd ending), or oblivious to it (3rd ending), the tension between the inheritance and the soul's longing for freedom from it will continue to serve as a pivot point around which the image evolves. Thirdly, though the union of opposites is possible, it is necessarily a temporary condition, since as long as the soul is in a body – which is to say, as long as one is alive – a higher level of integration will always be possible, and the soul will always gravitate, consciously or unconsciously, toward that possibility. When the soul stops seeking this integration, it begins to die – or put another way, the tenuous fusion between Spirit and body begins to unravel. Sophocles might argue for a fourth lesson – namely, that it doesn't pay to try to outsmart the gods, but that is merely another way of saying that the complex inner pantheon of psychic forces within us will seek integration, one way or another, despite our resistance, or even the generations of resistance that are passed down to us by our ancestors and the culture at large.

Though he failed to grasp the deeper implications of the Oedipus myth for the soul's journey, Freud's contribution to our collective understanding of the image is not to be underestimated. At a time when the emergent science of psychology was prepared to interpret the image in purely objective, external and physiological terms, Freud insisted that it must be approached subjectively through an exploration of internal soul space, and discussed not just physiologically, but also psychologically. At a time when his colleagues were concerning themselves only with conscious processes and behavioral consequences, Freud suggested that the process was actually mostly unconscious. He further began mapping the psychic "structure" of the unconscious, and identifying mechanisms by which the subjective image of the world was formed. He evolved a sexual theory of the underlying tension beneath the formation of the image which was too literal, but which taken metaphorically, goes straight to the heart of the soul's dilemma.

Freud would not have articulated his ideas in the way that I have here, nor does his contribution to psychology end with what I have outlined, but if we can borrow these ideas, and adapt them to our immediate purpose – understanding the use of imagination as a cornerstone of any true language of soul – we have a hopeful trail that we can begin to follow through the history of psychology toward our goal. This trail was simultaneously broadened and articulated in greater detail by Freud's disciple, Swiss psychoanalyst, Carl Jung.

The Symbolist Contribution To a Cultural Embrace of the Image

Before we take a closer look at Jung's contribution, it is worth noting that as Freud was beginning to articulate the subjective image-making process of the unconscious, there was a parallel revolution going on in the arts throughout Europe, particularly in France. In keeping with the increasing dominance of the scientific worldview, and the Victorian moral codes that attempted to dictate social behavior, the arts in the latter half of the 19th century were subject to strict rules of formalism and literal interpretation. Art was expected to accurately mirror objective reality, and there was very little tolerance for subjective liberties, or flights of imaginative fancy. In breaking out of this cultural straitjacket, several French poets, including Baudelaire, Verlaine, and Rimbaud, began to introduce into their work a more impressionistic strain, evocative not of the literal external world, but of the more ephemeral, irrational, and ineffable inner life. Instead of interpreting reality through exposition and narrative, they employed liberal use of imagery and metaphor, suggestive of mysteries that could not be articulated by direct reference.

Following in the symbolist tradition, American poet, James Wright, says:

> While I stood here, in the open, lost in myself,
> I must have looked a long time
> Down the corn rows, beyond grass,
> The small house,
> White walls, animals lumbering toward the barn.
> I look down now. It is all changed.
> Whatever it was I lost, whatever I wept for
> Was a wild, gentle thing, the small dark eyes
> Loving me in secret.
> It is here. At the touch of my hand,
> The air fills with delicate creatures
> From the other world.

The early French poets and many since were, in short, exploring the same image that Freud was beginning to unveil, but in an artistic rather than a psychological way. A century earlier, the Romantic poets – Wordsworth, Keats, Byron, Shelley, Coleridge, and others – had celebrated the emotional and sensory realms in support of Kant's declaration that the rational mind was inadequate to understand metaphysical truths. Now, in the late 19th century, the Symbolists, as they later came to be called, were inadvertently lending similar support to Freud's assertion that in order to understand the human psyche, we had to go down into its unfathomable depths to find the image that governed it.

Though the arts have historically been granted more latitude than the sciences, including scientific psychology, there was quite a backlash to both Freud and the Symbolists. In the wake of the Clark University lectures, which made him famous, Freud was called "a dirty, filthy man" and accused of advocating "a relapse into savagery" (Hunt 191) by his detractors, while the Symbolists were judged to be decadent bohemians, and dismissed as fin-de-siecle folly. Meanwhile, they had touched a nerve in the collective psyche and launched a movement that would spread throughout Europe to the United States, and stretch from poetry to the literature of Joyce, Yeats, Eliot, and Woolf, to the theatre of Maeterlinck, Claudel, and Strindberg, to the impressionist painting of Monet, Gauguin, and Van Gogh to the music of Debussy, Ravel, Delius, and Wolf (EB 11: 458-459). After World War I, Surrealist painters - such as Chagall, Klee, Picasso and Dali, and writers such as Eluard, Aragon, Crevel, and Soupault carried this tradition was carried forward into a more overtly psychological age (Sanchez). The Surrealists were directly influenced by both Freud and Jung, and their intention was to give expression to images emerging directly from the unconscious, without undue interpretation by the conscious mind.

In the 20th century, the tradition was carried forward by film directors such as Fellini, Bunuel, Bergman, Wenders, Herzog and many others, remaining very much alive in the present day, as witnessed, for example, in the 1999 award-winning Sam Mendes film, *American Beauty*. In the film, Wes Bentley plays Ricky, a young dope-smoking photographer-voyeur, living at home with his rigid, neo-Nazi father, who maintains tight control over the tumultuous forces in his own repressed psyche, and tries unsuccessfully to do the same with his son. At one point, toward the end of the film, Ricky shows Jane, his girlfriend, a short film of a paper bag floating upon the wind. If we remember the ancient association between wind and Spirit, then the paper bag – a fragile and utterly temporary carrier of goods – can easily become a symbol for the postmodern embodied soul, cast adrift in a world of forces beyond its control. At the same time, however, the bag somehow possesses a numinous vitality of its own that creates an image with the capacity to move the world – if only in the psyche of a young, impressionable teenager armed with a digital camcorder. In the grand tradition of the Symbolists, the bag also becomes a metaphor for all the ephemeral beauty and irrational magic that has been cast aside by a society under pressure from the superego.

One might think we'd be beyond that now, given the cultural revolution of the last 40 years, but the battle delineated by Freud between the natural subjective expression of the sensual, emotional, imaginative soul, and the fear-based forces of rational, literal, consensual objectivity, rages on. It rages on, as Freud was one of the first to point out, because it is not out there somewhere. It is in here, inside every one of us, hardwired into our psyche.

Jung's Contribution
To a Psychological Understanding of the Image

Freud's work with the image was extended and deepened by Jung. Jung explored many avenues into the heart of the image-making process, including dreams, mythology, astrology, alchemy, Taoism, Native American shamanism, Christian iconography and Tibetan mandalas, to name just a few of the many sources that he tapped. Once a space is made for the image, it is not hard to find echoes of it everywhere, since the world is a most accommodating mirror. Jung's big breakthrough into the realm of the image came in mid career, however, not through his professional work within the world, as we might expect, but when his own psychic ferment drew him inward, and he honored it by withdrawing from the world.

The process began, appropriately enough, after Jung had his falling out with Freud. He saw that Freud was unwilling to confront certain aspects of his own psyche, and realized that it was time for him to move on. Freud had a dream, which Jung interpreted and then suggested that he could take it to a deeper level, if Freud would supply him with additional details about his life. When Freud responded, "But I cannot risk my authority," Jung knew that it was over. As he wrote in his autobiography, *Memories, Dreams and Reflections*, "That sentence burned itself into my memory; and in it, the end of our relationship was already foreshadowed. Freud was placing personal authority above truth" (158). To go further with his own process, Jung would have to separate from his mentor and find his own way forward. This is, of course, in microcosm, a reflection of the first task of the soul as suggested by the myth of Oedipus, where in order to individuate, as Jung would put it, the soul must first separate from the voice of the collective past, turn within, and find an image of self and of the world that is truly its own.

Jung's quest began from a place of uncertainty and disorientation. As Jung described the awkward transition, "I felt totally suspended in mid-air, for I had not yet found my own footing" (Memories 170). This statement can, in one sense, be interpreted to mean that Jung believed he lacked the confidence to proceed in his professional life without the guidance and support of a mentor. On a deeper level, however, Jung was reaching for something within himself that he was not yet sure existed. By this point in his career, he had helped many patients with their psychological problems; he had written books about psychological theory, mythology, the quest of the hero as a metaphor for the soul's journey, and for all intents and purposes, would have already begun to appear in the eyes of the world as an authority on psychological process. Yet, in the aftermath of his split with Freud, he felt compelled to turn inward and ask himself the same question that he asked of all his patients: "What is your myth – the myth in which you live?" If after all, he could not be accountable to himself in the way that he expected Freud to be accountable to him, then he had no more right to his authority than he was willing to grant his former mentor. Jung was chagrined to find that he had no answer to this question, and despite all the professional credibility he had already garnered in the eyes of the world, he suddenly found himself standing on the edge of an intimidating abyss. "At this point," he says, "the dialogue with myself became uncomfortable, and I stopped thinking. I had reached a dead end" (Memories 171).

During the next several years, Jung entered deeply into his own subjective soul space. He had a series of potent dreams and visions, which he dutifully recorded and struggled to understand. Amidst an ongoing sense of disorientation, and mounting fears that he was undergoing a psychotic breakdown, Jung bravely chose to continue exploring his experiences and learn what he could. He could not, however, maintain the same professional distance to his own process that he dispassionately exercised with his patients, nor could he assume his usual scientific objectivity in the face of experiences that were deeply subjective and overwhelming in their emotional intensity. In order to explore the realm of the image that was trying to communicate with him from deep within his own psyche, Jung had to abandon everything his conscious, rational mind thought he knew, and begin again from scratch. " 'Since I know nothing at all'," he reasoned, " 'I shall simply do whatever occurs to me'. Thus I consciously submitted myself to the impulses of the unconscious" (Memories 173).

What occurred to him first was a childhood memory of playing with blocks, accompanied by the reawakening of a passion to resume this activity. So Jung began gathering stones from the lakeshore where he lived, and starting building – cottages, a castle, a church with an altar, and eventually a whole village. As he engaged himself in this activity, which to his conscious mind often seemed childish, his unconscious mind began speaking to him in earnest – through ongoing dream activity, disturbing visions, dialogues with inner figures he later recognized as the archetypal denizens of his own psyche, through strange drawings he felt compelled to render, through sessions with modeling clay in which he attempted to give shape to the image as it was revealing itself to his conscious mind. "To the extent that I managed to translate the emotions into images," he tells us, "that is to say, to find the images which were concealed in the emotions – I was inwardly calmed and reassured. Had I left those images hidden in the emotions, I might have been torn to pieces by them... As a result of my experiment, I learned how helpful it can be, from the therapeutic point of view, to find the particular images which lie behind the emotions" (Memories 177).

Jung eventually developed his subjective experiences into an elaborate psychological theory based upon an illumination of the images behind the troubling emotions to which all human beings are prone. He came to understand these images to be representative of universal psychic forces within the collective unconscious, which he called *archetypes*. He identified several key archetypes, most notably the *shadow*, the *anima* and *animus*, the *wise elder* and the *Self* – all of whom are key residents of the psyche, with the capacity to facilitate various phases of the individuation process. Lastly, he made the potent connection between these internal archetypes and the various symbols appearing in dreams, myth, folklore, magic, astrology, alchemy, and many other places as evidence of human effort to bring the image, as we have been discussing it here, into more tangible form, accessible to the conscious mind.

These discoveries are well documented through Jung's own writings, and the prolific evolution of subsequent generations of Jungian psychologists, and I feel no compelling need to describe them in more detail here. I do want to suggest that in taking this road, which began in the subjective realm of his own psyche, Jung opened a door to the only serious alternative to the scientific approach to the psyche that has dominated psychology before and since. He was the first to place the image at the very heart of the attempt to understand soul, and to take seriously the imagination (image-making power of the soul).

Where others were ready to relegate the images produced by the psyche to the realm of nonsense, hallucination, or indigestion, Jung took them seriously, admonishing anyone who would listen that "the images of the unconscious place a great responsibility upon a man. Failure to understand them, or a shirking of ethical responsibility, deprives him of his wholeness and imposes a painful fragmentation on his life" (Memories 193).

In the midst of this subjective process, Jung realized that what he was doing could not be called science, in the way that science is normally understood. Despite the widespread application of the theories that evolved out of his experiences, the experiences themselves were too personal, too deeply rooted in numinous, ineffable mystery, too sacred to attempt to capture in final form, or communicate within the context of the rational, objective, causal worldview that his scientific training demanded of him. *The Black Book*, consisting of six black-bound leather notebooks in which he recorded these experiences, and *The Red Book*, an embellished version of the same material in the form of a medieval manuscript, were never published. Jung eventually returned to his scientific training, which provided sold ground and a much needed psychic anchor to his soul's inner journey, and left a trail of bread crumbs for anyone in his wake, who might dare to make the journey for themselves.

The Further Cultivation of the Image in Jung's Wake

Other pioneers left additional bread crumbs, and some have taken pains to describe some of them in great detail. Several of Jung's students and successors have focused on one or more of the archetypes, and explored their mythological history, contemporary manifestations, and psychological implications in prodigious and important expositions. Esther Harding, for example, explored the archetypal feminine in great depth in her landmark book, *Woman's Mysteries: Ancient and Modern*, while Jung's wife, Emma, focused more explicitly on the anima and animus. In a similar spirit, Erich Neumann tackled the Great Mother, Paul Radin, the Trickster, and Joseph Henderson, the archetypal process of initiation, to name just a few of the many threads that now weave together the rich tapestry of contributions to a Jungian understanding of the source material for the image that each of us recreates in our own way.

Other pioneers within the humanistic psychology movement of the 1960s and 70s, most notably Fritz Perls and Roberto Assagioli, have focused on a cultivation of skill in drawing forth the image, as a centerpiece of their approach to psychotherapy. Perls pioneered a modality he called Gestalt therapy (no relation to Wertheimer's earlier school of Gestalt psychology), in which he attempted to evoke and sometimes provoke heightened awareness of emotional process in his clients. His primary technique for doing this involved dialogue between various inner voices, each of which had their own set of values, and beliefs, and a surprising amount of psychic autonomy. Whereas Jung preferred consigning his dialogues to the privacy of his journals, Perls had a more in-your-face style that insisted on exteriorizing them, often with an audience, to help his clients cultivate a more authentic sense of self. This technique, called the *two-chair exercise*, had the client move back and forth from one chair to the other, giving each side of the polarity under exploration its own literal space, until the voices converged in a creative synthesis that promised a more integrated cooperation in the future.

While the dialogue technique is useful in bringing to consciousness the various intrapsychic polarities responsible for producing the image, Italian psychoanalyst, Roberto Assagioli pointed out that the actual inner dynamic that produces the image is often more complicated than that. Assagioli observed that the classic Freudian ego is only one voice among many sub-personalities, and often not the focal point of consciousness, as Freud contended that it was. Nor did the ego necessarily follow a neat progression from shadow to anima or animus to wise elder to individuated Self in its assimilation of unconscious contents, as was implied in Jung's work. Instead, Assagioli observed that there was "a constant osmosis" taking place within the psyche as various sub-personalities made their way to the forefront of consciousness and took charge of the melodrama of life. By becoming more aware of this process – which is the image-making process, as understood from the perspective of a relatively sophisticated model – Assagioli hoped to help his clients achieve "objective" understanding of their own soul space, and greater control over the inner conflicts and ambivalences that plagued them.

In actual practice, Assagioli began with an extensive psychic inventory of everything that was known about the individual, as a soul, from the perspective of the conscious mind. He had his clients tell their story and eventually write an autobiography, respond to questionnaires which helped them trace presenting problems to their family of origin or other possible sources, and keep a personal journal throughout the course of therapy. In addition, Assagioli asked his clients about their heroes and heroines, favorite books, songs, pictures or statues, public buildings, games and sports, and other potential sources for material within resonant soul space, as well as attitudes toward various aspects of life, beliefs, and values, from which the psyche might draw the raw material out of which it would fashion the image. As a last step in the preparation process, he would help his clients identify any polarities within their own psychological make-up, which might possibly be the source of conflict or ambivalence.

Once this foundation had been established, Assagioli then began leading his client into the realm of the image, through the usual psychoanalytical tools – word association, dream analysis, projective techniques such as the Thematic Apperception Test, the Rorschach, the Szondi Test and others, free drawing exercises, writing exercises and hypnotherapy techniques. In the tradition of all psychoanalysts, Assagioli sought to strengthen the ego, or as he preferred to think of it, the conscious will, since he felt that a strong, clear set of intentions was necessary to successfully enter the realm of the unconscious without getting lost in the tumultuous currents one often found there. At the same time, Assagioli guided his clients in cultivating the imagination through visualization exercises, techniques for enhancing awareness of auditory, kinesthetic, tactile, gustatory, olfactory and other sensory experiences, and increasing familiarity with symbols, especially those drawn from nature, religion, mythology, and personal dreams. Included in the work with symbols was an attempt to help each client get in touch with the spiritual core of his or her being – a core that I would call the soul, but that he called the *superconscious*. Lastly, he helped each client cultivate the faculty of intuition he deemed necessary to comprehend the wholeness of the symbols that could be used to evoke an image of the soul.

Other psychologists emerging from the confluence of Jungian psychology and the humanistic and personal growth movements in the 1960s and 70s gave rise to an additional plethora of techniques, which more or less revolved around the use of active imagination, as practiced by Jung, and/or techniques for cultivating sensory, emotional, and intuitive awareness pioneered by Assagioli and others. An important contribution to this growing field of image-making has been made by Jean Houston, through elucidation of the mind-body connection, and several books of techniques for increasing somatic awareness, integration of the left and right hemispheres of the brain, and the cultivation of what she calls *evolutionary memory* (96) – reaching back into the limbic brain for our connection to the thread of life as it has been unwinding since the beginning of linear time. Jungian psychologist, Robert Johnson, has also written a useful book, entitled, *Inner Work: Using Dreams and Active Imagination for Personal Growth*, which incorporates Assagioli's awareness of subpersonalities with a Jungian sensibility. These are only a few resources among many that have become available since Jung opened the door to a more subjective exploration of the inner confluence of psychic streams that inform and shape the image projected by the soul.

The Potential For Astrology's Contribution To an Understanding of the Image

Astrology has for centuries facilitated the exploration of the image, which arises from soul space. But except for a few notable exceptions, astrology has been primarily focused on the rational interpretation of symbols, as opposed to the exploration of their sensory, emotional, and imagistic roots in personal experience. While we all naturally desire to know what symbols mean, interpretation of them actually renders them less useful for purposes of soul work. I'm sure this will seem like a statement of heresy to most astrologers, since the interpretation of symbols is generally understood – by astrologers and the general public alike – as the essence of what astrologers do.

Yet, if we understand symbols as Jung understood them, as windows into a level of being that is mostly unconscious, then interpretation merely provides the conscious mind a foothold within a vast unknown territory that otherwise has no familiar solid ground. To the extent that the astrologer clings to that foothold as the only possible source of information to be extracted, then the chart soon goes flat and lifeless, and the symbols turn into signs, or a mere shorthand notation for a static truth the astrologer is attempting to decode. As pre-eminent Jungian psychologist, James Hillman warns us, "We sin against the imagination whenever we ask an image for its meaning, requiring that images be translated into concepts. The coiled snake in the corner cannot be translated into my fear, my sexuality, or my mother-complex, without killing the snake" (39). If we kill the snake – that is to say, the image laden with subjective meaning born of individual sensory and emotional associations to the image – then we cut off a primary source of nourishment to the soul. If we kill enough snakes, then eventually we starve the soul that feeds upon them. Though Hillman was not talking about astrological symbolism per se, the same caution applies to the reading of any birthchart.

To be sure, most contemporary astrologers have at least a rudimentary appreciation for the fact that within the span of one hour, not everything that *can* be said about the birthchart *will* be said. Many, if pressed, would acknowledge that the same chart would not have the same meaning for the same individual at age 7 that it will at age 47. Nonetheless, within the omnipresent model of astrology in which a client comes to an astrologer for a reading, expecting her to decode the strange, undecipherable markings on the piece of paper called a birthchart, the snake is often the sacrificial victim of the process. To render astrology truly useful as a language of soul, we must learn to work with the birthchart, not as a static statement of psychological or spiritual fact, but as the point of departure for an ongoing process of exploration. The goal of this work should not be interpretation, through decoding symbols, but rather glimpsing more clearly the unconscious current out of which the image of the soul constantly evolves.

The symbols of a birthchart are not mere shorthand signs for discrete packets of information that can be regurgitated at will. They are synergistic conduits to the image-making process, which can only be known to the extent the individual provides the story that underlies the formation of the image. The truth to be found in a birthchart is not within the chart itself, but in that which can be glimpsed through the chart of the individual's sensory, emotional, imagistic response to the experiences that shape the soul. This response is constantly changing, revolving in kaleidoscopic fashion around an ancient intention, which takes a wide range of potential shapes, depending on the situation in which it is evoked. We can't possibly know the image once and for all. We can at best hope to form a more conscious relationship to it, so that our response to life increasingly becomes a matter of choice and intention. The birthchart can help with this to the extent that it is approached as an invitation to more deeply enter the psychic undercurrents that shape the image. In order to do this, we must constantly refer back to the actual experience of the person for whom the birthchart is merely a conscious opening to a deeper, more unconscious place of knowing.

The most important of all these images, of course, is the one that connects the embodied soul to its source in Spirit. In Chapter Nineteen, we will explore how astrology can be used in a more poetic way to find and illuminate such an image. First, we must examine how psychology has failed not only as a language of imagery, but also as a language through which the most meaningful questions posed by soul – about its ultimate identity and its source in Spirit – can be addressed.

Endnotes

[1]   This curse was compounded by an already existing curse on the house of Labdacus (Laius' ancestral lineage) that began when Pentheus (Oedipus' great-grandfather on his mother's side) imprisoned Dionysus because of his capacity to arouse the women of Thebes to orgiastic frenzy. In exchange for defying the god, Pentheus was stoned to death by the Maenads, female devotees of Dionysus, among them Pentheus' own mother. When Labdacus (Pentheus' cousin and Oedipus' paternal grandfather) succeeded Pentheus, he sought to repeat his predecessor's policies against Dionysus, and met the same fate. After two generations of opposition on both sides of the family, Dionysus did not look upon Laius, Jocasta, or their son, Oedipus with great favor.

[2]   Dionysus – whose worship was inspired by wine, and generally resulted in orgiastic fervor and indulgence of every possible sensual desire – can be understood as the mythological embodiment of the id. Opposition to Dionysus – which was the sin of Oedipus' ancestors, who sought to pass laws prohibiting the Dionysian rites – can in turn, be understood to represent the tyranny of the superego.

Chapter Fifteen
The Pathology of Soul
And Psychology's Response to It

The central questions, which every soul is born to spend a lifetime addressing, are "Who am I?" and "Why am I here?" Or as Zen master, Hoshin, is reputed to have said on his deathbed, "I come from brilliancy and return to brilliancy. What is this?" (Reps 14) – presumably meaning human life, death, and the embodied soul apparently sandwiched between experiences of brilliancy. As seen in Chapter Thirteen, before William James postulated the existence of an empirical self, psychology was oddly the study of "this" without reference to the one experiencing "this," nor to the "I" at the heart of all these questions about "this". Since Kant and Hume had declared the soul to be unknowable by scientific observation back in the 18th century, science stopped asking questions about who it was that was being observed, much less who it was that was observing, and all subjects simply became objects. When psychology emerged in the scientific mold a century later, the study of the human psyche continued along these same stilted lines.

From the scientific perspective, adopted by behavioral psychologists, the life of the psyche was construed as the impersonal interplay of internal forces that somehow procceded independently of the individual whose psyche hosted them. The human *being*, in other words, was not considered necessary to an understanding of human behavior. This did not change, even when James proposed the empirical self to try to rectify what he felt was a serious omission in the scientific worldview, for the empirical self became immediately identified with its response – primarily its physiological response – to external stimuli. The empirical self was not important to the behaviorists, only its visible behavior. In theory, the empirical self was an attempt to turn science inward to study what previously lay beyond its scope. But science's bias against the validity of subjective information was so strong, that in practice the empirical self was confined to the observable aspects of external behavior without reference to the self who behaved.

Psychopathology and the Soul

As discussed earlier, the psychoanalytical school, led by Freud, took this self more seriously, giving it a name – *ego* – and declaring that it had to be reckoned with, in order to understand the subjective response (or image) that was causing the dysfunction under treatment. The empirical self had been rendered inert through a scientific mindset that approached it as a passive, mechanical responder to external stimuli. But the ego could actively participate in creating and orchestrating its own experience, and this was a definite step forward in restoring "soul" to "the study of soul" that psychology's etymological and philosophical roots suggest it ought to be.

Through its gradual acceptance of the ego as a valid focal point for observation of psychological process, the psychoanalytical community began to give the soul – though it dared not call it that – a foothold somewhere near the center of its own experience. To be sure, the ego is not the soul. As a concept, it actually embodied more of the Victorian mistrust of those aspects of soul that were rooted in its connection to the body, than it did a recognition of the soul itself. Ego, no less than the mind that came before it, was in fact, a psychological barrier to everything we have identified in this book as being relevant to embodied soul, including sensory experience, emotion, and the imagination. But the concept of ego nonetheless allowed a more serious consideration of the activity of the soul within the psyche to enter the back door of psychological scrutiny.

As discussed in Chapter Fourteen, the healthy ego was actually the antithesis of a truly subjective sense of individuality. Nonetheless, by the same irony turned inside out, the more psychoanalysts tried to strengthen the ego as a barrier to the emergence of soul, the more soulful the pathological dysfunctions it was compelled to analyze and treat, and the more idiosyncratic the subjective selves that presented themselves for analysis. The more the image-making capacity of the soul was feared, the more pathological and distorted the image-making process became.

On the other hand, if we step back a moment and realize that psychopathology is nothing more or less than the soul's attempt to reconcile the internal polarities it is faced with, then perhaps even the grossest distortions can be understood as part of the soul-making process. As James Hillman has dared suggest, despite the pejorative connotations we have to the term, psychopathology is a legitimate, even central activity of the soul (55-56):

> Perhaps our psychopathology has an intimate connection with our individuality, so that our fear of being what we really are is partly because we fear the psychopathological aspect of individuality. For we are each peculiar; we have symptoms; we fail, and cannot see why we go wrong or even where, despite high hopes and good intentions . . . The study of lives and the care of souls means above all a prolonged encounter with what is broken and hurts – that is, with psychopathology.

As difficult as it is to integrate the broken pieces into the whole fabric of our identities, they are the very places within our lives where the embodied soul is most active, where death in the metaphorical sense has claimed us, and we are stripped to the bone. When life breaks down, and doesn't work the way it us supposed to, that is our opportunity to find out who we are at the core of our being. For what we discover when we are brave enough to go down into the pain, to own the depression, to find out where the anger really wants to take us, to look the tumultuous psychic forces in the face even as they threaten to tear us apart, is that there is something deeper, older and wiser within us than that which has us in its grip. This something is the soul, and the apparent source of our anguish is the rite of passage necessary to bring us to a recognition of it. A true psychology of soul ought to help us realize what is really going on in the midst of our pain, and teach us how to take advantage of the opportunity our psychopathology presents to us. Instead, we are met by fear in the very places where the soul is most alive and fervently seeking our attention.

The Institutionalized Fear of Psychopathology

This fear became institutionalized by the psychoanalytic movement, which treated psychopathology as illness, instead of the important soul-making activity that it is. Just as religion sought to keep soul in check 2,500 years earlier by labeling soul-making activity sinful, psychoanalysis asserted a parallel brand of control on the soul through endlessly categorizing the various pathologies it was possible for the soul to act out, and then attempting to "treat" them, so that they disappeared behind a soul-less facade of normalcy. The more subjective the message at the heart of the pathology, the more intense the effort toward objective classification, and the more pathological the symptoms of soul-making activity became. Within a religious culture that feared the soul, one had to commit sin in order to find one's soul. Within a psychoanalytical culture, rooted in a scientific model that denied the existence of the soul altogether, one had to psychopathologize and become "abnormal."

Or as Freud would have put it, one had to occasionally break the taboos imposed by the superego in order to allow the id enough breathing space to keep the ego from breaking down under its unconscious pressure. During the half-century or so in which psychoanalysis asserted its primary influence, peaking during the 50s and early 60s, the Eisenhower/pre-Kennedy assassination era of conformism and normalcy, psychopathology became the last refuge of the soul. In a society dominated by the institutions of the superego – church, state, school, and military-industrial complex – the psychoanalytical couch became a safe haven for the id, in all of its raw, dysfunctional glory - a place where the soul could expose itself and get some sympathy.

To be fair, Freud did understand that the superego could also be overbearing. He routinely recognized and treated patients whose problems were caused, not by a rampant id, out of control, but by a tyrannical superego that suppressed the very lifeblood out of the individual. The symptoms of such a condition were depression, excessive guilt or shame, severe inhibition, timidity and overly apologetic behavior, or conversely, strong, angry judgments projected toward other people, and self-righteous moralism. When the superego dominated to the point that the id was no longer functional, the ego's job was to tone the superego down, so that the soul was given some reprieve. The ideal, within the Freudian system, was to allow the id just enough slack so that a "normal" life of nondescript conformity, in which the passions were held in check by reason, was possible.

While postmodern society tends to mock the quaint retro sensibilities of the Freudian era, keeping the rampant, unpredictable, sometimes troubling individuality of the soul in check is still the goal of modern psychopharmacology. Any deviation from the norm, any discomfort – physical, emotional, psychological, or social – any experience of death in the metaphorical sense is increasingly labeled as illness, amenable to treatment. In the 21st century, we no longer expect to keep the troubled rumblings of the soul in check by reason; instead, we simply treat the biochemical machine with drugs. Social anxiety, for example, used to be part of the process by which the soul found its place within the realm of interpersonal relationships. Now, as the drug companies would have us believe, the inability to be outgoing in social situations is a painful "disorder," treatable only by medication. Though the technology is new and constantly evolving, this is merely the current incarnation of the same ancient fear of emotion and its power to evoke the soul that motivated religious authority, armchair psychologists, and behaviorists to avoid the topic altogether. This new generation of psychoactive drugs is merely the current avoidance mechanism of choice. Just as religious authority, armchair psychologists, and behaviorists have previously failed to keep the soul in check, however, so too will this new strategy inevitably fail.

Beneath the symptoms of pathology are core issues, which are irrepressible. The soul has incarnated, in part, to explore these issues, and a willingness to do so is a critical first step on the path to the conscious embodiment of Spirit. As painful as these issues often are, they contain within them the vitality of the soul's relationship to death and to its shaping influences. To face these issues takes great courage, because they expose the embodied soul to the very forces of death, in the metaphorical sense, that threaten its demise. To buffer ourselves against core issues through the use of drugs – or in any other way – is to essentially put the soul into a psychological coma, or living death, which is far more damaging to the soul than the fate it hopelessly seeks to avoid. When drugs are used as a substitute for addressing core issues, chemically-induced comfort is confused with resolution. Our issues don't disappear, because we have become numb to the pain they would normally generate. They merely go underground, where they fester in anticipation of our eventual return to consciousness.

I do not doubt that there are situations in which emotional pain becomes so intense that the ability to cope with everyday life – much less the capacity to deal with core issues – is severely compromised. In such cases, the limited use of medication can perhaps be helpful, provided it is anchored by a firm commitment to face the psychological trauma at the source of the pain. But there is a long stretch from debilitating emotional pain to discomfort, and as we slide toward the mild end of the spectrum in our use of drugs, we blunt the innate feedback mechanism that tells us there is soulwork to be done. Discomfort is not a signal that we are in need of medical treatment; it is a signal that the soul is seeking to rebalance its relationship to Spirit and/or the embodied world. Without that signal, the price to be paid for comfort is increasing imbalance, which will one day take its toll.

Dealing with discomfort can be inconvenient, because it requires us to break with the habitual routines of business as usual, pay attention to what is going on inside, and do something different in response. Drug companies promote the illusion that by popping a pill, we can get on with our extroverted lives and not have to concern ourselves with whatever was bothering us before we copped our legal fix. But taking the trouble to address the issues triggering our pain is a small price to be paid for bringing the soul into balance, and where we are not willing to suffer inconvenience to care for the soul, we trade the spiritual opportunity of our embodiment for the chemical illusion of well-being.

It is the fear of inconvenience, discomfort, and vulnerability in the face of core issues, and the money to be made in preying upon these fears, that allows a scientific psychology to insist that the pathway to happiness is the medication of pain. When a psychoanalytic attitude that treats the symptoms of core issues as illness teams up with the technology of a pharmaceutical industry intent on selling drugs, the end result is an institutionalized fear of the soul that becomes extremely profitable. But medication of pain is a strategy for happiness that will ultimately backfire, as the divine intelligence within the soul seeks increasingly ingenious counter-strategies for breaking through the barriers of repression. The end result, though perhaps postponable for awhile, will not be a pretty sight.

A more conscious cooperation with the soul's agenda – as Jung was brave enough to point out – is ultimately a much smarter choice. Paradoxically, the most effective pathway to the alleviation of pain is not up and away from one's most disturbing symptoms, but down into them with as much consciousness as one can muster. In order for the soul to find itself, it has to somehow break through this fear – both personal and culturally conditioned – that makes the raw experience of the dark, troubled areas of the psyche a persistent societal taboo. As psychological issues are increasingly treated as medical problems in the brave new world that scientific psychology has spawned, this means more specifically that one has to stop using one's meds as a crutch to avoid facing the issues through which the soul explores its subjective image of the world.

The soul does not find itself by conforming to the prevailing societal definitions of normal, nor by repressing the emotional cataclysms that tear the façade of normalcy asunder. Quite the contrary. The soul's primary task, according to Jung, is to separate itself from the collective pressure toward conformity, and find its own way into an individuated and more psychologically integrated personality – a process that is often inherently painful because it requires one not only to confront, but also to claim all those aspects of the psyche that seem to make one abnormal. No doubt, this understanding arose as a consequence of Jung's own "breakdown" as discussed in Chapter Fourteen. As confused and as frightening as this process was for Jung, it nonetheless became the approach to a brand of psychoanalysis that did not stand back in superior judgment of the psychopathology of the soul, but understood it instead to be a healthy sign of spiritual vitality.

The Shadow as the Gateway to Soul Process

Jung employed the term *shadow* to encompass the psychological damage that the superego caused within the psyche through repression of various vital aspects of the id. Jung recognized the ugliness inherent in the shadow to be commensurate to the pressure with which it had been suppressed. Unlike Freud, however, who sought to treat this ugliness as something pathological, Jung was clear enough to recognize it as the guardian of the threshold of soul space. The shadow – or put another way, the pathologized image of the soul – was a gateway necessary to traverse on the way to the embrace of a more authentic sense of self that was intimately personal, and much larger, and deeper than the ego. As Jung tells us (Archetypes 21-22):

> The meeting with oneself is at first, the meeting with one's own shadow. The shadow is a tight passage, a narrow door, whose painful constriction no one is spared who goes down to the deep well. But one must learn to know oneself in order to know who one is. For what comes after the door is, surprisingly enough, a boundless expanse full of unprecedented uncertainty, with apparently no inside and no outside, no above and no below, no here and no there, no mine and no thine, no good and no bad. It is the world of water, where all life floats in suspension; where the realm of the sympathetic system, the soul of everything living begins; where I am indivisibly this and that; where I experience the other in myself and the other-than-myself experiences me.

The shadow is the gateway to that place inside of us where the polarities begin to reconcile, where an invitation to the *hieros gamos* or sacred marriage of opposites that is the holy grail of the psychological process is extended. It is through reclaiming the bits and pieces of ourselves relegated to the shadow that we begin to experience ourselves as a being endowed with integrity and wholeness, and learn to cultivate a dynamic sense of interconnectedness between the various projected images of self within the world. This, however, is only the beginning of a process that intensifies before we have had a chance to adjust to the bright lights of soul space. Once we are able to entertain the pathologizing process without judgment, as the heart of soul-making activity that it is, then everything we do suddenly becomes soul-making activity, and soul is encountered everywhere. Moving through the shadow requires a new set of eyes capable of seeing what lies on the other side. The guide to the development of these eyes, Jung called *anima* (or *animus*).

The Anima/Animus as Guide to Soul Space

Jung originally conceived the *anima* in mythological terms as a nixie (half-human fish), mermaid, siren, wood nymph or succubus – a magical feminine creature with the erotic power to enchant, as well as the capacity to suck the life force from its victim. At the root of everything banished to the realm of the shadow by the collective forces of the superego is the fear of the fundamentally erotic nature of life, in which the interplay of the opposites requires a lascivious, passionate embrace of both sides of any polarity, without guilt, remorse, or judgment. This erotic dimension, teeming just below the surface of ordinary life, is ever elusive, unpredictable, uncontrollable, irrational, playfully mischievous, and much more powerful than any barrier the ego might construct against it. It often erupts of its own accord, and the *anima*/animus is the trigger to its release. From the standpoint of the ego, the *anima* is more dangerous than the shadow, because it knows the ego to be nothing more than a cork bobbing in an ocean way over its head, and will use that knowledge to saturate the ego with a subjective truth it is powerless to resist. While the ego can consciously at least keep some distance from the shadow, which tends to remain out of sight unless provoked, the *anima* will intentionally seek the ego out and play with it like a sex toy.

As Jung informs us, "everything the *anima* touches becomes numinous - unconditional, dangerous, taboo, magical. She is the serpent in the paradise of the harmless man with good resolutions and still better intentions . . . Because the *anima* wants life, she wants both good and bad. These categories do not exist in the elfin realm" (Archetypes 28) and in her presence the whole notion of moral correctness begins to break down. The rational order and controlled dispassionate powers of neutral observation deemed essential to understanding by the scientific community also prove useless within the *anima*'s world. For as Jung observes (Archetypes 32):

> [I]n actual reality, we do not have at our command any power of cool reflection, nor does any science or philosophy help us, and the traditional teachings of religion do so only to a limited degree. We are caught and entangled in aimless experience, and the judging intellect with its categories

proves itself powerless. Human interpretation fails, for a turbulent life-situation has arisen that refuses to fit any of the traditional meanings assigned to it. It is a moment of collapse . . . 'a kind of voluntary death.'

This of course, is quite a frightening prospect to the psyche that is conditioned, at every turn – by religion, by philosophy, by science, and by psychoanalytical psychology – not to trust its own innate instincts. The *anima* also invites the soul, however, to return to that pre-moral state where following *dharma* was not a matter of conforming to external laws, but of learning to feel the internal balance within oneself at every step along the way (<u>Archetypes</u> 28-31).

> *Behind all her cruel sporting with human fate there lies something like a hidden purpose which seems to reflect a superior knowledge of life's laws. It is just the most unexpected, the most terrifyingly chaotic things which reveal a deeper meaning. And the more this meaning is recognized, the more the anima loses her impetuous and compulsive character. Gradually breakwaters are built against the surging of chaos, and the meaningful divides itself from the meaningless . . . In this way, a new cosmos arises.*

This new cosmos is a much more potent reflection of the soul than the old, because it is not artificially bound by morality, rational objectivity, or linear, causal explanation. Everything within this cosmos becomes an image of soul – not a soul that is pathologized into hideous distortion through repression – but a soul that is free to be itself, in all the raw erotic beauty of its wholeness. Wholeness includes warts, rampant desires, and gaping holes, as well as proud badges of identity. The sense of self that begins to emerge within this cosmos is a self in relationship to everything else, one that participates in the life of the Whole, and partakes of a larger sense of Self. If there is an eventual return to Spirit within the soul's destiny, as postulated by many religions and the perennial Neoplatonist revival of each new age, then it will undoubtedly come not through transcending this world, but through cultivating the relational self of the *anima*, which infuses the world with pulsating intercourse between souls in meaningful resonance with each other and with the very soul – the *animus mundi* – of the world itself.

In the *anima's* world, the ego's boundaries become permeable, and the limited sense of identity to which the ego clings becomes untenable. The rational order begins to break down, and a new way of thinking is required. Says Jung (<u>Archetypes</u> 31):

> *In elfin nature, wisdom and folly appear as one and the same; and they are one and the same as long as they are acted out by the anima. Life is crazy and meaningful at once . . . There is . . . little sense and little nonsense either. When you come to think about it, nothing has any meaning, for when*

*there was nobody to think, there was nobody to interpret what happened.
Interpretations are only for those who don't understand; it is only the things
we don't understand that have any meaning. Man woke up in a world he did
not understand, and that is why he tries to interpret it.*

Jung is speaking primarily of the realm of the collective unconscious here, and not
directly of the external world inhabited by the awakening soul, but within the context
of the image-making process, the two essentially become one and the same. The world
becomes a living mirror in which the psychic streams converging in the underworld
become more visible and more tangible. In the midst of this process, everything has
symbolic implications that go beyond the thing itself, and understanding comes as these
implications are assimilated – not by the conscious, rational mind – but through the
senses, the emotions, the projective imagination, and the intuition.

Intuition, in particular, is a way of grasping levels of symbolic meaning that elude
the rational mind. Intuition only becomes possible, however, when the *anima* shatters
the ego's illusion of control, and the soul is forced to learn who it is within the content
of a process that lies far beyond its ability to rationally comprehend. We like to think of
intuition as a refined mental capacity, or a function of "higher mind," as it has been called
by 19th century Theosophists. But from the soul's perspective, higher mind is still mind,
and as such, incapable of understanding, much less explaining the soul's reality. It is only
when something snaps within the mind, and breaks its hold upon the psyche, that true
intuition can emerge. True intuition, as I am discussing it here, is not a mental process,
but a holistic function encompassing not just mind, but also heart, belly, and bones.

Zen Buddhists wrestle with *koans*, or riddles that have no answer that the rational
mind can comprehend. "What is the sound of one-hand clapping?" "Who were you
before you were born?" And so on. The mind that earnestly engages these questions
eventually snaps in the face of its inability to answer them, and then out of that snapping
comes a more organic way of seeking answers that speaks more directly to the soul. The
same thing happens from a Jungian perspective, when the *anima* seduces the ego into an
"elfin world" where nothing makes sense. The mind cracks open in such a world under
the pressure of its own inability to grasp what it happening, and true intuition gradually
begins to seep through the cracks. Before this cracking open of the mind, the intuition as
a function of higher mind only confirms what the lower conscious mind already knows.
The intuitive wisdom that the soul is seeking can only be found in what the mind doesn't
and can't know through the usual channels by which it processes information.

The rational mind serves the ego because it reinforces a belief in the solid boundaries
of consensual reality. Once the ego comes under the spell of the *anima*, however, reality
slips through the fingers of the rational mind like a school of minnows, and reveals

291

itself to be something other than what the ego thought it was. New Age practitioners are sometimes found of saying that "we create our own reality," but this is really only true in a subjective sense, and only then, when the uninitiated ego believes itself to be in charge. Anyone who has ever experienced death in the metaphorical sense, knows how untenable this belief is, yet we all cling to it with tenacity. From a psychological perspective, it is the ego that clings, and its effectiveness at clinging is hailed as the mark of success in a world that is conditioned by science and New Age thought alike to respect the primacy of the rational mind.

Once the illusion of control has been shattered by the *anima*, and the mind is revealed to be the ineffective minnow catcher that it is, however, the ego becomes a measure not of our power and capacity as creative beings, but of our fear – the extent to which we perceptually and conceptually wall ourselves off from the rest of the sentient universe. It becomes the gatekeeper for what British author and pioneer in the study of consciousness, Aldous Huxley called, "the doors of perception." As Huxley pointed out, "each person is at each moment capable of remembering all that has ever happened to him and of perceiving everything that is happening everywhere in the universe. The function of the brain and nervous system is to protect us from being overwhelmed and confused . . ." (Doors 22-23).

What the brain and nervous system accomplish on a physiological level, the ego accomplishes on a psychological level, filtering out those memories, feelings, and unconscious streams of subjective truth with which the individual is not prepared to deal. When the *anima* has cracked the mind, and the numinosity of the world begins to shine through the broken shards of identity, the doors of perception begin to open of their own accord, and consciousness begins to expand, despite the ego's resistance. Or put another way that is more in keeping with the perspective I have elaborated in this book, the soul begins to embody Spirit more completely and take its place within an integrated embodied world of transparent boundaries. It should be noted here, that this only happens to the extent that the psychological ego – which is the primary conceptualization of the self in psychoanalytic understanding – becomes permeable, and thus a less effective gatekeeper, a development that ironically runs counter to the stated goal of psychoanalysis.

The Wise Elder and the Individuation Process

Once this happens, according to Jung's theory, a new archetype enters the picture, and the unraveled ego is relieved of its duties by the wise old man or woman, who becomes a more reliable guide through the new cosmos of meaning than the ego could ever be. The ego is incapable of comprehending symbolic images - particularly disturbing images such as a hungry wolf, or a bloody glove, or a dark shadowy figure with no recognizable face – on any level other than that within which they appear as separate entities in the external world, or better still in the safe pages of a magazine, on TV or in a movie. When they start to show up in the psyche itself and assert an influence that rivals the ego for dominance within the psychic process, a new, more intuitive and permeable center of consciousness is required to facilitate an integration of these experiences. This center of consciousness is not the ego, but the soul itself, that is learning to fully embody Spirit - in all of its crazy, omnipotent wisdom. The wise elder is the internal compass that guides the soul through the embodiment process, emerging in earnest when the ego has been sufficiently tenderized by the *anima*, and the soul is ready to pursue its spiritual agenda with conscious intention.

On a psychological level, conscious embodiment is not something that happens all at once, but rather takes place gradually, and often involves a great deal of backtracking. Even though Jung has identified these various stages of the process, it should be noted, if it is not already obvious, that we do not simply graduate from one stage to the next. We move back and forth between the stages, and one or more archetypes will take center stage at any given time. On a good day, the ego will be surrendered to the *anima*, there will be a larger opening to Spirit than there was the day before, and the wise elder will be actively pointing the way. On a difficult day, however, the ego may be struggling with some aspect of the shadow it has not yet integrated, the opening to Spirit will begin to close as the ego asserts its protective function, and the wise elder will retreat. Once the *anima* has given the ego a glimpse of the meaningful cosmos, however, there is no going back, especially when the ego compares its "normal" life within the collective world of societal expectations and the life of subjective meaning and individual purpose to which it is being enticed by the *anima*.

Once the soul develops the strength of will to intentionally open itself to these more dangerous and subversive areas of the psyche, and to go where the rational mind has no foothold, the archetype of the wise elder, or inner teacher, comes increasingly into play. This archetype, Jung tells us, ". . . symbolizes the pre-existent meaning hidden in the chaos of life. He is the father of the soul, and yet the soul, in some miraculous manner, is also his virgin mother, for which reason the alchemists called him the 'first son of the mother'" (Archetypes 35). If the soul is understood to be embodied Spirit, as we have been discussing it, then the wise elder becomes an important link between Spirit and the soul.

When the ego looks out into the world, it sees a material universe of separate forms, in which survival is the goal. When the wise elder looks out into the world, it sees a magical universe, in which everything is filled with Spirit, and through Spirit is intimately connected to everything else. Spirit flows through and between the various apparently separate forms, and a full cultivation of conscious relationships becomes the vehicle for bringing Spirit more completely into embodiment. The goal is no longer survival, since at this level, Spirit is recognized to be indestructible - not as a theory or belief, but as fact -

◇◇◇

and this recognition serves as a psychologically potent antidote to the fear of death. When the fear of death begins to dissipate, the goal becomes full conscious participation in the cycle of life *and* death, out of which comes a personal wisdom that cannot be undone. The wise elder is ultimately a guide to the cultivation of this wisdom, and will provide a counterbalancing voice within the psyche to the fear-based ego. The wise elder is born of the soul to the extent that it represents a perspective that fills the embodied world with Spirit. To the extent that it is able to impart this wisdom to the individual in whose psyche it dwells, then it becomes the father of the soul.

The Individuated Self and the Soul

In Spirit, the polarities that infuse the life of the embodied soul cease to have meaning – a psychological fact that represents a great paradox to the soul, and a threshold beyond which the soul cannot go. Just as the physical death of the body makes it impossible for the soul to continue its journey on Earth, so too, on a psychological level, does the soul dissolve into Spirit once the integration of polar opposites is complete. Because the soul exists as a mediation of opposites, when the opposites cease to exist, there is nothing for the soul to mediate. But the soul's journey is toward this ultimate *hieros gamos*, this final reunion with Spirit, which on a psychological level is the very thing that ensures its demise. Popular western spiritual teacher, Ram Dass calls this journey of the soul "the crisp trip," suggesting that it is a process we are all called to, in one way or another, despite the fact that when it is over, "there's going to be no adventurer left to have had the adventure" (9).

The soul's journey an adventure that ironically renders everything that psychology – at least analytical psychology – is supposed to be about, a moot point. The object of this journey is not a stronger, more integrated personality, nor a healthy ego, nor even a fully functional self, but rather the dissolution of everything the psychological soul strives to become while alive in a body. The individual soul, if it exists at all at the end of "the crisp trip," is an utterly transparent Self that reveals the world to be a simple vehicle through which Spirit can freely function. This transparent Self is unimpeded by the fear-based ego, the personality, or even the identity – the sense of self that propels the soul through 99% of its journey. That last 1% is a place that psychology does not go. It is also a phase of the journey that cannot be discussed in a way that anyone on this side of that last threshold could possibly comprehend.

Jung intimated that he knew this when he spoke about this last phase of the soul's psychological journey (Archetypes 106-107):

> [W]e enter the realm of the syzygies, the paired opposites, where the One
> is never separated from the Other, its antithesis. It is a field of personal

experience which leads directly to the experience of individuation, the attainment of the self. A vast number of symbols for this process could be mustered from the medieval literature of the West and even more from the storehouses of Oriental wisdom, but in this matter words and ideas count for little. Indeed, they may become dangerous bypaths and false trails. In this still very obscure field of psychological experience, where we are in direct contact, so to speak, with the archetype (of the Self), its psychic force is felt in full force. This realm is so entirely one of immediate experience that it cannot be captured by any formula, but can only be hinted at to one who already knows.

After going through his own personal soul journey, and finding his roots in the archetypal realms he described in *The Archetypes and the Collective Unconscious*, Jung had become "one who knows." Jung was also living in a world that was not ready to fully embrace the process he was describing, except in the abstract. In the years following World War I, during which Jung had his transformative experiences, he started writing about the collective unconscious and the archetypes, and over the course of the next four decades, finally brought his ideas into increasingly cogent form – a process that culminated in 1954 with the first publication of the masterwork cited above. During this period, psychology in general was strongly behavioristic in its biases, and where individual psychologists attempted to break out of that mold, their focus was predominantly a psychoanalytical concern with strengthening the ego to be able to withstand the very encroachment of the unconscious that Jung was describing as necessary to individuation.

Only a handful of hardy souls of Jung's generation were prepared to take the journey he had taken, and so as Jung attempted to hint at the ineffable process to others "who already knew," his words fell upon many deaf ears. His teachings, as is true of all soul teachings, reached the ears of those who were ready to embrace his ideas, but perhaps not the process itself. It was one thing to talk about the archetypes as psychological theory, but few were prepared or brave enough to invoke them, and submit the ego to the dismembering process they required of it, before the Self could be revealed. Jung was really writing for another generation, one eager to blast through the doors of perception by whatever means available, and it wasn't until after his death in the early 1960s that his ideas really began to find an audience willing to take them to heart.

Even now, as many casualties of the reckless days of rampant experimentation with psychedelics might attest, the journey he laid out is fraught with peril, and not for the faint of heart. Far too many souls set their sights on the ascendant heights of Spirit, without realizing that when they get there, if they ever do, they are going to be crisped just as surely as Icarus was when he attempted to fly into the Sun. Too many souls strain toward enlightenment, hoping to avoid the necessary trip down into the underworld, where the

295

◇◇

roots of the embodied Spirit are intertwined. Too many souls harbor an antiseptic image of the soul's journey, sterilized through thousands of years of conditioning by religion, at least a hundred year's of psychology's idolatry of the ego, and more recently through the romanticized notions of popular New Age culture and the rosy seductions of the pharmaceutical industry. Jung's journey was downward into the belly of soul space, where the ego was digested so that soul could be nourished. Few then or now are willing to make that sacrifice. In Jung's day and on into our own, the collective effort instead has been toward enshrining the ego within the measurable and more secure parameters of personality.

Psychology's Obsession with Personality

Though it is mostly understood by psychologists as the primary expression of the self, personality can be more accurately conceptualized within the psychoanalytical model, to be the visible evidence of the ego's effort to keep the id under control. It is the ego's attempt to channel the abundant energy of the id (which is, after all, the life force – the *ch'i* of the Taoists, the *prana* of the Hindus, the *elan vital* proposed by Bergson – under a distinctly psychological name) in ways that are acceptable to the superego. As an adaptation to external expectations, personality allows only a limited expression of soul, which remains mostly hidden at the innermost (often repressed) areas of the psyche. Personality is not the soul, nor even the psychological self, but essentially the compromise that the individual makes in order to function in the world of social convention. Personality theorists focused on the various forces shaping this compromise, but the compromise itself was generally mistaken throughout the psychological community for the more essential identity of the soul that was compromised. The soul itself remained largely beyond the scrutiny of psychologists who studied the personality only at the very surface of the interface between soul and world. The object of their interest was not the soul, but a mask the soul wore to be able to function in the world that Jung called the *persona*.

To the scientific mindset, this study depended on measurable parameters of personality, and the derivation of tests that could measure them. Curiously enough, the first personality test, the Personal Data Sheet, relied on subjective evaluation of psychological symptoms, hardly conducive to the kind of information science considered reliable. Robert Woodworth, an experimental psychologist at Columbia University, was commissioned by the army in 1917 to devise a psychological test that could identify emotionally disturbed recruits. Woodworth came up with a simple questionnaire that asked such bare-faced questions as "Do you feel like jumping off when you are on high places?" (Hunt 314-315). Those recruits who were self-aware and honest enough to answer yes to enough of these questions were labeled unfit for military duty.

Following in Woodworth's footsteps came a small army of "trait theorists," as they were called, devising clever questionnaires that coordinated answers with various psychological traits. Jung's earlier work with personality types gave rise to one such test, the popular Myers-Briggs inventory. Myers-Briggs measures the relative dominance of the four primary psychological functions identified in Jung's theory - thought, feeling, sensation, and intuition, as well as the predominance of two basic attitudes toward life - introversion and extroversion. A test devised by Robert Bernreuter similarly measured identification with another set of pet traits - dominance, self-sufficiency, introversion and neuroticism - while many others divided the personality pie in increasingly sophisticated ways. When behaviorists discovered in the late 1920s that different behavioral traits would tend to manifest in different situations, personality tests simply adapted by becoming more situational. Instead of asking, "Are you aggressive by nature?" they began asking, "What would you do if someone cut in front of you in line?"

A leading proponent of this type of test was Gordon Allport, who developed an elaborate theory involving cardinal, central, and secondary traits, each of which occupied a different niche in the hierarchical structure of personality. Allport and a colleague once counted all the words in the dictionary that could be associated with personality traits or various expressions of personality, and found about 18,000 (Hunt 319). Subsequent efforts to measure personality have largely revolved around distinguishing which traits are important and finding ways to measure them. One of the most popular of such tests, the omnipresent MMPI (Minnesota Multiphasic Personality Inventory) contains 550 statements, empirically determined through testing of hospital patients to distinguish between "normal" people and those prone to mental illness. Another common test, the CPI (California Psychological Inventory) was adapted from the MMPI and modified to measure personality within a more "normal" population.

A more daring school of personality testing evolved in the 1930s with the introduction of projective tests such as the Rorschach and the TAT (Thematic Apperception Test), which attempt to measure not just the personality, but also the image-making process that gives rise to personality. If, for example, one were to look at an ink-blot and see two elephants mating in the bushes, then this would tell the researchers something about the convergence of memories, feelings, and fantasies taking place in the more unreachable depths of the unconscious. These techniques actually hold great promise in recognizing the soul-making process that gives rise to the image, especially as they are employed within the context of a soul-based theory such as Assagioli's psychosynthesis. In the hands of most psychoanalysts of the 1930s, 40s, and 50s, however, they became an elaborate attempt to use the image-making process not to connect with soul, but as a tool for analysis of personality syndromes. Complex systems of interpretation were devised for the Rorschach Test, for example, in which responses were studied, characterized, and then rigidly assigned to dogmatic interpretations - so that two elephants mating in the bushes meant this, while a butterfly shedding its cocoon meant that. The subjectivity, in other words, was soon squeezed out of these tests, or reinterpreted to satisfy science's demand for measurable objectivity.

The Merging of Schools in the Scientific Vein

Meanwhile, by the 1940s, the trend became to combine projective tests with trait tests, and look for larger patterns of correspondence within batteries of tests, that could in turn serve as empirical evidence for sets of traits then called syndromes, now called profiles. English psychologist and statistician Charles Spearman developed a technique known as factor analysis, by which correlations between groups of variables were measured. These ideas were then applied by Hans Eysenck, a German-born psychologist who escaped to Britain during Hitler's rise to power. Eysenck used factor analysis to elaborate Jungian personality theory, and discovered how to interpret the MMPI in comparison to his own personality test to measure the correlations he found. Others who followed in his footsteps devised more sophisticated sets of correlations, so that by 1945, British-born psychologist, Raymond Cattrel was able to identify sixteen source traits that were "necessary and adequate to cover all kinds of individual differences of personality (I.e., surface traits) found in common speech and psychological literature. They leave out no important aspect of total personality" (qtd. In Hunt 331), or so he was bold enough to claim.

Behaviorists stayed out of the general feeding frenzy over personality traits, at least for the first 30 years or so. They considered personality to be something that was not innate to the individual, but rather a set of conditioned responses to repetitive stimuli. If, as a child, you were rewarded for the expression of your curiosity, for example, you would become a curious adult, and register high on the curiosity scale of any test that measured it. The cultivation of such a personality trait had nothing to do with who you were, but evolved instead in relation to the feedback you got from your environment. There is some truth to this perspective, since we do respond to feedback, and we do adapt ourselves accordingly – as Freud pointed out in his discussion of the superego. As I suggested earlier, this adaptation is the very essence of personality as it must be understood from a soul-based perspective. To assume, however, that we are *just* the product of the environmental stimuli that shapes us, as the behaviorists have done, is to deny the existence of the soul, or the self, or even a distinct personality that we could call our own.

By the 1950s, even behaviorists caught the personality fever, and began reframing learned sets of behavior in terms of personality traits. A psychotherapist and professor at Ohio State University, John Rotter observed a fundamental difference between those who felt they had control over their lives, and those who did not, and developed a test, called the Internal-External Locus of Control Scale to measure it. This test became popular in the 60s and 70s, and led other theorists to explore the relationship between attitude and personality. While personality theorists in general, believed that personality traits were innate to a central self, behaviorists tended to believe that they were acquired through conditioned patterns of response, which in turn led to attitudes and expectations about outcomes, and then to habitual ways of being. Nonetheless, by the mid 1960s, both schools of thought were investigating personality as the locus of identity. Since then, the two schools of thought have begun merging, and now, most personality theorists believe personality to be partly innate and partly due to environmental influences.

In the 1940s, a new breed of psychologists began investigating personality from a biological perspective. At the New York University Medical Center, psychiatrists Alexander Thomas and Stella Chess observed nine differences in infant behavior that were manifest within the first few hours after birth, and speculated that these differences in personality were hereditary. Out of this research, gradually evolved a new field of science called behavioral genetics, which though outside the domain of psychology, has asserted a profound influence on its practice, especially among those pushing to make psychology a hard science. During the 1950s and 60s, mountains of data were accumulated showing correlations in mental abilities, personality traits, achievements and patterns of success or failure in life, and habitual emotional responses, between children and their parents, and between twins separated at birth.

One such set of twins, documented in Hunt's history of psychology, Jim Lewis and Jim Springer, separated at birth and raised by different families, were discovered later in life to have "chosen" parallel lives. It turns out, at age 39, after having had absolutely no contact with each other, nor even being aware of each other's presence, "both had wives named Betty, were heavy smokers of Salems, drove Chevrolets, bit their fingernails, and had dogs named Toy" (Hunt 345). What is more, they both had nearly identical responses to a battery of personality tests. This, and other less spectacular instances like it, were taken to be evidence of the genetic basis of personality. Personality theorists within the psychological community itself tend to shy away from this view, since it seems too deterministic for most tastes, and has not contributed to the refinement of testing. No doubt as genetic engineering extends to humans later in the 21st century, however, efforts will be made to mold personality through genetic manipulation – just as Aldous Huxley predicted it would 60 years ago (Brave New World).

Astrology's Contribution to the Cult of Personality

Though I am promoting a modified form of astrology in this book as the empirical basis for a language of soul, in actual practice, astrology has largely been a study of personality, both in the popular understanding of what astrology is, and in the minds of many of those who are attracted to want to learn it. The signs of the zodiac, which are normally the first exposure any layperson will have to the subject, are almost universally construed as descriptive of personality traits. Geminis are curious, socially gregarious, and easily distracted; Scorpios are emotionally intense, psychologically complex, and mentally focused; Libras are sensitive, indecisive, and sophisticated in their aesthetic tastes. And so on. Syndicated sun sign-columns give pithy behavioral prescriptions for the day, week, month, or year, based on personality characteristics associated with various signs. Astrological cookbooks abound, giving more detailed descriptions of personality characteristics associated with the placement of various planets in the signs. Most astrologers, reading the natal chart of a new client for the first time, will routinely give information about expected personality traits, also depending primarily upon planetary placements in signs.

Many astrologers also interpret houses, planets, and aspects between planets in terms of personality characteristics, as though by outlining a detailed description of personality, they will have helped their client to get a better handle on who they are. As discussed earlier, this approach to an understanding of soul is superficial at best, and symptomatic of a systemic confusion between the soul and the compromises the soul must make in order to function within a particular environment of societal expectations. Astrology has been no less confused in this regard than psychology, using a sign-based interpretation as the springboard for its own focus on personality assessment. Worth mentioning here, as notable exceptions, are Dane Rudhyar's *Astrological Signs: The Pulse of Life*, which discusses signs as phases of a rhythmical interplay between light and dark, within the context of the annual cycle of the Earth's revolution around the Sun; and Liz Greene's *The Astrology of Fate*, which masterfully correlates the meaning of each sign to mythological themes and psychological processes depicted in these myths.

Before astrology can be useful as a language of soul, astrologers must wean themselves from their collective preoccupation with personality traits, and reinterpret signs in terms of adaptation to collective norms and the compromise that soul must make in order to be in the world. This is not just my opinion, nor simply an arbitrary demand, but rather a natural tenet of astro-logic that derives from the symbolic implications of the astronomical reality of signs. Signs refer to phases of the Earth's apparent motion around the Sun, which is generally considered by most astrologers to represent the psychological ego, the central protagonist in any individual's life story, and the sense of personal identity that revolves around the "I" that I believe myself to be. The living Earth represents the embodiment of Spirit, or the soul about which we have been speaking in this book. Within the context of these symbolic equivalencies, then, the signs of the zodiac are formed as the soul revolves around the ego. The Sun represents an *external* focus, and as the Earth revolves around the Sun to form the signs, the signs reflect who we are as we orient ourselves to this external focus. The metaphor is one that fits the ego well, since ego is the psychological faculty that mediates between soul and the external, collective norms assimilated through the superego.

I believe it is also possible to understand the Sun as a representative of Spirit, as was in fact the case with many 16th and 17th century astronomer/astrologers such as Copernicus, Galileo and Kepler, in which case we have the symbolic equivalent of the soul revolving around Spirit. But Spirit within this metaphor must be understood to be transcendent Spirit, and not the immanent Spirit of embodied life, since the Sun is still an *external* focus, and as such must be understood as symbolic of something that is outside of the context of embodied life. Dane Rudhyar called the motion of planets through signs "*motion in space*, or objective motion, as it brings about change in location and displacement of the center of the being . . . It is the substratum for all relationships, for all interchanges. Through motion in space, through actual displacement of one's own center, one... becomes aware of the reality of the larger collective whole of which one is but a part" (162-163). Thus when we speak of signs, we are essentially discussing the way in which the individual adapts to an external reality shared by the collective.

The relationship between the embodied soul and immanent Spirit, on the other hand, is one that evolves from a consideration of the daily rotation of the Earth about its own *internal* axis – a motion which gives rise not to the signs, but to the houses. For a more complete discussion of this point, I would refer the reader to my article, "The Clockwise Interpretation of Houses. " Meanwhile, in the wake of Rudhyar's monumental influence within the astrological community, there was a movement in the 1960s and 70s away from emphasis on signs, and toward a recognition of the primacy of planets and planetary patterns. More recently, however, the pendulum has begun swinging back in the other direction, triggered by a resurgence of interest in Western medieval and Vedic whole-sign techniques.

I do think signs are important, since the incongruity between the soul's intimately personal nature and the compromises to that nature, required of anyone living within a society shaped by collective norms, is an important catalyst to soul growth. Any soul must also seek to find its place within the whole of which it is part, in order to truly understand who it is and what it has taken birth to do. To some extent, the signs – and especially the relationship between the signs – hold the key to understanding this web of relationships and the soul's place within it. But soul growth cannot be understood on the level on which the signs are defined in terms of personality traits alone. Even at the level of personality, soul process is not a static phenomenon, but rather a perpetual balancing act requiring conscious and deliberate choice between compromise for the sake of social adaptation and natural self-expression. Personality evolves mostly out of compromise, but can become an arena for soul growth to the extent that one becomes aware of the compromises being made and chooses to swim upstream toward a more natural expression of soul.

The sign, Sagittarius, for example, is often associated with the personality trait of optimism. Yet as Liz Greene points out, through her discussion of the sign in relation to the myth of Chiron, beneath this optimism is a profound sense of woundedness and susceptibility to the darkness in the world, which in turn fuels "a kind of depression or despair beneath the surface of the sign" (240). Optimism then, can be understood to be the adaptation that Sagittarius makes, in order to function in the world, while the true soul work that is required of this sign, may well entail finding the courage to go down into this underworld, where the depression being masked by personality is rooted.

As with Sagittarius, so too with the personality characteristics associated with each of the other signs. The domesticity of Cancer may well mask a fear of the embodied world; the eccentricity of Aquarius, a missing sense of core identity; the fastidiousness of Virgo, an internal chaos that feels dangerous. To reach the soul, each of these signs will need to risk moving beyond the coping mechanisms available on the personality level, and plumb the depths of whatever inner reality is being kept at bay.

We will have more to say about signs in Part Four, when we explore in more depth the astrology of soul. Meanwhile, it should be clear that personality in general is a limited psychological construct that must be interpreted within a more enlightened context, in order to be meaningful to the soul. Personality is often merely the compromise that the ego makes in order to meet society's expectation of normalcy, while beneath the façade of normalcy are the core issues through which the soul comes to know itself on the deepest level possible. Neither behaviorists, social psychologists, psychoanalysts, nor cognitive psychologists have been prepared to enter these depths or recognize the pathology generated by these issues as the important soul-making activity that it is. The impetus to do so has only arisen within the psychological community within the last 35 years or so, as the humanistic psychology movement struggled to shed what had become yet another layer of conceptual baggage on the way to a more useful understanding of soul.

Chapter Sixteen
Through Inanna's Seventh Gate
Into Embodiment of Spirit

Humanistic psychology arose as a "third force" during the 1960s and 70s in reaction to the two mainstream 20th century trends in psychology to that point, behaviorism and psychoanalysis. Humanistic psychologists felt that behaviorists were too concerned with the scientific study of the biochemical machine, to the neglect of all those aspects of being that were most intrinsic to our humanity. Humanistic psychologists also took issue with psychoanalytic theory for its deterministic stance that defined human beings predominantly in terms of shaping influences from childhood. What appeared to be missing within psychology, that the humanistic movement sought to remedy was a central sense of self – affirming the fact that human beings were not just the consequence of the physiological, psychological, and social forces impinging upon them, but that they were also autonomous, creative agents in their own right, endowed with the capacity to make intelligent choices, and to intentionally determine the course of their own lives.

Humanistic psychologists concerned themselves with aspects of the human experience that previously had little space within the tradition – such as individuality, intention, growth, freedom, spontaneity, play, humor, creativity, love, affection, intimacy, ecstasy, self-transcendence, meaning and purpose. The psychological center for this broader range of experiences encompassed by this new orientation was not the ego, nor the personality, but the "authentic self" – a more inclusive concept, which recognized that something intrinsic to the individual and autonomous was at work beneath both the behavior being studied by behaviorists and the dynamics of ego formation emphasized by psychoanalysts. The soul was generally discussed by humanistic psychologists only within the context of mystical and transcendent religious experiences, which they attempted to bring within the province of psychology. But the concept of the authentic self nonetheless became the psychological equivalent of the soul in many of the ways in which we are talking about it in this book.

The Influence of Existentialism on Humanistic Thought

The nature of the psychological self embraced by the humanistic psychologists borrowed heavily from the existentialist philosophy of Søren Kierkegaard, Martin Heidegger, Karl Jaspers, Jean-Paul Sartre, and others. Like the existentialists, the humanistic psychology movement emphasized the personal nature of individual existence, and proposed that the individual's primary task in life was in coming to terms with the pain and suffering inherent in existence in order to create a life of meaning and purpose. These, of course, are the very forces that I suggested in Chapter One shape the soul. The defining historical event for many existentialists was World War II, and particularly the atrocities of the Holocaust. Like the social psychologists of the 1950s and 60s, the existentialists and the humanistic psychologists who drew upon existentialist thought for inspiration recognized that pain and suffering could be a rich catalyst to the soul's experience. Unlike the social psychologists, who were primarily concerned with the impact of historical events upon the collective psyche, existentialists and humanistic psychologists affirmed the individual nature of the soul's pain. Many of those most active in shaping the humanistic psychology movement were of another generation, for whom the historical events shaping social psychology were not quite so indelibly etched in memory and personal experience. The existentialist idea that there was meaning and purpose to be found not just in historical events, but also in *individual* suffering, however, became a basic cornerstone in the humanistic understanding of the self. To be a self, within both existential and humanistic philosophies meant to emerge through the pain and suffering that were unavoidably part of any life, as a more authentic being.

Becoming a more authentic self demands confronting the inevitability of one's death, making intentional choices within the context of this awareness, and taking responsibility for those choices. It also involves understanding that life is part of a continuum with death, and that the polarity between life and death, male and female, Spirit and matter, and all other polarities is not a matter of either-or, but a simultaneous embrace of both. Hegel, who was a source of provocation to many existentialists, argued that the process of human evolution was *dialectical* – that is to say, one in which opposites constantly evolved into each other – and sought reconciliation and synthesis at each step of the way. While most existentialists rejected this idea, preferring to believe that the opposites were irreconcilable, they nonetheless laid the foundation for a psychology in which the opposites were a centerpiece.

Søren Kierkegaard, widely recognized as the founding father of existentialism, rebelled heavily against Hegel in developing his own philosophy, which nonetheless involves the Hegelian notion that life is an endless stream of choices in which emptiness and boredom, despair and anguish, and all unpleasant emotions become motivating factors for personal growth, and the discovery of a more meaningful and purposeful existence. "Paradox," he is reputed to have said, "is the source of the thinker's passion, and the thinker without paradox is like a lover without feeling, a paltry mediocrity" (qtd. in Christian 211). Whereas, for Hegel, the goal of a meaningful life was the resolution of paradox at a higher level of synthesis; for Kierkegaard, the goal was keeping the edge alive at which resolution lay one step beyond reach. If we did not consciously cultivate the intention to do this, life would see to it anyway, perpetually propelling us beyond synthesis to another edge, where paradox required a fresh round of choices. Regardless of their differences, both Hegel and Kierkegaard affirmed the value of a life in deliberate relationship to the opposites, in contrast to the perpetual discomfort in the face of the opposites shared by religion, science, and scientific psychology.

Kierkegaard parted company with Hegel in his insistence that this process of existential choice in the face of paradox was an irrational, and entirely subjective process. As discussed in Chapter Five, Hegel was a champion of objectivity and reason, taking Descartes' idea that thinking and being were one, to a new level of sophistication. As a rationalist, Hegel proposed that the synthesis of opposites was ultimately the rational triumph of *Geist* (translated in German as both *mind* and *spirit*). By contrast, Kierkegaard, argued that reason and objectivity were mostly derived from collective conditioning. Reason was irrelevant to the discovery of the authentic self, which was subjective and often eccentric in nature. Kierkegaard celebrated the irrational and emotional nature of choices, a sentiment echoed by Nietzsche, Sartre, de Beauvoir, Camus, and other existentialists, then later picked up by the humanistic psychologists. Most notable of these was Fritz Perls, whose quest for emotional authenticity evolved out of provoking dialogue between the subjective polarities within his clients.

Humanistic Psychology and the Study of Consciousness

Humanistic psychology's celebration of the subjective self as the center of experience owes a second philosophical debt to Edmund Husserl, founding father of an influential school of philosophy called *phenomenology*. Trained as a mathematician, Husserl was searching for a scientific approach to a study of consciousness, when he developed phenomenology as a theoretical system. In practice, phenomenology is the art of subjective perception without preconceived notions about what one is perceiving. This art, also referred to as *epoché* (a Greek word meaning the wise and deliberate suspension of judgment), took root in the imaginations of several existentialists, notably Martin Heidegger, Jean-Paul Sartre, and Maurice Merleau-Ponty. These existentialists were less interested in questions about epistemology and cognition, and more concerned with using subjective information as a basis of choice in a life of meaningful action. Husserl nonetheless gave those who followed in his wake philosophical permission to live and think subjectively, without regard to rational, objective, and collective notions of truth.

Husserl also brought new legitimacy to the study of consciousness, and the idea that the psychological self was first and foremost a conscious being growing toward a higher level of integration through the intentional exercise of choice. This idea became a cornerstone of the humanistic psychology movement, largely because of Husserl's influence on the existentialists. Behaviorists and cognitive neuroscientists insist that consciousness is simply an epiphenomenon of brain function, and what is important is not the subjective interpretation of these internal experiences, but their physiological, neurological and potential genetic correlates, which can be quantified, measured, controlled, and manipulated. With philosophical support from Husserl and the existentialists he influenced, the humanistic psychologists rebelled against this idea by asserting that consciousness was an expression – perhaps the primary expression – of the psychological self at the immaterial, subjective, often irrational, and immeasurable center of human experience.

Consciousness encompasses all those experiences of sensation, feeling, desire, thought, belief, memory, fantasy, and insight that are the object of scientific and psychoanalytic scrutiny. But it also implies something else – the subject around which these experiences cohere in discernible patterns – the "I" at the center of the experience. A neuroscientist would claim that this "I" is a largely a mythical function of memory, lodged in the prefrontal cortex, which dissipates as the integrity of the prefrontal cortex is weakened or impaired (Hobson 100). A psychoanalyst would say that this "I" is the product of childhood experiences which shape it and in most cases, wound it, causing distortions called neuroses which must be worked through before the "I" can be itself. An existentialist such as Jean-Paul Sartre, who is famous for his pronouncement that "existence precedes essence" would argue that this conscious "I" does not exist as an innate focal point of being, but rather evolves out of the choices that the individual gradually makes over the course of a lifetime worth of experience.

While any of these theories could be true, and probably all are true on the level of experience on which they are being considered – they are only of peripheral relevance to the "I" itself, seeking to know itself. Consciousness is the vehicle through which the self recognizes itself within the patterns of resonance that occupy soul space in any given moment. Consciousness can shape itself in any number of ways – as brain waves, painful memories of childhood experiences, a choice or a series of choices, or within the conceptual framework of any number of potential models for understanding how consciousness works. It will more often than not shape itself on all these levels at the same time. All the individual soul seeking self-knowledge needs to know is that consciousness is constantly working to produce information relevant to the quest, and that the key to harvesting it is not some theory, but the willingness to be aware of the process, and be open to the information in whatever form it chooses to come.

Awareness of the various theories by which consciousness precipitates self-knowledge can be helpful, but it can also get in the way. If any theory, however astute, becomes mistakenly construed as the sole source of information of relevance to the self seeking to know itself, that theory becomes an impediment to the soul's process. The soul is better served by having access to as many different sources of information as it can encompass within the resonance of its own space, especially when this access is accompanied by an open-mindedness that is free to choose among them. And where theory is lacking, the conscious self, with the help of the unconscious mind, is perfectly capable of generating its own theory, to be used as long as it is useful, and then discarded, or allowed to mutate, or be replaced by some other theory of greater resonance. The theory is not important. What *is* important is the willingness to exercise a flexibility of the mind in contemplating new frameworks out of which information useful to the soul might emerge. This is the essence of consciousness – which is nothing more or less than the direct experience, beyond theory, of the soul.

The Two-Shark Theory of Consciousness

As an example of how this process works, I'd like to relate an experience I had on the eve of writing the perspective I just shared with you. Last night, I had a dream in which it became clear to me that the unconscious was populated by an unruly school of semi-autonomous sharks. Each time there was a reverberation on the surface of the water, through some experience that evoked a strong emotional reaction, an asymmetrical pair of sharks was born below. Each pair contained a big-fin shark, encompassing a greater amount of psychic energy, but in a more diffuse way, and a little-fin shark, encompassing less energy, but with greater focus. One of the two sharks in each pair would provide creative momentum to the psyche, while the other served the function of deconstructing those areas of psyche that were no longer useful to the soul. A big-fin shark that was creative would produce a positive, constructive mood, while a creative little-fin shark would produce a more focused creative momentum in response to some specific project or life task. A big-fin shark that was deconstructive would produce a sense of restlessness, malaise, anxiety, irritability, or some other diffuse momentum toward change, while a deconstructive little-fin shark would act like a psychic saboteur, causing accidents, derailments, and breakdowns in the world above.

After birth, these sharks would eventually break free from their partners and seek out new partners. Big fin sharks would tend to gravitate toward little fin sharks, and vice versa, while creative sharks of any size would seek out other creative sharks, and deconstructive sharks would seek out other deconstructive sharks. In this way, as these various couplings came together and broke apart, the sensations, feelings, memories, thoughts, beliefs, fantasies, insights and other psychic phenomena we associate with consciousness, would ripple through the water and gradually find their way to the surface, where we consciously experienced them.

◇◇◇

Upon awakening, I knew I was onto something important, since I rarely remember dreams, and this one seemed so clear. In retrospect, I realize that I've now got my own theory of how consciousness works. Who knows? This dream might potentially have objective relevance, which could be elaborated and expounded at great length. Or it could just be an example of how the psyche is capable of providing, not just its own information, but also its own theory about how that information might best be internally processed. Perhaps, instead of putting this theory out there to vie with the others for supremacy, it could be more usefully understood as a subjective message from my soul to the psychological self that processes these messages, suggesting that I might potentially learn something valuable by considering whatever comes up in the next few days or so in light of this dream.

Earlier today, for example, I spoke on the phone with a friend, who told me he would be unavailable to help co-lead a workshop we had already planned and advertised. Within the context of the theory proposed by my dream, this feels like the work of a little-fin deconstructionist shark. If the theory is correct, then this little fin shark is out looking for a big-fin deconstructionist shark to pair with. Indeed, it has already produced a mood in me that is restless, anxious, and teetering on the edge of strong emotion. If I follow this strong emotion in my imagination, however, it seems to want to take me to a new underwater birth. Emerging from this angry, frustrated burst of energy that seems to be mounting in the wake of my friend's revelation comes a little-fin creative shark propelling me toward a concerted round of action – getting on the phone, calling people, rearranging my schedule to make this workshop happen anyway despite this roadblock; and a big-fin deconstructive shark, compelling me in general to let go of some of the many irons I perpetually have in the fire, in order to allow the little-fin creative shark the attention that he deserves.

I can see, in following this little exercise to its illogical conclusion, that the two-shark theory of consciousness is useful to me, on a subjective level, in making personal sense of my own life process. Whether or not it has relevance to anyone else is beside the point, although I include it here, and invite you to play with it, if it has any resonance for you. Meanwhile, the dream can obviously be interpreted in any number of ways, according to any number of theories, without ever recognizing that the dream contains within it the theory necessary to its own utility as a subjective resource.

A behaviorist might insist that the dream is simply a physiological reaction to the baked shark I ate a few days ago, and on the level on which psyche is connected to gastrointestinal sensations, I don't see why that couldn't be true. An Adlerian psychoanalyst might interpret the big fish to be compensatory for the powerlessness of the little fish, and I suppose, even within the context of my current dilemma in relation to my upcoming workshop, this might also be true. A Gestalt therapist might have the big fish and the little fish dialogue, while a therapist versed in psychodrama might have me act out the fish with whom I least identified, and a Jungian therapist might confront me with my ambivalence about my Christian upbringing. As I tried to make my way through the external smorgasbord of options available to me in processing the dream and becoming more conscious of the message, I might be distracted (through the activity, no doubt, of a big-fin deconstructionist shark) from realizing the power of my own subjective process (creative little-fin) to guide me.

The Value of Humanistic Eclecticism

One reason why the humanistic psychology movement was so appealing, and represented a significant step forward in articulating a useful language of soul was the fact that its proponents were willing to be eclectic and inclusive in their embrace of theories. They gravitated to the existentialists largely because they reasserted the primacy of the self as the arbiter of its own experience. Their goal in doing so was not to deny that experience was in part, a product of brain chemistry, or that early childhood experiences beyond the control of the individual did not shape human behavior, but rather to assert that all these experiences, and others worked together simultaneously in multiple dimensions to anchor, trigger, and direct consciousness to shed kaleidoscopic light on the nature of the self at the center of them all.

Where scientists were being too objective, humanistic psychologists embraced Kierkegaard's ideas about the validity of subjective experience. Where behaviorists were being too literal in their understanding of the body, humanistic psychologists opened themselves to Merleau-Ponty's idea that the body was the mediating link between the self and its experience of the phenomenal world. Where psychoanalysts were too focused on what had happened in the past, humanistic psychologists found Heidegger's future-oriented notion of being, or *Dasein*, an attractive source of balance. Where Freud and Darwin had articulated the human predicament in terms that were too deterministic and limiting, humanistic psychologists gravitated toward Sartre's reaffirmation of the power of choice.

Not afraid to cross boundaries between disciplines, or between contradicting theories within disciplines, the humanistic psychology movement, as a whole, sought to explore consciousness in as many ways as possible – not so their theories would be better, but so that the authentic self might have as many avenues to self-exploration open to it as it might find useful. In this, as much as in the content of their discoveries using these new tools, they are to be applauded for laying the foundation for a truly useful subjective language of soul.

This eclectic approach to consciousness is embodied in the amazingly wide range of programs and workshops conducted at Esalen Institute, the prototype and still in many ways the pre-eminent example for hundreds of similar retreat and personal growth centers that have sprung up around the country and throughout the world over the last 40 years. From noisy, confrontational encounter groups to mediation retreats conducted in silence; from Bioenergetics, Feldenkreis and Alexander techniques focused almost exclusively on the body to classes in guided imagery, hypnotherapy, and Zen, which approach the psyche from a more internal standpoint; and in a series of topical workshops ranging from the male grieving process to self-defense for women to creative sexuality for couples, the humanistic psychology movement opened a huge field of exploration which continues nearly unabated to this day.

The Limitations of Humanistic Psychology's Worldview

There are two basic limitations to this worldview. First, although humanistic psychology emphasizes the primacy of subjective experience, and has produced a plethora of techniques for entering more deeply into subjective experience, it has also ironically helped spawn a culture which increasingly defines itself in terms of extroverted activity that in some ways is antithetical to its original intent. As the humanistic psychology movement met the counterculture of the 1960s, then merged with the human potential movement of the 70s and 80s, then mutated into the New Age of the 80s and 90s, it has increasingly become defined by an outwardly focused, consumer mentality. The quest for a deeper connection to soul has in many circles become a quest for the right teacher, the right books, the necessary crystals, feathers, drums, CDs, and other accoutrements, and attendance at the right workshops – all of it very much focused out there, rather than in here where the soul actually lives.

The search is apparently no longer for the authentic self of the existentialists, much less for the sense of soul that arises as the meaning at the heart of pain and suffering is realized. Instead, many contemporary postmodern seekers have become workshop junkies, perpetually on the prowl for ego-gratification, sensory indulgence free of deeper meaning, quick painless fixes to psychological problems, and transcendence of suffering altogether in an endless stimulation of endorphins experienced in the gregarious company of fellow seekers. I don't mean to imply here that the soul necessarily demands misery suffered in isolation, but to the extent that the soul is bound to the mortal body, and the limitations that time and space impose upon the mortal body, then the soul does require a journey to the underworld of the psyche (as it was outlined so eloquently by Jung) in order to complete itself.

Although we can all use all the help we can get in taking this journey, and Jung's ideas have perhaps fallen out of fashion, in the end, it is still a journey that we must take alone. As discussed in Chapter Fifteen, it is furthermore a journey that will take us to the heart of the core issues which cause pain and suffering in our lives. To the extent that the psychological establishment (and the culture as a whole) has shied away from this journey – either through the palliative wonders of pharmacology, or through an attempt to apply wishful New Age thinking to a transcendence of these issues – the ideas of humanistic psychology must remain of limited use to the soul. It is not the outer whirlwind that moves the soul to these necessary depths, but the searing emptiness that remains when the whirlwind has come and gone, and all that is left is a stranded, broken tumbleweed at the side of an abandoned desert highway.

The second limitation of the humanistic worldview is the subtle absence of Spirit. This absence comes primarily through the dual influence of existential philosophy and science upon humanistic psychology, both of which categorically refuse to embrace the metaphysical dimensions of soul. To be sure, humanistic psychologists avoid the *nihilism* of extreme existentialists like Nietzsche, and the worst pitfalls of science. The movement as a whole has laudably seen through the limitations of *logical positivism*, in which all psychological phenomena that cannot be reduced to measurable quantities are dismissed as unreal; and *reductionism*, in which all manifestations of consciousness are considered secondary epiphenomena. Humanistic psychologists are, however, still very much within the existentialist, scientific mold, with regard to those aspects of soul that might be considered spiritual. That is to say, they still tend to dismiss metaphysical questions about the roots of soul in Spirit, preferring instead to place human beingness at the center of the equation by which the soul is understood. In fact, they rarely speak very much about soul at all. Humanistic psychology insists upon the essential wholeness and integrity of the human being at the center of its quest, but it makes little connection between this wholeness, and the greater Wholeness of Spirit out of which it evolves, and of which it is a microcosm.

To do so would complete the circuit between body and Spirit that is required in order to produce a soul in the sense that we have been talking about it. But to introduce Spirit into the psychological equation would, as we have seen, also amount to scientific heresy, and entail the risk of marginalization. To the extent that humanistic psychology is bound by the strictures of science, it can edge up to this line, but cannot cross it. Typical of this dilemma is the statement by Abraham Maslow – often considered the founding father of the humanistic psychology movement – who says (92):

> *The neurotic person seen from a godlike vantage point, can . . . be seen as*
> *a wonderful, intricate, even beautiful unity of process. What we normally*
> *see as conflict and contradiction and dissociation can then be perceived as*

inevitable, necessary, even fated. That is to say, if he can be fully understood, then everything falls into its necessary place and he can be aesthetically perceived and appreciated. All his conflicts and splits turn out to have a kind of sense or wisdom.

The statement hints that there is meaning and purpose to be found at the heart of suffering, and that it is possible to discern this meaning and purpose from a "godlike vantage point" – an attitude I suggested earlier was intrinsic to a humanistic/existentialist worldview. But it stops short of saying that the resolution of suffering and the discernment of meaning and purpose are both a matter of actually evolving to this godlike state by bringing Spirit down more consciously into the embodied state. Not that this is the only way to understand the human predicament. But if we are willing to entertain this possibility, then we have the basis for a psychology that addresses the human experience in a language that is meaningful to the soul. To the extent that psychology, even the most liberated of humanistic psychologies, is prohibited from speaking about the psyche in these terms, because of its pretension to scientific credibility, then it strips the human experience of its spiritual underpinnings, and falls short of providing the soul with the conceptual framework it needs to make sense of the embodied life.

The Immense Promise
Of the Transpersonal Psychology Movement

This shortcoming was partially rectified in the late 1960s and early 70s, as humanistic psychology began to encompass and evolve into a larger, more overtly spiritual perspective known as transpersonal psychology. In 1969, humanistic pioneers Abraham Maslow and Anthony Sutich first published the Journal of Transpersonal Psychology, in order to better explore the relationship between the psychological self and Spirit. The Association for Transpersonal Psychology was founded in 1972 by Sutich, James Fadiman, Michael Murphy and Miles Vich, thereby establishing the transpersonal perspective as a distinct though integral voice within the larger humanistic movement. Over the course of the last 30 years or so, transpersonal psychologists have drawn from a wide range of sources outside the scope of a strictly scientific psychology, seeking to incorporate not just modern psychological insight, but also Eastern and Western mystical practices, the naturalist philosophy of Ralph Waldo Emerson and Henry David Thoreau, and the most enlightened insights that Jung had to offer. More recently the field has also expanded to encompass the wisdom of "allied health disciplines (counseling, medicine, nursing, psychiatry, social work), social sciences (anthropology, economics, political science), and practical arts (business, governance, law)" (ATP Homepage). Certainly this healthy eclecticism can only breathe new life into what would otherwise be a sterile one-dimensional scientific exploration about the nature of psyche.

The reintroduction of Spirit into the psychological discussion, and the reawakening of psychology to its rich and varied philosophical roots must also be understood as vitally important developments. If transpersonal psychology is committed to explore a "recognition of how the sacred is imbedded in all experience," as the Mission Statement posted on the web site of the Association for Transpersonal Psychology suggests that it is, then I believe the ideas that evolve out of this movement can be of great benefit to the embodied soul, who seeks an intimate connection to the immanent Spirit within this manifest world.

I also think it necessary, however, not to lose sight of the existential side of the humanistic equation in attempting to develop a psychology that is more overtly spiritual. For the presence of Spirit within the embodied world means little if it does not mean the presence of Spirit within the depths of our darkest, most wounded and most despairing moments. The goal of a spiritual psychology should not be the transcendence of suffering, but the wondrous discovery of sacred resources at the very heart of suffering – for this is where the omniscience of a transcendent Spirit and the vulnerability of a mortal body come together to produce the embodied soul who stands to benefit from whatever a spiritual psychology might have to offer.

Bringing Spirit Into the Darkness Of Our Most Intractable Core Issues

It seems to me that as souls – that is to say, as embodied Spirit – we are faced with an immense, inescapable paradox. On the one hand, we are bound to the body in which we are housed, and so we must somehow come to terms with the pain and suffering, and the limitations that embodiment entails. On the other hand, we are conscious beings, endowed with intelligence, creativity, inventive ingenuity and every other psychic resource necessary to address any problem we are capable of creating, or experiencing. While it is perhaps possible to understand these faculties strictly in terms of the body's response to pain and suffering, as a scientific psychologist would, or of transcendent human capabilities, as most humanistic and transpersonal psychologists do, unless we make a conceptual connection between consciousness or Spirit and the inherent vulnerability of being alive in a mortal body, the circuit through which soul becomes activated remains incomplete.

Unless we can understand that the pain and suffering we experience *is* the opportunity given to the embodied soul to awaken to its spiritual potential in this life, then a transpersonal perspective that merely seeks to understand the psyche's connection to Spirit can't really help us. Spirit is free from pain and suffering; as embodied souls, we are not. Human existence is, however, an opportunity to awaken within our pain and suffering to the presence within us of Something beyond the one who suffers, then meld the two halves of our being together. It is the melding of the opposites - of the omniscient, immortal, inviolable Spirit and the vulnerable, mortal, easily breakable human self - that constitutes the miracle that transpersonal psychology, or any truly soul-based psychology, must attempt to articulate.

For what is this wisdom that Maslow senses at the heart of human suffering, but the presence of Spirit functioning as consciousness within the fragile embodied experience, leading the soul step by step toward a recognition of its true nature? Yes, it is bound to this body that is suffering; but it is also one with the Spirit in which all suffering is obliterated. Does this not suggest that as the soul exercises with clear intent the gift of consciousness Spirit provides, it will find the meaning and purpose inherent in that suffering, and then gradually learn how to awaken within it? The bad news, at least from the perspective of most religions, is that we don't simply get to shed the body and merge with Spirit without having to endure the pain and suffering inherent in our core issues, and in our humanity. The good news, at least from the perspective of any psychology willing to step outside its scientific straight-jacket, is that by bringing consciousness into our core issues, we will gradually learn how to embody Spirit in a way that elevates these issues in the light of an increasingly inviolable wisdom.

In this regard, the Sufi poet, Hafiz has an insightful confession to make to the transpersonal psychologist who would mistakenly seek a purely spiritual understanding of the human predicament:

> One day the sun admitted,
>
> I am just a shadow,
> I wish I could show you
> The Infinite Incandescence
>
> That has cast my brilliant image!
>
> I wish I could show you,
> When you are lonely or in darkness.
>
> The Astonishing Light
>
> of your own Being!

It is this Infinite Incandescence at the core of our being that each of us, in our own unique way, is attempting to find - "the core of every core" as Rilke called it. The paradox at the heart of the human predicament seems to be that we cannot find this Astonishing Light within, without first entering into darkness - that is to say, without addressing the core issues that darken our lives with pain and suffering. To do this, we must access this same incandescence we are seeking, which within the context of our embodied existence, takes the form of consciousness. These core issues are not the curse of our existence, but the catalyst to the discovery of this incandescence, and the awakening of consciousness. Out of our pain comes the necessity for reaching down deeply inside ourselves for something we never knew we had before we reached for it. Out of the reaching and the longing and the wailing desire for the release from pain, comes the growth in consciousness necessary to pull us up by our own bootstraps. As we then bring this hard-won gift of consciousness to bear upon the core issues that stand as guardians of the threshold to the Astonishing Light within, over the course of a lifetime, we gradually awaken to the sacred knowledge that we *are* this Light. And in this knowledge, this wisdom born of soul, the core issues of the underworld that previously plagued us, reveal themselves to be the radiant jewels out of which the meaning and purpose of our existence emanate to light our way forward.

Who are we? We are the Incandescence of Spirit, blessed with an embodied existence so that we can awaken within matter as souls, endowed with consciousness and capable of infusing any worldly predicament with Astonishing Light. Why are we here? To do just that: to bring our light into the heart of darkness, first our own, and then the world's, so that this entire creation can shine with Incandescence of Spirit. The goal is not an end to suffering or an obliteration of darkness or a transcendence of this world, but rather a conscious awakening of soul within the suffering darkness of the world.

The world is like a circus of candles waiting to be lit. Each of us is a match, and Spirit the flame. Any true language of soul must speak simultaneously to the match and to the flame that has not yet emerged from the match, essentially providing a personalized crash course in spontaneous combustion, while simultaneously leading us toward those candles that have our name on it. In Chapter Seventeen, we will recapitulate everything we know so far about such a language, and then begin to explore how a modified form of astrology might teach us how to strike the match, so that we can light the candles that we - and we alone - have taken birth to light.

PART FOUR

FROM
ASTROLOGY
TO
ASTROPOETICS

Chapter Seventeen
Taking Astrology Into the Realm of Soul

To this point, we have been slowly winding our way through a history of ideas about the soul, demonstrating how various conditioned habits of mind acquired during the course of this history are actually antithetical to a genuine understanding of soul. In my introduction, I evoked the mythological image of Inanna, passing through seven gates on her way to the underworld, and suggested that this image might provide a suitable metaphor to our process of liberating the soul from its conceptual baggage. Thus far, we have traced the contribution of religion, philosophy, science, and psychology to our collective attitude toward soul, and shown how each of these worldviews in its own way, is prone to get stuck at one or more of these gates. In Part Four, I want to walk astrology through the same process, in order to show how the practice of astrology, must be altered before it can become a suitable template for the language of soul we are attempting to construct.

Celebrating the Fertility of the Astrological Field

Just as psychology has absorbed, partly by osmosis and partly by design, many of the same misconceptions we have extracted from religion, philosophy and science to unearth our emerging language of soul, so too has astrology been subject to the same developmental distortion. Thus, before astrology can pass through Inanna's seven gates, it must shed many of the same conceptual limitations. Astrology carries the additional burden of intellectual ostracism, since it is demonized by religious authorities, ridiculed by scientists, trivialized by the media, and grossly misunderstood by the general public, because of the charged and distorted images projected onto it from all quarters. Before we can intelligently discuss astrology's potential as a template for the language of soul we are hoping to create, we must first extricate it, from its own blindness, and from the aspersions and misperceptions cast upon it by others, most of whom actually know very little about it.

These problems are intensified by the fact that there is very little philosophical unity within the astrological community itself, nor is there a coherent, universally accepted methodology, such as that employed by science, which would identify astrology as a disciplined approach to the understanding of reality. As mentioned earlier, some within the astrological community are pushing for a program of concentrated research, based on a scientific model, to establish once and for all, a cogent, proven standard of practice that can be used as the criteria for professional licensing – another hallmark of any profession that is also missing from the astrological world. Within a movement pioneered by Robert Hand of Project Hindsight, Robert Zoller, and Robert Schmidt – others believe that such professional criteria should more appropriately be taken from astrology's own buried history, which predates that claimed by science, and are making a concerted effort to recover and translate ancient texts. Still others have adopted a psychological model, based largely on the pioneering efforts of Dane Rudhyar in the 1960s and 70s to reinterpret astrological principles in terms of Jungian, humanistic, and transpersonal psychologies.

Beyond these three primary astrological paradigms, many other schools of thought have emerged during the 30 years I have worked with astrology representing merely the current wave of a perpetual flux in philosophical outlook that has informed astrological thought, since the earliest known astrological texts were written in the late third and second centuries BCE (Tester 12). Among the more intriguing offerings available in the current astrological smorgasbord are:

- the Brotherhood of Light, founded by C. C. Zain and rooted in Egyptian and Hermetic magic

- the soul-centered astrology of Alan Oken, based on the teachings of Tibetan master, Djwhal Khul

- a number of schools which emphasize astrology's inextricable association to ancient Greek mythology and the mythopoetic world, most notable among them the Centre for Psychological Studies, founded by Jungian psychologist, Liz Greene and the late Howard Sasportas

- the legacy left by Carl Payne Tobey, and carried forward by Naomi Bennett, approaching astrology as a form of sacred geometry

- various schools of Vedic astrology, articulating astrology as part of the larger healing tradition of Ayurveda, which in turn is thoroughly rooted in Hinduism

- the Huber Method taught by the Astrological Institute of Great Britain, integrating astrology with the psychosynthesis of Assagioli and the esoteric theosophy of Alice Bailey

- evolutionary astrology, an approach pioneered by Jeffrey Wolf Green and Steven Forrest, discussing astrological principles in terms of reincarnation, past lives, and the evolutionary history of the soul

- experiential astrology, introduced by Barbara Schermer, which explores astrology in a non-intellectual way through the medium of dance, music, art, drama, ceremonies, rituals, meditations and games

- shamanic astrology, developed by Daniel Giarmario, which as the name implies, brings a shamanic sensibility to an astrology derived through a visceral connection with the night sky.

This list does not include schools of thought that revolve around specific techniques, such as Harmonic Astrology, pioneered by John Addey; Cosmobiology, or the study of midpoints, popularized by German astrologer Reinhold Ebertin in the 1940s and 50s; or Uranian astrology of the Hamburg School, an earlier German approach developed by Alfred Witte and Friedrich Sieggruen in the 1930s, which focused on hypothetical planets. Most of these are more scientifically-minded, although scientists not well-versed in astrology might dispute that assertion. Nor does my list include the many branches of astrology which do not concern themselves specifically with the human experience from a psychological or spiritual perspective – among them *mundane astrology*, or the study of historical and natural processes; *horary astrology*, or the use of astrology as a divinatory technique not rooted in the natal birthchart; *financial astrology*, which has been used quite successfully by a handful of Wall Street brokers as a guide to investment in the stock market; and *electional astrology*, or the timing of events.

Astrology is often criticized for its lack of philosophical coherence by a small army of detractors, and this criticism has been taken seriously by a vocal minority of astrologers, who have agreed that a unified presentation is a necessary precondition for acceptance in the eyes of the world, and that the lack of unity within the astrological community is a problem. On the other hand, few astrologers agree on what the basis for a more coherent presentation might be, while many admit there may not be one. To call oneself an astrologer is to claim membership in a relatively anarchistic community, many of whose colleagues with whom one might vehemently disagree about what the practice of astrology actually entails. Meanwhile, the field as a whole has remained vital, alive, and amazingly flexible for a discipline that is thousands of years old. The proliferation of perspectives outlined above – of which I have only mentioned the most uniquely distinguishable – attests to the creative fertility (some would say, the intellectual chaos) that enriches and at times confuses the field

Although a minority of individual astrologers may practice their craft with dogmatic allegiance to a particular technique or belief system, in practice most astrologers draw together their own synthesis of principles and techniques, eclectically sampling and synthesizing bits from those streams and tributaries with which they feel a sense of resonance. Personally, I feel that this creative ferment within the community is healthy, and despite the fact that I am adding my own paradigm to the stew, I encourage as much diversity as possible. Just as the soul thrives on access to a polymorphous universe, so too does anyone wishing to use astrology as a template for a language of soul, thrive in an environment where philosophical speculation and innovation are encouraged. If the price of admission into the ever-elusive circles of respectability to which some astrologers aspire requires a codification of our art, then I say that is too high a price to be paid.

Having said that, however, I also believe there are certain common assumptions within the astrological lexicon, taken as a whole, that must be questioned before astrology can be useful as a point of departure for the language of soul we are constructing. These can perhaps best be outlined by returning to the task at hand, and walking astrology at a relatively brisk pace, through Inanna's seven gates, so that we might get a sense of what an astrology of soul would look like, according to the principles set forth in this book. First, it will be helpful to briefly retrace our journey through the seven gates, and outline the nature of this language, as we have envisioned it.

Passing Through Inanna's Seven Gates On Our Way to a Genuine Language of Soul

Passing through Inanna's first gate, we shed the religious notion of immortality, which can be seen with an appropriate level of detachment, as a lopsided identification of soul with Spirit. We defined soul instead as an alchemical fusion of Spirit and body, which is subject to the vulnerability that necessarily comes with mortality, but which also presents a unique opportunity to bring Spirit more deeply into the embodied world through our conscious participation in it. We noted that a language of soul must encompass the experience of the body and the embodied life, and at the same time, provide a window through which we might glimpse Spirit at work within ourselves and within the world.

At Inanna's second gate, we left behind all the conditioned patterns of judgment that religion, and later psychology, have projected onto the soul's process. Tracing the history of early religious thought throughout all the major traditions, we arrived at the conclusion that the soul's job was not to be good in a moral sense, but to attune itself from moment to moment to the ever-shifting balance of yin and yang that characterizes the embodied life, on every possible level of manifestation. We affirmed the value of the innate human desire for pleasure, and demonstrated how the pursuit of pleasure invariably triggers the entire continuum between pleasure and pain as an optimal learning environment within which the soul could gravitate toward a state of natural balance. Lastly, we observed that a true language of soul would be nonjudgmental, and provide for a compassionate observation of this balancing process.

Moving from religion through philosophy into the scientific paradigm that dominates our culture, we arrived at Inanna's third gate, and gave up the requirement that our language of soul speak exclusively to the rational mind. We discussed the limitations of the rational mind in handling the paradoxes inherent in a dualistic universe, and showed how its analytical approach to truth was antithetical to an intuitive understanding of the whole and of the soul's place within the whole. We affirmed the value of sensory information, emotion, and the images we project onto the screen provided by objective reality, as mechanisms more conducive to the soul in its quest for self-understanding, belonging, and interconnectedness. Finally, we concluded that a useful language of soul must be able to speak intuitively to the soul through the heart on all three levels of communication.

At Inanna's fourth gate, we gave up science's demand for objectivity, affirming that the soul's experience instead was highly subjective, and not necessarily in conformity with consensual notions of reality shared by society or the culture at large. From the scientific worldview, we extracted the idea of empiricism, and suggested that it could be equally useful to a process of subjective exploration. Any application of empirical process to subjective experience would ideally provide an intimately personal window of self-observation, while encouraging us to discover whatever repetitive patterns we could glimpse through it. We concluded that it would be especially helpful to notice patterns related to the actualization of purpose – which would universally entail bringing Spirit more consciously into matter, yet vary considerably from individual to individual. Lastly, we affirmed that while observing purpose, we should pay particular attention to the evolving quality of our experience, and describe that quality with fine poetic attention to subtlety and nuance.

At the fifth gate, we shed the scientific preoccupation with causality. Instead, we proposed a model of resonance, borrowed in part from biologist Rupert Sheldrake, but adapted more specifically to the task of discussing the soul's experience. We acknowledged the difficulty of stepping outside of the causal paradigm, but noted the value in approaching the embodied world as a complex web of relationships in which the soul gravitated, through the acausal mechanism of resonance, to those people, places, and life experiences that held the greatest potential for soul growth. We then showed how astrology might be understood as a language of resonance through which we could describe this web of embodied relationships.

At Inanna's sixth gate, we shed our causal notions of space and time. We noted how a positivist, causal understanding of space has left the soul stranded without a sense of place, and suggested that redefining space as a resonant field of relationships could be helpful. We spoke of time as a qualitative experience, which moved in cycles, and was measurable subjectively through the use of basic astrology. Lastly, I demonstrated how this might work, using my own experiences as an example.

After moving through Inanna's sixth gate, we moved out of the scientific realm into the psychological, noting that many of the same conceptual handicaps we had discussed in relation to science had been adopted by psychology through its identification with the scientific paradigm. We traced the history of psychology's fitful attempts to free itself from this unnecessary burden – through Freud's focus on the human predicament and discovery of the unconscious, through Jung's brave mapping of the journey to the underworld in a generic sense, through Assagioli's reaffirmation of the value of subjective imagery and the multidimensional nature of the psyche, and through humanistic psychology's attempt to restore creativity, identity, autonomy, and purpose to the soul.

Arriving at Inanna's seventh gate, we found ourselves compelled to shed the notion that human life could be anything but a spiritual experience, since the source of our being and the beginning and the end of the journey were to be found in the Incandescence of Spirit that we are. We furthermore affirmed the value of the core issues studied by psychology as the vehicle through which soul was compelled to access and embody this incandescence.

As we move astrology through these same seven gates, we will gradually transform it into a new discipline, which I am calling *astropoetics*, to differentiate it from common practice. Addressing the issues raised at each of these gates will allow us to use astrology as a template for a language of soul, capable of mapping the spiritual opportunity within everyday experience in exquisite, intimately personal detail. Though I have hinted at this possibility at various points throughout this book, in Part Four, I will focus exclusively on the challenges astrology must meet before it can pass through Inanna's seven gates, and culminate our discussion in demonstrating the deeper connection to soul that astropoetics affords on the other side of that passage.

Walking Astrology Through Inanna's First Gate

Moving through the first gate brings us to the question of astrology's relationship to the concept of immortality. It is interesting to note that the astrology we practice in the West today, passed down to us from the Greeks, emerged through the convergence of two primary streams (Tester 12). One stream came from Egypt, which as we saw in Chapter Two, was also the main source of our Western religious ideas about immortality. The other stream came from the Mesopotamian river culture of Babylon in what is now the

Middle East, circa 2,000 BCE. Central to the Mesopotamian worldview of that era was the opposite idea – that the life of the soul ended with the death of the physical body.

This belief is illustrated in the story of Gilgamesh, the great king/hero of Sumerian myth. When an aging Gilgamesh loses his best friend, Enkidu, he sets off to visit Utnapishtim, who with his wife, was the only mortal to have achieved immortality. In order to appease his fears about his own impending death, Gilgamesh decided to seek the ancient sage's guidance. On the way, he meets Siduri, the wine maiden, who exhorts him to make the most of the present for "the life which thou seekest thou wilt not find." Undeterred by this answer, Gilgamesh kept going, endured the usual arduous journey to the underworld, crossed the obligatory poisonous river, and asked the same questions of the Immortal One, himself.

After insulting Gilgamesh about his uncouth appearance, and telling him his story, Utnapishtim puts Gilgamesh to a test before answering his question by challenging him to stay awake for six days and seven nights. When Gilgamesh inevitably fails, Utnapishtim asks him, "If you cannot conquer Sleep, the little brother of Death, how do you expect to be able to conquer Death?" As a consolation prize for failing to get the answer Gilgamesh wanted, Utnapishtim told him of a prickly herb that grew deep in the sea that would restore youth to an old man. As heroes are wont to do, Gilgamesh promptly dove to the bottom of the ocean, retrieved the plant, and began his journey home. Unfortunately, he lost the plant to a serpent when he stopped to bathe in a well, but that is another story. Meanwhile, upon reaching his home, he carved his story on a stone, grew old and died, just like every other mortal before and since (Powell 46-48).

If Gilgamesh can be understood to be the mythological embodiment of the soul – as most heroes are in mythology – then, it is clear the Babylonians were not of the immortalist tradition. The Egyptian primary contribution to astrology was the soli-lunar calendar of 12 months out of which arose the astrological notion of the zodiac; and the 24-hour day, which later became the wheel of houses. Meanwhile, from the Babylonians, the early Greek astrologers absorbed a more fated understanding of the plight of the soul, which tied it intimately to the life of the body. Out of the Mesopotamian culture also came the idea that terrestrial events could be mirrored by celestial motions, which under Greek influence became the Hermetic axiom, "as above, so below," that serves as astrology's most essential cornerstone.

From about 2,000 BCE, these cultures began accumulating a vast body of omen-literature, which predicted various fates for nations as a whole, or for the king. These pronouncements were codified in a body of work called the *Enuma Anu Enlil*, circa 1000 BCE, and were further elaborated through another 500 years of observation. In the late 5th century BCE, astrology began to be tentatively applied to the fate of ordinary

✕✕

souls, other than the king, and gradually evolved to become the art of interpretation of personal destinies most laypeople associate with astrology today. Through all of these developments, very briefly outlined here, astrology encompassed the notion of fate, absorbed from the Babylonians and Chaldeans, and taken to heart by the Stoics, with whom astrology became most closely associated in the fertile Hellenistic period in ancient Greece. Though my discussion here is focused on Western astrology, it is worth noting that Vedic astrology, based on the idea that the birthchart is a depiction of *karma* (the Eastern equivalent of fate), and oriented toward the prediction of specific life events, is no less deterministic.

Ironically, astrology was also embraced in the West by Plato, who was greatly instrumental in anchoring the notion of immortality in western religious tradition. The Stoics, Plato, and Aristotle all saw in astrology a reflection of the essential Greek concept of *kosmos*, and looked to it to provide information about the order within the universe, both celestial and terrestrial. The Stoics, who believed that human life was strictly predetermined by natural law, also gravitated to the astrological assumption that natural law was immutably etched in the cosmic patterning of the sky and could be read in relation to the fate of an individual soul. Plato and the immortalists believed that this was true to a point, but that God ruled the planets, and through the individual soul's relationship to God, the influence of the planets upon human affairs could and would be mitigated. This caveat was in keeping with the Platonic idea that the body and this world was a prison, from which the soul was to be liberated at death. The fine point about God's role in the process eventually became a sore spot between the immortalist tradition – especially as it was taught and passed on to Western religious culture by Augustine – and the Stoic astrologers.

While the Church's antagonism toward astrology is worthy of its own history, and beyond the scope of this book, we can glimpse something of this conflict in the words of Marsilio Ficino, 15th century Catholic priest, founder of the Platonic Academy in Florence, and a discriminating student of astrology. Railing against what he considered the astrological abuses of his day, he said (164):

> These astrologers in declaring every single thing is necessarily brought to pass by the stars, are themselves absorbed in three highly pernicious errors, and they involve the public in them too. For insofar as they are able, they take away from God, Almighty and Supreme, his own providence and his absolute sovereignty over the universe. Next, they deny the justice of the angels, for according to them, the angels move the celestial bodies in such a way that from thence come forth all the crimes of men, all evil events for good men, and good events for evil men. Lastly, they take away from men their free will and

deprive them of all peace of mind, for it seems to the astrologers that men, no less than beasts, are driven hither and thither.

Toward an Astrological Definition of Fate Capable of Empowering the Soul

Ficino's concerns have reverberated not just among the religious, but also within the astrological community itself. There seems to be a real division between those astrologers who consider prediction to be the rightful province of astrology, and those that do not. Through the influence of Dane Rudhyar and others, the trend, at least in natal astrology, over the last 30 years or so has been to shy away from fated pronouncements and toward greater recognition of the individual's freedom of choice with regard to personal destiny. The concept of fate, however, need not be antithetical to the idea of free will, and the whole argument – as Jung and others have pointed out – is based on a false dichotomy.

Fate ultimately arises as a natural consequence of the fact that death is inevitable. This life – the embodied life of the soul – is, by definition, fated by this incontrovertible fact, and by the equally unavoidable necessity for living this life on a physical planet, bound by space and time. It would also appear that certain other factors impinging upon the quality of existence – our heredity, the family into which we are born, the society that conditions our education, the world at large in which we seek to self-actualize and fulfill our sense of purpose – are all beyond our control. The embodied life is fated by all these factors.

Astrologers would also say that we are born with certain innate predispositions, natural talents, blind spots, core issues, and a spiritual agenda that impels us in a certain direction. While this level of fate is not immutable in the same way that the death of the body, or gravity, or the parents to which we are born, it does condition the process of becoming, and determines the quality of our experiences. To the extent that we push against our own nature, or deny it, or attempt to mold it into some shape that doesn't really fit who we are at the core of our being, we will suffer. To the extent that we are able to discover who we are, and consciously and intentionally create a life in harmony with our nature, we will be more likely to enjoy success, fulfillment, well-being, and abundance.

This discovery of self and giving of intentional consent to be who we are, within the range of possibilities that are encompassed by our fate, constitutes the soul's journey. As we bring ever-deepening levels of awareness to this process, we draw Spirit more deeply into the body, and grow the soul that we are here to be. Not coincidentally, the quality of our life evolves to reflect our growing embodied alignment, and we experience less a sense of being imprisoned by fate, and more a sense of being free within it. As Liz Greene puts it, "It would seem that consciousness . . . is the fulcrum upon which the relationship between fate and freedom balances, for this quality of consciousness permits fate to unfold in a richer and more complex tapestry which is at the same time more supportive of the ego and, paradoxically, more honouring of the unconscious" (155-156).

The possibility of freedom within a fated existence is a paradox, which nonetheless must be embraced as the price of admission to Inanna's first gate. The immortalist gets stuck in assuming that freedom is a liberation from fate, rather than something to be achieved within the parameters and the boundaries that fate imposes. When astrologers err in the opposite direction, assuming that fate is a limitation of freedom, or a negation of the power of conscious choice, they will also get stuck at this same gate. To be sure, it has become astrologically incorrect to say that the birthchart is limited by fate, but the attitude persists nonetheless in countless seemingly innocent forms. Sun sign columns, computer-generated readings, astrological cookbooks, and any other form of astrology that exists in a vacuum without input from the recipient of such information is a disservice to the soul, because it presupposes that it is possible to read fate in a meaningful way, without any reference to the consciousness of the person attempting to become free within the context of that fate.

The idea that human behavior is predictable solely on the basis of astrological indications emanating from a birthchart implies that the freedom to make choices, learn from those choices, and evolve toward a higher level of possibility is limited by fate. Fate provides the container within which the learning process takes place, but it does not dictate how much consciousness an individual will bring to that process or how far he will go with it. Utilized consciously, astrology can help tremendously with an understanding of fate – that is to say, of the life conditions that appear to be beyond our control. To the extent that the astrologer attempts to read the chart and predict future behavior, without reference to the actual experiences of the living person behind the chart and the opportunity for growth within those experiences, then in the hands of that astrologer, astrology will fail as a language of soul.

It is not the astrologer's rightful business to suggest anything other than the possibility that what appears to be fated is a disguised opportunity for the soul to embody Spirit more fully, more consciously, and more creatively. This is not to say that fate is always easy to bear, and the astrologer who focuses only on positive potentials without acknowledging the real life struggles of the soul to actualize those potentials will ultimately be no more help than the astrologer who sees fate as a limitation of freedom. It is important to recognize life as a learning process, shaped both by fate and the exercise of consciousness, before any birthchart can be interpreted in a way that is truly useful to the soul.

Fate can be predicted in broad outline, but the response to fate – which is a matter of consciousness – cannot. As Dane Rudhyar says (448):

> The value of astrology does not depend upon its predictive accuracy . . . It depends rather upon the fact that it provides us with 'formulas' of being . . . and of becoming . . . which enable us to extract the most significance out of what is happening or what has happened. If we assimilate that significance thoroughly, we are then able to face whatever will happen: 1) with an integrated, unified front; 2) as a bestower of creative significance.

The "formulas of being and becoming" that astrology provides are a description of fate, of the embodied condition into which the soul is born. Being and becoming are entirely a matter of how much consciousness the soul can bring to her fate, or how intentionally she can bring Spirit into her body and the embodied world. How much creative significance is bestowed within a given life depends not on the birthchart, but on the soul living the birthchart. If astrology is practiced on the basis of this understanding, the soul will be empowered to face its fate as the ingenious, customized opportunity for learning and growth that it is.

Walking Astrology Through Inanna's Second Gate

At the second gate we must consider astrology's relationship to the concept of judgment, for as we saw in Chapter Three, it was the moral codes adopted by both Eastern and Western religious traditions that rendered them unfit to provide a useful language of soul. Spirit was considered good, body was considered bad, and it was decided in various ways by various traditions that the coming together of Spirit and body – which we have identified as the very condition necessary for the existence of soul - was some kind of cruel cosmic joke, to be endured and eventually transcended.

Considered as a language descriptive of fate, astrology is morally neutral, though each astrologer will bring her own personal sense of morality to its practice. To utilize astrology as a language of soul, then, it is necessary for the practitioner to be aware of her moral biases and hold them in suspension while addressing her life process as it is reflected in the birthchart. This will, of course, be difficult, especially to the extent that these biases are unconscious. On the other hand, for the practitioner who sets this intention, the symbolism itself will offer a wide range of possible meanings, which taken in their entirety, can increase appreciation for the power of creative choice. The greater the range of options in a given situation, the less likely that situation will be approached in rigid moral terms.

Beyond the personal biases that the individual astrologer brings to the neutral mirror that the birthchart provides, astrology itself has evolved through its own history of judgment in relation to the relative desirability of various fates. More specifically, through a series of judgments about *benefic* and *malefic* placements, aspects and planetary configurations, astrology suffers from a conditioned tendency to judge certain factors as good and others bad. Though countless astrologers have attempted to steer our collective thinking toward a more neutral attitude, the problem persists, as evidenced by a recent submission to an e-mail newsletter I subscribe to, in which one astrologer complained that "sometimes God scrambles the planets in such a rotten combination, life can only become better, one might think. Question arises, how? . . . One can be as sophisticated and esoteric as the Dalai Lama, but here on the surface of planet Earth this cluster of aspects really sucks!" (Kluter).

The question of "how" is an important question to ask. The answer, regardless of the particulars of a given birthchart is always a matter of bringing more consciousness into the fated situation that appears to suck. What really sucks, however, is not fate itself – regardless of what it looks or feels like – but the attitude, apparently deeply ingrained in astrological thinking, that certain patterns of fate are good and others are bad. If fate is an opportunity for the soul to learn and grow into the fullness of its Being, then any fate – all fate – is good. It is only when the opportunity is missed, or willfully ignored, that fate itself grows ugly. But this depends not on the birthchart, which is inherently neutral, but on the individual soul living the fate reflected by the birthchart.

Where then does this attitude come from? Aside from being deterministic, the Mesopotamian omen literature dating from about 2,000 BCE – out of which astrological lore evolved – often contained dire pronouncements of doom and gloom. Typical of these would, for example, be this prediction (qtd. in Tester 13):

> *When the Moon occults Jupiter (Sagmigar), that year a king will die (or) an eclipse of the Moon and Sun will take place... When Jupiter enters the midst of the Moon there will be want in Aharru. The king of Elam will be slain with the sword: in Subarti... (?) will revolt. When Jupiter enters the midst of the Moon, the market of the land will be low. When Jupiter goes out from behind the Moon, there will be hostility in the land.*

One might speculate that it was by predicting dire consequences and subsequently helping their royal employers to avert catastrophe that astrologer-priests grew in political stature, although as with any discipline, there were also undoubtedly practitioners whose love of truth was their only guiding star.

By the end of the 5th and the beginning of the 4th century BCE, astrology had evolved to include similar omens for individuals, and eventually grew to encompass the full reading of individual birthcharts, a practice that probably didn't really catch on in ancient Greece until the 2nd century BCE, or the beginning of the Hellenistic period. During this exciting era (discussed elsewhere in this book), the intermingling of cultures in the wake of Alexander the Great's conquests produced a fertile, open-minded, experimental atmosphere conducive to astrology's acceptance. By the time astrology as we know it began to be practiced, it was thoroughly cast in a highly judgmental mold: this aspect is good and will bring good fortune; that placement is bad and will bring disaster. Vedic pronouncements, evolving separately in India, were equally stark in their assessment.

By the time that the Alexandrian astrologer Claudius Ptolemy wrote his four-volume *Tetrabiblos* (Four Books on the Influence of the Stars) around 150 CE - a masterwork which represented a compendium of astrological lore gathered to date; the virtual Bible of astrology at the time, and still covertly influential to this day - the judgmental pronouncements of astrology had solidified into a set of interpretive rules. Certain planets (notably Saturn and Mars) were declared to be *malefic*, while others were pronounced *benefic* (notably Jupiter and Venus). The placement of planets in certain signs was considered to be *exalted*, while other in other signs, the same planets were considered to be in *detriment* or *fall*. *Hard aspects* - particularly squares, oppositions and certain conjunctions were thought to be *malefic*, while *soft aspects* - sextiles and trines - were deemed *benefic*. In this way, the astrological judgment rendered on a given birthchart was based on an elaborate assessment of good and bad influences, which by the 2nd century CE had begun to crystallize as astrological dogma.

Revisioning the Birthchart as the Optimum Game Plan For a Personal Embodiment of Spirit

Though countless astrologers over the course of the last 35 years or so have begun moving away from this highly polarized mindset, the judgmental attitude persists. It persists in part, because of the efforts of a small cadre of dedicated scholars who have taken on the monumental task of translating and making available the Hellenistic and medieval texts in which this mindset was first formalized. It also persists because of resurgent interest in the West in Vedic astrology, which is perhaps even more judgmental than Western tradition, routinely prescribing mantras, gemstones, the intermediation of a trained priesthood, and other remedies for the mitigation of *malefic* influences. Certainly the efforts of the scholars have helped all astrologers to appreciate their historical roots, which are routinely and systematically denied by society at large, while the integration of East and West has broadened our collective outlook. But if we are to evolve a language of soul that empowers the individual to embody Spirit, using the astrological birthchart as a guide, then it is time to embrace the new paradigm initiated by Dane Rudhyar and others a generation ago.

As clear-thinking, popular astrologer Donna Cunningham bluntly states (58, 52):

◇◇

The division of planets into malefics and benefics is wrong - any planet properly used has its constructive function in our lives and any planet improperly used can be destructive.... Each planet in each sign has its positive and negative expression.... Rather than putting down or praising any planet in any particular sign, you should try to put each planet and each aspect in your chart to work in its most positive form.

Obviously this advise is more conducive to the soul's embodiment of Spirit than pronouncing a given placement "rotten," or telling someone that their chart basically "sucks," and if we are to cultivate astrology as a language of soul, this is the direction in which we must move. Instead of merely paying lip service to the power of conscious choice to mitigate an otherwise difficult astrological signature, then decrying the curse of that signature in the very next breath, we must evolve an astrology that assumes every astrological signature to be the optimum path of evolutionary fulfillment for the one who is fated to live with it.

If we can assume for the moment that the soul is an embodiment of the Creative Intelligence that pervades this manifest universe at every possible level, then we might assume that the birthchart - which is a snapshot of the moment when Spirit chose to enter a particular body – is also a reflection of this Intelligence at work. If so, then your birthchart must necessarily provide the best possible game plan for the actualization of your soul's purpose, which is to embody Spirit in a way that only you can do. If we also assume that the process by which you fulfill your life's purpose will be pleasurable, then however this process is mapped out for you in your birthchart, to live in harmony with the birthchart, whatever it might be, will be your optimum path to pleasure, balance, and well-being.

This does not mean that the process of coming into alignment with your birthchart will always be easy. Quite the contrary: any chart worth the paper it is printed on will challenge you through the pain and suffering you experience, to reach down into yourself and access a deeper connection to Spirit, so that you can embody the creative intelligence that is there to be expressed. In this way, difficult charts often become a potent catalyst to spiritual growth, while easier charts can reflect the curse of contentment, under which the individual will coast and stagnate. In the end, it all depends on you. How hungry are you to take advantage of the opportunities that are presented to you? How fiercely are you committed to the growth that your challenges will demand of you? The chart, whether easy or hard, is merely an invitation to the soul to live in harmony with its nature. It is up to you to take this invitation to heart, or not. If the desire to bring as much Spirit into the embodied experience as possible is not there, benefics cannot save you or provide the spiritual will necessary to adequately address your fate. If the desire *is* there, then malefics will only serve to spur you on, and provide the driving engine behind your transformation.

If astrology is to serve as a template for a language of soul, it must sever itself from the Ptolemaic mindset, which is bound by rules dictating what is good and what is bad. From the soul's perspective, good is what facilitates growth, and any chart will do that, provided we have the eyes to see it that way, and the will to actualize its potential. The chart must be read not as the interplay of benefic and malefic influences, but as an ingenious signature for the optimal path to an intimately personal embodiment of Spirit. This means that where difficult placements, aspects, or planetary configurations occur, we train ourselves to perceive them as potent opportunities for soul growth, and approach them accordingly. Where the astrological terrain is easier, we rejoice in the opening to pleasure that comes through the cultivation of our natural affinities, preferences, and instincts. Whatever our astrological lot in life, we realize that what we make of it is entirely up to us. We won't be able to make lemonade with rotten lemons, but we can make compost, and out of that compost may grow a strong and resilient life of great beauty. If we approach astrology with a nonjudgmental attitude, and pay attention to our own experience of it, it can teach us how to grow this life of beauty with the Earth beneath our feet, out of the substance of our own embodied lives, however difficult or painful they may seem to be.

Chapter Eighteen
Creating an Astrological Epistemology Independent of Science

At Inanna's third gate, our task is to free astrology from the requirement that it speak specifically to the rational mind. This might seem like a strange request to make of a discipline that is widely viewed by scientists, sociologists, historians, and the vast majority of the uneducated public alike as an irrational vestige of primitive superstition, a pesky holdover from a pre-rational era. The irony here is that astrology's great appeal – both during the early days of its coalescence in ancient Greece and now, in the postmodern era – is that it helps bring order to the chaos of life in difficult and uncertain times in a way that reason is supposed to, but often does not. At its best, astrology helps the individual to make sense of those aspects of his experience that defy rational explanation. Astrology's many detractors discuss it as a "belief system," as though its tenets were a matter of blind faith in some irrational set of misperceptions about the nature of reality, but if we look at the way astrologers – then and now – understand what they are doing, it is as a *logical* delineation of correspondences between celestial events and terrestrial phenomena that astrology developed, and has been practiced through the ages. Despite the easy dismissal of astro-logic by its supposedly rational detractors, Inanna's third gate is actually one of the most difficult rites of passage faced by any potential astrology of soul.

Walking Astrology Through Inanna's Third Gate

Though many scholars attempt to denigrate astrology as the embarrassing bastard progeny of the classical Greek mind, the fact is that astrology appealed to the early Greeks precisely because it dovetailed nicely with their passionate efforts to understand the rational order of the cosmos. As historian George Sarton describes this relationship, "One might almost claim that Greek astrology was the fruit of Greek rationalism. At any rate, it received some kind of justification from the notion of cosmos, a cosmos which is so well arranged that no part is independent of the other parts and of the whole," and "the basic principle of astrology, a correspondence between stars and men, enabling the former to influence the latter, was not irrational" (qtd. in Tester 18). This sentiment is echoed by science historian Otto Neugebauer, who observes that "compared with the background of religion, magic and mysticism, the fundamental doctrines of astrology are pure science" (qtd. in Tester 18). Though Neugebauer and Sarton are both critics of astrology, their cynical acknowledgment of its pivotal role in the ancient Greek world is often lost on modern critics without this historical perspective. Indeed, until about the 7th century CE, the same word – *astrologia*, which means "logic of the stars" – was used to identify both astrology and astronomy (Tester 19). Far from being the antithesis of the emerging rational proto-science of the time, astrology was very much at the heart of it.

When Ptolemy codified astrology as a systematic body of knowledge in the 2nd century BCE, he did so not because he was seized by some irrational belief to which he felt compelled to give expression, but because he saw astrology as a practical, logical approach to the understanding of the rational order he believed to exist within the manifest universe being studied by science. As philosophical historian Richard Tarnas notes (83):

> *For Ptolemy and his colleagues, astrology seems to have been regarded as a useful science – a straightforward study of how specific planetary positions and combinations coincided with specific events and personal qualities. Ptolemy noted that astrology could not claim to be an exact science like astronomy, since astronomy dealt exclusively with the abstract mathematics of the perfect celestial movements, while astrology applied that knowledge to the necessarily less predictable imperfect arena of terrestrial and human activity. But while its inherent inexactness and susceptibility to error left astrology open to criticism, Ptolemy and his era believed it worked. It shared with astronomy the same focus on the orderly motions of the heavens, and because of the powers of causation exercised by the celestial spheres, astrology possessed a rational foundation and firm principles of operation, which Ptolemy undertook to define.*

Astrology was further embraced by the Neoplatonists, who saw it as Plato and Aristotle had – as evidence of the Divine Intelligence at work, and as a point of entry into the understanding of that Intelligence. The banner was carried forward through the medieval era into the Renaissance of the 14th and 15th century by the Humanist tradition, which championed the use of the imagination as a vehicle for understanding the archetypal meaning behind the rational facts of concrete, material existence. While the more literal-minded of the Renaissance astrologers were ridiculed and ostracized by religious authorities and Aristotelian scholars for their predictive audacity, much as they still are today by modern critics, astrology had nonetheless woven itself into the very fabric of everyday discourse. Says Tarnas (216):

> *Horoscopes abounded, and references to the planetary powers and zodiacal symbols became ubiquitous. It is true that mythology, astrology, and esotericism had never been absent from even orthodox medieval culture:*

allegories and artistic images, the planetary names for the days of the week, the classification of the elements and humours, and many other aspects of the liberal arts and sciences all reflected their continuing presence. But now they were rediscovered in a new light that served to revivify their presence.

This new light was essentially the appreciation of the imagination, or the image-making capacity of the soul, as a faculty of equal value to the rational mind. Astrology's renaissance, within this context, was not strictly as a rational system, but as a language through which the imagination could speak freely. What made astrology seem so useful to 15th century Humanists was their recognition of its potential as a non-rational language of soul. To be sure, astrology had its own internal logic, which made it attractive as a system. This logic, however, was not an Aristotelian exercise in rationality, but rather an affirmation of the mythopoetic order of classical Greece, in which the self-contradictory, polymorphous nature of the human soul was rediscovered and celebrated anew.

To the extent that astrologers of the day attempted to cling to an Aristotelian black-or-white logic in making deterministic predictions, they were lambasted by the Aristotelian scholars themselves for an invasion into territory where they did not rightfully belong. The newly emerging scientific paradigm was beginning to define the literal, rational order of the external world, while astrology's real value, as recognized by the Renaissance Humanists was in mapping the imaginal, archetypal logic of soul space. This differentiation was apparently lost on the more predictive astrologers of the era, and continues to elude many practicing astrologers today, even though the art they practice could not exist except as an exercise of the projective imagination. The signs of the zodiac, for example, are images projected onto groupings of stars that have no rational basis for association. Planets are endowed with mythological features that the actual physical planets obviously do not possess. All astrological interpretation proceeds by way of analogy and metaphor, which are not inherent in a strictly rational or literal understanding of the cosmos.

Many contemporary astrologers continue to insist that astrology is a science, while most scientists insist that it is not. Scientifically-minded astrologers talk about planetary forces, and scientists scratch their heads because there is no way to measure or even identify these forces in any other than a metaphorical way. To the scientist, such assertions appear irrational, because they are – if by reason, we mean the nominalist view, derived from Aristotelian logic, that the language we use ought to refer to the tangible things of this world that we can identify and measure. Astrology is not such a language, nor does it do itself justice to pretend to be. To take astrology through Inanna's third gate, we must strip it of the residual rationalist pretensions it carries forward from its early embrace by Plato, Aristotle and Ptolemy.

Toward an Astro-Logic of the Soul

Astro-logic is predicated not on the identification of distinct things that we can name, but upon a recognition of the patterns of resonance between things considered metaphorically. As discussed in Chapter Five, this depends first, on the recognition that it is the birthchart as a whole that provides the astrological context in which the particulars must be understood, since the whole is what binds the particulars together in an astro-logical way. The unconscious scientific metaphysic passed to astrology through Ptolemy and others inclines us to want to dissect the chart, and then attempt to put it back together. Indeed, this is the way that beginning astrology students often learn, but then soon find themselves confused and overwhelmed, when the pieces don't quite fit, or present contradictory perspectives that fail to neatly reconcile. If instead, we train ourselves to begin with an overview of the chart as a whole, and then work our way down to particulars, we will be approaching the chart in a way that is more conducive to a glimpse of Spirit, which is nothing if not a living metaphor for the Whole pulsing holographically within each individual embodiment of it.

Secondly, beginning astrologers often also look for ways to simplify the astrological language, in order to reduce the complex interweaving of multiple levels of symbolism – represented by signs, houses and planets – into a more manageable system the rational mind can grasp. One such approach – the 12-letter alphabet – was introduced by Zipporah Dobyns in the early 1970s. The rationale behind this system is a recognition of affinity, through rulership, of the various parts of speech that compose the astrological language. Says Dobyns (8):

> [W]hether the first letter of the astrological alphabet is represented by Mars or its nodes, by the first house of the chart, by the sign Aries or the Aries dwad of a sign, it is still the drive toward individual self-expression. 'I do my thing.' Since any planet can be in any sign in any house, a real chart involves complicated mixtures of the twelve parts of life. If the student has a clear understanding of the basic alphabet, its mixtures can be **analyzed logically**, and a range of possible consequences can be **deduced**. (boldface emphasis mine)

The intent behind this approach is to make the birthchart more accessible to analysis by the rational mind. But the logic of astrology is very different than the rational logic which Dobyns and many others – indeed most other astrologers – use to approach a birthchart, and demands its own allegiance to the syntax of metaphor. Signs derive from a consideration of placement within the zodiac, which in turn, represents a division of the Earth's revolution around the Sun. Houses derive from a division of the Earth's rotation about its axis. The planets move in relation to their own unique *synodic periods* (the time it takes each planet to revolve completely around the Sun) and to their various cycles with each other. These are all very different metaphorical contexts, and to be true to the astro-logic of a birthchart, the astrologer must be careful not to mix her metaphors.

The sign Aries, for example, is not symbolically equivalent to the 1st house, or to the planet Mars, because the first describes a style of being, while the second describes an area of soul space, and the third a focal point of consciousness (or resonant attractor) through which soul becomes aware of Spirit and a process through which Spirit can be more consciously embodied. As discussed in Chapter Fifteen, all three of these symbols are often interpreted as though they were descriptive of personality, but that is strictly true – within the syntax of astro-logic – only with signs, and even then only to the extent that we understand personality to be an adaptation and a compromise.

To put it in Dobyns' terms, we might say that where Aries is prominent in the birthchart, the individual will tend to "do his thing." In the 1st house, by contrast, the life task before the soul is discovering who he is. Doing one's thing is only one way to go about this task. For someone with Libra on the cusp of the 1st house, the path to self-knowledge may well involve helping someone else to do their thing; with Pisces on the cusp, the path to self-knowledge will come through surrendering the desire to do one's thing in order to attune to the will of Spirit. Dobyns might conceive of these distinctions as mixing two letters of the 12-letter alphabet, but within the syntax of astro-logic, they actually involve understanding a given symbol – in this case, the 1st house – within the context of a distinct system of metaphors – the zodiac. While the distinction might seem to be splitting semantic hairs, intermingling signs, houses, and planets as though they were interchangeable flattens the astrological language into a single dimension, while placing symbols within various astro-logical contexts opens up multiple dimensions within which the same symbol can be understood.

Approaching Astrology as a Language of Imagery

Lastly, it is important to realize that astrological symbols derive their meaning not as literal equivalencies, but as metaphors with subjective powers of suggestion. As we saw in Chapter Six, when we say that Mars is the god of war, we do not mean that Mars equals war in any way the rational mind can identify. Mars is not a code word or synonym or shorthand notation for war; Mars does not cause war; Mars and war are not interchangeable in meaning. The whole constellation of experiences we associate with war, however, can provide an imagistic point of entry into a deeper understanding of Mars when Mars shows up in a prominent position in a birthchart or specific astrological context. What this resonance means will depend on three factors: 1) the place that

Mars occupies within the overall pattern described by the birthchart as a whole; 2) the time, considered astro-logically in terms of cycles, at which the pattern of resonance is contemplated; and 3) the consciousness that is brought both to the contemplation and to the embodiment of that aspect of soul symbolized by Mars.

The way to get at the meaning behind this pattern of resonance is not through reason, but through an empirical process of subjective association in soul space and soul time, using sensory information, emotion, and imagery to evoke intuitive recognition. The soul must first experience truth within the body as an awakening of Spirit through sensory awareness. As this awareness registers somewhere on the scale between pleasure and pain, the heart translates the experience into an emotional response. The emotions evoked are connected to a network of resonant memories within soul space, and linked cyclically in soul time. As sensory information triggers emotion rooted in memory, images begin to arise which contain within them information that is wholistic in nature – that speaks to the whole being having the experience. These images can then be accessed by the intuition, which speaks directly to the soul through insight, revelation, and instinctual impulses toward meaningful and purposeful action. Intuition does not function, however, until Spirit and body come together, and Spirit and body do not come together when the rational mind is employed to bypass the connection.

Any symbolic language of soul must approach the soul through the body, by deliberately engaging the sensory, emotional, and imagistic levels of input, before the rational mind is engaged as an organizing faculty, if it need be engaged at all. When we honor astro-logical symbols in this way, they evoke a deeper level of recognition that transcends the intellectual knowing of the rational mind. This recognition serves as an intuitive touchstone we can take into our lives in order to explore the patterns of resonance we find there. We did this, for example, in Chapter Twelve, when we tracked the cyclical history of the Mars/Mercury cycle through my life, and identified a pattern related to the challenge of learning to communicate without antagonizing others.

It is also possible to simply allow the imagination to create images that embody the feeling states that the recognition of an astro-logical pattern has evoked. Both types of information can be valuable in different ways. Memories will help to identify those areas of soul space being triggered by a given pattern. Images generally contain within them an abundance of resources to help us more effectively deal with the pattern in question. Both processes will be intertwined as dual threads winding around each other in soul space, like the snakes of the caduceus, through their astro-logical association with the symbolism related to the pattern.

Each resonant memory is itself an image which carries not just literal but also metaphoric associations. If I remember physically falling down in relation to a specific astrological pattern, for example, that literal event may then serve as a metaphor encompassing all the ways it is possible to fall down - on the job, in keeping promises, or in sticking to a diet. If I repeatedly encounter a flock of birds during key stations of a cyclical history, these repeated encounters may be telling me something beyond the literal appearance - that I can fly more freely than I am allowing myself to, that I have more in common (birds of a feather) with those from whom I am distancing myself, or that it is time to migrate to a more hospitable climate, among myriad other possibilities that may or may not be relevant in a given context. If I become aware of a particular sensory quality within the context of a given cycle - say, of something smooth - it can be an indication that I am in some way being drawn to consider all things sensual, superficially manipulative, or flowing with intuitive ease, depending on my associations to the sensory experience and the context in which it occurs. The same is true for repetitive emotional states. Often the images that repeat themselves in my cyclical memories will have sensory, emotional, and imagistic correlates, any or all of which can have metaphorical implications.

Going Beyond Strictly Astro-logical Imagery In Order to Explore a Pattern

Any set of memories capable of revealing an identifiable pattern will be a potent source of transformation, simply because it not only speaks to the soul on all three data streams that feed the intuition, but also because it evolves out of the soul's own life experience. But the realm of imagery transcends the literal events of life, and within the reach of astropoetics, there is no reason why our understanding of a given symbol or pattern cannot be illuminated by images generated through their resonance with a given sensory and/or emotional state. In general, the images that come from real life experience will be the most potent. But in the event that the memories related to a specific feeling state are blocked - which they may well be to the extent that they are connected to painful core issues - then free-association to spontaneously arising images that share the same sensory and emotional correlates can be helpful.

If we return to the accident I had while Mars was conjunct Mercury in August, 2001, we might, for example, use the experience of being broadsided - with all of its attendant sensory and emotional correlates - as a potential metaphor, capable of generating a wider range of images relevant to the pattern it reveals. We will explore this possibility in more detail in Chapter Nineteen in relation to the actual events of my life. But assuming for the moment that I cannot remember any specific events that might fit this metaphor, I can still easily plumb my imagination for suitable images. If I simply close my eyes, and get back into the sensory and emotional soul space I associate with being broadsided, for example,

⬦⬦⬦

I see an image of a man gasping in horror as he is stabbed in the back. Clearing that image from my imagination's palette, I see the image of another man climbing a ladder while flames slowly rise and lick at his heels. And yet one more time, I see the image of a bat with red eyes, swooping through the darkness into my face. These are not actual memories. But each of these images is nonetheless a fertile source of information – not to my rational mind – but to the intuition, which in turn, can plumb them for insight relevant to my predicament in moving through the troubled soul space related to Mars/Mercury and the pattern of being broadsided.

There are many techniques for evoking and working with these images, as outlined in material from numerous sources on the Jungian technique of active imagination (Johnson, Houston), dreamwork (Williams), and various cutting edge astrological practices (Nevin, Schermer, Bogart). The essential core of all techniques is simply the willingness to sit with the images, however uncomfortable they might be, and see what happens. These images have a life of their own, and they come bearing gifts of insight, latent resources, and hints at empowering possibilities yet to be explored on the path to wholeness and self-actualization.

If, for example, I simply sit with the image of the bat with red eyes, swooping into my face, I initially feel fear. But as I muster the courage to focus my attention within my fear, I find this troubling emotion gradually changing into exhilaration as I unexpectedly become the bat, discovering that these red eyes have the power to "see" in the dark and that as a bat, I can fly. If I could, in fact, see in the dark and fly, I would have another set of resources at my disposal with which to approach the challenge of being broadsided. There is nothing here that my rational mind can easily comprehend, since becoming a bat is not within the range of literal possibility. Identification with the bat and its unique set of powers is nonetheless a resource that my imagination can readily embrace in soul space. In some mysterious way, this image and each of the others holds the potential for teaching me something about how to deal more effectively with the experience of being broadsided.

Traditional astrology will take us into no bat caves, but an astrology built around resonant images can and will take us to many exotic and unexpected places where a fitting metaphor for the soul's process might be found. Within these images is the wisdom that we have available to us, without knowing that we do. Tapping this wisdom, or helping others to tap this wisdom, ought to be the first order of business for any astrologer intending to use her knowledge of astrology to speak directly to the soul, and a strictly rational approach to the symbolism of a birthchart won't allow us to make the necessary imaginative leaps.

Before astrology can become useful as a language of soul, we must back away from the idea that the birthchart is something to be interpreted or rationally decoded, and approach it instead as a complex labyrinth of openings to a sensory, emotional, and imagistic exploration of soul space. In this way, its symbols become potent catalysts to intuition, insight, and meaningful changes capable of bringing more Spirit into the embodied life. The astrology that we practice in this way will be very different than the astrology we practice now. But given its own sphere and *modus operandi*, this approach to astrology may prove to garner more respect as a language of soul than any well-intentioned, but misguided attempt to squeeze it into a rational mold to which it is ill-suited, except by historical default and conceptual habit.

Walking Astrology Through Inanna's Fourth Gate

At Inanna's fourth gate, we are compelled to give up science's insistence on objectivity. As Jung has suggested, all symbols are conduits to the collective unconscious where a universal set of archetypes conditions the human experience. Yet, as his own experience bears testimony, the actual journey through that conduit is intimately personal to each soul brave enough to take it. My associations will necessarily be different than yours, even if we pass together through the same symbolic gateway. If, for example, we both contemplate Jupiter's mythological association to lightning, or Venus' association to doves, we may well have different sensory and emotional experiences, which will elicit a unique constellation of memories and secondary images. Our exploration of these memories and images will take us into different resonant fields, and lead to entirely different sets of insights.

In contrast to this understanding, it seems reasonable to assume that from its origins, astrology developed not as a subjective language of soul, but as an attempt to understand the objective order of the external cosmos, as it was reflected in outer events of external lives – first of entire nations and the rulers who held the fate of those nations in their hands, and later of individuals. Then as now, such individuals approached an astrologer to assess their personal fortune – "Will I be successful at such and such an endeavor? When will I meet the person I am supposed to marry? How can I appease the gods, who have afflicted me with such and such a disease?" The answers to these questions traditionally depended less, if at all, upon reference to the individual's actual life process, and more, if not exclusively, upon the interplay of symbols within a strictly astrological frame of reference. Ptolemy codified the rules by which this interplay was interpreted, and subsequent astrologers adapted them to changing cultural contexts, only rarely doubting their veracity and universal application to whichever soul happened to show up for a reading.

Yet as Dane Rudhyar pointed out to a new generation of astrologers, beginning to hunger for a more intimately personal understanding of the birthchart, "Astrology of itself has no more meaning than algebra. It measures relationships between symbols whose concreteness is entirely a matter of convention, and does not really enter into the problems involved – just as the symbols of algebra, x, y, n, are mere conventions" (48). Just as the algebraic equation, xy = 3, means nothing unless we know something about the nature of the context in which this equation is applied, so too do we know nothing about Mars square Mercury or any other astrological statement, except in a purely abstract sense, until we place these statements in the context of the actual life of a specific individual.

To be sure, the astrological context – that is to say, the birthchart as a whole in which the aspect occurs – partially accounts for the differences in meaning between one Mars-Mercury square and another. Mars in Virgo square Mercury in Sagittarius must necessarily be understood differently than Mars in Cancer square Mercury in Aries. Mars in the 9th house square Mercury in the 1st house must necessarily refer to a different life process than Mars in the 11th house square Mercury in the 8th house. A Mars square Mercury that exists as part of a t-square with the Moon must necessarily function differently than a Mars square Mercury that does not form a larger pattern with another planet. And so on. But by far, the greatest differences in meaning between one Mars-Mercury square and another evolve out of a larger consideration that transcends astrology or any other conceptual system.

Even if our charts were identical, Mars square Mercury would not mean the same thing for you and I, because our lives – and thus the overarching life context in which the aspect derives its specific resonant connotations – would necessarily be different. This overarching life context can only be understood with reference to our individual subjective experiences. Evolutionary astrologer Steven Forrest drives this point home most poignantly when he points out that a cockroach born under the manger at the moment of Christ's birth would have the exact same birthchart as Christ, but these birthcharts would hardly merit the same interpretation (Measuring the Night 2). The same will be true to a lesser extent for any two souls born with the same birthchart.

This has been proven true in various studies of the charts of identical twins, born close enough in time to register little difference in their respective birthcharts. The results of such studies have been used to conclude that environmental factors are of greater importance in accounting for individual differences than astrological considerations (Dean 527-543), but such conclusions assume that symbols must have consistent correlates that are the same for everyone. Actually they don't. Astrological factors must be considered within the context of the environment or specific life context in which they apply in order to be meaningful at all. And they must be understood as a reflection of the consciousness through which they are expressed. These are not shortcomings of astrology, but the very nature of the astrological language.

As Forrest reminds us, "Each astrological symbol represents a spectrum of possibilities; each birthchart contains the roots of ten thousand personalities. This is the key to the system. An individual can respond to a birthchart in an unimaginative way, or vibrantly and creatively. His or her response can never be known in advance" (Inner Sky 4). The response of the individual to her birthchart cannot be predetermined by reference to the chart alone. Which of the ten thousand personalities actually blossoms is a reflection of the quality of consciousness an individual is able to bring to the chart and to her life. The chart will describe the broad objective outlines of this life, but the subjective act of embodiment itself – which is the necessary secret ingredient that brings the chart to life – colors, fills and reshapes these broad objective outlines in highly idiosyncratic ways.

Putting the Soul Back at the Center of Astrological Process

Just as the scientific preoccupation with objectivity left the subject at the center of its observation out of the equation, so too does the astrologer enamored of astrology's universal, objective application, leave the soul out of her interpretation. Before astrology can be useful as a language of soul, it must revolve around the subjective experiences of the individual. Astrology can provide a lens through which the meaning and purpose of those experiences can be discovered, but it does not work when the lens is mistaken for the life of the soul it is intended to clarify. Just as Assagioli gathered extensive information about each client before attempting to provide perspective on their process, so too does it behoove the astrologer wishing to use astrology as a language of soul to spend a comparable amount of time listening to the story behind the chart, before attempting to fit the soul into an astrological mold.

Having said this, I would also note that the astrologer has at his disposal a set of tools that the psychologist does not. Because everything astrological can be understood with reference to a cyclical process through which its meaning unfolds, the astrological lens can be focused to capture the subjective process related to any given symbol or set of symbols. Using the birthchart in this way, one need not resort exclusively to a set of objective interpretive rules, but can simply look to see what is happening in the life of the individual that reflects the fundamental astro-logic of the symbolism. The essence of this process – which is an astro-logical form of subjective empiricism – will involve tracking memories related to key moments in the cycle being studied, observing the interplay of astro-logical dynamics in real time, and exploring the images that arise within the memories and observations as metaphors for the soul's process. We did a bit of this in Chapter Twelve, when we tracked some of the memories related to Mars' transits to my natal Mercury, and will do a bit more in Chapter Nineteen, as we take the process to a deeper level. A more thorough exploration of the various cyclical histories weaving through the story of any life can yield an exquisite multi-dimensional picture of the soul unavailable either through the tools offered by psychology or through a more theoretical approach to astrology.

Before astrology can pass through Inanna's fourth gate, it must learn to hold its objective rules lightly, focusing instead upon a subjective observation of the soul's experience in relation to the chart that reflects it. The rules codified by Ptolemy evolved through thousands of years of observations, which were then sifted and sorted by astrologers through the ages for repeating patterns that could objectively be associated with a given planetary placement, aspect, or configuration. Astrologers since have added a vast body of empirical data to the literature out of which interpretations are derived. To render astrology useful as the template for a subjective language of soul, we need not throw out all these observations. We do need to continue observing, however, with the understanding that what has proven objectively true in the past is only the point of departure for a subjective exploration that will take us more directly into our own soul's experience. What we find there may not conform to objective expectations, but if we can get our preconceived rule-based ideas out of the way, it may reveal the soul at work in a more intimate way than a strictly objective mind ever could.

Because this process is necessarily subjective, it is best done by individuals by themselves and for themselves, where the intuition is free to meander without the undue influence of others standing outside the process. Some outside influence is unavoidable, since we are all in relationship to others who influence us in various ways. But the most valuable bits and pieces of subjective truth will come to us in moments of quiet contemplation, during which we are brave enough to approach the events of our lives with self-honesty and clear intent. While most practicing astrologers tend to be primarily interested in using astrology to help others, it is my contention that astrology is most useful as a language of self-reflection, the fundamentals of which can be taught, but the real work of which must be done in the privacy of subjective soul space. This is not to say that a knowledgeable astrologer cannot be a useful resource to anyone wishing to explore their own chart in more depth, but she will be more useful as a guide to a process than as a mere dispenser of information.

Walking Astrology Through Inanna's Fifth Gate

At the fifth gate, we are invited to trade our scientifically-conditioned preoccupation with causal explanations for a more poetic model of resonance. According to this model, learning and soul growth take place within a field of relationships, where we naturally gravitate toward that with which we feel an affinity, and away from that with which we feel an antipathy. Such an understanding translated astrologically means that to make a statement correlating the Moon, for example, with its mythological association to menstruation, childbirth and menopause does not mean that the Moon causes these experiences, but rather that these feminine rites of passage create a metaphor for the kind and quality of experience we might associate with the Moon. Wherever the Moon is emphasized either natally at birth, or through some subsequent activation by transit or progression, this and other metaphors associated astro-logically with the Moon provide a conduit through which the imagination can enter soul space, particularly if they are associated with real life experiences with which they share a resonant affinity.

Though there are few astrologers today who believe that the Moon actually causes menstruation, to the extent that we fail to distinguish an alternative metaphysical basis for astrology's usefulness as a way of knowing that is different than and independent of the dominant scientific paradigm, we will revert by default to the unconscious metaphysics of science. We will adopt the causal paradigm considered gospel by science, because the history of astrology is intimately intertwined with the history of science – not just at its origin, but on through to the development of the scientific method that we recognize as the antithesis of astrology today. Even though the Greeks began differentiating *astrologia* from *astronomia* and science in general around the 7th century CE, it would take another thousand years to sort through the entanglement, during which time astrology was thoroughly steeped in the same causal philosophy in which science as we know it was fomenting.

During this period, astrology and science were parallel approaches to a delineation of the causal order that science would ultimately claim as its exclusive turf. During this transitional period, astrology was of enduring interest – not just to the masses seeking their fortune, but to the very men who were defining the scientific paradigm as a causal order. As astrological historian Jim Tester points out (17):

> [I]t was not the uneducated and superstitious who accepted and developed (astrology). It was the philosophers, like Plato, who prepared the ground, and the Stoics – who were among the greatest logicians and physicists of their times – who most fully worked it into their system. It was the doctors and the scientists like Theophrastus who accepted it and developed its associations with medicine and plants and stones, and with the science of alchemy, which was then nearer to chemical technology than to the magical search for the philosopher's stone it much later became.

Aristotle, Paracelsus, Bacon, Copernicus, Kepler, Gallileo and other pioneers at the cutting edge of science were all versed in astrology, and did not dismiss it categorically as their more arrogant descendents have, simply because it did not fit the paradigm they were articulating. On the contrary, in astrology they saw the possibility for reconciling the new causal order with the metaphysical underpinnings of the cosmos they were describing in scientific terms. Even those who were skeptical did not dismiss astrology out of hand. Francis Bacon, writing in 1623, complained that "as for astrology, it is so full of superstition, that scarce anything sound can be discovered in it. Notwithstanding, I would rather have it purified than altogether rejected" (qtd. in Phillipson 5-6). Others found it more unequivocally useful.

Through the Middle Ages, astrology's relevance to medicine was undisputed. A physician of 17th century Europe was expected to know astrology, since there was no more accurate mechanism to indicate the appropriate remedies corresponding to various elemental imbalances, or the timing for their administration. This influence persisted, despite mounting scientific opposition to astrology, well into the 19th century (Tester 186). If we stop to consider that medicine is one of the most causal of all the sciences, then it seems safe to assume that astrology developed along with the science with which it was intermingled, as a causal worldview.

This is not to say that astrology is appropriately understood as a causal language. As Copernicus proved that the Sun, and not the Earth, was the center of the solar system, and subsequent discoveries through Galileo's telescope showed that the "harmony of the spheres" that enraptured Kepler was more metaphorical than literal, it should have became painfully obvious that scientists and astrologers were not describing the same universe at all, and astrology should have taken a distinctly different road. Astrologers should have differentiated themselves from scientists and developed an alternate epistemology, based on symbolic resonance, metaphor, and intuitive processing of the poetry of science, rather than its literal interpretation as rational, causal fact. The fact that this did not happen attests to an inextricable commingling of these two distinct disciplines in the minds and hearts of scientists with lingering metaphysical sensibilities. As science increasingly divorced itself from metaphysics, astrology became an embarrassing reminder of science's mythopoetic past, and had to be vehemently denied in order for science to establish itself as the sole arbiter of truth.

To distance itself from astrology, metaphysics, and mythopoetry, science adopted a strict adherence to nominalism, rational causality and objective empiricism, and declared that any truth or attempt at discovering truth that fell outside of the range of this theory and/or did not lend itself to science's methodology either did not exist or was not worthy of investigation. Given this exclusionary attitude, an astrology that could or would not establish itself as an independent epistemology was forced to measure itself in terms of literal causal relationships that did not fit, and would be perpetually doomed to fall short by those criteria. Scientists continue to attack astrology as being unscientific because it does not conform to the causal model, and astrologers defensively scramble to try to prove that it does. Like a lover in denial in the midst of a relationship gone bad, a small but vital subculture of scientifically-minded astrologers cling to the notion that if only astrology can prove its validity on scientific grounds, science will take it back. Meanwhile, the very notion leaves astrologers open to endless rounds of abuse.

The most famous incidence of this abuse in recent history is a statement by B. J. Bok and L. E. Jerome, published in 1975 in *The Humanist*, endorsed by 186 leading scientists, and later expanded into book form. In the book, entitled *Objections to Astrology*, the authors argue that astrology is absurd because the gravitational and electromagnetic forces emanating from the planets are too weak to causally affect anything happening on Earth, including human behavior. They also argue that because the Sun, Moon, planets and stars are all made of the same material, there is no scientific basis that could account for the different effects that these bodies had on individuals with different charts.

Astrology's Failure to Measure Up Within a Causal Paradigm

The truth is they are right. The planets do not cause anything to happen; they do not produce effects that can be quantified; nor is there a scientific explanation for astrology's utility in helping to shed light on the human predicament. This does not mean, as scientists assume, that because astrology cannot measure up to scientific standards, it is invalid. It does mean that as long as astrologers and scientists alike assume that astrology ought to be able to conform to a scientific paradigm to which it is ill-suited, the arguments on both sides will go round and round, while astrology remains marginalized because it is inherently non-scientific, but ambivalent about this status.

As psychotherapist and astrologer Glenn Perry describes the problem (27):

> Starting with the premise that 'astrology can't work, therefore it doesn't,' there have been countless attacks on astrology based entirely upon the now obsolete billiard-ball cosmology of Newtonian physics . . . Unfortunately, many astrologers have fallen into the same trap as their critics. There have been countless experiments designed within the framework of mechanistic science that do not support astrological claims. It is, however, understandable that such attempts should be made. Unless the astrologer is well-versed in the limitations of the experimental method, he is apt to respond to criticisms in the same language as his attackers.

So it was, for example, when three scientifically minded astrologers Geoffrey Dean, Arthur Mather and Rudolf Smit set out to validate astrology's claims using scientific methodology. "We started in much the same way as any astrologer starts – we calculated charts, saw that they seemed to work, and were hooked. Astrology became our passion

◇◇◇

. . . we became more and more convinced that astrology worked." After their research, however, they state, "We were dismayed to find that artifacts and errors seemed to explain everything. Our beautiful world of astrology began to collapse" (qtd. in Phillipson 4). Now the three are among the most vociferous critics of astrology, convinced that unless astrology can prove itself scientifically, it is no longer worthy of their passionate attention.

The most famous and most successful of all astrological researchers to date is French statistician Michel Gauquelin, noted for his studies of the correlation between rising and culminating planets and various professions. If anyone ever had the power to vindicate astrology on scientific terms, this brave pioneer, who was well versed in the scientific method, ought to have settled the argument between science and astrology once and for all, or at least opened the door to a meaningful dialogue. This did not happen. Instead, Gauquelin's studies were picked apart and endlessly dissected for flaws by scientists with a fierce bias against astrology that would necessarily cloud any objectivity that might otherwise have legitimized their investigation.

Even Gauquelin came to conclusions that were not always favorable to astrology. In the wake of a less famous study of Sun signs, for example, Gauquelin concludes that "the influence of the signs of the zodiac is not confirmed by an objective study of the behavior of thousands of people - or, to put it crudely, the signs of the zodiac are valueless" (131). If such a vital piece of the astrological language can be so unambiguously dismissed by the best scientific champion the astrological community has yet produced, then what hope is there that astrology will miraculously prove itself scientific, according to the causal model Gauquelin was investigating, if additional research is done?

The problem is not necessarily that astrology is unscientific, although I believe that to be true. The real problem is that in order to establish itself as the sole arbiter of objective truth, science has found it necessary to sever all ties with its historical sibling, and no amount of scientific proof can ever mend this rift. The effort to discredit astrology is not a dispassionate, objective venture, but an irrational obsession pursued by scientists trained to discount their own emotional biases. Trying to overcome these emotional biases with rational arguments is like trying to explain the beauty of a sunset to a blind Frenchman by showing him a movie in English with French subtitles. In attempting to establish astrology on scientific ground, astrologers are only digging themselves more deeply into the quicksand of scientific ridicule and rejection. Efforts in this direction are a losing proposition for all concerned. Of far more benefit to the astrological community - and to any language of soul we might hope to base on astrology - will be for us to admit that astrology has no causal basis that can be measured by science, and then proceed to develop it instead as a sophisticated methodology of subjective exploration of images and metaphors, capable of poetically mirroring the soul back to itself. At the very least, before we can squeeze astrology through Inanna's fifth gate, this is the collective paradigm shift I believe we must make.

Walking Astrology Through Inanna's Sixth Gate

Once this paradigm shift has been made – not an easy task, given the 2,500 years or so it has taken astrologers to dig themselves into the hole we are in now – passage through Inanna's sixth gate becomes much easier. If astrology can wean itself from the necessity for defining astrological "influences" in causal terms, it then becomes free to reconceptualize space and time in a way that is more conducive to soul growth. Because of the confusion that prompts scientists and astrologers alike to hold astrology to inappropriate scientific standards, however, there has been an awkward attempt to translate the qualitative poetry of astrology into a more static language of definition and immutable law. This attempt has distorted the way in which some astrologers tend to think about soul space and time. Before we can take astrology through Inanna's sixth gate, these distortions must be addressed.

In causal space, forces act upon other forces according to well-defined laws to produce well-defined results. When astrologers interpret a birthchart according to a causal model, however unconsciously that model is held, the symbols of the birthchart are understood to have set definitions which reveal themselves in distinct, clearly demarcated packages. A planet in a house for example is understood as a force operating within a neatly circumscribed area of life circumstances. A planet in a sign is understood as a force operating a specific way. Two planets in aspect are interpreted as though they assert some kind of constant influence upon each other, locked in a static embrace that defines once and for all the meaning of the symbolic association. When this happens, all sense of the interconnected wholeness of soul space is lost, and the soul's movement becomes inhibited by expectations of conformity to definition. The Moon in Libra, Venus in the 5th house, and Sun conjunct Pluto all become shorthand notations for static truths, and cease to function as a viable description of the soul's complex evolutionary process.

Missing from such an approach is any appreciation of the fact that these symbolic signatures are what they are, because they are in relationship to a larger cycle that binds them together. To the extent that the language of astrology attempts to cast itself into a scientific mold, demanding consistent definition, each phase of the cycle is treated as though it were a distinct and separate category of experience, while the dynamic interplay between all phases of a cycle that connects each phase to the whole is ignored. Meanwhile, it is this reference to the whole cycle that must give all astrological symbols their meaning in a soul-based language, and any cycle is nothing if it is not an ingenious holographic device that connects every piece of the astrological puzzle to every other piece, and to the whole that contains all the pieces. Understood in this way, each planetary placement within astrological soul space is not just what it is. It is also a gateway into an experience of the wholeness and interconnectedness of soul space itself. Conveniently, everything astrological is based on some cyclical process – the zodiac on the cyclical revolution of the Earth around the Sun, the houses on the cyclical rotation of the Earth around its axis, any aspect on the cyclical interplay of the two planets moving in relation to each other, and so on. It is impossible to explore anything astrological without being led intuitively around the whole cycle of which each piece is part.

This awareness seems to have been latent in the very origins of astrology, although in practice, it was often lost among the definitions that came to characterize astrological knowledge. Before the Alexandrian scientist-astrologer Ptolemy codified astrological definitions in his masterwork *Tetrabiblos*, the Roman poet-astrologer Manilius hinted at the dynamic fluid primacy of the cycle in his early 1st century CE masterwork, written as a poem in five volumes. Says Manilius in describing the zodiac (qtd. in Tester 31):

> From Aries shining in his golden fleece
> Wonders to see the back of Taurus rise,
> Taurus who calls, with lowered head, the Twins,
> Whom Cancer follows; Leo follows him,
> Then Virgo; Libra next, day equalling night,
> Draws on the Scorpion with its blazing star,
> Whose tail the Half-horse aims at with his bow,
> Ever about to loose his arrow swift.
> Then comes the narrow curve of Capricorn,
> And after him, Aquarius pours from his urn
> Waters the following Fishes greedily use,
> Which Aries touches, last of all the signs.

Throughout his book, Manilius displays his Stoic sensibilities in the affirmation of a strictly causal worldview, and in his own way, is every bit as rule bound as the other astrologers of his day. Yet, in this passage, and others, it is clear that Manilius understands and appreciates the dynamic interplay of the cycle that must necessarily lie at the heart of any astro-logical attempt at definition. The cycle has been brought to the forefront of astrological awareness in more recent times by Dane Rudhyar, who reinterpreted the signs, houses, aspects, and phases of the Moon all in terms of cyclical processes. Astrologers since Rudhyar give obligatory lip service to the cycle, but in practice often revert to interpretations that treat signs, houses, and aspects as discrete and static entities unto themselves, often forgetting that they take their definition from the larger cycles in which they participate.

Astrologers, for example, will routinely describe the Moon in Libra as though it possessed certain qualities, which in turn essentially define it. Typical of such a definition would be this interpretation, taken from one of the best astrological cookbooks available: "You like life to be beautiful and prefer not to think about things that aren't pleasant. You are affectionate, warm and friendly, but you may overlook other people's faults that you should keep in mind. Your strong need to be agreeable may cause you to give in when you shouldn't. You are a peace-loving person and do not like to start fights with others" (Hand, <u>Planets in Youth</u> 106).

While this may be true, on the level of personality - that is to say, on the level on which the soul has learned to adapt to the expectations of society - from the soul's perspective, the Moon's placement in Libra is really only a point of departure for the journey toward a more complete embodiment of Spirit. The placement is not only to be taken literally as a definition of where the soul happens to be at the moment, but must also be understood as the focal point of a cyclical process of change which points beyond itself to a much more dynamic fluctuation of possibilities. Within the context of the larger cycle in which the Moon in Libra participates, it is actually moving from a prior identification with Virgo into a more liberated identification with Scorpio, and the placement itself is insufficient to describe that section of soul space where the Moon is resonating. At times, the soul will be recognizable as the cookbook interpretations suggest it ought to be, but at other times it will not.

It may be that the reason why someone with Moon in Libra "like(s) life to be beautiful and prefer(s) not to think about things that aren't pleasant" is because when her Moon was in Virgo, she was overly involved in attempting to address the pain and suffering of the world, and now she needs a break. As the soul with Moon in Libra continues mutating and evolving, she may eventually reach a place in Scorpio, where she feels strong enough to walk through the valley of the shadow of death and fear no evil, but she is not quite there yet, so she is nourishing and fortifying itself with beauty and pleasant thoughts. At times, she may revert to her old habits, and seem more Virgoish than Libran - fussing with details, worrying endlessly about decisions yet to be made, seeking beauty in order and organization. At other times, she will jump ahead of herself and display a Scorpionic intensity of passionate certainty that surprises her and everyone around her, finding beauty not in balanced patterns of symmetry and pleasantry, but in the courage to break free from those patterns.

If you observe this soul's process more clearly during various key moments, especially when then Moon is being transited by an outer planet, it is likely that you will see empirical evidence of such back-and-forth momentum. The Moon's participation in a cycle can be taken literally, since it will move constantly after birth - by transit and progression, where it can be felt mutating through various qualitative changes by those who are sensitive enough to register such changes. It can also be understood figuratively, as a recognition that any placement of the Moon is a statement about its participation in a cyclical process. The Moon in Libra, or any other sign, is not a static description, but an evolutionary snapshot, taken as the Moon moves from one state to the next. Moon in Libra will at times act like Moon in Virgo – not necessarily because it has been there in its movement through a literal cycle – but because the qualities associated with Virgo are implicit in Libra's evolutionary status, just as the child is implicit in the adult.

Depending on what else is happening in the chart, someone with the Moon in Libra might also find her behavior rooted in Aries (its polar opposite), Gemini or Aquarius (signs with which Libra shares a natural sense of resonance), Cancer or Capricorn (signs with which Libra shares a natural sense of antipathy), Leo or Sagittarius (signs with which Libra also resonates, but more dynamically), or even Taurus and Pisces (signs in which Libra is not likely to experience a reflection of itself), or some combination of the above. When this happens – and it will tend to be the rule rather than the exception – Moon in Libra must be understood from a variety of perspectives, for it can potentially have a wide range of motivations, needs, desires, impulses, tendencies, and intentions, the scope and depth of which cannot possibly be encompassed by any definition, however astutely or insightfully it is constructed. The fault is not with the definition, but with the attempt to define – a conditioned pattern of response to symbolism that limits the soul unnecessarily, and that is a natural by-product of a causal understanding of space. In causal space, the soul seeks to define itself as a discrete entity; in resonant space, definition is only possible through an exploration of relationship with everything else with which it shares a pattern of resonance.

Shifting Our Astrological Focus From Events to Processes

The other major limitation that arises out of an unconscious default to the language of causality, is in focusing on events rather than processes. In linear time, we tend to think of our lives as a chronological sequence of events, stretching from birth perhaps to the birth of siblings, to the first day of school, to graduation, to our first full time, job to marriage, to the birth of a child, to the death of a parent, to the onset of illness, to death. Our movement through soul time, however, is not marked by events, but rather on subtle shifts in awareness that may or may not correspond to anything happening on the outer planes of our experience. We tend to remember events, but the reason why we remember them is because they are associated with sensory experiences, strong emotional responses, and/or enduring images, which in turn, are the evidence within the embodied life of Spirit awakening within us. It is this awakening we are attempting to track through soul space, within the context of the various cycles that weave through soul time. The awakening itself is not an event, but a process that unfolds gradually, in various ways, over the course of a lifetime. If we are to successfully use astrology as a language of soul, we must shift our collective attention away from events and toward a more nuanced attention to process.

The way through Inanna's sixth gate is pointed out very clearly by Liz Greene, when she says (319):

> The events of 'real life' and the flow of inner images are both regulated in some mysterious fashion by the Self, and the 'stuff' of which both inner and outer experiences are fashioned is symbolized by the horoscope.... It would seem that this thing Jung calls the Self makes its arrangements using the astrological chart as a weaver uses his threads.

To follow these threads through soul space, we track their emergence in soul time – as events when they occur – but also as processes. These processes are often symbolized by the events themselves considered metaphorically. But in any case, they can be discerned with reference to astrological patterns being triggered at any given time, and the sensory, emotional and imaginal experiences related by subjective observation to those patterns. The patterns are best understood by tracking them through key stations of the appropriate cycle (or cycles) as we did very briefly with my Mars-Mercury cycle in Chapter Twelve.

We will continue this exploration in the next chapter in order to demonstrate how astrology might be used to explore the connection between the embodied soul and the Divine Intelligence that quickens it to life. For now, we can simply note with confidence that astrology will be incapable of facilitating such an exploration unless it is divorced from scientific assumptions about the nature of reality. Astrology is not a science – and in no small measure, this is its great advantage as the template for a language of soul. Where science is rational, astrology is thoroughly steeped in imaginative imagery with identifiable sensory and emotional overtones. Where science is objective, astrology is free to celebrate the nuanced subjectivity of the individual soul. Where science depends upon static causal explanations for its authority, astrology practiced poetically opens an ever-widening circle of resonant relationships through which the soul can find itself. Where science measures the quantitative impact of events in physical space and linear time, astrology can be used to track the cyclical evolution of meaningful processes in qualitative terms. With modifications as suggested in this chapter, we can cultivate an astro-logical form of empiricism that takes it through the scientific gates into a resonant space where soul can be more clearly seen and appreciated for the evolving subjective entity that it is.

Chapter Nineteen
Using Astrological Imagery To Make a Connection to Spirit

The more awareness we can bring to this astro-logical process of subjective exploration, by observing the various cycles that weave through our lives, and playing with the images that arise spontaneously in the focused contemplation of life patterns, the more conscious we become of an indisputable Intelligence at work in the smallest of details, as well as throughout the global picture. This Intelligence is Spirit - not Mind, as conceptualized by the rationalists - but Creative Ingenuity with a wonderful sense of humor, a taste for irony, and an uncanny sense of timing. Nearly everyone with whom I share the astrological process has marveled at the way moments in cyclical time dovetail in order to reveal a deliberate calling of attention to some aspect of our soul's process that in retrospect seems almost intentional. Spontaneously arising images that speak to the soul in moments of synchronicity often carry the same spiritual potency, and hint at the possibility of conscious design flowing beneath the surface of seemingly unconnected events. To attempt to discern this design, and align ourselves with It is the surest path to a more complete embodiment of Spirit.

Walking Astrology Through Inanna's Seventh Gate

It is also the essence of an astropoetic approach to astrology. Astrology practiced astropoetically holds great potential for providing a window through which we can glimpse this intelligent design at work at the beating heart of a life in progress. There is no guarantee, however, that astrology will fulfill this potential, unless we who use it, are able to pass through all seven gates ourselves. For it is the consciousness that each of us brings to the language that determines what the language will reveal. Just as science can be used to build a better, safer, more harmonious world, or to destroy it, so too can astrology be used to guide the soul toward a more radiant embodiment of Spirit, or to reinforce a sense of entrapment and victimhood.

While many astrologers and students of astrology focus on the cultivation and mastery of technique, the heart and soul of astropoetic practice is the cultivation of awareness. It is ultimately what one brings to the mirror that astrology provides, and not astrology itself that is the deciding factor determining the quality of information that is reflected. If one approaches the mirror convinced that life is a struggle against impossible odds, the birthchart will confirm and more deeply entrench that attitude. On the other hand, if one is intent upon seeing the handiwork of Spirit as it infuses the embodied world with life, vitality and the opportunity to evolve, then the birthchart becomes a detailed reflection of that promise, as well as an intimately personal guide to its realization in soul space and time.

Astrologer Stephen Arroyo sums up astrology's most enticing potential when he suggests (xi):

> [A]s one becomes attuned to that center, to that higher Oneness, one perceives with increasing clarity that the birthchart is a whole, unified, living symbol; that the individual person is not merely a composite of many diverse factors, but is a living unit of divine potential. And the growth-processes with which astrology deals . . . are not isolated cycles that happen occasionally to overlap; rather they are all aspects of a unified and developing consciousness operating simultaneously at many different levels and in many different dimensions.

The beauty of the astrological language is that once we set the intention to use the birthchart as focal point of awareness, so that we might align ourselves with the Intelligence of Spirit functioning through us, we will begin to see it everywhere. Grasping the whole is important, as discussed earlier, but once we are clear that it is Spirit that we are witnessing in the genius that weaves the whole together, then each thread of astro-logic that we explore also leads toward a deeper recognition of the Whole and our place within it. Regardless of where we focus our attention within a birthchart, we will be lead step by step to that place where there is no separation between the individual soul and the Spirit that animates and inspires the embodied life. It is not useful to simply assume, as does religion, that no separation exists. But it is valuable to pursue the gradual discovery of this ultimate truth through an intentional process, for which astrology provides an opportunity. Since all things astrological are circular, and everything is connected to everything else, each thread within the warp and woof of the cosmic design leads back to the Intelligence at the heart of that design. It is not possible to approach that design with clear intention without eventually making a tangible connection to its Source.

Once the connection has been made and thoroughly integrated, the chart is no longer necessary, for the same information is available everywhere in each moment throughout the embodied world – in the movement of clouds, the random spilling of beans out of a bag, tea leaves at the bottom of a cup, the flow of traffic through an intersection, the flight of birds, on the page of any book we are randomly drawn to open, in the daily news, and through a thousand other everyday sources of common metaphor.

Using Astrology as a Path to Metaphoric Vision

Astrology is not ultimately an end unto itself, but a methodology for training the student of life to see the embodied life in metaphorical terms through the eyes of Creative Intelligence. By taking the time to explore the sensory and emotional correlates to the basic symbolism of astrology, we cultivate the art of paying attention to the moment. By tracking cyclical histories related to planetary patterns being activated in soul time, we discover the images that reflect back to us who we are in the various interpenetrating dimensions of our being. The deeper we go with this process, the closer we come to the very core of Being, that silently reverberating pulse at the Heart of the embodied world that also beats within us.

Astrology is traditionally practiced as an art of great complexity. Many astrologers pride themselves on the breadth of their esoteric knowledge, which encompasses not just the Sun signs superficially familiar to the average layperson, nor the basic vocabulary of houses, signs, planets and planetary aspects, transits and progressions known by the modest student of astrology, but also an arcane body of additional information encompassing asteroids, hypothetical planets, midpoints, harmonics, minor aspects, Sabian symbols, return charts, composite charts, relocation charts, astrocartography maps and many more layers of information too numerous to mention. While judicious use of these techniques can be helpful in the appropriate situation, it is all to easy to substitute a wealth of information for a depth of understanding, All this information means nothing, if we do not feel its meaning in our bones, and experience that small shiver of recognition that Spirit is afoot in the intimate workings of our life process.

If the particular path through the astrological maze that you are following does not lead to Spirit's doorstep, perhaps it is because you have become too enamored of technique and the quest for rational interpretation. A focus on technique will invariably take you up into your head, while the path to subjective truth is through the breath into a simple awareness of astro-logical truth. Once you set the intention to bring an awareness of Creative Intelligence at work into the present moment, where Spirit is always pulsing at the heart of the embodied experience, the astro-logical process becomes easier, and much more organic. What are the sensory and emotional correlates to the symbols involved in the pattern that you are tracking? What are the images that arise within your own experience that seem to embody these sensory and emotional correlates? How are these images a reflection of Spirit at work in your life? These three questions encompass the essence of astropoetic practice, and one need not be an intellectual acrobat or a master of complex technique to ask them at each step of the astrological journey.

Getting lost in the maze is easy, if we insist upon approaching astrology as a linear intellectual exercise. But the way back to awareness is even easier, provided we are willing to pay astro-logical attention to the abundance of clues provided within our own experience. It is perhaps human nature when faced with difficult or painful situations to seek intellectual understanding as a way to rise above our suffering and gain perspective, and astrology will readily lend itself to this instinctual response. The way to deeper understanding, however - understanding that can actually be used to transmute the pain and suffering into growth - is down and into the sensory and emotional roots of the image in which the pain and suffering are encompassed. For this, traditional astrology - with its emphasis on interpretation and rational decoding of symbols - is a less effective tool than astropoetics, which focuses instead upon using the symbols as an intuitive point of entry into the spiritual essence of embodiment.

What will surely be disconcerting to some is that unlike traditional astrology, astropoetics offers no hard and fast rules or definitions. There is no specific formula or technique that will work in every instance. Instead, focused practice in the light of principles outlined in this book will teach you the intimacies of your own process. With clear intention, all roads will ultimately lead to Spirit, or more precisely to the specific way in which Spirit has chosen to inhabit the embodied soul that you are. Everything you discover on the way to this ultimate realization will also be useful, since there are no wasted gestures in the grand scheme of things. Learning to see this life from an astropoetic perspective, you will slowly grow in your capacity to appreciate the exquisite choreography of Spirit at work in the tiniest of details and the most magnificent of visions. Passing at last through Inanna's seventh gate, you will one day enter a blessed world of revelation, where there is no longer any separation between the you that is seeking answers and the You in which they are implicitly revealed.

The Application of Astropoetic Technique To a Deeper Understanding of the Image

Guessing that my description of this process will sound rather cryptic to some, and naively optimistic to others, it seems appropriate to conclude astrology's passage through Inanna's seven gates with a real life example. To illustrate how we might use an astropoetic approach to astrology to lead us toward a deeper and more conscious connection to Spirit, let's return for a moment to my experience of transiting Mars conjunct my natal Mercury during the period from August 18-20, 2001, as discussed in Chapter Twelve. During this transit, I was in a car accident in which my partner Ann and I were broadsided by a woman whose car had no brakes.

If I were simply going to *interpret* this event from an astrological perspective, I could say that it was a reflection of the fact that the potential for accidents (Mars) was high while traveling (Mercury), and that angry (Mars) communication (Mercury) was caused in a conflict between two people moving at cross purposes to one another (a description of the square between transiting Mars and natal Mars). An apt cookbook interpretation for this transit admonishes me that "if (I) drive anywhere in a car, (I should) be careful not to speed. (I) may be inclined to recklessness and risk-taking while (I) travel, which can lead to accidents." Of course I would argue that it was the other driver that was speeding and being reckless, but the cookbook interpretation of this transit does point to the need to be careful while traveling, and most astrologers would could consider it to be uncanny in its relevance. The same interpretation also suggests that "today (my) ego is unusually involved in communication with others. Consequently, (I am) unusually touchy and irritable and likely to get involved in disputes...." (Hand, Planets in Transit 232) – another appropriate reference to my actual experience.

Meanwhile, the car with no brakes was aptly symbolized by Mars, while Mercury represents awareness which, in this case, was peripheral. Mercury never saw Mars coming, in other words, and was broadsided because of it. If you consider the fact that we were hit by a vehicle moving at right angles to us, the whole accident can be construed as a graphic depiction of the square between natal Mars and transiting Mars (two vehicles entering the intersection perpendicular to each other). All of this is of little help to me after the fact, although it does accurately describe what happened in a way that validates traditional astrological technique – as far as it goes.

From the astropoetic perspective, however, an accurate description of the event itself is less important than the sensory and emotional content of the image evoked during the experience, and so that is where we will begin our exploration. On the sensory level, all I really remember when I close my eyes and recall the event is the sound of crunching metal, breaking glass, and a horn – sensory cues the reader may recognize as the loud, staccato, piercing, palpable, sharp, metallic sensory signature for Mars, tinged perhaps by the agitating, disorienting, ozonous flavor of Mercury. Emotionally, I am aware of a progression of three distinct states of being. First, before the accident, I felt calm, relatively content with life in general, and looking forward to what I was planning to do that evening. Immediately after the accident, I felt vulnerable in the midst of forces beyond my control that literally smashed into my contentment. As the event itself began to register, it was my anger that came to the surface, seeking an appropriate outlet. This response is related to the issue identified in Chapter Twelve as a process of learning how to effectively communicate and discharge my anger.

What emerges from a consideration of the emotional content, however, is a new piece of the puzzle, for this is not just anger directed toward another, traceable to a specific incident – although in this case, it was that. It was also anger experienced in the face of a situation I could not have seen coming and that was beyond my control. The vulnerability I felt in the midst of this experience, and at the core of my anger was an opening to soul – to that place where the impending, but unpredictable fact of my mortality potentially creates a deeper connection with my own essence. I say "potentially" because in order to benefit from this opportunity, I will have to go through the opening, and experience the

✕✕

nexus of images waiting to be explored.

Sorting Through the Relevant Cyclical History For Resonant Memories

From an astro-logical perspective, this opening seems related to Mars square Mercury in my chart, so it makes sense to begin with this clue, and see what else I might be able to discover. But a simple astrological interpretation of Mars square Mercury won't do very much for me, unless I use my conscious understanding of the symbolism to take me into the realm of the unconscious, where the deepest metaphorical meanings of the symbolism are waiting to be discovered.

To move more deeply into this unknown territory, I might begin, as Assagioli would, with a conscious inventory. Rather than reconstruct an entire biography, I can assume that this experience is but one station of a cyclical process, and using my knowledge of astrology, track that process with greater precision. More specifically, I can track the cardinal points (conjunction, waxing square, opposition, and waning square) of the Mars-Mercury cycle, and in this way, flesh out an entire history of experience, which is symbolically related to this one thread I am trying to follow into soul space.

I did a bit of this in Chapter Twelve. Now that I have identified a feeling tone related to the thread I'm tracking and an appropriate metaphor, I also have an emotional attractor to take with me into soul space, around which additional relevant experiences will resonate. As I search through my memories of the cyclical history of Mars transits to my natal Mercury, I will intuitively feel a sense of resonance with those experiences that evoke a sense of vulnerability and anger in the midst of some prior state of relative well-being, and fit the metaphor of being broadsided. I call these experiences of recognition, *resonant memories*.

Obviously, it helps in doing this, to have a journal. Since I've been keeping one for 25 years, I have plenty of material to draw from, although I have found that whenever I take an intention into soul space – in this case, the intention to track the pattern related to being broadsided – memory tends to gravitate automatically to the relevant experiences, especially when I use the dates of the related cyclical history as a point of reference. If, for example, I know that from December 24-27, 1986, transiting Mars was square my natal Mercury, and I can remember the general time frame – say, in this case, as the Christmas holidays, then more specific memories related to the pattern being tracked will begin to emerge. For the sake of this illustration, I won't list every memory this exercise evokes, nor even every memory with which I resonate in relation to this thread I am tracking. Nor will every period of the cyclical history I am using as a template for my memory produce something of significance. Nonetheless, with just a few examples, the reader should be able to see where this is going, and how this approach to astrological symbolism opens up a fascinating portal into the more unconscious dimensions of soul space.

Looking for Reenactments of the Original Metaphorical Scene

First, let's start with my memories. Sometimes it happens that the pattern in question repeats itself literally, or at least, uses the same literal symbols to make its point. In April, 1997, for example, as transiting Mars was square my natal Mercury, a woman hit my truck in a parking lot of a store where I was shopping. This time, I was not in the vehicle, nor did I get angry afterwards, since there was little actual damage to my truck. The anger was played out, in this case, by those who saw the accident and urged me to call the police. In any event, here was another situation in which I was broadsided by forces beyond my control, using the same symbolic equation, Mars = moving vehicle. I did not see it coming, and I could only react after the fact. I choose this situation, out of all the memories connected to my Mars-Mercury story, because of these similarities, and the sense of resonance they evoked.

More important than the literal repetition of symbolic elements, is the metaphor of being broadsided, and the emotional and visceral response that this kind of experience tends to trigger in me. I was broadsided in this larger, metaphorical sense, for example, in February, 1998, as Mars was square my Mercury, when I got a call from my sister in Florida to inform me that my father had just been diagnosed with terminal brain cancer and was fading fast. I was broadsided in August, 1976, as Mars square my Mercury, when I tripped over a rock I didn't see on the beach in California, while playing football, and broke my elbow. I was broadsided in late spring/early summer of 1953, possibly while Mars was opposed my Mercury, as the neighborhood kids ganged up on me, and stuffed ashes in my mouth.

I don't remember the exact date of this last incident, since it happened when I was three-and-a-half years old, well before I started keeping a journal. The familiar progression of emotions from relative contentment and well-being to extreme vulnerability to anger (which emerged later over the course of the next 3-4 years) marks this incident as one that belongs to this particular track through soul space, regardless of the exactitude of the corresponding transits. In all three incidents, and others I have not mentioned, the experience is one of being broadsided by a twist of events I did not foresee, and perhaps could not have foreseen; moving through this familiar emotional pattern at various levels of intensity; and often undergoing major changes in my life, as a consequence of these triggering events. As I sift and sort through my memories of this Mars-Mercury cycle, I become more conscious of the pattern, and grow in my capacity to recognize its essence throughout its many permutations.

CHAPTER NINETEEN

◇◇

Moving Beyond Pattern Recognition
To Explore the Unconscious Dimensions of Soul Space

Now it is time to go back into the same cyclical history for additional clues that are less obvious to the conscious mind, but somehow still resonant within the context of this pattern. Just as Freud, Jung and many other psychologists have used dreams as a point of entry into soul space, so too can dreams correlated with a given cyclical history be used as a point of entry into a deeper understanding of the pattern. In June, 1998, as Mars was opposed by Mercury, I had a dream that an airplane lands in a clearing next to my house, crashing its wing through my roof. I tell the pilot, "You can't park here," but he ignores me, so we get into a fist fight. Meanwhile, people are starting to move in and out of my house, looting my possessions. Eventually the plane leaves, but not before my house is trashed. Although the particulars are unlike anything experienced in waking life, it should still be easy to see the familiar themes at work: I am broadsided by the plane crashing into my house; my emotional state shifts from relative tranquility to vulnerability to anger; and I am challenged by a crisis in communication. Here we have the same pattern, rendered in the dream language of the unconscious.

This dream reminds me of another I had in September, 1986. In this second dream, I am walking home in semi-darkness, being followed by, and sometimes following, a gray wolf with red eyes. I manage to elude him and get inside my house (which reminds me of the house in which I lived, right after I was born), when I notice that a door on the second floor is open. In trying to secure the door, I inadvertently knock down the entire wall, and can only surrender myself to the inevitable encounter with the wolf that I know is coming.

As it happened, this second dream took place on the opening night of an annual gathering in the New Mexico desert to celebrate the turning of the seasons. The gatherings are loosely structured around Native American ceremonies, and attended by people from all walks of life who find the ceremonies a meaningful way to mark the passage of soul time. Among these traditions is the practice of forming a more conscious relationship with one or more animal spirits, called *totems*, with which one feels a sense of resonance. Once such a relationship is identified, the qualities and ways of being associated with the animal often serve as a pivot point around which important life lessons are absorbed. In the Native American traditions in which totems are a central feature, individuals often adopt or are given names – called medicine names – that reflect the relationship with their totem animal, and perhaps with some quality in particular, possessed by the totem animal that they wish to more consciously embody. Choosing a totem animal and a medicine name is often not a rational decision, but rather a process of opening to a sense of resonance in a moment of synchronicity. My dream felt like such a moment and in its wake, I felt inspired to adopt the medicine name, Redwolf.

At the time, the name seemed to embody the masculine side of my nature, an energy I felt compelled to call on more intentionally, as an antidote to my vulnerability. I chose the color red, in part, because in my dream the wolf's eyes were red, but also because red is associated with Mars, traditionally understood to be the archetypal embodiment of masculine energy. Sitting at the apex of a major pattern in my chart, as pointed out in Chapter Eleven, Mars represents an area in my psyche I consider to be most in need of healing and integration. My adoption of this name in the wake of this dream was in part, a conscious nod to this ongoing healing process.

There was much more to the adoption of this name, however, than my conscious mind could assimilate, and by choosing it, I also opened a door to soul space that I did not previously know was there. This became evident to me immediately, for the morning after I had this dream and assumed this name, I felt great sadness. I went off into the desert and cried. My sadness stemmed in part from a lingering sense of vulnerability from the dream, but my vulnerability also had a deeper source that seemed to belong to the embodied world and everything in it. In that moment, I cried not just for myself, but also for all the suffering that filled the world. This sense of the world as a vulnerable place of suffering, and my emotional response to it, was the essence of the image that I was projecting into the world at that time, and accessing that essence was an intensely powerful experience.

At the time that I had this dream, transiting Mars was not at one of the cardinal points of its cycle with Mercury, though it was exactly *semi-sextile* (an aspect of 30 degrees) Mars and *quincunx* (an aspect of 150 degrees) Mercury, while four other planets (Sun, Moon, Jupiter and Uranus) were within *orb* (range) of an exact hard aspect to both natal planets. It was, in fact, the night of a full Moon, which itself was opposed natal Mars and square Mercury. Given this powerful convergence of astrological factors simultaneously triggering my natal Mars-Mercury square, I feel safe in assuming this experience was part of this same resonant pattern I have been discussing in relation to these planets.

Though astrological patterns can be helpful as a point of entry into the unconscious dimensions of a given resonant pattern, the farther in we go, the less rigidly attached to astrological correlates it behooves us to be. Traditional astrologers, in fact would not necessarily recognize the wolf as a symbol for Mars, nor does this particular symbolic equation necessarily mean anything in a generic sense. It does, however, evoke a powerful sense of resonance within the context of my subjective soul space, so for me, it is a fitting image of Mars through which I am able to project that aspect of my soul into the world.

I worked through a great deal of vulnerability with this medicine name over the course of the next ten years or so, as I asserted myself into situations that initially felt beyond my control. Instead of being a victim of circumstances, I learned to access a place of deeper strength and resourcefulness within my self – symbolized by the wolf, and to work with it, to create a space in which something positive could happen. One might say I was learning, in the context of this resonant pattern, to function more effectively in the face of situations that could potentially broadside me. I learned to think on my feet, respond to the unexpected in the moment, and flow with whatever was happening in the here and now. I still often call on this energy – which is now a part of me – whenever I feel I need the strength of my wolf totem in situations of great vulnerability.

Exploring the Interface Between Personal Soul Space And the Collective Unconscious

In making this association between Mars and the wolf, I was simply following my intuition – moving from a dream that actually occurred during the cyclical history I am tracking to a memory of a similar dream, which in retrospect, proved to be part of the same astrological pattern. This is typical of the way the intuitive mind moves through soul space, as it weaves together the image that represents the resonant pattern it is trying to identify and explore. The movement is instinctual, and though it may follow an identifiable astro-logical pattern, there is often no rhyme nor reason to it, other than the fact that this is the way my subjective soul space happens to be arranged.

What gives the arrangement its resonance is partly the uncanny fact that as I perceive the landscape of my soul space, I also tap into the collective unconscious in ways that amplify the spiritual vitality of my resonant memories. When I find my way into soul space, I also find my place within the whole. The tears of Redwolf are personal tears, but they are also more than that. Just as Mars is connected to Mercury in my chart, the image of the wolf is also connected to a richer, more synergistic web of images that speak to the possibility for a higher level of integration within the resonant soul space that the wolf occupies. Let's track this pattern a little farther to see more clearly how this works.

As I was moving back through the memories of my cyclical history, I was drawn to make note of a book I happened to be reading at the time of the accident in August, 2001. The book was entitled *The Mind of the Raven*. Why I felt compelled to note this particular book, I don't know. I just trusted the fact that I did, and then moved on with the cyclical history. Often this is the way we begin to flesh out aspects of the resonant pattern that are inaccessible to our conscious mind. If something intuitively seems important, it probably is, at least within the subjective context of soul space. In any case, it turns out that I had bought the book on a trip to Arizona, when Mars was opposed my Mercury, one half cycle before I actually started reading it. Now my sense of resonance is aroused, since buying and reading the book are part of the same astrological cycle. In light of this information, I feel fairly certain I have stumbled onto an important clue that will take me more deeply into the area of soul space associated with this pattern.

It was also interesting to me to note how I bought this book, for it was an unusual process. Normally, when I buy a book, I either know what I am looking for, or I find something while browsing in an area of general interest, but this book caught my attention somehow out of the corner of my eye, as I was about to leave the store. I could not see the title, nor even the cover when I was pulled to walk over to it, but once I picked it up, I knew I had to read it. So I bought it – one of the few impulse buys I have ever made. Though it would not have occurred to me at the time, I can see now how this kind of peripheral vision is, in its own way, an antidote to the vulnerability I experience when I am broadsided, albeit in a very different way than through the assertive focus of the wolf.

As I discovered when I read this book, which is subtitled *Investigations and Adventures with Wolf-Birds*, wolves and ravens have a long-standing symbiotic association. Ravens follow wolves, because at the end of the trail, they know they will likely find a fresh kill, of which they may be lucky enough to partake. But wolves also follow ravens, because ravens can see what wolves cannot - namely potential prey too far away to be seen on the ground. The ravens find food, and the wolves secure the food for themselves and the ravens, while keeping competitors away. Without the wolves, the ravens would often be last in the pecking order of those in line to eat, but without the ravens, the wolves would be less successful in finding food. It is a symbiotic arrangement between two radically different species, in which strengths and weaknesses complement and counterbalance each other.

As pointed out in Chapter Eleven, the astrological square between Mars and Mercury in my chart is also an arrangement between two radically different species, where the challenge is to find ways to counterbalance weaknesses and synergistically complement strengths in order to more effectively deal with whatever opportunities for learning and growth – such as the tendency to be broadsided – the square might attract in soul space. Could it be that this symbiotic relationship between wolves and ravens might somehow serve as a symbolic model for handling this challenge? Could it be that bringing peripheral vision together with an assertion of masculine energies associated with Mars would provide a more effective antidote to being broadsided than either resource could alone? This, at least, is what the symbolism suggests – something I did not consciously recognize, by the way, before I began this foray into the unconscious dimensions of soul space.

As it turns out, the raven has many attributes that are traditionally associated with Mercury - it is highly intelligent, curious, resourceful, socially gregarious, mischievous, and playful. Ravens are also mythologically associated with the archetype of the trickster, which is a cosmic function associated with Mercury. Does this mean that Mercury and the raven are somehow generically equivalent? No, not necessarily. Intellectually it is tempting to make this connection, although others far more deeply versed in these matters have cautioned against it (Kerényi 188-191). More important than a recognition of any intellectual rationale for this symbolic equivalency, however, is the fact that within the context of my own experience, these two symbols seem to converge. In fact, during the years that I was identified with the medicine name of Redwolf, I remember being "followed around" and taught valuable lessons by ravens.

Once while handing a raven feather to a woman whom I wanted to acknowledge for her contribution to a workshop I taught, a raven swooped down to buzz us, something I had never seen a raven do. Years later, when I was contemplating doing something foolish that would have taken me on a detour far removed from the path I had chosen through life, I walked out to my car to find the biggest raven I had ever seen, perched on the hood, cawing loudly with a sound that I could have sworn was laughter. During the first Gulf War, when I was camping in a remote spot in New Mexico, I had an important encounter with ravens, in the midst of one of those broadsided experiences of vulnerability related to this pattern I am exploring.

About that experience, I previously wrote ("Raven's Joy" 171):

> I was standing in a field of green,... the sky was ultra blue, and the serenity was tangible. Into the midst of this idyllic scene ripped two stealth bombers, burning through the entire expanse of sky in seconds. One of them flew directly overhead, its sleek robotic underbelly displayed in frightening detail. I went numb. A Pavlovian ripple of fear coursed up my spinal column. It was instinctual. I thought immediately of the war now going on in the Persian Gulf, and felt my fear smolder at its core with anger.

This will no doubt by now be familiar to the reader as yet another expression of the pattern we are exploring – complete with emotional transition from well-being to sudden vulnerability to anger. What happened next was the symbolic antidote to this habitual response offered by the ravens (172).

> In exactly the same formation the jets before them had taken, two ravens flew above me - one directly overhead, the other to its left at a distance. This in itself would not have caught my attention, as ravens fly overhead all the time in this place. But these ravens were not just flying. They were riding the thermals, wings outstretched, effortlessly. Most remarkable of all, as they caught an air current, these ravens would abandon themselves to it, roll onto their backs, and coo. I had never seen or heard anything like it.

In that moment, I knew that the ravens knew something that I didn't know, but that I was eager to learn. I was consciously beginning to integrate the energy of Redwolf, and was feeling less and less vulnerable as time went on. But there was still something missing, and in that moment, I felt certain that the raven provided the symbolic key to that missing piece, though I didn't understand what that piece was until just now. Ravens and wolves are inextricably connected to one another – in life, and in the same resonant soul space in which my Mars-Mercury square operates. Wolf provides the courage, the focused intention, the strength and the vigilance; raven provides the peripheral vision necessary to keep the intensity of this concentrated form of masculine energy from becoming a liability.

Wolves hunt, while ravens play. When wolves and ravens run together, the hunt turns playful, and the play becomes productive. If I happen to be broadsided in the midst of a focus that gets derailed, my inner raven offers me the opportunity to ride the thermals, roll on my back and coo. This, of course, is in stark contrast to my habitual pattern of getting angry, and often a more effective strategy for dealing with the situation. Then when I've been on my back too long and my focus begins to unravel, my inner wolf helps me to pull it back together. Or put in more basic sensory terms, when Mars gets too hot, heavy, and deep, the raven can teach me how to keep my cool, lighten up, and rise high above the intensity. When Mercury starts to flutter, agitate or disorient me, my wolf can sharpen my focus, pierce to the heart of the matter, or bring my process down to a more palpable level.

Out of this synergistic combination of energies comes a perspective and a combination of resources that are otherwise not possible. How I incorporate this understanding in the living of my life is an ongoing challenge that does not end with a simple moment of understanding. But the understanding itself is a direct consequence of my foray into the unconscious dimension of soul space, using the symbolism of my chart as a point of entry. The understanding itself is less important than this inner connection with the energy of wolf-birds and raven-trackers, which will continue to infuse my soul space to the extent that I allow it to, and provide me with options that I would not otherwise have.

Following the Confluence of Astropoetic Images To a More Intimate Identification With Spirit

But the trail does not end with this discovery of the association between wolves and ravens, or even the relationship between this natural symbiosis and my Mars-Mercury square, for there are additional dimensions of this puzzle yet to be unraveled. Wolves and ravens, for example, come together in the mythology surrounding the Teutonic god, Odin, who was often accompanied by both species – a raven on each shoulder and a wolf by each side. As pointed out by Kveldulf Gundarsson, "The name Odhinn means 'fury' or 'inspiration' and is related to the modern German *wuetend* and archaic English *wood*, both of which carry a meaning of 'furious,' 'mad,' and 'wild.' His name has been suggested to be roughly cognate to that of Vata, Lord of the Winds, in the Rig Veda" (223).

Fury, of course, can be associated with Mars, while Mercury is associated with the element of air, or wind – and Spirit. Fury comes from the body; it is a physiological response to danger, chaos, forces beyond control. Wind comes from Spirit, and is the force that animates the body, giving birth to the soul. All of this is apparently implicated in the relationship between my Mercury and my Mars, providing a fertile nexus of images that are at once personal and universal, in which I can find a meaningful reflection of my soul space. From this reflection, I can learn – not just how to handle situations in which I might potentially be broadsided, although that is one important practical application, but also something about myself – who I am as a soul, and what it is that I have come here to do.

Within the area of soul space associated with my Mars-Mercury square, I am in some way which cannot be entirely articulated, in resonance with the god, Odin – who incidentally, somewhere down the line was also likely the god of my German ancestors. It can sound somewhat contrived and presumptuous to make a statement like this, and in making it, I certainly don't mean to imply that I am a member of some spiritual elite. Quite the contrary, we all have similar inner connections waiting to be discovered and more consciously assimilated. When I follow my Mars-Mercury trail through soul space, I land on Odin's doorstep. Your trails will likely take you to other gods or goddesses. But we are all born of Spirit, and our awareness of the resonant connections to whatever gods and goddesses inhabit our respective soul spaces gives the soul's quest a certain numinous intensity and a deeper spiritual context it did not have before.

This is not a rational process; it does not yield an objective truth that can be applied to anyone else; it does not describe a causal relationship between inner experience and anything in the outer world. It is not a truth that a scientist, a scientifically-oriented psychologist, nor even a traditional astrologer, would necessarily recognize as an orthodox interpretation of my experience. In some circles, it might even be considered hallucinatory or delusional. Following these threads of symbolic meaning through my Mars-Mercury story does, however, enrich my understanding of the subjective truth of my being. And hopefully, it also demonstrates how astrological symbolism can be used in an empirical way to bridge the gap between conscious knowing and the unknown opportunities for learning and growth to be found in soul space.

Making a Distinction
Between Traditional Astrology and Astropoetics

In closing, I would like to reiterate – to lay readers and practicing astrologers alike

– what has most likely become obvious by now: the approach to astrology that I have demonstrated in this chapter and throughout this book differs, at times radically, from traditional astrological practice in several important ways. Just as the soul moving through Inanna's seven gates must necessarily be utterly transformed by this process, so too must the practice of astrology undergo a radical transformation to be useful to the soul. I have outlined the necessary changes throughout this book, and discussed them in a more concentrated way in Part Four, but they are worth summarizing here.

While traditional astrology understands the birthchart to be a signature of fate, an astropoetic approach to astrology understands fate to be but an elaborate opportunity for evolution of consciousness within the embodied state. This opportunity is a learning process that transcends traditional astrological judgments about good and bad placements, benefic and malefic signatures, and the relative ease or difficulty of birthcharts considered in their entirety. Astropoetics assumes that each chart is an expression of Creative Intelligence at work, delineating the optimum path to conscious embodiment for the soul to which it belongs.

While traditional astrology is largely a matter of rationally decoding signs that have become shorthand notation for known qualities, astropoetics is oriented more toward the discovery of the sensory and emotional correlates to symbols, and of the images that embody these correlates. The process is by nature a journey into the unknown, and the outcome is not something that can be predetermined according to standardized definitions for astrological symbols. Traditional astrology aims at an objective understanding of the symbolism; astropoetics assumes that the symbolism must be referenced to both an astrological context (the birthchart considered as a whole) and an intimately subjective life context that is unique to the individual soul, before it can mean anything at all.

To the extent that traditional astrology strives to be scientific, it will adopt science's insistence on causal explanations for its interpretations, even if the language that it uses emphasizes individual choice. Astrologers that are sensitive to this issue might say as Paracelsus did, for example, that "the stars incline; they do not compel" (qtd. in Tillet). Actually the stars do nothing but provide an endlessly intriguing mirror to the idiosyncratic organization of soul space. Instead of attempting to articulate the causal relationship between heaven and earth, however euphemistically it might be phrased, astropoetics assumes instead that everything astrological is a reflection of an interconnected web of resonant relationships, which reflect back to the individual soul who it is and where it belongs within the Greater Whole of which it is part. These relationships are not causal in nature, but expressions of natural metaphorical logic. The entire web of relationships is encompassed astro-logically by the interconnected nature of the birthchart, which reflects the coherent internal logic of subjective soul space. Each resonant relationship evolves cyclically through soul time, reflected astrologically in the various cycles of planets that are connected by aspect in soul space. While traditional astrology tends to understand the birthchart as a static description of personality undergoing a series of discrete events, astropoetics views it instead as descriptive of a process that deepens and transmutes in cyclical time as increasing awareness is brought to the experience of embodiment it describes.

Lastly, while traditional astrology – at least that which is psychologically oriented – strives toward an understanding of the human predicament and an alleviation of suffering through enlightened perspective, astropoetics aims a bit higher. Astropoetics strives toward an understanding of how the human predicament is thoroughly infused by the presence of Spirit. This is true, especially where the human predicament is most difficult, most painful, most intensely vulnerable, and where the seemingly intractable core issues that mark the embodied life are encountered. Without attempting to romanticize or otherwise dismiss the suffering inherent in such experiences, astropoetics aims toward a vision broad and deep enough to encompass them as the portals to a deeper, more conscious and more creative embodiment of Spirit that they ultimately are.

While the difference between astrology and astropoetics is largely a matter of attitude, there are also specific differences in technique and approach that are important. Some of these I have outlined in this book, but my primary goal here has been to show what an astropoetic language of soul might look like in general, once it has shed the conceptual baggage absorbed by osmosis from religion, philosophy, science, psychology and its own tradition. In my next book, I will explore the astropoetic process itself in much greater detail. Meanwhile, it has been my pleasure to demonstrate how opening a passage through Inanna's seven gates can provide a point of entry into the mysterious heart of this endlessly fascinating life, where the soul vibrates in living embodiment of Spirit. Astropoetics – or astrology transmuted by its passage through these same seven gates – can be an intriguing portal through which this sacred experience of embodiment comes into focus and can be translated into the poetry of everyday life.

EPILOGUE

Epilogue

Like every other budding young astrologer, I began my study of astrology voraciously reading all the best books, attending all the right conferences, and sitting at the lotus feet of anyone with a reasonable claim to mastery. Yet, although there were a number of good professional astrologers out there, some of whom also wrote quite well, and/or taught from a place of deep personal wisdom, I soon came to the conclusion that getting to the heart of what astrology had to offer could not be accomplished by reading books, or attending conferences, or feeding at the trough of someone else's understanding. Instead, it slowly dawned on me, I would have to discover or develop my own relationship to the symbolism, one that was rooted in my own experience and that provided reliable access to my own internal wisdom.

It was then that I began to suspect that astrology, in its essence, was actually a rather solitary and sometimes frightening pursuit. Sure, everyone likes to feel as though they belong to a community of peers, and for a long time, having a comprehensive library at my elbow lent a certain amount of intellectual security to my quest. But ultimately, I began to realize that the practice of astrology is not about gathering and disseminating information. It is about standing at the very edge of what is known, and then facing the unknown with an open mind and heart. This is not necessarily an easy, or comfortable thing to do.

The symbols my conscious mind so desperately hoped would eventually become known and familiar friends suddenly revealed their true identity as thresholds to a realm no one had yet explored, even though thousands had looked through the same portal before. It was a realm, in fact, that no one else could explore but me, because what I was really asking - although I did not know it then - were the questions about soul that led to the writing of this book. What I realized in that moment was that even though I might stand shoulder to shoulder with hundreds of other astrologers, each facing a similar opening, once I had stepped over to the other side, I would be alone. I knew what I would find there would be a discovery and a revelation, and I could not possibly know before stepping across the threshold, exactly what I would find. Once I knew of the existence of this secret passageway, I could no more refrain from going back and forth through it than I could taking my next breath, but I also knew that moving through the door would change everything. And it has.

My life since then has been a process of mustering my courage and stepping through that gateway, not once, but again and again and again. Each astrological consultation that I have done, each lesson I have prepared for a student, each time I have sat before my own chart, faced with some new crisis or personal dilemma, the same gaping abyss has stared

◇◇

me in the face. And the same task has called me forward. Each time I have passed through this mysterious opening has been the first.

I have not always been disengaged enough from my conscious mind to enter the realm of soul, but each time I have, I have been amazed, energized, and empowered. Each time, what I have found there has been unexpected and new. The answers that come back to me from the other side are never what my conscious mind thinks they ought to be. The symbolism has proven itself to have many more faces than could ever be revealed in all the books that have ever been written. To enter the inner world at all, I have had to put my books aside, let go of everything I thought I knew, and approach the symbolism of the birthchart before me as though it were a Great Mystery worthy of great reverence.

It is human nature to want to believe that once we pass through the door to a deeper understanding of the soul, by whatever means - astrological or otherwise - we will be home. That is to say, we want to believe that the journey we are each somewhere in the middle of, has a final destination, and that when we arrive there, we will have definitive answers to the riddle of our existence. Who are we and why are we here? Inquiring minds want to know, and the quest for answers has brought us to the end of yet another book where we hoped to find them. But here is another door before us, and life is still a relatively inscrutable mystery.

Yesterday, as I was struggling with an earlier version of this epilogue, which was turning into a second book, and feeling stuck with it, an early Christmas present arrived in the mail from my sister. Opening the box, I found the most amazing gift - one that I could never have imagined my sister, or anyone else for that matter, sending me. In the box was a life-like, full-size replica of a raven, made out of plastic and feathers, but somehow with a presence that was tangible and real. If you have read this far, you will, of course, recognize the raven as an important denizen of my personal soul space. As discussed in Chapter Nineteen, I associate the raven with Mercury, which traditionally governs the art of communication, and of writing. In many cultures, Mercury also assumes the role of psychopomp, leading souls from life into the realm of death. This raven, I could not help but intuit, had apparently arrived just in time to suggest it was time to wrap this writing project up.

I wish I could say that the message was an instantaneous revelation to me, but the truth is, I am only now just getting it as I write it down for you. For I woke up this morning, still feeling stuck, and sat down to write as I have on many such mornings throughout this past year. The difference was - this morning, there was a raven sitting on top of my bookshelf, with a message that my conscious mind was not expecting. Communing silently with the messenger, I decided to scrap what I was writing, and start again from scratch. Within a few hours, I had the epilogue you are reading now, and the rough draft of this book was finished. You can call it a meaningless coincidence, but for me, it was an astropoetic moment – a confirmation that the art of mapping planetary energies to the extraordinary images that somehow manage to find their way into our resonant soul space at significant moments is an idea worth exploring with passion.

I sincerely believe that if we develop the principles of astropoetics as the basis for a non-dogmatic language of soul, we will be able to bring the mystery closer to us - so that we might glimpse a few of its many faces, hear more clearly the sweet siren song it is singing to us, and feel the timeless beating of its omnipresent heart. In fact, I intend to pursue this beckoning promise myself in a series of subsequent books outlining the theory and practice of astropoetics in much greater detail. But despite the delightfully unexpected moments of synchronicity and revelation this way of looking at the soul is capable of producing, I would be misleading you if I told you that astropoetics will answer these eternal questions – posed by every religious teacher, philosopher, scientist and astrologer mentioned in this book – once and for all. It will not.

One reason that religion and science have been the two dominant influences shaping the dialogue about soul for the past three millennia is because they offer the illusion of certainty. Certainty is a popular concept, a perennial best-seller, especially in times like these when everything we have taken for granted for so long suddenly seems up for grabs. I am here to tell you there is no such thing. The God of religion, spoken of as Spirit in this book, is not a final destination, but an evolving mirror into which we project our highest sense of what is possible. But what is impossible now will be routine tomorrow, and who knows what God will look like then? For every answer science has given us, it has created a host of new questions – most of which we did not even have the vocabulary to ask a few short centuries ago. Who knows what questions science will be asking tomorrow, when it empties its in-basket of the questions that seem to have no answers today?

The quest does not end with this or that answer to this or that question. It goes on – as it always has and always will – in this present moment, the only moment there is, or ever can be. And even as you close the last door and put out all the lights, I venture to guess that there will be another door somewhere, for You to enter – if you choose. What lies beyond that door will be just as much a question with no answers as the ones you struggle with today. Religious teachers, philosophers, scientists, traditional astrologers and astropoets may all offer you answers, and some of these – hopefully many of them – will prove helpful. The best and most honest among them all will offer you tools with which you can approach the questions yourself. If and when they offer you certainty, however, I recommend you run the other way.

For beyond the answers will be more questions, and beyond the questions will be the need for new, more penetrating ways of approaching them. And in the end, no one out there will have answers for you, but you. No matter which belief system you subscribe to, no matter which avenue of approach makes sense to you, no matter how many books you read, or workshops you attend, or therapy sessions or readings or transformational experiences you have, in the end, you – the soul that you are – will be face to face with the Great Mystery. This will be true for you as long as You exist. The Final Door, if there is a final door, is one that you will have to go through alone. In that moment, none of the religions, philosophies, scientific truths, or astro-logical discoveries that have comforted you on this side of that door will mean anything. If anyone tells you differently, they are either trying to sell you something, or they are still on the comfortable side of Inanna's seven gates.

At the outset of the soul's journey, I think it is important to acknowledge that there may never be a final moment in which the larger picture is completely clear. Ultimately, despite my own relentless quest and dedicated work as an astropoet, helping others to make sense of their lives, I still believe that Life is a Great Mystery. In fact, I believe this more fervently than I did 30-plus years ago when I started my study of astrology, and the raven on my bookshelf agrees. I also believe that the meaning and purpose of any life is to gradually circle in on the meaning and purpose of Life, knowing in advance, that we may never actually arrive at a definitive understanding. The Mystery forever remains a mystery, and we forever remain travelers on the road into the heart of the Unknown. But that is okay. I have made my peace with the Unknown, even if I am not always comfortable when face to face with it.

I also believe that it is in staying connected to the ultimately inscrutable wonder of it all, and being brave enough to actually take the impossible journey into the heart of the Unknown, each of us in our own way, that we become most alive, and most attuned to our purpose in this life. To the extent that you are on the road, meaning reveals itself along the way, and your life will become meaning-full. The meaning and purpose of a life in progress does not reveal itself all at once, nor will it stand still for your attempts to grab hold of it. There are secrets within secrets within secrets to be unveiled, and regardless of where you start, the task will involve entering more deeply into each one as you come to it, and integrating the surprises it contains. Once you do that, the you that asks the next question will not be the you that asked the last one. Your deepest truths will change as the one who seeks answers changes, and tomorrow what you think is true today will only prove to be the horizon toward which you were moving yesterday.

Within the context of this perspective, to attempt to find meaning in the ephemeral snapshot we call a birthchart might seem an exercise in absurdity. Yet, as a student once suggested, "the part of us that loves mystery is only slightly larger than the part of us that needs clarity," and so we persist in attempting to make sense of, or feel our way into, that which cannot be explained, using any language that holds forth the promise of revelation. Some flock to science, others to religion. I prefer astrology, because astrology at its best is one that honors the Great Mystery anew as it reveals itself through each living being whose birth has been marked by time. The astrology of which I speak, of course, is the one I have been speaking of in this book – an astropoetry of the soul that has relinquished the illusion of certainty, and stands willing to give up everything it thinks it knows for a glimpse into the mystery that connects heaven to earth, Spirit to body, soul to soul.

Such an astrology is a pathway to knowledge that must constantly renew itself with each civilization it informs, each generation that rediscovers it, and each individual astrologer that is drawn to contemplate its bottomless symbols. An astrology that can be captured within some dogmatic system may bloom for a season, and entertain a few shallow minds with its fleeting, clever beauty. By contrast, an astrology that stands perpetually trembling on the threshold through which the Great Mystery reveals itself is one that is perennial, despite the endless comings and goings of its detractors.

Why is it, I must continue to ask myself, that some form of astrology continues to survive paradigm shift after paradigm shift, when other systems come and go? When the Earth was flat, there was astrology; when the Earth suddenly became round, there was also astrology. When the Sun revolved around the Earth, there was astrology; when the Earth began revolving around the Sun, there was still astrology. When philosopher-scientists believed there were only seven planets, there was astrology; now that we have infinitely greater knowledge of the heavens, including the existence of black holes, quasars, pulsars and other astronomical realities no one dared dream of a short time ago, there will continue to be astrology.

Even were we to scrap everything that we know or think we know about astrology and begin again, the basic premise on which any astrological system is based – namely that each soul is part of a larger universe with which it has a meaningful connection – would still be valid, and would reassert itself. The desire to explore this relationship between heaven and earth would appear to be hard-wired into the driving mechanism of the human soul. Scorned though it is, it would appear that the impulse toward astrology – toward articulating the Mystery through an exploration of the exquisite network of interconnections within the resonant space occupied by the living soul – is as basic to our nature as the religious impulse toward God or the scientific impulse toward objective truth.

Despite the centuries of effort by those who would wish it away or banish it, the astrological premise is universal in its appeal, and implicit in life upon a material planet formed by cosmic forces. As we make our way through this material realm, we cannot help but look for signs and signals capable of taking us back to our origin; we cannot help but believe those signs and signals are everywhere, and that everything that happens within the earthly realm arises from and mirrors a cosmic process unfolding. Astrology, in its most essential urge, is the longing to understand this process and its mirror image upon the Earth, despite the fact that such a connection may not ultimately be knowable in any lasting or definitive way.

Astrology is ultimately not just about making sense of life, although at its best, it is that. It is also about learning to see with the kind of peripheral vision that allows the shimmering, invisible Essence at the heart of the embodied life to coalesce into a pattern, release another aha! experience into the cerebral cortex, and then disperse for another round of unknowing. It seems that when these patterns do come together, the experience we have is somehow astro-logical. That is to say, in the moment of coalescence, the recognizable patterns that form on planet Earth are echoed by recognizable patterns in the sky. Perhaps we are all just projecting collective fantasies here, responding to a kind of cosmic Rorschach Test, but if the projections trigger a deeper knowing of the Self, a recognition of who we are as souls embarked upon a mysterious journey, then what should it matter that tomorrow these patterns will be gone. It is the recognition of a Self with endless faces we are after, and in the context of this quest, astrology becomes the art of squeezing recognition out of coalescing patterns in the sky.

How we go about doing this, and the understanding that we ultimately attain, will change from era to era, from culture to culture, and from individual to individual, but I cannot conceive of a time or place where there will not – in one way, shape, or form – be this quest for soul-recognition and understanding. Beyond the rise and fall of civilizations; beyond relentless attempts to discredit and suppress astrology by the powers that be, both religious and scientific; beyond revolution after revolution in our quest for understanding of life's mysteries; beyond even the inevitable choking of its own vitality with dogma, astrology will play its part in our collective attempt to penetrate the Great Mystery that enfolds us, because at heart, that attempt is astro-logical in nature and origin.

Or as astropoet Rilke observed:

> Again, again, even if we know the countryside of love,
> and the tiny churchyard with its names mourning,
> and the chasm, more and more silent, terrifying, into which
>   the others
> dropped; we walk out together anyway
> beneath the ancient trees, we lie down again,
> again, among the flowers, and face the sky.

Introduction to Astropoetics
The Annual Workshop

For those who wish a more intensive introduction to astropoetics, there will be an extended weekend workshop held each fall at Phoenix Ranch, a retreat center in the beautiful Ozark mountains. Beyond exposure to more in-depth theory, each participant will also have the opportunity to apply the principles of astropoetics to their own life process with the collective wisdom of the group as a support and resource. Participation in the workshop will be purposely limited to create a more intimate atmosphere for sharing. Additional workshops will be scheduled throughout the year wherever sufficient interest warrants, and a correspondence course will be available for those who wish to continue their studies and soul-exploration beyond the workshop experience.

More detailed information and a current workshop schedule can be found at:

www.astropoetics.com.

WORKS CITED

Works Cited

Ali, Ahmed, Trans. <u>Sacred Texts: The Qur'an</u>. New York: Quality Paperback Book Club, 1993.

Allport, Gordon. Preface. <u>Man's Search for Meaning</u>. By Victor E. Frankl. New York: Pocket, 1963.

<u>The American Heritage Dictionary</u>. 2nd College Ed. Boston: Houghton Mifflin, 1991.

Ariès, Philippe. <u>The Hour of Our Death</u>. New York: Oxford UP, 1981.

Aristotle. "On the Soul." <u>The Philosophy Source: Classic Readings</u>. CD-ROM Version 3.0. Ed. Daniel Kolak. Wadsworth, 2004.

Arroyo, Stephen. <u>Astrology, Karma & Transformation: The Inner Dimensions of the Birthchart</u>. Reno, NV: CRCS Pubns, 1978.

<u>Association of Transpersonal Psychology Homepage</u>. 17 June 2003. <http://www.atpweb.org>.

<u>Association of Transpersonal Psychology Mission Statement</u>. 17 June 2003. <http://www.atpweb.org/mission.html>.

Augustine. <u>Confessions</u>. Trans. R. S. Pine-Coffin. Middlesex, England: Penguin 1961.

"Augustine." <u>Encyclopedia Britannica</u>. 15th ed. Vol. 14. Chicago: Encyclopedia Britannica, 1997.

Bogart, Greg. <u>Astrology and Meditation: The Fearless Contemplation of Change</u>. Bournemouth, England: The Wessex Astrologer, Ltd., 2002.

Bok, Bart Jan and Lawrence E. Jerome. <u>Objections to Astrology</u>. Amherst, NY: Prometheus Books, 1976.

Burtt, E. A. <u>The Metaphysical Foundations of Modern Science</u>. Atlantic Highlands, NJ: Humanities P, 1952.

Campbell, Joseph. <u>The Masks of God: Primitive Mythology</u>. New York: Penguin, 1959.

——, <u>The Masks of God: Oriental Mythology</u>. New York: Penguin, 1962.

Capra, Fritjof. <u>The Tao of Physics: An Exploration of the Parallels Between Modern Physics and Eastern Mysticism</u>. 4th Ed. Boston: Shambala, 2000.

Carey, Ken. <u>Starseed, the Third Millennium: Living in the Posthistoric World</u>. New York: Harper, 1991.

Castenada, Carlos. <u>A Separate Reality: Further Conversations With Don Juan</u>. New York: Simon & Schuster, 1971.

——. <u>The Teachings of Don Juan: A Yaqui Way of Knowledge</u>. New York: Simon & Schuster, 1973.

Chodron, Pema. <u>Start Where You Are: A Guide to Compassionate Living</u>. Boston: Shambala, 1994.

Christian, James. <u>The Wisdom Seekers: Great Philosophers of the Western World</u>. Vols. 1-2. US: Thomson Learning, 2002.

Covey, Stephen R. <u>The 7 Habits of Highly Effective People: Powerful Lessons in Personal Change</u>. New York; Simon & Schuster, 1989.

Craig, Gregory, ed. "Morphological Analytics for Inflected Greek Words." The Perseus Digital Library, Tufts University. 5 January 2002. <http://www.perseus.tufts.edu/cgi-bin/morphindex?/lang-greek>

Cunningham, Donna. <u>An Astrological Guide to Self-Awareness</u>. Sebastopol, CA: CRCS Pubs., 1978.

Dass, Ram. <u>Be Here Now</u>. San Cristobal, NM: Lama Foundation, 1971.

——. <u>Grist For the Mill</u>. Santa Cruz, CA: Unity Press, 1977.

Dawkins, Richard. <u>The Selfish Gene</u>. New York: Oxford UP, 1990.

Dean, Geoffrey and Arthur Mather. <u>Recent Advances in Natal Astrology: A Critical Review 1900-1976</u>. Kent, England: Astrological Ass., 1977.

"Death," <u>Encyclopedia Britannica</u>, 15th ed. Vol. 16. Chicago: Encyclopedia Britannica, 1997.

de Chardin, Pierre Teilhard. <u>The Heart of Matter</u>. San Diego: Harcourt, Brace Jovanovich, 1976.

Descartes, René. "Meditations on First Philosophy". Ed. Louis P. Pojman. <u>Classics of Philosophy</u>. 2nd ed. New York: Oxford UP, 2003, 497-524.

——. "Passions of the Soul". <u>The Descartes Web Project</u>. Ed, Patricia Easton. Claremont Graduate U, Dept. of Philosophy. 30 August 2003. <http://www.cgu.edu/hum/phi/descartes/Passions_Part_Two.html>.

Dobyns, Zipporah Pottenger. <u>Finding the Person in the Horoscope</u>. Los Angeles: T.I.A. Pubs., 1973.

"Doctrines and Dogmas, Religious." <u>Encyclopedia Britannica</u>, 15th ed. Vol. 17. Chicago: Encyclopedia Britannica, 1997.

Eliade, Mircea, ed. "Breath and Breathing." <u>Encyclopedia of Religion</u>. Vol. 2. New York: Macmillan, 1987.

——. "Hades," <u>Encyclopedia of Religion</u>, Vol. 6. New York: MacMillan, 1987.

——. <u>A History of Religious Ideas: Volume 1 - From the Stone Age to the Eleusinian Mysteries</u>. London: U of Chicago P, 1978.

——. <u>A History of Religious Ideas: Volume 2 - From Gautama Buddha to the Triumph of Christianity</u>. London: U of Chicago P, 1982.

——. <u>Shamanism: Archaic Techniques of Ecstasy</u>. Bolligen Series 76, New York: Pantheon, 1964.

Epicurus. "Letter to Menoeceus." Pojman, Louis P. <u>Classics of Philosophy</u>. 2nd ed. New York: Oxford UP, 2003, 358-360.

Espenak, Fred. "Solar Eclipses of Historical Interest." NASA/Goddard Space Flight Center Eclipse Page. 20 February 2002. <sunearth.gstc.nasa.gov/eclipse/SEhistory/SEhistory.html>

<u>The Essene Gospel of Peace - Book Two: The Unknown Books of the Essenes</u>. Trans. Edmond Bordeuax Szekely. Cartago, Costa Rica: International Biogenic Society, 1978.

"European Religions, Ancient." <u>Encyclopedia Britannica</u>. 15th ed. Vol. 18. Chicago: Encyclopedia Britannica, 1997.

Ficino, Marsilio. <u>Meditations on the Soul: Selected Letters</u>. Rochester, VT: Inner Traditions International, 1996.

Fieser, James. <u>A Historical Introduction to Philosophy</u>. New York: Oxford UP, 2002.

Forrest, Steven. <u>The Inner Sky: How to Make Wiser Choices for a More Fulfilling Life</u>. San Diego: ACS Pubs., 1988.

——. <u>Measuring the Night: Evolutionary Astrology and the Keys to the Soul</u>. Vol. 1. Chapel Hill, NC: Seven Paws Press, 2000.

Fox, Matthew. <u>The Coming of the Cosmic Christ</u>. San Francisco: Harper & Row, 1988.

Fox, Matthew and Rupert Sheldrake. <u>Natural Grace: Dialogues on Creation, Darkness, and the Soul in Spirituality and Science</u>. New York: Doubleday, 1996.

Gauquelin, Michel. <u>Birthtimes: A Scientific Investigation of the Secrets of Astrology</u>. New York: Hill and Wang, 1983.

Gibson, James J. <u>The Ecological Approach to Visual Perception</u>. Boston: Houghton Mifflin, 1979.

Greene, Liz. The Astrology of Fate. York Beach, ME: Samuel Weiser, 1984.

Griffith, Ralph T.H., Trans. Sacred Writings: The Rig Veda. New York: Quality Paperback Book Club, 1992.

Grof, Stanislav. The Adventure of Self-Discovery: Dimensions of Consciousness and New Perspectives in Psychotherapy and Inner Exploration. Albany, NY: State U of New York P, 1988.

——. Beyond the Brain: Birth, Death, and Transcendence in Psychotherapy. Albany: State U of New York P, 1985.

Grossinger, Richard. The Night Sky: The Science and Anthropology of the Stars and Planets. San Francisco: Sierra Club, 1981.

Gundarsson, Kveldulf. Teutonic Magic: The Magical & Spiritual Practices of the Germanic Peoples, St. Paul, MN: Llewellyn, 1990.

Hafiz. "My Brilliant Image." I Heard God Laughing: Renderings of Hafiz. Trans. Daniel Ladinsky. Oakland, CA; Dharma Printing Company, 1996. 13.

Hand, Robert. Planets in Transit: Life Cycles For Living. Rockport, MA: Para Research, 1976.

——. Planets in Youth: Patterns of Early Development. Rockport, MA: Para Research, 1977.

Harding, M. Esther. Women's Mysteries: Ancient and Modern. San Francisco: Harper Colophon, 1971.

Harner, Michael. The Way of the Shaman. New York: Bantam Books, 1980.

Harris, Stephen L. Classical Mythology: Images and insights. 3rd ed. Mountain View, CA: Mayfield, 2001.

Henderson, Joseph L. Thresholds of Initiation. Middletown, CT: Wesleyan UP, 1967.

Herrnstein, Richard J. and Edward G. Boring, eds. A Source Book in the History of Psychology. Cambridge, MA: Harvard UP, 1965.

Hillman, James. Revisioning Psychology. New York: HarperCollins, 1975.

Hobson, J. Allan. Consciousness. New York: Scientific American Library, 1999.

Horgan, John. "Quantum Philosophy." 28 May 2003.
<http://www.fortunecity.com/emachines/e11/86/qphil.html>

Houston, Jean. The Possible Human: A Course in Enhancing Your Physical, Mental and Creative Abilities. Los Angeles: J. P. Tarcher, 1982.

Hunt, Morton. <u>The Story of Psychology</u>. New York: Doubleday, 1993.

Huxley, Aldous. <u>Brave New World</u>. Rev. ed. New York: Harper Perennial, 1998.

——. <u>The Doors of Perception</u>. New York: Harper, 1954.

James, William. "On the function of consciousness." <u>A Source Book in the History of Psychology</u>. Eds. Richard J. Herrnstein and Edward G. Boring. Cambridge, MA: Harvard UP, 1966. 483-495.

Jenkins, John Major. "The How and Why of the Mayan End Date in 2012 A.D." <u>The Mountain Astrologer</u> December, 1994/January, 1995, p 52-57+.

John of the Cross. "The Spiritual Canticle." <u>The Collected Works of St. John of the Cross</u>. Trans. Kieran Kavanaugh and Otilio Rodriguez. Washington, D.C.: ICS Pubns, 1979.

Johnson, Robert A. <u>Inner Work: Using Dreams and Active Imagination for Personal Growth</u>. New York: HarperSanFrancisco, 1986.

Jones, Alexander, ed. <u>The Jerusalem Bible: Reader's Edition</u>. New York: Doubleday, 1968.

"Judaism," <u>Encyclopedia Britannica</u>. 15th ed. Vol. 22. Chicago: Encyclopedia Britannica, 1997.

Jung, Carl. <u>The Archetypes and the Collective Unconscious</u>. Trans. R. F. C. Hull. Bolligen Series XX. Princeton, NJ: Princeton UP, 1959.

——. <u>Memories, Dreams and Reflections</u>. Ed. Aniela Jaffé. Trans. Richard and Clara Winston. New York, Random House, 1961.

——. <u>Symbols of Transformation</u>. Trans. R. F. C. Hull. Bolligen Series XX. Princeton, NJ: Princeton UP, 1956.

Jung, Emma. <u>Animus and Anima</u>. Dallas: Spring, 1957.

Kabir. "The Hopeful Spiritual Athlete." <u>The Rag and Bone Shop of the Heart</u>. Ed. Robert Bly, James Hillman and Michael Meade. New York: Harper Perennial, 1993. 281.

Kalweit, Holger. <u>Dreamtime & Inner Space</u>. Boston: Shambala, 1984.

Kerényi, Karl. Commentary: "The Trickster in Relation to Greek Mythology." <u>The Trickster: A Study in American Indian Mythology</u>. By Paul Radin. New York: Schocken, 1956.

Keyes, Ken Jr. "The Hundredth Monkey." Testament. New Consciousness Research Organization. 13 May 2003
<http://www.testament.org/testament/100thmonkey.html>

Kinsley, David. <u>Ecology and Religion: Ecological Spirituality in Cross-Cultural Perspective</u>. Englewood Cliffs, NJ: Prentice Hall, 1995.

Kluter, Benjamin. "Ten of Swords." Online posting. October 6, 2002, Previous Emailletters: International Society of Astrological Research. 23 October 2002. http://www.isar. demon.nl/page021.htm#Anchor199

Krupp, E. C. <u>Skywatchers, Shamans, and Kings: Astronomy and the Archaeology of Power</u>. New York: John Wiley and Son, 1997.

Kuhn, Thomas S. <u>The Structure of Scientific Revolutions</u>. 2nd Ed. Enlarged. Chicago: U of Chicago P, 1970.

Laing, R. D. <u>The Politics of Experience</u>, Middlesex, England: Penguin, 1967.

Landwehr, Joe. "The Clockwise Interpretation of Houses." <u>The Mountain Astrologer</u>. 93: (October/November, 2000). 90-98+.

——. "The Raven's Joy," <u>Full Moon Meditations: Musings on the Journey Toward Godbeing</u>. Mountain View, MO: The Light of the Forest Primeval, 1993.

Lao Tzu. <u>Tao Te Ching</u>. Trans. Gis-fu Feng and Jane English. New York: Vintage Books, 1972.

——. <u>Tao Te Ching</u>. Trans. D.C. Lau. Middlesex, England: Penguin, 1963.

Leo, J. "The Sins of the Fathers." <u>US New & World Report</u> 11 Feb. 2002: 57.

LeShan, Lawrence. <u>How to Meditate</u>. New York, Bantam, 1974.

Levine, Stephen. <u>A Year to Live: How to Live This Year As If It Were Your Last</u>. New York: Bell Tower, 1997.

Lovelock, James. <u>Gaia: A New Look at Life on Earth</u>. 3rd Ed. New York: Oxford UP, 2000.

Maddox, John. "The Prevalent Distrust of Science." 28 May 2003. <http://www. fortunecity.com/emachines/e11/86/maddox1.html>

——. "A Book for Burning." <u>Nature</u> 293 (1981): 245-246.

Mair, Victor H., Trans. Afterword. <u>Tao Te Ching</u>. By Lao Tzu. New York: Quality Paperback Book Club, 1990.

Matt, Daniel. <u>The Essential Kabbalah</u>. New York: Quality Paperback Book Club, 1995.

Maslow, Abraham. <u>Toward a Psychology of Being</u>. 2nd Ed. Melbourne, Australia: Van Nostrand Reinhold, 1968.

McFague, Sallie. <u>Models of God: Theology for an Ecological, Nuclear Age</u>. Philadelphia: Fortress, 1987.

Melchert, Norman. The Great Conversation: An Historical Introduction to Philosophy. 3rd ed. Mountain View, CA: Mayfield, 1999.

Metzner, Ralph. The Well of Remembrance: Rediscovering the Earth Wisdom Myths of Northern Europe. Boston: Shambala, 1994.

Monod, Jacques. Chance and Necessity: An Essay on the Natural Philosophy of Modern Biology. New York: Knopf, 1971.

Moore, Thomas. Care of the Soul: A Guide for Cultivating Depth and Sacredness in Everyday Life. New York: Harper, 1994.

Morford, Mark P. O. Classical Mythology. 5th ed. White Plains, NY: Longman, 1995.

"Mormon Scandal" Weekend Edition. Rep Howard Berkes. NPR. WACU, Abilene, TX. 7 July 2002.

Muktananda. Satsang With Baba. Vol. 2. Oakland, CA: SYDA Foundation, 1976.

Myss, Caroline. Anatomy of Spirit: The Seven Stages of Power and Healing. New York: Three Rivers Press, 1996.

"Myth and Mythology." Encyclopedia Britannica. 15th ed. Vol. 24. Chicago: Encyclopedia Britannica, 1997.

Narby, Jeremy. The Cosmic Serpent: DNA and the Origins of Knowledge. New York: Tarcher/Putnam, 1998.

"Native American Peoples." Encyclopedia Britannica. 15th ed. Vol. 13. Chicago: Enclyclopedia Britannica, 1997.

Neumann, Erich. The Great Mother: An Analysis of the Archetype. Princeton, NJ: Princeton UP, 1955.

——. The Origins and History of Consciousness. Boligen Series XLII. New York: Princeton UP, 1954.

Nevin, Bruce. Astrology Inside Out. West Chester, PA: Whitford Press, 1982.

Nietzsche, Frederich. Beyond Good & Evil: Prelude to a Philosophy of the Future. New York: Random House, 1966.

Olson, Geoff. "The Hundredth Monkey Meme." The Globe and Mail. 28 January 1995. 13 May 2003. <http://www.testament.org/testament/100thmonkey.html>

"177 Priests Resigned or Removed From Ministry Since January." America. 13 May 2002: 4-5.

"Origen." Encyclopedia Britannica. 15th ed. Vol. 8. Chicago: Enclyclopedia Britannica, 1997.

Oxtoby, William, ed. <u>World Religions: Eastern Traditions</u>, 2nd ed. Ontario, Canada: Oxford UP, 2002.

——. <u>World Religions: Western Traditions</u>. 2nd ed. Ontario, Canada: Oxford UP, 2002.

Pelikan, Jarsalav, ed. <u>Sacred Writings, Vol. 1 - Judaism: The Tanakh</u>. New York: Quality Paperback Book Club, 1992.

——. <u>Sacred Writings, Vol. 2 - Christianity: The Apocrypha and the New Testament</u>. New York: Quality Paperback Book Club, 1992.

——. <u>Sacred Writings, Vol. 5 – Hinduism: The Rig Veda</u>. New York: Quality Paperback Book Club, 1992.

Perry, Glenn. "How do we Know What we Think we Know? From Paradigm to Method in Astrological Research." <u>Astrological Research Methods</u>" Volume 1: An ISAR Anthology. Ed. Mark Pottenger. Los Angeles: The International Society for Astrological Research, 1995. 12-48.

Phillipson, Garry. "Astrology and the Anatomy of Doubt." <u>The Mountain Astrologer</u> (Mercury Direct). 104: (August/September, 2002. 2-11.

"Philosophical Schools and Doctrines." <u>Encyclopedia Britannica</u>. 15th ed. Vol. 25. Chicago: Enclyclopedia Britannica, 1997.

Plato. <u>The Last Days of Socrates</u>. Trans. Hugh Tredennick. London: Penguin, 1969.

Powell, Barry B. <u>Classical Myth</u>. Englewood Cliffs, NJ: Prentice Hall, 1995.

Radin, Paul. <u>The Trickster: A Study in American Indian Mythology</u>. New York: Schocken Books, 1956.

"Reincarnation." <u>Encyclopedia Britannica</u>, 15th ed. Vol. 9. Chicago: Encyclopedia Britannica, 1997.

Reps, Paul, Compiler. <u>Zen Flesh, Zen Bones</u>. Garden City, NY: Doubleday, nd.

Rilke, Ranier Maria. "Again, again!" <u>Selected Poems of Rainer Maria Rilke</u>. Trans. Robert Bly. New York: Harper & Row, 1981. 167.

——. "Buddha Inside the Light." <u>Selected Poems of Ranier Maria Rilke</u>. Trans. Robert Bly. New York: Harper & Row, 1981. 151.

——."I live my life...." <u>Selected Poems of Ranier Maria Rilke</u>. Trans. Robert Bly. New York: Harper & Row, 1981. 13.

"Rites and Ceremonies." <u>Encyclopedia Britannica</u>. 15th ed. Vol 26. Chicago: Encyclopedia Britannica, 1997.

Roberts, Jane. <u>Adventures in Consciousness: An Introduction to Aspect Psychology</u>. Englewood Cliffs, NJ: Prentice Hall, 1975.

Rudhyar, Dane. <u>The Astrology of Personality: A Reinterpretation of Astrological Concepts and Ideals in Terms of Contemporary Psychology and Philosophy</u>. New York: Doubleday, 1970.

Rumi. "The Turn: Dance in Your Blood." <u>The Essential Rumi</u>. Trans. Coleman Banks. New York: Quality Paperback Book Club, 1995. 280.

——. "The Sheikh Who Played With Children." <u>The Essential Rumi</u>. Trans. Coleman Banks. New York: Quality Paperback Book Club, 1995. 44-46.

Sanchez, Monica. "History of Surrealism," 27 May 2003. <http://www.bway.net/~monique/history.htm>.

Schermer, Barbara. <u>Astrology Alive!: Experiential Astrology, Astrodrama and the Healing Arts</u>. Northhamptonshire, England: Aquarian Pr, 1989.

Scofield, Bruce. "Planetary Circuits: An Astro-Biological Model of Human Development." <u>The Mountain Astrologer</u>. February - March, 2002, p 45+.

Sdorow, Lester M. <u>Psychology</u>. 3rd ed. Dubuque, IA: Brown, 1995.

Searleman, Alan, and Douglas Herrman. <u>Memory from a Broader Perspective</u>. New York: McGraw-Hill, 1994.

Semeniuk, Ivan. "Cat in the box." New Scientist. 9 March 2002. 28 May 2003. <http://www.newscientist.com/hottopics/quantum/quantum.jsp?id=23334400>

Seymour, Percy. "Astrologers by Nature." <u>The Mountain Astrologer</u>, February - March, 2002: p 58+.

Sheldrake, Rupert. <u>A New Science of Life: The Hypothesis of Formative Causation</u>. Boston: Tarcher, 1981.

——. <u>Sheldrake Online</u>. Controversies. 14 May 2003. <http://http://www.sheldrake.org/controversies>

Singer, Peter. "Hegel." <u>German Philosophers</u>. New York: Oxford UP, 1983.

Stevens, Wallace. "Six Significant Landscapes." <u>The Palm at the End of the Mind: Selected Poems and a Play</u>. Ed. Holly Stevens. New York: Vintage Books, 1990. 17.

"Symbolist Movement," <u>Encyclopedia Britannica</u>. 15th ed. Vol. 11. Chicago: Encyclopedia Britannica, 1997.

Tagore, Rabindranath. "Gitanjali." Eulogos Project. Intratext Digital Library. 19 February 2002. <http://www.intratext.com/IXT/ENG0230/$20.htm#87p>

WORKS CITED

Tarnas, Richard. <u>The Passion of the Western Mind: Understanding the Ideas That Have Shaped Our World View</u>. New York: Ballentine, 1991.

Tester, Jim. <u>A History of Western Astrology</u>. New York: Ballentine, 1987.

<u>The Tibetan Book of the Dead</u>. Trans. Robert A. F. Thurman. New York: Quality Paperback Book Club, 1998.

Tillet, Rob. <u>Astrology on the Web</u>. "A Nexus of Probabilities." 23 October 2003. <http://www.astrologycom.com/nexus.html>

Underhill, Evelyn. <u>Mysticism: The Nature and Development of Spiritual Consciousness</u>. Oxford, England: Oneworld Publications, 1999.

Vivekananda. <u>Lectures on Raja Yoga and Other Subjects</u>. New York, 1899.

von Franz, Marie-Louise. <u>Creation Myths</u>. Dallas, TX: Spring Publications, 1972.

Wertheimer, Michael. <u>A Brief History of Psychology</u>. 3rd ed, New York: Holt, Rinehart and Winston, 1987

Whitman, Walt. "I Sing the Body Electric." The Academy of American Poets. 17 October 2003. <http://www.poets.org/poems/poems.cfm?prmID=1732>

Wilbur, Ken. <u>The Marriage of Sense and Soul</u>. New York: Random House, 1998.

Williams, Strephon Kaplan. <u>Jungian-Senoi Dreamwork Manual</u>. Berkeley: Journey Press, 1980.

Wilson, Andrew A. "A Treasury of African Folktales." Marcus Garvey Tribute Website. 17 December 2003. < www.marcusgarvey.com/taf15.htm>

Wolf, Fred Alan. <u>Taking the Quantam Leap: The New Physics for Nonscientists</u>. New York: Harper, 1981.

Wright, James. "Milkweed." <u>The Rag and Bone Shop of the Heart</u>. Eds. Robert Bly, James Hillman and Michael Meade. New York: Harper Perennial, 1993. 424.

Yeats, William Butler. "A Dialogue of Self and Soul." <u>The Rag and Bone Shop of the Heart</u>. Eds. Robert Bly, James Hillman and Michael Meade. New York: Harper Perennial, 1993. 505.

——. "Discoveries." <u>Essays and Introductions</u>. London: Macmillan, 1961, 261-297.

Zukov, Gary. <u>The Dancing Wu Li Masters: An Overview of the New Physics</u>. New York: Bantam, 1994.

INDEX

INDEX

Index

A

active imagination 342 *See also* Jung, Carl.

Addey, John 321 See also astrology: harmonic.

Adler, Alfred 251 *See also* psychoanalysis.

agnosticism 130

alchemy 7, 85, 274, 276

Allport, Gordon 297 See also trait theory.

American Beauty (Mendes) 274

Alexander, the Great 46, 331 *See also* Hellenistic culture.

anatomy of soul 148, 150

Anaximander 198, 201, 222

anima/animus 276-277, 289-293 *See also* archetypes *and* Jung, Carl.

animal totems 364-366

animism 32, 266

animus mundi 123, 290 *See also* embodied world.

anticipatory resoluteness 224 *See also* Heidegger, Martin.

Aphrodite 96, 130-131

Apology (Plato) 142

Aquinas, Thomas 94, 145

Aragon, Louis 274 *See also* Symbolists.

arché 95-96, 104 *See also* cosmologists.

archetypes 10, 131, 276-277, 293, 295-296, 343 *See also* Jung, Carl.

   anima/animus 276-277, 289-293

   Self 276, 278, 290, 294-296

   shadow 80, 276, 278, 288-289, 293

   trickster 277

   wise elder 293-294

Archetypes and the Collective Unconscious, The (Jung)

Aristotle 105, 108, 144-150, 158, 178, 181, 184, 189, 202-203, 210, 219, 239, 250, 326, 336-337, 347

   affirmation of astrological worldview 144, 326, 336, 347

   affirmation of polytheism 144

   affirmation of subjective truth 144-146, 157

   as precursor to objective empiricists 121, 148-149

   as rationalist 105, 146, 163-164

   conflict with Christianity 144-145

◇◇◇

C

◇◇

∞∞

F

G

J

N

◇◇◇

◇◇

U

V